RESOLVING INTERNATIONAL CONFLICT

Resolving International Conflict rethinks the dynamics of conflict escalation and continuation by engaging with research from the wide range of subfields in this area.

The book suggests a new framework for understanding conflict as a particular form of situation, interaction and tension. It shows how conflicts are shaped by varied dynamics relating to emotion, securitization, incentives, digital technology and violence; even attempts at monitoring, resolving or remembering conflicts may end up contributing to their escalation or continuation. Split into two sections, the first part focuses on the question of why and how conflicts escalate, while the second part analyses the continuation of conflict. The book features several case studies of conflict escalation and continuation – in Bahrain, Israel–Palestine, South Sudan, Northern Ireland and, most prominently, the case of the Syrian uprising and subsequent civil war. Throughout the book, and, in particular, in the conclusion, the consequences for conflict transformation are discussed.

This work will be of much interest to students of conflict resolution, peace studies, war and conflict studies, security studies and international relations, in general.

Isabel Bramsen is a Postdoctoral Researcher at the Centre for Resolution of International Conflict (CRIC), University of Copenhagen, Denmark.

Poul Poder is an Associate Professor of Sociology at the University of Copenhagen, Denmark, and the Deputy Director of CRIC (2013–2016).

Ole Wæver is a Professor of International Relations at the Department of Political Science, University of Copenhagen, Denmark, and the Founder of the research centres CAST (Centre for Advanced Security Theory) and CRIC.

Routledge Studies in Peace and Conflict Resolution

Series Editors: Tom Woodhouse and Oliver Ramsbotham University of Bradford

The field of peace and conflict research has grown enormously as an academic pursuit in recent years, gaining credibility and relevance amongst policymakers and in the international humanitarian and NGO sector. The Routledge Studies in Peace and Conflict Resolution series aims to provide an outlet for some of the most significant new work emerging from this academic community, and to establish itself as a leading platform for innovative work at the point where peace and conflict research impacts on International Relations theory and processes.

UN Intervention Practices in Iraq
A Discursive Approach to International Relations
Kerstin Eppert

Comparing Peace Processes
Alpaslan Özerdem and Roger Mac Ginty

State Domination and the Psycho-Politics of Conflict
Power, Conflict and Humiliation
Daniel Rothbart

Gender, Nationalism and Conflict Transformation
New Themes and Old Problems in Northern Ireland
Fidelma Ashe

Resolving International Conflict
Dynamics of Escalation, Continuation and Transformation
Edited by Isabel Bramsen, Poul Poder and Ole Wæver

For more information about this series, please visit: https://www.routledge.com/
Routledge-Studies-in-Peace-and-Conflict-Resolution/book-series/RSPCR

RESOLVING INTERNATIONAL CONFLICT

Dynamics of Escalation, Continuation and Transformation

Edited by Isabel Bramsen, Poul Poder and Ole Wæver

Routledge
Taylor & Francis Group

LONDON AND NEW YORK

First published 2019
by Routledge
2 Park Square, Milton Park, Abingdon, Oxon OX14 4RN

and by Routledge
52 Vanderbilt Avenue, New York, NY 10017

Routledge is an imprint of the Taylor & Francis Group, an informa business

British Library Cataloguing-in-Publication Data
A catalogue record for this book is available from the British Library

Library of Congress Cataloging-in-Publication Data
Names: Bramsen, Isabel, editor. | Poder, Poul, editor. | Wæver, Ole, 1960– editor.
Title: Resolving international conflict: dynamics of escalation, continuation
and transformation / edited by Isabel Bramsen, Poul Poder and Ole Wæver.
Description: Abingdon, Oxon; New York, NY: Routledge, 2019. |
Series: Routledge studies in peace and conflict resolution | Includes
bibliographical references and index.
Identifiers: LCCN 2018061184 (print) | LCCN 2019015927 (ebook) |
ISBN 9781351590761 (Web PDF) | ISBN 9781351590754 (ePub) |
ISBN 9781351590747 (Mobi) | ISBN 9781138104853 (hardback) |
ISBN 9781138104860 (pbk.) | ISBN 9781315102009 (e-book)
Subjects: LCSH: Conflict management—International cooperation—Case studies. |
Crisis management—International cooperation—Case studies. | Peace-building—
International cooperation—Case studies. | World politics—1989—Case studies.
Classification: LCC JZ5601 (ebook) | LCC JZ5601 .R47 2019 (print) |
DDC 327.1/72—dc23
LC record available at https://lccn.loc.gov/2018061184

ISBN: 978-1-138-10485-3 (hbk)
ISBN: 978-1-138-10486-0 (pbk)
ISBN: 978-1-315-10200-9 (ebk)

Typeset in Bembo
by codeMantra

CONTENTS

FIGURES

TABLES

CONTRIBUTORS

Dr. Martin Beck is a Professor of Contemporary Middle East Studies at the University of Southern Denmark. He has published extensively on Middle Eastern affairs, particularly the Arab uprisings, the Israeli–Palestinian conflict, international oil politics and international relations of the Middle East in general. His latest publications and activities can be found at http://www.sdu.dk/staff/mbeck.

Isabel Bramsen (PhD) is a Postdoctoral Researcher at the Centre for Resolution of International Conflicts (CRIC), Chair of the Danish Council for International Conflict Resolution (RIKO), and Operational Partner in Nordic Women Mediators (NWM). She is the Co-founder of and responsible for the Master's programme in international relations, diplomacy and conflict studies at the University of Copenhagen. She is the Co-author of *International Konfliktløsning* (Samfundslitteratur 2016). Her research is focused on Video Data Analysis and the micro-dynamics of violence, nonviolence and conflict resolution.

Nikolas Emmanuel is an Associate Professor in the Graduate School for International Peace Studies (SIPS) at Soka University of Japan. His work explores different ways in which external actors incentivize conflict management processes in Africa and beyond.

Troels Gauslå Engell is a PhD Fellow at the Centre for Military Studies, Department of Political Science, University of Copenhagen. His primary research areas include the UN Security Council, UN peace operations, human rights in security policy, diplomatic practice theory and the Responsibility to Protect.

Sune Haugbolle is a Specialist on political culture in the Middle East and a Middle East Region Head at Oxford Analytica. He holds a DPhil in Modern Middle Eastern Studies from the University of Oxford and is currently a Professor (MSO) in Global Studies at Roskilde University, Denmark. His research on Lebanon and Syria has been published in leading academic journals. He is the author of *War and Memory in Lebanon* (Cambridge UP 2010) and editor of *Visual Culture in the Modern Middle East: Rhetoric of the Image* (Indiana University Press 2013). He currently directs a research group on the history of the Arab Left.

Katja Lindskov Jacobsen is a Senior Researcher at the Centre for Military Studies, Department of Political Science, University of Copenhagen. Her research focuses on different practices of intervention, including conflict prevention, capacity building and stabilization. She has also published on refugee biometrics as a technology of intervention.

Dietrich Jung is a Professor and Head of Department at the Center for Contemporary Middle East Studies, University of Southern Denmark. His most recent book is *Muslim History and Social Theory: A Global Sociology of Modernity*, New York: Palgrave (2017).

Dr. Amir Lupovici is a Senior Lecturer in the Department of Political Science at Tel Aviv University and a Research Fellow in the Blavatnik Interdisciplinary Cyber Research Center. His book *The Power of Deterrence: Emotions, Identity and American and Israeli Wars of Resolve* was published in 2016 by Cambridge University Press.

Dr. Sara Dybris McQuaid is an Associate Professor in British and Irish History, Society and Culture and the Director of the Center for Irish Studies at Aarhus University. She was a Member of the steering committee and a Core Researcher in the Centre for Resolution of International Conflicts (CRIC) 2013–2016, Copenhagen University, funded by the Danish Strategic Research Council.

Her research area focuses on the role of memory in protracted conflict, conflict resolution and peace-building (particularly in Northern Ireland). She is currently doing comparative research examining contestations of the (violent) past, and the role of public policy in governing memory discourses.

Bjørn Møller is an Associate Professor at the Department of Culture and Global Studies at Aalborg University in Copenhagen.

Poul Poder Associate Professor Poul Poder has tenure at the Department of Sociology at the University of Copenhagen, Denmark. He has published on social theory, sociology of emotions and conflict theory.

Jakob Skovgaard-Petersen is a Professor at the Department of Cross-Cultural and Regional Studies at the University of Copenhagen. His field is contemporary Islamic media and thinking, and the contemporary role of the Muslim scholars, the ulama.

Ole Wæver is a Professor of International Relations at the Department of Political Science, University of Copenhagen, and a Founder of the research centres CAST (Centre for Advanced Security Theory, director 2008–2013) and CRIC (Centre for Resolution of International Conflicts, director 2013-). Much of his international repute stems from coining the concept of securitization and co-developing what is known as the Copenhagen School in security studies. Beyond security theory, his research interests include the history and sociology of the International Relations discipline, philosophy of science, sociology of science, religion, climate change, conflict analysis and the role of national identity in foreign policy. He has been a Member of policy advisory bodies in the areas of security, climate and research policy. Among his main books are *Security: A New Framework for Analysis* (with Barry Buzan and Jaap de Wilde, Lynne Rienner 1988, Chinese, Czech and Romanian translation); *Regions and Powers: The Structure of International Security* (with Barry Buzan, Cambridge University Press 2003; Chinese and Persian translations 2009); and *International Relations Scholarship Around the World* (ed. with Arlene B. Tickner, Routledge 2009).

Josepha Ivanka Wessels is a Visual Anthropologist/Human Geographer specialized in Syria where she worked and lived between 1997 and 2002 for her PhD (2008) dissertation. She carried out postdoctoral research at the University of Copenhagen for the Centre for Resolution of International Conflicts (CRIC) between 2014 and 2016. Her work focuses on audiovisual media and the role of YouTube videos in the Syrian uprisings. She carried out fieldwork in Turkey and northern Syria in 2014. She is a Senior Lecturer at K3 – the School of Arts and Communication, at Malmö University, Sweden. She is the author of the world's first history of Syrian documentary film entitled "Documenting Syria; Filmmaking, Video Activism and Revolution" published in 2019 with IB Tauris/Bloomsbury. Currently she is finalizing a longitudinal ethnographic film research project with Syrian Refugees in Europe.

1

INTRODUCTION

Revitalizing conflict studies

Ole Wæver and Isabel Bramsen

Conflict is endemic to social life, sometimes inescapable, often productive and occasionally disastrous. Violent conflicts are a major source of suffering in the world. Much relevant knowledge has been gained through conflict research, and the management of conflict has progressed in many respects. Yet, conflicts continue to surprise, erupting with unexpected force and resisting attempts at resolution, often recurring again and again. An overview of the insights and challenges regarding international conflict can therefore be structured usefully around two topics: *escalation* and *continuation*. The former concerns the question of why large-scale, violent conflicts occur in the first instance: Why do many minor, seemingly manageable conflicts turn into self-reinforcing, often lethal processes that drastically limit the potential for human achievement of other aims? The second question is why conflicts continue – often long after they have been generally seen as counterproductive, destructive or fruitless: Why do they not lose momentum, but continue to reproduce, often against determined efforts to end the conflict?

This book aims to make a novel contribution by focusing on the dynamics of conflict as such. During escalation, something *happens* when actors, relations and the general situation increasingly become shaped according to the logic of conflict. While this 'becoming conflict' is central, it is often seen as self-evident in contemporary scholarship that the most powerful approach – not least in order to ensure sustainable conflict transformation – is to look 'before' the conflict for its 'causes'. This common approach entails a risk of making an error that is simultaneously logical, methodological and practical, where causality is attributed to pre-existing features that only became causes of the conflict because the conflict became a conflict, which was not a determined outcome. It was only as the conflict escalated that these pre-existing conditions gained their clear direction. Further exploration of the transformative powers of self-reinforcing conflict escalation is therefore required. Similarly, concerning conflict continuation, it is crucial to focus on the dynamics of the conflict itself: dynamics rendering it not only resistant to resolution but actually enabling the generation of new energy, which reinvigorates the conflicting parties. Escalation and continuation are the key observation points of our dynamic approach to analysing conflict; they enable novel insights into conflict prevention and conflict resolution/transformation, respectively.[1]

If conceptualized as distinct from its causes and effects, conflict can only be captured analytically. We do so by viewing conflict as a mode of being, as a form of social relations. In this volume, we define conflict as a social form comprising a *situation of contradiction, interaction* and *tension* (SIT).[2] The heart of conflict is the ongoing communication of a 'no' in relation to a 'no' (Luhmann 1984, 1997; Messmer 2003a, 2003b, 2007; Stetter 2008, 2014), that is, a conflict exists only when a communication offer is refused and the first party also refuses the refusal (more on this later). Unshackling the concept of the conflict itself as distinct from its causes and effects is a precondition for locating social mechanisms in the conflict itself, thereby seeing the effects of a situation becoming *conflictualized* (taking that distinct social form) and the processes and effects of change within the conflict along the main dimensions that constitute it, that is, changes of *situation of contradiction, interaction* and *tension*.

Does the preceding approach and our further reflection regarding conflict apply to conflicts of all types and scale? Or specifically to 'international conflicts'? The theory of conflict is general; the focus here is narrower. A central idea of the volume is that conflict is a generic social phenomenon; it has characteristic features across scale and can therefore be theorized and studied in settings ranging from local to global. The purpose of the present volume is to show the value of conflict as concept and to approach cases of 'large-scale social conflict' that touch upon violence in the sense of having been (or being) violent conflicts or threatening to turn violent or return to violence. To keep the volume focused, we use our distinct approach to speak to the range of cases that are typically held to be the domain of both International Relations and mainstream Peace and Conflict Research: 'International Conflicts'. However, we do so by drawing on theories and ideas that in some cases have evolved out of research on smaller groups. The book thus repeats the move of the founders of modern peace and conflict research in the 1950s and 1960s (e.g. Boulding, Galtung and Rapoport), who theorized about conflict in general, with the international arena as their main motivation (Boulding 1963; Galtung 1958, 1969; Rapoport 1960).

The central assertion is that conflict is a particular social form that rebuilds social identities, subjectivities, energies and emotions as part of a conflictualization of situations. While numerous factors condition this process in significant ways, it is important to avoid linear causality and instead carefully study the process whereby a given conflict gains increasing hold of a development (escalation) and how it continues to reproduce as social formation (continuation). Many elements normally seen as 'causes' of conflict are better understood by our perspective, which still ascribes importance to the pre-existing elements but avoids the widespread tendency to impute causality to relationships that are much more contingent and only appear clear by unjustified selection on the basis of outcomes. Closer attention to what makes a case a conflict, how it took that shape and why it continues sheds new light on familiar cases.

The book is driven by this attempt to refocus conflict studies on the dynamics of conflict itself. It is therefore primarily organized around the issue of conflict dynamics rather than a particular selection of cases or variables. Coherence of analysis is achieved around dynamics rather than variables. This chapter introduces a series of key concepts and mechanisms associated with these dynamics. Different chapters place their emphasis differently, but all draw on this perspective on endogenous dynamics. In accordance with the shift in explanatory focus from underlying causes to endogenous dynamics of conflict, the methodological approach shifts from variables to mechanisms.

Our approach recognizes the importance of identifying the underlying factors that create higher or lower general probability for conflicts to escalate, especially important when devising structural policies that can influence these factors and thereby, at the aggregate level, the number of violent conflicts in the world. If the likelihood of violent conflict increases with economic inequality (Cederman, Gleditsch and Buhaug 2013) or climate change (Hsiang, Burke and Miguel 2013), this certainly should enter into political decisions that impact inequality and climate change. However, the effects of such factors on conflicts are basically 'statistical' – that is, they influence the frequency of the outbreak of violent conflict – but specific conflicts cannot be traced back to such statistical factors. Such large-scale understanding of causes is important for systemic policies preventing conflicts; and in relation to specific conflicts, part of peacebuilding can be the address of such factors to reduce the risk of a return of violence. However, this hunt for underlying causes has often hindered a sufficiently close look *into* the dynamics of the conflicts, as such, and exploring the dynamics of escalation and continuation in conflicts therefore holds great promise for conflict transformation.

The book addresses *two times two* questions:

1. Why and how do conflicts escalate? And what does that suggest in terms of how to achieve conflict transformation[3]/violence prevention?
2. Why and how do conflicts continue? And what does that suggest in terms of how to achieve conflict transformation/violence prevention?

Not all chapters give equal weight to these questions of how conflicts escalate and/or continue on the one hand and how this could be addressed on the other. Some chapters focus mainly on the first part of the question, touching only on the consequences for transformation/prevention at the end, while other chapters focus entirely on efforts at resolving or de-escalating conflicts. Given that the subtitle of the book lists escalation, continuation and transformation, some might

have found it more logical to divide the book into three sections: one on escalation, one on continuation and one on transformation. Nevertheless, we argue
that conflict transformation is too interconnected with the dynamics of escalation and continuation for them to be treated separately, both because causes of
conflict escalation and continuation have implications for conflict transformation
and because attempts at transforming conflicts in and of themselves often end up
being parts of the dynamics escalating or continuing the conflict, as several of
the chapters will show.

While 'escalation' is rather self-evident as focus and terminology, the second part is not: why 'continuation'? The two terminologies most often used to
describe continuing conflicts are 'protracted' and 'intractable' conflicts. While
there are advantages to connecting to established, specialized terminology,
there are also reasons for deviating from this practice. Firstly, our idea of 'continuation' is more general (the other two terms are only used for conflicts that
have already continued for a long time and proven hard to resolve, whereas
the issue of continuation already appears rather early in a conflict as in Syria);
and secondly, the conceptions of protracted and intractable are too closely tied
to the notion that these conflicts have been exposed to attempts at resolution
and proven resistant to such efforts, which again is a secondary feature to the
characteristic that they are able to regenerate energy to continue as conflicts.
'Protracted conflict' is usually a label that points towards particularly strong,
underlying sources of conflict (in terms of human needs or incompatible identities), thus rendering a conflict 'intractable' in the sense of being 'resistant' to
efforts at resolution that would work in other cases. Edward Azar's concept of
'protracted social conflict' has become part of ordinary parlance. He developed a theory of protracted conflict focusing on deep-seated cleavages, hatred
and fear among social groups that cause hostile interactions often turning into
violence. The main route to the solution of such conflicts goes through meeting underlying human needs (Azar 1990; Ramsbotham, Woodhouse and Miall
2011). 'Intractable' conflict is a concept that has been used rather systematically
by several scholars, including Coleman et al. (2012) and Crocker, Hampson and
Aall (2005). While the focus is on the difficulty of resolving these conflicts,
thereby emphasizing the importance of prevention, labelling some conflicts as
inherently difficult to solve is problematic, as this will always depend on specific
dynamics of both conflict and conflict transformation rather than a particular
feature of the conflict in the first place. Finally, our intention is that the use of
'continuation' will trigger productive puzzlement and guide people towards
considering the perspective on conflict – the mode of asking – presented in
this book.

The book does not follow a conventional approach to causal explanation,
where it posits 'variables' that are then tested for their explanatory power. Beyond
general meta-theoretical reasons for not doing so, it would in the present case risk
putting excessive emphasis on causes 'prior' to conflict, where this book shifts
the focus towards the dynamics of conflicts themselves, but also on dynamics of

conflict transformation, as analysed in Chapters 9 and 10 on Northern Ireland and South Sudan, respectively. In principle, it is therefore open to any kinds of factors that are demonstrated to be relevant in the empirical chapters. However, we intend to pay special attention to some particular elements: emotions, external actors, new social media, religious actors, modern subjectivity formation and collective memory. Some of these are inherently linked to the concept of conflict (especially emotions and memory), while others are brought in because we find that they have not been given as much attention as deserved (new social media, religious actors, modern subjectivity formation) or not properly linked to the analysis due to the dominant approaches to conflict studies that place factors as external to the conflict that really should be conceptualized as part of the conflict itself (external actors, conflict expertise). Most attention is paid to the three factors: emotions, memory and media.

The approach in this book can be characterized in three steps that are connected but do not fully determine each other (and *are* therefore three moves, not one):

1. We focus on the dynamics of conflict as such – how conflict organizes social relations. In contrast to an emphasis on causes outside the conflict, it is the conflictualization and de–conflictualization itself that we study through the phases of escalation, continuation and transformation.
2. The SIT triangle is a more operational, specified articulation of one possible way of studying conflict that satisfies the principled demand from the first point. This model is presented in detail below.
3. We privilege three particular factors that are usually given insufficient attention: emotions, memory and media. This does not exhaust the possibilities opened by the first two moves, but these processes become particularly important in light of our interest in conflict dynamics and their unfolding in situations, interactions and tensions.

Positioning the book in contemporary conflict research

Peace and Conflict Research is generally eclectic and inclusive, which is often productive and pleasant. In contrast to a discipline like International Relations, which routinely cultivates 'great debates' and a strong sense of internal contrast (Wæver 1996), the general intellectual style in peace and conflict research is broadly inclusive, which probably relates to its solution-oriented self-understanding and that 'whatever works' is therefore welcome (Bramsen 2017). Among the costs of this is a tendency to pile models and insights on top of each other, with little attention to the basic assumptions and principled status of different elements. This complicates our effort to position ourselves. Especially any claim of novelty is likely to be met with the objection, 'No, we include that too'. However, it is one thing to mention, say, dynamics of conflict, and to possibly depict them as part of some diagram, it is another to put the emphasis there. Most studies have a plot, an underlying narrative that links elements in a manner that makes particular flows, dynamics and points of action particularly important. Along these lines, it is possible to identify some broad traditions or main approaches, each of which places their main emphasis in a particular place. At the risk of oversimplifying, we will briefly use the typology presented by, amongst others, Peter Wallensteen (2015:37–62), and relate it to our project. Wallensteen presents three basic approaches to conflict resolution focused on, respectively, human needs, rational calculations and conflict dynamics. Each includes both a conception of what conflict *is* and what conflict *resolution* should focus on. These are not active research traditions or 'schools' that most scholars consciously identify with; rather, they are ideal types that remain relevant as characterization of most work in peace and conflict research (we will discuss some recent contributions that have important similarities or contrasts to our approach but do not fit well into these three approaches).

The first approach is about basic human needs, fundamentally arguing that conflict is the expression of unmet needs that find expression in violent behaviour towards other social groups (Burton 1990). This approach has generated much useful research and practice. Like the founder of the approach, John Burton, a leading second-generation scholar like John Paul Lederach (1995), is also a scholar-practitioner, and much insight has been gained from this approach as a result of its application in actual conflict resolution attempts and problem-solving workshops. Moreover, scholars interested in rethinking foundational theoretical questions have found it useful to revisit this approach, address the criticisms and develop the theory (Avruch and Mitchell 2013). However, the two main limits of the approach remain. First, theoretically, that it is problematic to give any context-free, general measure of human needs (also exemplified by the fact that different scholars identify different basic needs, e.g. Galtung 1996:197; Burton 1990); the analysis therefore tends to become trapped between a subjectivist hostage to what people see as their needs and an objectivist 'view from nowhere' of true human needs that is ultimately imprinted by power through dominant conceptions of subjectivity and sociality. The second problem is that which we have already hinted at: 'deep causes' is mostly relevant for understanding what comes before conflict, not necessarily the self-propelling dynamics of conflictualization. In many cases, deprived human needs might not be an issue at all, whereas everything in hindsight can be interpreted in this framework. Still, this approach is complementary to ours, not incompatible. It is important to conflict resolution, not least in a peacebuilding perspective where peace agreements and the processes that back them up are well advised to consider the more continuous concerns in society that can favour a remobilization of violence; only it will always remain one step removed in the understanding of any given conflict.

The second approach is defined by rational calculations. Wallensteen illustrates this with reference to the work of I. William Zartman (1991), whose concepts of ripeness and mutually hurting stalemate are among the most immediately useful and operative ideas in contemporary conflict resolution. Zartman argues that violent conflict typically continues as long as the parties believe it is possible to win the conflict; the moment first becomes ripe for mediation when they reach the realization that the situation has evolved into a 'mutually hurting stalemate'. While this in itself does not ensure that they find a way out, at this point they become open to help to finding an exit from a trajectory that has become unattractive. Another rationalist scholar who several of the contributors to the present volume draw upon is James D. Fearon. Some of his most influential analyses (1994, 1995) showed how, in principle, a peaceful solution always existed for both parties that would be preferable to war. His rational choice-based analysis helped identify some of the main mechanisms preventing such peaceful solutions, pointing specifically to the difficulty of communicating private information and commitment problems in the face of future power shifts. While the Zartman and Fearon analyses might initially appear very different from ours, as they approach conflict basically as a rational choice and not a complete social process, they are actually relevant in our perspective: the moment agreement is reached is important in a conflict process – not necessarily the final word, but an important one, nevertheless. This means that one should regard an agreement as an element in the history of the conflict, as a step that often reconfigures the dynamics and energies of the conflict – but in what direction and how successfully can only be understood by embedding the 'rational' analysis of agreements in a more dynamic and more complete picture of the conflict as a whole. It is also hard to deny that self-consciously rational calculations play a role in conflicts, even if we will argue from our perspective that they are always emotionally charged (as argued below). Thus, 'rational' decisions make up a particular form of conflict behaviour, not because they reflect some form of abstract, pure rationality, but by being constituted as a specific modality of reasoning that is energized emotionally in distinct ways.

The third approach in Wallensteen's typology is the dynamic one, associated with Johan Galtung, and maybe especially 'the middle Galtung' (i.e. the work that followed his first more conventional phase and predated the later often absolutist and culturalist work (1990), especially the seminal pieces in *Journal of Peace Research* like Galtung 1969) who developed the conflict triangle (more on this later). In this approach, there is no single 'source' of a conflict; once a conflict has evolved, it becomes a combination of perceptions, conflict behaviour and contradictory demands; we become our conflict, and it defines our identities and agendas. The conflict becomes a way of life. In this perspective, the main challenge is to somehow interrupt the self-reinforcing dynamic of the conflict, and then it will often become evident that what seemed like an absolute contradiction was actually amenable to 'win–win solutions'. Our work mostly belongs in the tradition of dynamic conflict theory, however, trying to make it even more dynamic than in the original version (more on this later).

A possible fourth approach to conflict could be called structural analysis or transformation. This is related to versions of the human–needs approach taking more of an interest in the deep socio-economic-political roots of conflict and to other sides of Galtung's work than those stressed in the ideal–typical dynamic approach, with more attention to how some cultures and societies generate more violence than others (Galtung 1996). Structural analysis points towards the middle- and long-term causes of violent conflict, such as the ethno–demographic composition, unequal distribution of resources or the political system (Mucha 2012:3, Rubenstein 2017) and identifies societal conditions such as transnational relations (Gleditsch 2007; Svensson and Nilsson 2018), ethnicity (Wucherpfennig et al. 2012), horizontal inequality (Steward 2010), unemployment (Gallo 2013) or poverty (Justino 2012), primarily in the explanation of the onset and duration of civil wars. Interestingly, the research frontier in the overall quantitative analysis of the causes of civil wars seems to move in this direction – forming a somewhat surprising alliance with some of the more radical, structural approaches: after a period where 'grievances' as explanation seemed to lose out to 'greed' (Collier 2007; Fearon 2008), a strong case is currently being made that with refined data and methods, the political exclusion of ethnic groups and economic inequality would appear to explain ethnic conflict better than it had been assumed for more than a decade (Bartusevičius 2014; Cederman, Gleditsch and Buhaug 2013). While it certainly can be argued that some spiritual value systems, economic orders and political regimes generate more violence than others, addressing such elements in order to transform a conflict is usually an excessively indirect strategy – both too slow and too prone to become politicized and thus a part of the conflict itself ('your religion is the problem', 'neo-liberal economic policies are to be blamed', etc.). Thus, the possibility of structural transformation removing some of the fuel for future conflict is better seen as part of processes growing out of conflict transformation from within the conflict.

Our emphasis on the dynamic approach does not mean that the others become irrelevant; basically, they just have to be reconceptualized as part of conflict dynamics. This means that while some of the following chapters will include elements that might initially seem more fitting for one of the other approaches, these moments are reinterpreted in the context of the present volume in terms of the dynamics of the conflict, including the networks of emotional energy.

Some bodies of work in contemporary peace and conflict research are difficult to fit into the three or four approaches discussed, and some of them have interesting points of contact to our approach that make future collaboration promising. Resource mobilization theory, one of the main approaches in the study of social movements, has become a major contender for explaining especially non-violent uprisings, but potentially also other conflicts (Chenoweth and Ulfelder 2017). This approach places much emphasis on the social dynamics involved in the process of people becoming mobilized by 'movement entrepreneurs' and creating self-sustaining processes. Even if it is currently often used to identify variables that can subsequently be tested quantitatively, the understanding of conflict and conflict resolution has some links to the dynamic and especially our neo-dynamic approach. Many of the criticisms raised against resource mobilization theory might be remedied by closer collaboration. Stathis N. Kalyvas has spearheaded a growing body of work on violence that demonstrates how the main cause of violence is very often not the underlying grievances in a given situation but rather the previous violence and confrontations between the groups. It is a dynamic approach, especially in how it sees the formation of the parties to a conflict as a complex process whereby local feuds and patterns of grudges channel choices into the formation of the larger groups that then emerge with major fault lines, that were not really the cause of the conflict (Kalyvas 2006; Kalyvas, Shapiro and Masoud 2008). Despite some clear methodological contrasts, there are points of contact from which we have benefited and see future potential in exploring. Similarly, there is a literature on wars (especially in Africa) which argues that especially the *continuation* of war is explained less by the importance of what the parties allegedly fight over than by the advantages for important actors on both sides in continuing them (Keen 2012; *cf.* Kaldor 2012). While this is similar to standard Marxist critique, these newer works are more dynamic in not anchoring their analysis in a deep social structure with pregiven interests, placing instead greater emphasis on constellations that emerge and distribute the interest in conflict continuation in complex ways. They tell us less about the emotional mechanisms that enable these conflicts to mobilize and therefore to continue on a large scale. A final 'like-minded' approach to be mentioned is the work by Oliver Ramsbotham on radical disagreement, which we return to later in this chapter. It is interesting to mention here, in the section on general approaches, because it has evolved in the direction of attention to intra-conflict dynamics, the possible mutations at the difficult end of very conflictual relations. It is also relevant to our approach because it pays attention to situations in which the intensity of the conflict is very high in terms of the kind of relationship without this necessarily correlating with the level of violence. Thus, it points to the independent importance of how a conflict is constituted linguistically, emotionally and socially distinct from its causes and effects.

In many quarters, peace and conflict research has become increasingly mono-disciplinary in recent decades due to the dominance of political scientists, including the two most influential journals in the field: *Journal of Peace Research* and *Journal of Conflict Resolution* (Desrosiers 2016). In this situation, the book shows the relevance of a range of approaches from the humanities, sociology, anthropology and area studies. The methods used and the processes of enquiry employed vary among the chapters (video analysis, interviews, action research, quantitative data, reflection on own experiences as practitioners). While they are all specialists in different fields, the authors have adopted a not-too-technical style of presentation, and the chapters are not written in the typical research article format with detailed reporting on one specific research finding fitted narrowly into some specialist agenda. In this way, the book is designed for further scholarship and teaching and stimulate general debate in the field of peace and conflict research on the identity, direction and core assumptions of the field.

Moreover, the concluding chapter collates some general lessons concerning conflict dynamics and implications for research and conflict resolution practice.

The concept of conflict

A central part of the Peace Research tradition, and this book in particular, is to look through the conflict-prism, to understand something *as conflict*. The notion of conflict is central in Peace and Conflict Research and has different connotations than in other traditions (*cf.* Wæver 2014). In sociological conflict theories, for example, conflict refers to the ongoing, ever-present struggle over resources and power in society (Collins 2015), whereas in Peace and Conflict Research, conflict often refers to a specific conflict with a beginning and end in time and space, including two or more parties striving to obtain incompatible goals (Ramsbotham, Woodhouse and Miall 2011; Wallensteen 2015). In the sociological context, one would typically have conflict as defining for one's general approach ('conflict theories', in contrast to consensus-defined approaches), paradoxically making it difficult to generate a distinct conception of a discrete object called conflict. Peace and Conflict Research wants to understand 'conflicts'. It matters whether something is considered a conflict rather than, for example, a revolution, an uprising, a war or analysing other aspects of international relations. There is an element of reciprocity inherent in the concept of conflict (Roy, Burdick and Kriesberg 2010). Tempting as it may be to perceive only one party as an aggressor – which is often the perspective, especially if you are involved in the conflict – perceiving the situation as a conflict implies recognizing the reciprocity, such as how Western policies stimulated the Russian annexation of Crimea or Al-Qaeda's attack on the World Trade Centre in 2001.

In the (predominantly) English-language scholarly world, most work has based itself on ideas of conflict from the 1950s and 1960s (Burton, Galtung, Boulding, Curle), from there pushing forward to add new empirical insights, leading to a sprawling network of specializations on the role of religion, media and various other important factors, on lessons from different strategies for resolution and so forth. However, the 'core' in the sense of understanding conflict has thinned out. Those specializing in 'religious conflict' emphasized 'religion' but took 'conflict' to be a trivial concept; the study of 'gender and conflict' or 'media and conflict' similarly; the specification and new link-up became defining, whereas a cross-cutting continuous development of the understanding of 'conflict' disappeared. One of the problematic effects of this has been a weakened sense of *the difference conflict makes*. It was part of the original intervention by conflict research to try to create awareness of the fact that conflict shaped relations, and the parties to a conflict therefore tended to be locked into focus on the 'substance' of the conflict, unable to see how the problem had become a constellation of which they had become a party themselves. Similarly, external parties trying to address a conflict need to understand the conflictness of the issue in order to avoid naïve assumptions about how it can be 'solved'. A conflict perspective can bring this out in ways that a security or development perspective on the same situation cannot. It is therefore important to keep cultivating a sense in conflict studies of what conflict is and what conflict does.

The status of conflict theory is paradoxical. Peace researchers often point out how policy debates on international conflicts ignore basic insights from textbook conflict theory. However, while it is true that even quite rudimentary conflict theory could improve practice, conflict theory has not evolved that productively; after a creative 'founding phase', conflict research did little to deepen its core theories. Parts of research floated 'upwards' to global structures, whereas work on conflict management and mediation drifted 'downwards' towards operational accumulations of ('how to') experiences and advice. Whilst parallel bodies of theory in fields such as Sociology and IR went through dynamic periods of theory development, less happened at the heart of conflict theory. An unambitious eclecticism has become fashionable within conflict research.

An important exception to the general decline in theorizing has especially unfolded in the German-speaking part of the world. Inspired by the systems theory of Niklas Luhmann, scholars like Heinz Messmer, Stefan Stetter and Mathias Albert have paid renewed attention to the question of what characterizes conflict as a particular social form (Luhmann 1984, 1997; Messmer 2003a, 2003b, 2007; Stetter 2008, 2014), thereby continuing the classical sociological insight from Simmel (1904) that conflict is not a lack of sociality but a particular form hereof. From Luhmann's communication-centred approach to social systems, the defining feature of conflict is the lack of agreement involved in jointly developing a differentiated social world. In contrast to the wide variety of social communication that can take place through media like money, love, power, law or faith, the form of social relationship that is characteristic of conflict is a communication offer that is not accepted.

How emotions matter

One of the ways we wish to advance the conceptualization and deepen the theoretical understanding of conflict is to include the importance of emotional dynamics that explain how parties to a conflict are energized or de-energized. Like Pearlman (2013), for example, we stress the role of emotions in relationship to agency, as various kinds of emotions either energize or de-energize actors (see also Barbalet 1998 for the basic sociological argument) (see Bramsen and Poder in Chapter 2). We treat emotions as an integrated part of normal social processes rather than as irrational aberrations (Lake and Rothchild 1996; Weingast and Figueiredo 1997). In so doing, we take a different approach than Eran Halperin (2016), for example, who discusses in *Emotions in Conflict: Inhibitors and Facilitators of Peace Making* why and how protracted conflicts become protracted, even though people actually want peace and are well aware of the manifold costs of protracted conflicts. Halperin's answer for understanding this puzzle lies in appreciating how emotions work as distinct psychological barriers to peacemaking.

The present book also addresses protracted or continuing conflicts but understands emotions basically as forms of energy rather than psychological barriers that hinder peacebuilding.

The sociology of emotions – especially the theory of interaction rituals by Randall Collins (2004, 2012) – suggests placing collective patterns at the centre of analysis. When studied sociologically, emotional dynamics can be linked to and integrated with other factors. It becomes possible to study specific groups and actors (neither individuals nor the abstract unit as such) in particular sequences of interaction that generate the emotional dynamics of a given conflict. Emotions float in networks between individuals, groups and things and should be understood as being located and transferred in such socio-material relations rather than arising from within 'the individual' (inside-out) or 'the society' (outside-in). Social networks can be understood as conduits for affect but also the reverse, as circulations of affect may also be constitutive of social networks alongside other factors (Ross 2013). Assuming that emotion configures conflict and vice versa, we can speak of an emotion-conflict assemblage that acknowledges the contingent, constantly changing and inextricable aspects of the emotion-conflict relationship. This conceptualization of conflict and emotion is applied in our analyses of how conflicts escalate and continue, respectively.

While emotion-centred research has a very marginal status in peace and conflict research, it has grown gradually within International Relations to the point where it has become common to talk of an 'emotional turn'. A substantial body of literature was spearheaded by scholars like Neta Crawford (2001) and Jonathan Mercer (2010) and well synthesized by Emma Hutchison and Roland Bleiker (2014). This literature usually tries to straddle psychological and political categories, encountering – and acknowledging – severe theoretical and methodological problems, especially in relation to problematic concepts of individual and collective emotions.[4] In the present book, we have placed the main emphasis elsewhere (although there are some overlaps, including inspiration from Barbalet 1998): our main reference point is Randall Collins's micro-sociological theory, which invests comparatively little in delineating particular emotions and ascribing political content to these, instead placing its main focus on the question of emotional *energy*, that is, the more aggregate effect of various emotions energizing or de-energizing actors to be more or less determined and forceful in their political acts. This focus on emotional energy and the production of agency is developed mostly in Chapters 2 and 3. One advantage of this approach is that it runs less risk of conflating psychological and political categories. Emotional *dynamics* are important to understand political processes, but political categories (like responsibility, protection, legitimacy, threats and justice) should not be replaced by psychological categories just because they seem to correlate (empathy, trust and fear). A conflict is basically a form of sociality, not an emotion, but the *dynamics* of conflict are understood best if emotions are included in the analysis, especially to understand which actors are energized or de-energized when and how. The possibility to delve into one specific emotion, humiliation, is explored in Chapter 4, and here it is shown how this can be done carefully to avoid reductionism.[5]

Conflict as a social form: introducing the SIT triangle

At their peril, analysts and practitioners alike often underestimate the value of understanding conflicts *as conflicts*. When a situation gets tense and laden with violence, the reaction from observers and parties considering intervention is to look at its 'content' right away, not its form, that is, the situation has become conflictualized. Therefore, they start discussing who is right or wrong on what, and in what direction the situation should develop in order to reach a just and stable outcome. This very often leads to political discussions on the values and interests at stake – what should be furthered or hindered – but ignoring that the situation has emergent collective qualities understood best as conflict (Galtung 1969; Simmel 1904). Similarly, the expertise drawn upon will often be specialized knowledge about the 'object' at stake (water scarcity, security experts or at best area specialists), but the distinct dynamics of conflict regularly upset expectations about the results to be obtained. When the situation has become conflictualized, the parties behave differently than expected based on their previous being and doing and their stated interests in relation to the object of the conflict, now overlaid by the dynamic of the conflict itself. In conflict studies, the question of what a conflict *is* is often confused with what *causes* conflict. The ubiquity of conflict has made us blind to it (Messmer 2003a, 2007). Most theories describe the larger field *around* conflict (causes and effects), but pay surprisingly little attention to what happens between input and output (i.e. the conflict as an independent entity). A useful definition of conflict must describe not what is *in* a conflict or what is affected *by* conflict (e.g. identities, interests and attitudes) but what *is* a conflict. Conflict is a specific type of social form, as already argued by Georg Simmel (1904). For the *intensity* of conflict to become a meaningful concept, it is necessary that *conflict*, in turn, is conceptualized with sufficient clarity that there can be more or less of it, that is, conflicts can be more or less conflictual or intense. Failing to achieve this, scholars fall back on violence as the sole measure of intensity, which, in turn, precludes meaningful research on the relationship between conflict and violence (Bramsen and Wæver 2016).

While many scholars declare that they see conflict as unavoidable or even constructive and that they only strive to keep it non-violent (Kriesberg and Dayton 2013; Ramsbotham, Woodhouse and Miall 2011), the majority end up making violence the primary gauge of conflict, thereby undercutting the logical space for intense, positive conflict (Sørensen and Johansen 2016). In Uppsala's data set, conflict intensity is literally measured as the number of battle deaths.[6] However, there is no evidence that higher levels of intensity lead to higher levels of violence (Chenoweth and Lawrence 2010). A non-violent conflict can nevertheless be very intense, marked by daily demonstrations, high levels of agonism, mobilization and confrontation. On the basis of comparative case studies of different patterns of non-violent and violent conflicts in liberation from French colonialism, Adria Lawrence concludes that neither time nor the level of repression and brutality can explain the emergence of violence; 'conflict does not eventually and inevitably produce violence if unresolved, the turn to violence may have little to do with the duration of the conflict, its intensity, or the level of antagonism between the parties to the conflict' (Lawrence 2010:145).[7]

This premise as the starting point – that violence is a *form* rather than *degree* of conflict – implies the need to rethink *conflict intensity* independently of the level of violence. Lumping conflict intensity together with violence obviously makes it very difficult to analytically understand the causes and dynamics of these distinct phenomena, respectively. Thus, there is much to be gained from theorizing conflict intensity as something independent of or at least *distinct* from the level of violence. And to make it even more challenging: while violence can be a form of conflict, it can also be a form of something that is not (primarily or principally) a conflict, such as a sports game or religious ritual. When combining this with the observation that conflict can assume violent or non-violent forms, the total picture covered by these two concepts becomes a fourfold table, but we will here only look at violent and non-violent conflicts, not violent and non-violent non-conflicts.

But how can intensity be measured or even described? Is it the level of conflictual discourses? Hardly, because silence can also indicate intensity. Descriptions of escalation often imply an increase in (emotional) tension, but this dimension is rarely articulated, specified or problematized. From a relational perspective, conflict is not merely a question of incompatibility (a third-party characterization of the constellation), but rather defined by a conflictual *relationship*, the rhythm of communication and the emotional tension that emerges *between* the conflicting parties. The challenge is to spell out these relational dynamics. Even sociological perspectives on escalation often focus on dynamics 'within' each party rather than *between* the parties. For example, framing approaches characterize a situation as increasingly conflictual, as the mental frames of the parties take on a series of features that make violence more likely and resolution more difficult (Elliott, Gray and Lewicki 2003), that is, dynamics that are ultimately anchored in the actors, not in the relationship between the respective parties.

Obviously, the question 'What is conflict intensity?' begs and begets the question, 'Intensity of what?'. Thus, we end up rehashing the question, 'What is conflict?'. To address this question, we revisit Galtung's conceptualization of conflict as attitude (A), behaviour (B) and contradiction (C). Galtung envisions conflict as a triangle consisting of three elements conveniently corresponding with the first three letters of the alphabet: (A) attitude, (B) behaviour and (C) contradiction. **A**ttitude is not to be understood (merely) in its commonsensical meaning, a settled way of thinking or feeling about something, referring instead to the emotional and cognitive dimensions of conflict from traumas to enemy images and mistrust. **B**ehaviour compromises the most visible dimension of conflict (i.e. what people do and say in conflict): from bullying to sanctioning and bombing. **C**ontradiction then refers to the issue about which the parties disagree, such as the ownership of territory or distribution of power in a society. While contradiction is sometimes (mistakenly) referred to as the root of the conflict, the original idea of the conflict triangle was that all three elements were equal, that is, no element was more central to the conflict, and a conflict could begin in any one of the 'corners' of the triangle and translate into the others (Galtung 1996). Bramsen and Wæver (2016) have proposed a more relational version of the ABC triangle, namely the SIT triangle. Rather than attitude (A), we suggest that **tension (T)** better grasps the emotional and cognitive dimensions of conflict, as it refers to a *field* or state of a relationship *between* the parties rather than within or adopted by the conflicting parties. Instead of behaviour (B), we suggest that **interaction (I)** is a more accurate description of what a conflict *is*, as this implies the actions and reactions of both parties. And finally, we propose that conflict is not a contradiction (C) *per se*, but rather a **situation (S)** of contradiction, which implies that it is the structure of the situation rather than the actual deprived needs or scarce resources that defines a conflict. While there might be behaviour and attitudes in conflict, we want to theorize not what is *in* a conflict but rather what a conflict *is*. All three elements – tension, interaction and situation – pass the test of saying 'conflict is a form of...', that is, conflict is a form of tension, a form of interaction and a form of situation.

That which is fundamentally different (and what this revision contributes to the framework) is that the three concepts are *relational* as opposed to one-sided and that they are *dynamic* as opposed to static, thereby better capturing the nature of conflict.

Figure 1.1 illustrates the triadic composition of conflict.

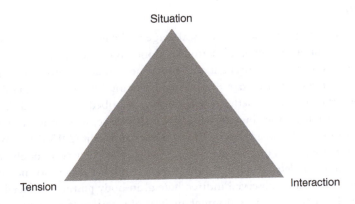

FIGURE 1.1 The SIT Triangle.

Situation of contradiction

Conflict is often described as a *situation* in different accounts for conflict theory. For example, Wallensteen (2011) defines conflict as a 'social situation', while Boulding (2012[1963]:5) defines it as a 'situation of competition' without further elaboration of the notion of a situation. What then characterizes the structure of a conflict situation?

The concepts of incompatibility and contradiction are often used interchangeably to describe a conflict, but we argue that contradiction more precisely grasps the structure of a conflict situation. The original meaning of contradiction is *contra dicere* – to speak against – which does not imply that goals or statements are necessarily incompatible, but rather that they oppose each other.

What does it imply to consider conflict a *situation of contradiction* rather than contradiction as such? Hopefully, without adding unnecessary complexity, the intention of the twist is that the issue at hand in conflicts is not scarce resources or deprived needs *per se* but the relative positioning of the parties. Similar to theories on relative deprivation (Gurr 1970) or relative gains (Waltz 1979), a conflict situation is not necessarily the one where parties do not have their needs met but rather the one where they stand in opposition to each other in terms of opposing wills, identities and/or discursive worlds. This can be the case in situations of scarcity and abundance alike. Conflict is characterized by the structure or composition of the situation, namely one of opposition and contradiction, not whether they are actually grounded in deprived needs or scarcity. A conflict is defined not by its causes but rather by its composition and structure, just as walls, a door and a roof characterize a house, not the construction workers building it or the motives of their employees. Regardless of whether a *situation of contradiction* has roots in underlying motives, these motives are not defining of the conflict and may very well emerge along with the conflict, as described by Collins (2008:337): 'Motives tend to emerge as the conflict heats up; once the situation has escalated, the persons involved start to form an idea of what they are fighting about'.

Tension

Despite the widespread commonsensical usage of the notion of *tension*, it is a notoriously difficult phenomenon to define let alone observe or measure.[8] While this speaks against using the concept at all, tension nevertheless captures an important dimension of conflict: the state of a strained relationship or tense situation. Furthermore, the fact that something is not easily described or measured should not prevent researchers from investigating it. In this sense, tension is similar to the concept of insecurity, as argued by Mearsheimer and Walt (2013:433): '[W]e cannot measure insecurity directly, because it is a mental state we cannot observe. But scholars can often detect evidence of its presence in what leaders do and say'. That said, emotions can be observed indirectly (e.g. in body postures or facial expressions) or alternatively in the sentiment analysis of utterings (e.g. on social media).

Tension is one of the most accurate descriptions we have of the feeling that 'something is wrong' in a relationship, be that between two ambassadors in a diplomatic meeting or in the beginning of a revolution. Tension has both cognitive and emotional aspects. The former would imply, for example, expecting conflictual actions from one's opponent (Goldmann 1974), whereas the latter hereof would be either fear or anxiety in the sense of a more diffusive kind of fear without a clear object. Fearing that the opponent engages in very particular counteractions can make the party tense but in a somewhat manageable sense, as certain precautions can be imagined; less so if the expectations as to what the counterpart will do are more diffuse and, hence, the tension will be experienced as more comprehensive and more intense (Rumelili 2014a). The concept of tension is a useful improvement on previous conceptualizations in conflict theory's triangles, because it is a quality of the relationship as such. It is the relationship (or the larger situation as a whole) that is 'tense', and this cannot be understood in an aggregate way as the sum of 'tense individuals'. Thus, 'tension' helps us to include an emotive and cognitive dimension of conflict that is located *in-between*, not *in* the actors.

Interaction

While Wallensteen describes the behavioural aspect of conflicts as 'actions' and Galtung identifies it as 'behaviour', we insist that *interaction* grasps the nature of conflict more accurately. Like a tango, a conflict requires (at least) two parties. A phenomenological exploration of what makes a conflict would reveal that it is exactly the dynamics of one party reacting to the other party's actions – and vice versa. The pattern of conflictual action and reaction of at least two parties has an almost rhythmical aspect to it, corresponding to a good conversation or dance (Bramsen in Chapter 3). This makes conflictual interaction inherently social rather than antisocial behaviour (*cf.* Simmel 1904). It is about responding to and often even mirroring the actions of one's opponent. Conflictual interaction may be both violent and non-violent but should be distinguished from domination, as the latter implies submission, whereas conflict implies counteractions by both parties. In a Luhmanian sense, "Conflicts are defined as the recursive rejection of communication offers, the repeated communication of a 'no'" (Stetter 2014:49). It is not easy to capture such 'no–no communication' in a precise understanding. What does conflictual interaction imply? That is, what does 'conflictual' mean apart from being part of a conflict? Words that point towards such interaction are negating, resisting, rejecting or colliding interaction, all illuminating different aspects of conflictual interaction.

Latent conflict and contradiction-free fights?

In Galtung's model, attitude (A) and contradiction (C) can be unconscious and, thus, people may be in conflict without even knowing it (Galtung 1996:74, 2009). This corresponds to the paradigms of Paulo Freire, Marxism and others, arguing that oppression is a form of conflict of which the parties are simply not aware (Freire 1970; Lukács and Lingstone 1971). In our model, a latent conflict of which the parties are not aware or upon which they do not act *is not a conflict*. If there is a *situation of contradiction* – if two or more parties want to have the same resources but there is no conflictual interaction or tension – we argue that there is no conflict.[9] Only if parties with contradicting goals *strive* to obtain these goals or attack each other then there is conflict (Ramsbotham, Woodhouse and Miall 2011; Wallensteen 2015). The original Latin meaning of conflict is 'to strike together', implying a 'no' that follows another 'no', a stance against another stance (Luhmann 1984).

While distinction can be drawn analytically and phenomenologically between *interaction*, *tension* and *situation*, it can be difficult to do so in practice, as the three corners of the triangle are highly interconnected. For example, conflictual interaction can be a sign of tension and you cannot entirely separate attempts at changing levels of tension from changing interaction, as interaction both produces and is reinforced by tension. Likewise, conflictual interaction and tension imply a situation of contradiction in which parties are positioned in opposition to each other, that is, after all, the point of bringing the three together in a triangle.

For Galtung, A and B can exist without C, but then it would not be a conflict:

> people may behave the way they tend to behave – like devils or angels, both or neither – depending on their personalities, which certainly may be shaped by conflicts in the past. Place two persons filled with ressentiment [resentment] next to each other, and verbal and/or animosity starts flowing. But for a conflict diagnosis to be justified there has to be an identifiable contradiction between the two that can be used to formulate reasonable hypothesis about the total formation and its dynamic under various circumstances, its transformation.
>
> *(Galtung 1996:7)*

Unlike Galtung, we would argue that if there is tension and conflictual interaction, there is also some form of situation of contradiction (unless it is a deliberately set-up game, such as a play or a sports game, in which case it can be said to be a way of playing with the conflict-ritual format). Contradiction does not necessarily imply any deeper, unconscious or substantial disagreement, as Galtung seems to argue, but may also imply the simple fact that the actions of one party contradict those of another.

In that sense, the contradictory situation, interaction and tension are dimensions of the same phenomena rather than elements that together make up a conflict. In other words, one dimension cannot go without the others, but you might have conflictual interaction producing only minimal tension, as where a non-violent group attempts to escalate a conflict but the repressive and silencing tactics of a regime keep the tension very low, as Bramsen writes in Chapter 3.

Conflict escalation

Previous conceptualizations of escalation either depict conflict escalation as a rational process wherein two parties deliberately escalate to prevail (Carlson 1995; Schelling 1960) or as a chiefly psychological process of personification and polarization (Pruitt, Rubin and Kimt 2003). Both approaches lack a handle on the relational dynamics of escalation. Escalation is not always about the same actors stepping up their conflict (vertical), but also about conflicts spreading into other locales, moving along various networks and flows (horizontal). It is also important to keep in mind that escalation is not merely a transitive process, as it also implies intransitive dynamics whereby escalation is driven by inherent conflict dynamics rather than rational calculations to raise the costs for the opponent; however, this does not imply that intransitive dynamics should be considered irrational. In fact, the line between transitive and intransitive mechanisms is very blurry, as rational calculations cannot be separated from the dynamics driving the conflict forward *per se* (Zartman and Faure 2005:8).

This book forwards a relational understanding of conflict escalation as conflictualization and increase in tension, conflictual interaction and the comprehensiveness of the contradictory situation. We especially emphasize the intransitive dynamics of a conflict 'taking on a life of its own' and theorize conflict escalation as a dynamic process of tension, interaction and situation of contradiction, where these dynamics reinforce each other in a spiral of intensification. Conflict interaction produces tension and objects of contention (contradiction), which further feed into the chains of conflict interaction rituals. While this may sound like an endless process, conflicts do end either when one party sufficiently dominates the other (wins) or when the parties engage in new forms of interaction rituals, redefining their relationship and transforming the conflict. Many conflict theorists tend to describe conflict as having roots that keep feeding its existence. To this, Collins (2008:337) rightly argues that 'multiple, shifting accounts of what the conflict is about are part of the texture of the action itself, not something that stands behind it and guides it like a puppeteer pulling the strings'. It is the elements of conflict itself – tension, conflictual interaction and a situation of contradiction – that keep feeding into the conflict. Conflict produces and reproduces its own prerequisite: 'the main elements and structures of conflict development are self-referentially 'produced' by conflicts themselves' (Messmer 2007:90).

In the Luhmannian tradition, conflict is described as a particular kind of parasitic social system that cannot organize in itself, because all (other) social systems are based on communication and conflict is in some sense the negation of communication or a form of communication that does not connect the way systems usually do.[10] Conflict is parasitic in the sense that it draws its issues and persons from the normal systems but recodes them according to the logic of conflict, thereby damaging its host system and tending towards absorbing it (Luhmann 2000). We have argued elsewhere (Bramsen and Wæver 2016; Wæver 1995,

2014) that this particular nature of conflict is well captured by the Clausewitz-inspired insight that, as a conflict intensifies, the conflict itself becomes the focus of attention at the price of less attention to that which the conflict was originally about (the *Zweck* (purpose) of a war is replaced by its *Ziel* (aim) – i.e. to win; Clausewitz 1982 [1832]). Conflict therefore has the odd duality of being simultaneously an intense aspiration for some object and a marginalization of this object in favour of the relationship to other parties that prevents the attainment of the object. It is therefore characteristic of a conflict that, seen from within by those who reason as parties to the conflict, an escalation or intensification reflects an increased commitment to the content of the conflict, its object; and at the same time, seen from without, both or all major parties very often get less, even of that which they struggle in the name of, which is because the conflict 'taxes' them – more energy, resources and social structuration are absorbed by the conflict itself as distinct from that which the parties see as the 'essence' of the conflict (i.e. which they are fighting for). For instance, in a 'value conflict' pitting freedom and liberal values against a particular vision of political Islam, we have seen both sides sacrifice their principles in order to fight more 'effectively'. And in classical state-to-state conflicts in previous centuries, wars were fought for the economic importance of territories, and both sides would be economically weakened after the war regardless of who 'won'. The paradoxical heart of conflict is a movement towards an object so intense and over-focused that it prevents the attainment of the object and instead becomes the organizing centre itself.

Conflict escalation is often portrayed as a staircase, with the conflict moving between different levels of increasing intensity. These escalation models are often useful for simplification but equally often raise more questions than they answer, such as why 'personification' is a step before 'enemy images' or whether two elements could occur simultaneously or in reverse order (Hammerich and Frydensberg 2006; Messmer 2007; Schmidt and Schröder 2001; Zartman and Faure 2005). Most problematically, the staircase or ladder models often have violence at the last stage, thus implying that every conflict will ultimately turn violent if further intensified and that violence is a degree rather than a form of conflict. An alternative to thinking in terms of staircases is to consider conflict escalation a process of increased 'conflictness' – of 'more and more conflict' – in a given relationship. In this mode of thinking, conflict escalation implies that the relationship is increasingly defined by conflict, as when the objects of contention are mentioned more (or remarkably silenced) in the public debate, if the communication about the opponent becomes more negative, and/or if more people engage in conflictual action. Hypothetical survey data questions to measure conflict intensity might be: 'How much does the conflict influence your everyday life?' and 'Are the group-solidarity rituals like displaying national flags related to promoting the group in opposition to an opponent?' or 'Are they simply national traditions?' Zartman and Faure (2005:7) summarize nine ways according to which escalation can occur, often simultaneously: escalation in means of conflictual interaction, ends of the parties, space within which the conflict takes

place, price, parties involved, demonization of 'the other', risks, costs, commitment and one could add time in terms of the amount of time that the involved
parties spend on the conflict. These parameters are helpful to specify the different
aspects of escalation. What they all sum up to is that the logic of the conflict
controls more social microunits and does so more intensely, thereby overriding
other logics more.

Conflict continuation

Both escalating conflicts and conflicts that vary or even decrease in intensity can
be seen as continuing conflicts. But the puzzle of escalation and the expansion of
conflictness are different than that of continuation.

Regarding conflict continuation, our approach has the productive effect of
making why a conflict continues a puzzle. In most prevalent perspectives, conflict is defined by its 'causes', and it is therefore hardly puzzling that a conflict
continues as long as these causes persist. For example, Ramsbotham (2010) suggests that some conflicts are 'essentially' more intractable and, thus, the puzzle is
not how the conflict continues to be protracted and intractable but rather how
peace-builders can navigate in such intractability. If conflict is instead considered
a particular social form, implying conflictual interaction and energy that fuel it,
it becomes a puzzle how and why conflicts continue. Just because the causes for
engaging in conflict, such as inequality, persist, it is not a given fact that a conflict will endure. For conflicts to continue, the actors also need to have sufficient
energy to continue conflictual action. If they are de-energized and hopeless,
conflict will not continue. The energy and concentration of attention necessary
for the production of conflict are often prone to entropy as opponents exhaust
their material resources, lack the conditions for solidarity and are unable to overcome confrontational tension/fear (Collins 2008, 2012). Often a conflict is not
'solved', but once its intensity drops below a certain level, it starts losing out to
other concerns and in hindsight it is forgotten how unresolvable it looked, and
the last of its decline mostly took the form of fading (e.g. the Danish-German
border conflict in the twentieth century; Wæver 2009). Consequently, conflict
continuation requires explanation.

Why and how do conflicts then continue? What continues to fuel conflictual
interaction and tension? The book discusses several examples of continuous
conflict, from the Syrian and Israeli-Palestinian conflicts to that in Northern
Ireland. Conflicts can continue in many different ways. For example, conflict
can continue, as in Israel-Palestine, where levels of tension and conflictual interaction vary over time. It can also continue in non-violent, political forms, as in
Ireland, where the conflictual interaction is transformed into politics but where
the situation of contradiction is institutionalized and thus continues to form
identities, actions and social hierarchies in opposition to 'the other' (McQuaid
2017; Mitchell 2011). Likewise, conflict can be locked in steady and more or
less continuous escalation and expansion, continuing to involve more actors and

affect more lives. The book addresses several diverse dynamics of how conflicts continue, from the incentives for conflictual engagement to the role of future scenarios and institutionalized contradiction. What all these have in common is that they focus on dynamic factors rather than root causal arguments that make conflict continuation a given as long as they persist.

Similar to the question of the causes of the conflict in the first instance, continuation can also be linked to various causal variables outside the conflict itself. When James Fearon (2004) asks, '*Why do some civil wars last so much longer than others?*', he can identify factors that correlate with length, which is important. However, the relationship is statistical, meaning that, for instance, a conflict has a higher probability of becoming drawn-out if it is a 'sons of the soil' type, where a peripheral ethnic minority is fighting state-supported migrants of a dominant ethnic group and the conflict has a short life expectancy if it stems from a coup. But since this is a relative difference between the cases, the single case remains open to becoming shorter- or longer-lived, and one should therefore always consider the actual socio-emotional dynamics that generate renewed energy for the conflict or let it fade – the underlying factors that cause the statistical variation among types should be included in such an analysis to see how they are mobilized and utilized concretely.

Regarding the SIT triangle, like escalation, conflict continuation is a process of the situation, interaction and tension continuously feeding into each other (although not necessarily expanding, as in conflict escalation). For this continuity to be disrupted or to change and the conflict to be solved, either of the three elements can be regulated and transformed, as described below.

Conflict transformation

In the framework of the SIT triangle, conflict transformation implies changing the interaction, the situation and the level of tension. These aspects of conflict are highly interlinked and cannot be completely separated due to the dynamic relationship between them, where a change in the situation will change the interaction and degree of tension. For analytical purposes, we will however theorize how each of these aspects respectively can be changed in conflict transformation.

Changing the situation

Seeing conflict as a situation of contradiction rather than contradiction *per se* has profound implications for conflict analysis and resolution. If conflict is structured around opposition and contradiction, then the objective of conflict transformation is not to address the incompatible goals but rather to change the structure of the situation, i.e. the opposing positioning of the parties. A change in the situation can, for example, resemble a shift from antagonism (where the other is non-recognized and ultimately to be eradicated) to agonism (as a legitimate opponent) (*cf.* Mouffe 2000, 2005, 2013; Ramsbotham 2010; Schmitt 1932). On a spectrum, it is possible to move further in the direction of a difference that is not purely conflictual, but a mix of identification and differentiation. Furthermore, it becomes important how self and other are differentiated – whether as external alternatives at an equal plane (State A and State B), or, for instance, in a hierarchical relationship or a temporal where one is eventually presumed to become like the other (Buzan and Wæver 2009; Gad 2010; Hansen 2006). Thus, it is central to think through the co-constitution of identities and conflictuality, but also to avoid a too-easy fixation on a dualistic 'self-other' set-up, as that tends to assume that there *are* these two positions in the first instance, whereas identity is even more performative than that, and in a world of multiple, overlapping identities, the real issue is often the degree to which different identities are accentuated and, thus, which plane of reality overrides the others.

A telling example of situational change that leads to a change from antagonism to collaboration is the Indonesia/Aceh conflict. Fought for almost 30 years, the conflict first ended after a 2004 tsunami 'changed the situation' in the country, partly due to how it forced the parties to work together to rebuild society (Le Billon and Waizenegger 2007). In this way, a change in the situation caused a change in interaction. Changing the situation is of course not an easy task, let alone changing it in the right direction. In Sri Lanka, the tsunami had the exact opposite effect on the situation and caused increased violence and tensions (accordingly due to the stage of the conflict). Thus, deep analysis of the specific conflict and its dynamics are needed for a strategy of 'changing the situation' to succeed.

Natural disasters and other circumstances external to the conflict are not the only hope for transforming the situation. Another option is to change the perception of the situation. When traditional conflict transformation theorists contest that an incompatibility has been transcended, was it then an incompatibility in the first place? Or was it rather a perceived incompatibility that was 'transcended' because the parties changed their perception of the situation? A good example is the transformation of the long-lasting conflict between Peru and Ecuador about territory in the Andes. Through mediation, the two parties agreed to construct a natural park in the area of contention among other things because Galtung challenged their perception of the situation by questioning whether every square meter of the world had to be owned by someone. In other words, what was perceived as an incompatibility was only an incompatibility within the framework of territorial thinking (Galtung and Fischer 2013).

Changing the interaction

One of the main priorities for transformation of violent conflicts is to change the interaction from violent to non-violent. Conflict transformation scholars like John Paul Lederach (2005:47) most explicitly contest that the goal should necessarily be to end the conflict, but rather to create a platform for handling conflict by non-violent and political means. Veronique Dudouet (2013) identifies several factors that can contribute to the transition from violent to non-violent conflict, i.e. how otherwise violent groups decide to pursue a non-violent strategy: (1) intragroup factors such as change of leadership, fatigue of fighting and organizational dynamics; (2) relational/environmental factors such as changing relations to allies and cross-border diffusion of new repertoires of action.

While the transition from armed to unarmed conflict is about continuing fighting with other means, a change in interaction can also imply changing conflictual interaction into collaboration or simply a lack of interaction (cf. Simmel 1904). Regarding the first option, parties can change their relationship through solidarity rituals in the form of dialogue, mediation, negotiation, conferences or other types of collaborative interaction, like trade. It is a well-known political strategy to promote cooperation on other issues (e.g. trade or environmental negotiations) in order to 'work around' and essentially transform a given international conflict. This was much discussed during the Cold War, with hefty disagreement regarding the utility of East–West cooperation and trade, as in the context of the so-called 'second basket' of the CSCE agreement (currently echoed in the US debate on strategy towards China), but also in relation to intra-Western developments such as the Franco-German relationship and the Monnet strategy for European integration. The second option, reducing conflictual interaction (e.g. with a ceasefire or a buffer zone) but without engaging in collaborative interaction, often equals a frozen conflict. However, the latter route might sometimes be assessed too negatively due to the bias that those cases where a ceasefire or buffer zone reproduced conflict are with us today (Korea and Cyprus), whereas those where the conflict faded tend to be forgotten or a then unproblematic agreement was reached later almost as an afterthought. The problem with disengagement as a strategy is that it risks taking the dynamics out of a peace process, but other social processes will sometimes do the work of weakening the conflict over time, and, if possible, disengagement can therefore be a useful step (Åkebo 2017).

Changing the level of tension

The objective of conflict transformation should not necessarily be "to remove tensions as to direct them into useful channels and to turn them to constructive social ends" (Bernard et al. 1957). In some cases, the most constructive approach may even be to increase tensions. As argued by Jabri (1996), Dudouet (2008) and others, conflicts may not always be ripe for resolution in asymmetric conflicts where power relations need to be challenged through conflict intensification for there to be a constructive solution. Violent actions very often escalate a conflict and generate tension, but also non-violent actions can be used to create tension and opposition. Martin Luther King Jr., for instance, contents that a non-violent direct action seeks to foster tension stating that "I am not afraid of the word 'tension'. I have earnestly opposed violent tension, but there is a type of constructive, non-violent tension which is necessary for growth" (King 1963). Non-violent conflict escalation can be achieved in many ways through demonstrations, civil resistance, strikes and other means of increasing the level of tension. When daily demonstrations become a part of a conflict for several years, it may no longer increase the intensity of the conflict, but simply be part of the status quo. Also, unlike violent events that tend to draw immediate attention, non-violent actions risk getting silenced by the opponents and outsiders. For non-violent actions to increase tension, they need to be sufficiently spectacular and unexpected, otherwise, as stated by the Bahraini activist Maryam Al Khawaja, e.g. non-spectacular, routinized demonstrations risk providing a

> space for people to go and protest, to you know get their anger out, which is bad for the revolution because it means people go out, they feel like they've done something and they go home, and in fact they haven't created any real pressure or escalation or anything like that.
>
> *(Maryam al Kawaja, Interview by Bramsen 2014)*

The SIT framework can be useful for non-violent activists to consider how to escalate a conflict, for example, how to initiate unexpected actions that would challenge the status quo.

When a conflict is very violent or in other ways destructive, conflicting parties and third parties may wish to de-escalate the conflict and reduce tensions. Détente mechanisms were most famously introduced during the Cold War, where the tensions between East and West were dangerous and counterproductive due both to the military dimension, with nuclear threats and various proxy wars, and the sociopolitical stifling effect of high tension (Kaldor, Holden and Falk 1989; Wæver 1989, 2003). Reduced tensions can resemble a hurting stalemate (Zartman and Berman 1982) where both parties are equally tired of fighting and have lost faith that they can win the fight. Similarly, Collins (2012) describes conflict de-escalation as a process of draining the conflict from energy in terms of allies, material resources and mobilization where both parties' internal solidarity falls apart. However, "new energy" can also be a source of de-escalation when courageous and energized groups or individuals change the situation in Liberia where the women's movement pushed the parties to a resolution through creative non-violent action.

Part 1: how and why do conflicts escalate?

The book is divided into two sections, one focusing on conflict escalation and the other analysing and discussing conflict continuation. The first section addresses the question of why and how conflicts escalate and what this suggests in terms of how to achieve conflict resolution/violence prevention. In Chapter 2, "How conflict escalation happens: three central interaction rituals in conflicts", Bramsen and Poder follow Randall Collins's methodological contention of taking the situation as the analytical starting point. On such a situational basis, the authors develop a model of three basic types of emotional dynamics central to conflict escalation: (a) solidarity interaction, (b) conflictual interaction and (c) dominating interaction (see also Bramsen and Poder 2014, 2018). They apply this framework in a discussion of emotional dynamics in conflict escalation in the context of the Arab Spring to illustrate how conflict is subjected to specific situational and emotional dynamics that form the interactions between regimes and protesters. This micro-situational approach is further applied and developed in Chapter 3, "Escalation or demobilization? Diverging dynamics of conflict displacement and violent repression in Bahrain and Syria", where Bramsen presents a comparative analysis of the first period of the Bahraini and Syrian uprisings, showing how the respective regimes attempted to displace the conflict from one between the people and a state to one between two sects, while at the same time violently repressing the uprising. Her puzzle is that while the conflict displacement and repression de-mobilized the uprising in Bahrain, it escalated the Syrian conflict. Bramsen argues that the displacement of conflict lines in Bahrain merely challenged the unity of the movement, whereas in Syria, the displacement caused significant splits *both* in the movement and in the regime and its security forces. Regarding repression, Bramsen suggests a division between a de-energizing form of repression and an energizing repression. While the Bahraini regime increasingly de-energized the protest movement by injuring, torturing and imprisoning, the Syrian regime continued to kill its challengers in the open streets, which spurred much more outrage and gatherings at funerals, further energizing the counteraction.

The role of emotion in the onset and escalation of conflict is further explored in Chapter 4, "Diverse humiliation dynamics in conflicts in our globalized world", focusing on humiliation as a latent basis of motivation for engaging in conflicts. Poder argues that understanding both content matter and mechanisms of contemporary humiliation issues is instrumental when trying to anticipate potential conflicts, which are often mobilized through different humiliation dynamics. He therefore examines Evelin Lindner's argument that humiliation proliferates due to the contradiction between human rights emphasizing the dignity of every human being and material conditions that negate these promises for many people; Jörg Friedrichs' exposition of culturally distinct notions of what defines basic human self-worth and consequently distinct notions of what is humiliated as people fail to accord the appropriate form of respect and Dennis Smith's diagnosis of humiliation as socially enforced displacement triggered by sociopolitical processes. While humiliation is often conceived in terms of interactional situations in which a perpetrator intentionally subjects a victim to degradation through actions or expressions, such understanding is not sufficient to understand contemporary humiliation dynamics. The chapter therefore further explains how current humiliation issues must be analysed in terms of: (1) symbolic humiliation, (2) representative humiliation, (3) humiliation qua non-recognition and (4) self-perceived humiliation.

Feelings of humiliation, anger and moral outrage are central topics in Wessels' Chapter 5, "Syria's moving images: moral outrage and the role of grassroots videos in conflict escalation". Wessels analyses how the uploading of user-generated videos on YouTube initially gave rise to a democratization of the Syrian media landscape, since the Syrian uprisings began in early 2011. These videos have provided documentation of human rights violations and, through their very graphic nature and rapid virality, enabled the escalation of conflicts and deeper confrontation between the authoritarian regime and the street protesters. This happened over vast distances within the country. Wessels' analysis focuses on how the viewing of these grassroots videos of human suffering triggered moral outrage. In particular, early videos documenting the torture of children by the regime led to more and bigger protests against the regime in other parts of the country, which rapidly spread throughout. With the uploading of every recording of funerals, grief and violence, more and larger groups reacted and felt compelled to organize multiple street protests, which the authoritarian regime answered with an even more brutal crackdown. This was consequently again recorded on video and uploaded on YouTube, resulting in a snowballing and escalating cycle of protests and regime violence.

Understanding the escalation of the Syrian conflict is also the effort of Petersen's chapter, "Clergy and conflict intensity: the roles of the Sunni ulama in the Syrian conflict". Petersen explores the role of "men of religion" – the carrier group of religious authority – in times of social and political tension. He analyses the roles they play in inter-religious escalation and in de-escalating religious dimensions of violent conflict with respect to Sunni Muslim scholars and preachers, the ulama, in Syria, who represent the majority religion, but not the religion of the dominant figures of the ruling regime in Syria. Instead of a unified whole, the ulama can be understood in terms of three ideal types. Firstly, the preacher as a Sufi wali, who draws his authority from his saintly charisma and intimate knowledge of the esoteric world. Secondly, the preacher as a scholar, whose authority is based on his learning. And thirdly, the preacher as a warrior, whose authority is based on his will to fight and sacrifice, and his opposition to the powers that be. Before 2011, this type was hardly present in Syria. Given this emergence of the warrior type of ulama and the complexity of roles, the analysis concludes that the contribution of the ulama is shaped and propelled by the overall conflict, while the peculiar nature of their authority has specific bearing on the dynamics of the conflict. In this way, Petersen's chapter provides clues to why and how conflicts turn violent.

An alternative approach to understanding violence and its relationship to conflict is elaborated in Chapter 7, "Foreign fighters: violence and modern subjectivity", in which Dietrich Jung critically examines the foreign fighter phenomenon. Rather than understanding persons fighting in foreign countries exclusively in terms of the radicalization of their minds and behaviour, such endeavours should be seen as alternative constructions of meaningful selfhoods. Analysing examples from civil wars in Spain and Syria, Jung suggests that the attraction of violent action in itself might be a decisive driving force behind joining foreign militias rather than extremist ideologies and personal grievances alone. To fully appreciate the war-prone history of modernity and the violent escalation of conflicts, the notion of the construction of meaningful violent selfhoods must be taken seriously, as not all forms of violence can be understood in terms of radicalization and pathological developments. War volunteers search for meaning in war. This finding implies that in order to properly understand the dynamics of conflict and issues of conflict transformation, it is necessary to consider violence as an independent cause and not merely an effect of some kind of pathological development, which is then to be remedied. The practical challenge also lies in addressing the various ways in which violence enters into cultural notions of meaningful subject formation.

The final chapter of the first section focuses more specifically on third-party possibilities and challenges conflict transformation in the escalation phase of a conflict. In Chapter 8, "Preventing violence escalation: international pursuit of conflict transformation", Katja Lindskov Jacobsen and Troels Gauslå Engell address the international conflict prevention initiatives in Burundi. They apply the SIT triangle presented in Chapter 1 to assess how the international community attempted to change the situation, conflictual interaction and level of tension, arguing that while it is difficult to point out whether the intervention has prevented a violent escalation or even a genocide, the intervention also had unintended consequences that must be considered in future attempts at preventing violent escalation. In particular, it can be discussed whether the conflict was ripe for détente or whether further (non-violent) escalation was needed for the unequal power relations between the government and the opposition (and their supporters) to be challenged.

Part 2: how and why do conflicts continue?

The second section addresses the questions of how and why conflicts continue. In Chapter 9, "'Nothing is agreed until everything is agreed': institutionalizing radical disagreement and dealing with the past in Northern Ireland", Sara Dybris McQuaid argues that the post-agreement transition in Northern Ireland is characterized by institutionalized radical disagreement wherein violent interaction has been transformed into political interaction and power sharing without changing the situation of contradiction. McQuaid argues that the maxim 'Nothing is agreed until everything is agreed' that characterized the peace talks leading to the 1998 agreement continues to impact subsequent attempts at and policies for dealing with the past. McQuaid thus identifies a 'Northern Ireland model' without any coherent framework for dealing with the violent past, but rather a more pluralistic and piecemeal series of interventions which are at once seriously circumscribed by the peace agreement but also in some ways manage to escape the entrenched diarchic order of the compromise to give shape to the ongoing transition.

Peace agreements are complex matters. Equally so – maybe even more so – are the roles played by third parties in conflicts. In Chapter 10, "'Third parties' and conflict resolution? Case study: Sudan", Bjørn Møller thoroughly analyses the various roles 'third parties' play in intra-state armed conflicts. A central point brought home is that conflicts often draw third parties into conflicts in ways that make them de facto parties to the conflict. Different dynamics unfold for different kinds of third parties and various intricacies are involved as they intervene in conflicts. In quite a few cases, third parties have made matters worse and their track record is generally unimpressive despite their good intentions. A sober attitude is therefore highly warranted. To ameliorate this sad but true condition, a significant recommendation may be to either seek to acquire sufficient understanding of the country, the protagonists and the culture – or refrain from intervening if the risk of prolonging and worsening the conflict seems high.

Caution is warranted considering the intervention of third parties, equally so when considering the range of possible external incentives that can be applied as discussed in Chapter 11, "External incentives and conflict de-escalation: negotiating a settlement to Sudan's North-South civil war". In this chapter, Nikolas Emmanuel explores the theoretical rationales behind the use of incentives in conflict management and subsequently develops a comprehensive typology of incentives applicable by external actors. A wide variety of incentive strategies are available to manage conflict and facilitate negotiation settlements, while external actors often do not consider the full range of options. Such incentive strategies can give interveners leverage and aid them in their efforts to mediate and hopefully bring conflict to an end. This leverage is frequently diplomatic in nature, providing an advantageous basis for soft intervention in conflicts, especially when the extremes of withdrawal and military intervention are inappropriate and possibly even counterproductive. The relevance of an incentive-laden approach is illustrated through a discussion of U.S. efforts to facilitate a negotiated settlement to the North–South Sudanese civil war (1983–2005). A central point in this analysis is that a crucial impact of the incentives was to get the conflicting parties from a belief in the meaningfulness of continuing previous conflict behaviour to first seeing the conflict as a mutually detrimental stalemate and ultimately as a 'mutually enticing opportunity'. This book's general thesis – that conflict dynamics *per se* are central throughout a transformation – is thus illustrated in Emmanuel's chapter.

The overall balance of incentives can sometimes lead to the continuation rather than termination of conflicts, as suggested in Chapter 12. Here, Martin Beck investigates the puzzle of how and why the Israeli-Palestinian conflict continues despite numerous attempts at different levels to solve it. In short, Beck argues that the incentives for continuing the conflict and status quo are higher than the incentives for ending the conflict, particularly for the Israeli part, as they hold the upper hand in the conflict. The chapter analyses how the situation of contradiction is structured as a graduated prisoner's dilemma, how the conflictual interaction is shaped by an asymmetric power relationship and how the Oslo Agreement in practice and the international and regional actors continue to support the conflicting parties sufficiently to continue the conflict, with little incentive to end it.

The continued Israeli-Palestinian conflict is also addressed in Chapter 13, "Ontological security as key to the continuation and connections among Israel's conflicts securitization and continuation of conflicts". Here, Amir Ludovici adds the lens of securitization, a process through which an issue is constructed as an existential threat. Ludovici accounts for two interrelated conflict-continuation mechanisms. Firstly, securitization and meta-securitization moves, both of which contribute to the perceived remaining threat and, thus, justify the conflict itself and the measures taken to address the (alleged) threat. Secondly, as the conflict is (meta-)securitized, this becomes a constitutive element of the self, thus validating the actors' ontological security. De-securitization moves aimed at overcoming conflict therefore challenge the actors' selves. Once the conflict becomes part of the actors' identities, the peace process contests both the ability of the parties to hold a coherent narrative of who they are and their ability to affirm their selves through their interactions with the enemy: their significant other. These dynamics, which are illustrated with references from the Arab-Israeli conflict, shed light on how conflicts endure. Discussing practical implications for conflict resolution, Ludovici underlines, firstly, that one form of means – de-securitization moves – is to block attempts to fuel conflict by incorporating new threats into them. This requires clearly specifying what the conflict is about and therefore how other threats are not necessarily part of it. Secondly, it requires preventing the usage of the (meta)narrative of the conflict to incorporate new threats into it (i.e. meta-de-securitization moves). Towards this aim, peace promoters can emphasize how specific de-securitization moves challenge the metanarrative of the conflict; for example, Israel's peace with Egypt can be used towards the development of a counter-narrative suggesting that not all of the actors in the Middle East wish to destroy Israel.

Challenging the present metanarrative is obliging to the promotion of future peace. The present is also concerned with the future, however, in terms of collecting potential transitional justice evidence. Such endeavours are analysed in Chapter 14 – "Holding out for the day after tomorrow: archiving, memory and transitional justice evidence in Syria" – in which Sune Haugbølle addresses how the collection of transitional justice evidence, and the future scenarios that such evidence gathering implies, shaped the development and continuation of the Syrian conflict. Based on ethnographic fieldwork, Haugbølle argues that processes of evidence collection have given hope to victims and activists alike, but also that it was part of generating two adversarial global narratives and camps with fundamentally different visions for the future of the country and the resolution of the conflict. Both the hope amongst activists and the created future scenarios have contributed to the prolonging and continuation of the conflict. While Emmanuel and Beck's short answer to the question of why conflicts continue (in this volume) is that conflicts continue when incentives for engaging in conflict are higher than the incentives for de-escalation, Haugbølle adds to the realist and rationalist explanations pointing towards dynamics of imagination and futurity.

We have now come full circle in this introduction of a new Situation-Interaction-Tension framework and the illustration of how it can revitalize our understandings of escalation, continuation and transformation in conflict studies. Consequently, we hope that the following chapters will provide food for thought and demonstrate that conflict studies need not remain idle, instead actively applying the SIT approach.

Notes

1 The book draws on several different sub-projects from a 3½-year interdisciplinary research project funded by (what was then) the Danish 'Research Council for Strategic Research' constituting the first phase of the 'Centre for Resolution of International Conflicts' (CRIC). All of the authors have been involved with the centre, most either having been in its employ or having directed a work package at the centre.

2 Our SIT conceptualization (the SIT triangle) has no relationship to the so-called 'social identity theory', which is also abbreviated SIT.

3 We have chosen the concept of conflict transformation instead of conflict resolution for two reasons. First for conceptual/theoretical reasons, this volume focuses on theoretically deepening the understanding of conflict dynamics, and transformation has a dynamic quality. Conversely, resolution is end-state-focused and, thus, more static. Second, in the case studies presented, we will see how conflict transformation processes can occur at moments throughout the spectrum of conflict, as in the case of Burundi; in the preventive stages of conflict through full-blown wars, as in Syria; to the post-violent conflict case of Northern Ireland, where the institutionalization of conflict dynamics offers both obstacles and opportunities for conflict transformation. As argued by Ramsbotham et al. (2011:14), conflict transformation is often considered a broader concept than resolution, also including early, preventive measures and post-conflict peacebuilding initiatives. Yet as witnessed by the name of the research project and research centre, from which this book springs, 'Centre for Resolution of International Conflicts', we also see merit in deploying the concept of 'resolution', first because it resonates with most media and policymakers, and secondly because the scholarly move from resolution to transformation is by now so old and subject to its own critique that 'resolution' is on the verge of becoming a self-aware label for the larger family of concepts, i.e. implicitly read as 'that which used to be called conflict resolution'. Thus, our current use of transformation should not be read as a definite rejection of 'conflict resolution' but closely tied to the particular argument of the present book.

4 In International Relations, the individual-collective dichotomy has been overcome best by Lacan-inspired contributions (notably Epstein 2013). An important future research agenda is to explore the potential synergy between this more principled theoretical work and the more operational approach in the present book, given that both promise to overcome the main impasse in the dominant strands of work.

5 Demertzis (2013) is a rare and interesting instance of a book in the politics/emotions field that moves in our direction, focusing on conflicts, even using the term 'tension' in the subtitle (more on this below). It draws mostly on the *sociology* of emotions, as we do, rather than a direct coupling of psychology and politics. In line with the tendency in the IR literature, however, most of the chapters try to straddle the individual-collective divide with a particular emotion as bridge (e.g. fear).

6 www.pcr.uu.se/research/ucdp/definitions/.

7 Recent quantitative analyses of civil war have distinguished with increasing clarity between what causes the conflict in the first instance and what then causes it to turn violent – and in some cases what thereafter explains conflict termination and post-war recovery (Bartusevičius and Gleditsch forthcoming, 2019; Cederman and Vogt 2017).

The most powerful variables are not the same, it turns out. It is promising that the study of the causes of civil war get beyond a set-up where it is assumed that conflict and violent conflict are degrees of the same phenomenon and therefore to be studied by explaining both in one take. Still, this has mostly been achieved thus far by defining several thresholds and explaining what causes each – so far not with a conception of degrees of conflictness or intensity. This, however, offers yet another promising point of possible contact between different strands of conflict research.

8 Demertzis (2013) has tension in the subtitle; yet, the book lacks not only a definition of the concept, it never reflects on the choice of concept – it is used as a self-evident way of selecting cases with a degree of conflictuality to them. Thus, the underlying intuition is similar to ours. However, this interesting book thereby also exposes the simultaneity of the attraction and the complexity of using the concept of 'tension'.

9 It is important to keep in mind that conflictual interaction might also imply the lack of interaction, as when countries withdraw diplomats from a country as an act of escalation. What counts as conflictual interaction, then, depends on the context and previous mode of interaction.

10 This also makes conflict a kind of 'immune system' for society, because it allows a continuation of communication in situations where the normal form has become impossible, and it allows for reorganization where the systems would otherwise be dangerously static.

References

Åkebo, Malin (2017) *Ceasefire Agreements and Peace Processes: A Comparative Study*. London: Routledge.

Avruch, Kevin and Christopher Mitchell (Eds.) (2013) *Conflict Resolution and Human Needs: Linking Theory and Practice*. London: Routledge.

Azar, Edward E. (1990) *The Management of Protracted Social Conflict: Theory and Cases*. Aldershot: Dartmouth Publishing Company.

Barbalet, Jack (1998) *Emotion, Social Theory, and Social Structure: A Macrosociological Approach*. Cambridge: Cambridge University Press.

Bartusevičius, Henrikas (2014) 'The Inequality–Conflict Nexus Re-Examined: Income, Education and Popular Rebellions', *Journal of Peace Research* 51 (1): 35–50.

Bartusevičius, Henrikas and Kristian Skrede Gleditsch (forthcoming, 2019) 'A Two-Stage Approach to Civil Conflict: Contested Incompatibilities and Armed Violence', *International Organization*, 73 (1), Winter: 225–248.

Bernard, Jessie, Tom Hatherley Pear, Raymond Aron and Robert C. Angell (1957) *The Nature of Conflict: Studies on the Sociological Aspects of International Tensions*. Paris: UNESCO. In collaboration with International Sociological Association.

Boulding, Kenneth E. (2012 [1963]). *Conflict and Defense: A General Theory*. Whitefish, MT: Literary Licensing, LLC.

Bramsen, Isabel (2017) *Route Causes of Conflict: Trajectories of Violence and Nonviolent Conflict Intensification*. PhD Dissertation, Copenhagen University.

Bramsen, Isabel and Poul Poder (2014) 'Understanding Three Basic Emotional Dynamics in Conflicts: A Situational Research Agenda', *Peace Research: Canadian Journal of Peace and Conflict* 46 (2): 51–86.

Bramsen, Isabel and Ole Wæver (2016) *Dynamic Conflict Theory Re-Animated: Conceptualizing Conflict Intensity as Distinct from Violence*. Paper presented at the International Studies Association (ISA) Annual Convention, Atlanta, GA, March.

Bramsen, Isabel and Poul Poder (2018) *Emotional Dynamics in Conflict and Conflict Transformation*. Berghof Handbook for Conflict Transformation, Online Edition. Berlin:

Berghof Foundation. www.berghof-foundation.org/fileadmin/redaktion/Publications/ Handbook/Articles/bramsen_poder_handbook.pdf.

Burton, John (1990) *Conflict Resolution and Prevention*. New York: St. Martin's Press.

Buzan, Barry and Ole Wæver (2009) 'Macrosecuritization and Security Constellations: Reconsidering Scale in Securitization Theory', *Review of International Studies* 35 (2): 253–276.

Carlson, Lisa J. (1995) 'A Theory of Escalation and International Conflict', *Journal of Conflict Resolution* 39 (3): 511–534.

Cederman, Lars-Erik, Kristian Skrede Gleditsch and Halvard Buhaug (2013) *Inequality, Grievances, and Civil War*. Cambridge: Cambridge University Press.

Cederman, Lars-Erik and Manuel Vogt (2017) 'Dynamics and Logics of Civil War', *Journal of Conflict Resolution* 61 (9): 1992–2016.

Chenoweth, Erica and Adria Lawrence (2010) *Rethinking Violence: States and Non-State Actors in Conflict*. Cambridge: MIT Press.

Chenoweth, Erica and Jay Ulfelder (2017) 'Can Structural Conditions Explain the Onset of Nonviolent Uprisings?', *Journal of Conflict Resolution* 61 (2): 298–324.

Clausewitz, Carl Von (1982) *On War*. London: Penguin Group.

Coleman, Peter T., Katharina G. Kugler, Lan Bui-Wrzosinska, Andrzej Nowak and Robin Vallacher (2012) 'Getting Down to Basics: A Situated Model of Conflict in Social Relations', *Negotiation Journal* 28 (1): 7–43.

Collier, Paul (2007) *The Bottom Billion: Why the Poorest Countries Are Failing and What Can Be Done about It*, 1st ed. Oxford: Oxford University Press.

Collins, Randall (2004) *Interaction Ritual Chains*. Princeton, NJ: Princeton University Press.

Collins, Randall (2008) *Violence: A Micro-Sociological Theory*. Princeton, NJ: Princeton University Press.

Collins, Randall (2012) 'C-Escalation and D-Escalation: A Theory of the Time-Dynamics of Conflict', *American Sociological Review* 77: 1–20.

Collins, Randall (2015) *Conflict Sociology: A Sociological Classic Updated*. London: Routledge.

Crawford, Neta C. (2001) 'The Passion of World Politics: Propositions on Emotion and Emotional Relationships', *International Security* 24 (1): 116–156.

Crocker, Chester A., Fen Osler Hampson and Pamela Aall (Eds.) (2005) *Grasping the Nettle: Analyzing Cases of Intractable Conflict*. Washington, DC: United States Institute of Peace.

Demertzis, Nicolas (Ed.) (2013) *Emotions in Politics: The Affect Dimension in Political Tension*. New York: Palgrave Macmillan.

Desrosiers, Marie-Eve (2016) 'A Sociological Look at the Evolution of Recent Scholarship on Ethnic Conflicts', *Journal of International Relations and Development* 21 (3): 580–607.

Dudouet, Véronique (2008) *Nonviolent Resistance and Conflict Transformation in Power Asymmetries*. Berghof Handbook for Conflict Transformation, Online Edition. Berlin: Berghof Foundation.

Elliott, Michael, Barbara Gray and Roy Lewicki (2003) 'Lessons Learned about the Framing of Intractable Environmental Conflicts', in Roy Lewicki, Barbara Gray and Michael Elliott (Eds.), *Making Sense of Intractable Environmental Conflicts: Concepts and Cases* (409–436), Washington, DC: Island Press.

Epstein, Charlotte (2013) 'Theorizing Agency in Hobbes's Wake: The Rational Actor, the Self, or the Speaking Subject?', *International Organization* 67 (2): 287–316.

Fearon, James D. (1994) 'Domestic Political Audiences and the Escalation of International Disputes', *The American Political Science Review* 88 (3): 577–592.

Fearon, James D. (1995) 'Rationalist Explanations for War', *International Organization* 49 (3): 379–414.

Fearon, James D. (2004) 'Why Do Some Civil Wars Last So Much Longer than Others?', *Journal of Peace Research* 41 (3): 275–301.

Fearon, James D. (2008) 'Ethnic Mobilization and Ethnic Violence', in Donald A. Wittman and Barry R. Weingast (Eds.), *The Oxford Handbook of Political Economy*, Oxford: Oxford University Press.

Freire, Paolo (1970) *Pedagogy of the Oppressed*. New York: Continuum.

Gad, Ulrik P. (2010) *(How) Can They Become like Us? Danish Identity Politics and the Conflicts of 'Muslim Relations'*, PhD Dissertation, University of Copenhagen, Department of Political Science.

Gallo, Giorgio (2013) 'Conflict Theory, Complexity and Systems Approach', *Systems Research and Behavioral Science* 30 (2): 156–175.

Galtung, Johan (1958) *A Framework for the Analysis of Social Conflict*. New York: Bureau of Applied Social Research, Columbia University (mimeo, unpublished).

Galtung, Johan (1969) 'Violence, Peace and Peace Research', *Journal of Peace Research* 6 (3): 167–191.

Galtung, Johan (1996) *Peace by Peaceful Means: Peace and Conflict, Development and Civilization*. London: Sage.

Galtung, Johan (2009) *Theories of Conflict: Definitions, Dimensions, Negations, Formations*. www.transcend.org/files/Galtung_Book_Theories_Of_Conflict_single.pdf.

Galtung, Johan, Dietrich Fischer (2013) *Johan Galtung: Pioneer of Peace Research*. Berlin: Springer Science & Business Media.

Gleditsch, Kristian Skrede (2007) 'Transnational Dimensions of Civil War', *Journal of Peace Research* 44 (3): 293–309.

Goldmann, Kjell (1974) *Tension and Détente in Bipolar Europe*. Stockholm: Esselte.

Gurr, Ted Robert (1970) *Why Men Rebel*. Princeton, NJ: Princeton University Press.

Halperin, Eran (2016) *Emotions in Conflict: Inhibitors and Facilitators of Peace Making*. London: Routledge.

Hammerich, Else and Kirsten Frydensberg (2006) *Konflikt og kontakt*. Gjern: Hovedland.

Hansen, Lene (2006) *Security as Practice: Discourse Analysis and the Bosnian War*. London: Routledge.

Hsiang, Solomon M., Marshall Burke and Edward Miguel (2013) 'Quantifying the Influence of Climate on Human Conflict', *Science* 341 (6151): 1235367.

Hutchison, Emma and Roland Bleiker (2014) 'Theorizing Emotions in World Politics', *International Theory* 6 (3): 491–514.

Jabri, Vivienne (1996) *Discourses on Violence: Conflict Analysis Reconsidered*. Manchester: Manchester University Press.

Justino, Patricia (2012) 'War and Poverty', *IDS Working Paper* 2012 (391): 1–29.

Kaldor, Mary (2012) *New and Old Wars: Organized Violence in a Global Era*, 3rd ed. Stanford, CA: Stanford University Press.

Kaldor, Mary, Gerald Holden and Richard Falk (1989) *The New Détente: Rethinking East–West Relations*. London, New York: Verso.

Kalyvas, Stathis N. (2006) *The Logic of Violence in Civil War*, 1st ed. Cambridge, New York: Cambridge University Press.

Kalyvas, Stathis N., Ian Shapiro and Tarek Masoud (Eds.) (2008) *Order, Conflict, and Violence*, 1st ed. Cambridge: Cambridge University Press.

Keen, David (2012) *Useful Enemies: When Waging Wars Is More Important than Winning Them*. New Haven, CT: Yale University Press.

King, Martin Luther, Jr. (1963) 'Letter from Birmingham Jail', *Liberation: An Independent Monthly* 8 (4): 10–16, 23.

Kriesberg, Louis and Bruce W. Dayton (2013) *Constructive Conflicts: From Escalation to Resolution*. Lanham, MD: Rowman & Littlefield.

Lake, David A. and Donald Rothchild (1996) 'Containing Fear, the Origins and Management of Ethnic Conflict', *International Security* 21 (2): 41–75.

Lawrence, Adrian (2010) 'Driven to Arms? The Escalation of Violence in Nationalist Conflicts', in Erika Chenoweth and Adria Lawrence (Eds.), *Rethinking Violence: States and Non-State Actors in Conflict* (143–172). Cambridge: MIT Press.

Le Billon, Philippe and Arno Waizenegger (2007) 'Peace in the Wake of Disaster? Secessionist Conflicts and the 2004 Indian Ocean Tsunami', *Transactions of the Institute of British Geographers* 32 (3): 411–427.

Lederach, John P. (1995) *Preparing for Peace: Conflict Transformation across Cultures*. Syracuse, NY: Syracuse University Press.

Lederach, John P. (2005) *Moral Imaginations*. Oxford: Oxford University Press.

Luhmann, Niklas (1984) *Soziale Systeme: Grundriss einer allgemeinen Theorie*. Frankfurt am Main: Suhrkamp.

Luhmann, Niklas (1997) *Die Gesellschaft der Gesellschaft* (2 volumes). Frankfurt am Main: Suhrkamp.

Luhmann, Niklas (2000) *Die Politik der Gesellschaft*. Frankfurt am Main: Suhrkamp.

Lukács, Georg and Rodney Livingstone (1971) *History and Class Consciousness: Studies in Marxist Dialects*. Cambridge: MIT Press.

Mearsheimer, John J. and Stephen M. Walt (2013) 'Leaving Theory Behind: Why Simplistic Hypothesis Testing Is Bad for International Relations', *European Journal of International Relations* 19 (3): 427–457.

Mercer, Jonathan (2010) 'Emotional Beliefs', *International Organization* 64 (1): 1–31.

Messmer, Heinz (2003a) *Der soziale Konflikt: Kommunikative Emergenz und systemische Reproduktion*. Stuttgart: Lucius Lucius.

Messmer, Heinz (2003b) 'Form und Codierung des sozialen Konflikts', *Soziale Systeme* 9 (2): 335–369.

Messmer, Heinz (2007) 'Contradiction, Conflict and Borders', in Stephan Setter (Ed.), *Territorial Conflicts in World Society: Modern Systems Theory, International Relations and Conflict Studies* (101–124), London: Routledge.

Mitchell, Audra (2011) *Lost in Transformation: Violent Peace and Peaceful Conflict in Northern Ireland*. Basingstoke: Palgrave Macmillan.

McQuaid, Sara Dybris (2017) 'Parading Memory and Re-member-ing Conflict: Collective Memory in Transition in Northern Ireland', *International Journal of Politics, Culture, and Society* 30 (1): 23–41.

Mouffe, Chantal (2000) *The Democratic Paradox*. London: Verso.

Mouffe, Chantal (2005) *On the Political*. Abingdon, NY: Routledge.

Mouffe, Chantal (2013) *Agonistics: Thinking the World Politically*. London: Verso.

Mucha, Witold (2012) *Why Do Some Civil Wars not Happen? Understanding Internal Violent Conflict as a Multilayered Phenomenon*. Villigst: AFK Nachwuchstagung.

Pearlman, Wendy (2013) 'Emotions and the Microfoundations of the Arab Uprisings', *Perspectives on Politics* 11 (2): 387–409.

Pruitt, Dean, Jeffrey Rubin and Sung Hee Kimt (2003) *Social Conflict: Escalation, Stalemate, and Settlement*, 3rd ed. New York: McGraw-Hill.

Ramsbotham, Oliver (2010) *Transforming Violent Conflict: Radical Disagreement, Dialogue and Survival*. Abingdon: Routledge.

Ramsbotham, Oliver, Tom Woodhouse and Hugh Miall (2011) *Contemporary Conflict Resolution*, 3rd ed. Cambridge: Polity.

Rapoport, Anatol (1960) *Fights, Games, and Debates – A Scientifically Grounded Method by Which We Can Understand Human Conflict in All Its Forms*. Ann Arbor: University of Michigan Press.

Ross, Andrew G. (2013) *Mixed Emotions: Beyond Fear and Hatred in International Conflict*. Chicago, IL: University of Chicago.

Roy, Beth, John Burdick and Louis Kriesberg (2010) 'A Conversation between Conflict Resolution and Social Movement Scholars', *Conflict Resolution Quarterly* 27: 347–368.

Rubenstein, Richard E. (2017) *Resolving Structural Conflicts: How Violent Systems Can Be Transformed*, 1st ed. London: Routledge.

Rumelili, Bahar (2014a) 'Identity and Desecuritisation: The Pitfalls of Conflating Ontological and Physical Security', *Journal of International Relations and Development* 18: 52–74.

Rumelili, Bahar (2014b) *Conflict Resolution and Ontological Security: Peace Anxieties*. London: Routledge.

Schelling, Thomas C. (1960) *The Strategy of Conflict*. Cambridge, MA: Harvard University Press.

Schmidt, Bettina and Ingo W. Schröder (Eds.) (2001) *Anthropology of Violence and Conflict*. London: Routledge.

Schmitt, Carl (1932) *Der Begriff des Politischen*. München-Leipzig: Verlag von Duncker und Humblot.

Simmel, Georg (1904) 'The Sociology of Conflict (I-III)', *American Journal of Sociology* 9 (4–6): 490–525, 672–689, 798–811.

Sørensen, Majken Jul and Jørgen Johansen (2016) 'Nonviolent Conflict Escalation', *Conflict Resolution Quarterly* 34 (1): 83–108.

Stetter, Stephan (2008) *World Society and the Middle East: Reconstructions in Regional Politics*. Houndmills: Palgrave.

Stetter, Stephan (2014) 'World Politics and Conflict Systems: The Communication of "No" and its Effects', *Horyzonty Polityki* 5 (14): 43–67.

Steward, Francis (2010) *Horizontal Inequalities and Conflict: Understanding Group Violence in Multiethnic Societies*. London: Palgrave Macmillan.

Svensson, Isak and Desirée Nilsson (2018) 'Disputes over the Divine: Introducing the Religion and Armed Conflict (RELAC) Data, 1975–2015', *Journal of Conflict Resolution* 62 (5): 1127–1148.

Wæver, Ole (1989) 'Conflicts of Vision: Visions of Conflict', in Ole Wæver, Pierre Lemaitre, and Elzbieta Tromer (Eds.), *European Polyphony: Beyond East-West Confrontation* (283–325), London: Macmillan.

Wæver, Ole (1995) 'Securitization and Desecuritization'. In Ronnie D. Lipschutz (Ed.), *On Security* (46–86), New York: Columbia University Press.

Wæver, Ole (1996) 'The Rise and Fall of the Inter-Paradigm Debate', in Steve Smith, Ken Booth, and Marysia Zalewski (Eds.), *International Theory: Positivism and Beyond* (149–185), Cambridge: Cambridge University Press.

Wæver, Ole (2003) 'Détente between Conceptual Analysis and Conceptual History', in Jan Hallenberg, Bertil Nygren and Alexa Robertson (Eds.), *Transitions: In Honour of Kjell Goldmann* (85–107), Stockholm: Department of Political Science, Stockholm University.

Wæver, Ole (2009) 'What Exactly Makes a Continuous Existential Threat Existential – And How Is It Discontinued?', in Oren Barak and Gabriel Sheffer (Eds.), *Existential Threats and Civil Security Relations* (19–35), Lanham, MD: Lexington Books.

Wæver, Ole (2014) 'Revisiting Classical Conflict Theory or How to Theorize Conflicts as Conflicts'. Unpublished paper presented at CRIC Research Seminar, February.

Wallensteen, Peter (2011) *Understanding Conflict Resolution: War, Peace and the Global System*. London: Sage.

Wallensteen, Peter (2015) *Quality Peace: Peacebuilding, Victory and World Order*. Oxford: Oxford University Press.

Waltz, Kenneth N. (1979) *Theory of International Politics*. New York: Random House.

Weingast, Barry R. and Rui de Figueiredo (1997) *The Rationality of Fear: Political Opportunism and Ethnic*. Institute for War and Peace Studies, Working paper.

Wucherpfennig, Julian, Nils W. Metternich, Lars-Erik Cederman and Kristian Skrede Gleditsch (2012) 'Ethnicity, the State, and the Duration of Civil War', *World Politics* 64: 79–115.

Zartman, I. William (1991) 'Conflict and Resolution: Contest, Cost, and Change', *The Annals of the American Academy of Political and Social Science* 518 (1): 11–22.

Zartman, I. William & Maureen Berman (1982) *The Practical Negotiator*. New Haven, CT: Yale University Press.

Zartman, I. William and Guy Olivier Faure (2005) *Escalation and Negotiation in International Conflicts*. Cambridge: Cambridge University Press.

2

HOW CONFLICT ESCALATION HAPPENS

Three central interaction rituals in conflict[1]

Isabel Bramsen and Poul Poder

Introduction: emotions emerging from interaction

We live in a world in which social and political conflicts emerge suddenly and unexpectedly. Within a few weeks in 2014, we witnessed a sudden rise in conflict as Russia intervened in Ukraine 'to take back' Crimea. The so-called Arab Spring uprisings (2010–2011) also exemplify a sudden onset of overt conflicts. Emotions are often considered as phenomena in need of control; we talk about putting a lid on them before conflicts escalate and run wild. Commenting on Russia's intervention in Ukraine, Swedish Prime Minister Fredrik Reinfeldt commented, 'We all have to do whatever we can in order to have those emotions that are now circulating attenuated ... [and] through diplomacy there are efforts to have the situation muted' (cited in Kott 2014 (own translation)). The circulation of emotions is considered dangerous, as it allegedly renders conflicts more destructive. However, emotions also drive non-violent action and diplomatic practice as well as violent action.

This chapter develops a model of three basic forms of interaction in conflicts: (a) cooperative interaction, (b) conflictual interaction and (c) dominating interaction. We focus on how emotions emerge in specific situations through ritual practices but also on how the ritual outcome of Emotional Energy (EE) has implications beyond immediate situations in terms of agency formation. Secondly, we formulate a research agenda for the study of EE dynamics in conflict escalation based on two themes: (1) the mobilization of collective EE and (2) emotional dynamics influencing political elites. While developing a situational research agenda for the study of conflict in general, we focus on a specific type of conflict: conflicts where a popular uprising challenges asymmetric power relations. We refer to events in the Arab Spring countries to illustrate how conflict is subjected to specific situational dynamics forming the interactions between regimes and the population.

Interaction rituals

We follow Collins's (2005) methodological contention that we can explain more by first analysing situations instead of assuming certain properties of individuals and entities, such as systems or discourses. Ultimately, such aggregated entities are engendered out of situations. The analytical challenge therefore becomes to investigate what is actually engendered in a specific social situation containing diverse elements, such as people (biological and psychological dispositions), interpretations, actions, emotions, locality, bodies and culture (presumptions). In this manner, we are able to specify how situations have their own local structures, dynamics and outputs (Collins 2005:32).

Collins conceptualizes situational dynamics in terms of interaction rituals, which are understood as the gathering of persons around a common action or event. Building on insights presented by Erving Goffman and Émile Durkheim regarding the ritual nature of social reality, Collins argues that a situation as an interaction ritual provides humans with motivation, agency, identity, symbols and community. It consists of mutually focused attention and emotion that engender a shared reality in terms of group emotion and membership (Collins 2005:7). An interaction can be symbolically productive when people represent their interaction through common symbols, such as the partisan scarf used in Palestinian intifadas (Collins 2005:17). The crucial situational point is to investigate how micro-social details interact in the situation at hand.

Collins's (2005:48) conception of social interaction as interaction rituals consists of different ingredients that can produce various outputs depending on the composition of inputs and the intensity and focus of the concerned interaction. The following model illustrates ritual ingredients and outcomes:

For Collins, the interaction ritual consists of four basic ingredients: (a) co-presence of at least two persons in the same place so that they affect each other by their bodily presence, whether or not they are aware of it; (b) barriers to outsiders where participants have a sense of who is (not) taking part in the interaction ritual; (c) people focus their attention on the same activity or object and become aware of each other's focus; and (d) people share a common mood or emotional experience (Collins 2005:48). The particular emotion they feel is insignificant; it is the sharing/contagion of the emotion that is the crucial dynamic. When people become

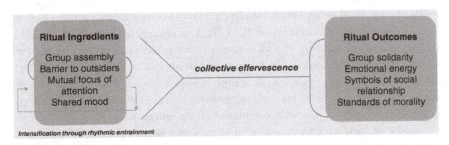

FIGURE 2.1 Interactional Ritual (Bramsen & Poder 2018).

aware of each other's focus, they become immersed in each other's emotions: 'As a result, the emotional mood becomes stronger and more dominant; competing feelings are driven out by the main group feeling' (Collins 1990:32).

Thus, bodily co-presence, barriers to outsiders, a common action or event, a mutual focus of attention and a shared mood that might be triggered by a transient emotional stimulus are needed to generate an interaction ritual. All of these ingredients, the latter two in particular, mutually reinforce each other. When interaction is focused, people can be carried along in the interaction, which establishes a rhythmic involvement such as a balanced exchange of speaking and listening among the participants. Alternatively, people's body language can become synchronized: their gestures, gazes and/or vocal pitch mirror each other in focused conversations (Collins 2005:75).

The right column in Figure 2.1 describes how focused and intense ritual interaction can generate (a) feelings of membership or group solidarity, (b) feelings of confidence, elation, strength, enthusiasm and initiative in taking action (EE), (c) symbols – visual icons, words and gestures – that members feel are associated with themselves collectively and (d) feelings of morality and a sense of rightness in adhering to the group. If the ritual interaction is part of a recurring pattern, it might also contribute to common standards of morality among the participating individuals (Collins 2005:49).

Interaction rituals not only generate emotions and EE, they also transform emotions (Collins 2005:107). Collins's theory is about the ritual processes involved in intensifying emotions or transforming participants' prior emotions as they engage in the interaction ritual. If a ritual is strongly focused and entrained, the individual emotions with which participants enter the ritual tend to converge into the arising group emotion. Collins's theory focuses on mechanisms that homogenize the emotional experience among the participants. His approach specifies the processes that engender a dominant group emotion in a given situation without assuming that social situations are characterized by the presence of very distinct emotions; it is useful for exploring how the relationship and balance between coexisting emotions are changed, as evidenced during the Arab Spring when fear and hopelessness were transformed into anger, hope and courage.

By referring to the situational causes of negative or positive EE and low EE as aggregated entities of mixed emotions, we avoid an overly abstract examination of the circulation of affect (which is Pearlman's basic criticism of Ross's approach; see Pearlman 2014) or an overly simplified analysis of emotion in political life by focusing on single emotions (Ross 2014:17). Consequently, emotional complexity (i.e. mixed emotions in Ross's terms) is best treated as an empirical question because different situations and interaction rituals make emotional experience either mixed or more focused. A combination of an empirical focus and the situational approach helps to determine how social processes are formed and established by either single or more mixed group emotions.

Like Pearlman, we link emotions to agency, but we develop this insight more systematically with respect to basic forms of interaction in conflicts. By stressing how such emotions can be enduring due to stable social circumstances, we provide a different framework than Pearlman, which works within the traditional paradigm of conceptualizing emotions as episodic. Theorizing the importance of emotions for individual and group agencies differs from Ross's focus on the circulation of affect and its significance for creativity and socialization.

Interaction rituals generate EE that differs from episodic and dramatic emotions, such as 'shouting or lashing out in anger, squealing and gesturing with joy, shrieking or running around in fear' (Collins 2005:134). The output of interaction rituals acquires a high degree of focused emotional entrainment that persists even after the individual has left the situation (Collins 2005:134). EE shows itself in bodily postures and movements, such as erect posture and moving firmly and smoothly (Collins 2005:135). According to Collins (2005:138), it can also be measured in hormone levels, especially in the relative increase or decrease of testosterone.

Collins's theory considers formal processes that characterize social life across cultural differences. We do not suggest that each situation is unique and can only be understood according to specific local conditions. Collins's theory addresses generic ritual dynamics with respect to how group identity, symbols and EE are generated and transformed in different cultures. In terms of ritual outcomes, what is important is how people behave when they gather together, not whether they gather around football or pray in a mosque. Moreover, interaction rituals reside on a continuum from highly focused and intensive interaction with several emotional and symbolic outcomes to dispersed or completely unfocused interaction with few or no ritual outcomes. On this formal basis, culturally variable interactions can be compared.

Positive background emotions contribute to agency

Collins's innovative notion of EE explains how agency is based on emotion. Barbara L. Fredrickson's and Jack Barbalet's respective theories further explore this insight into agency as an emotional matter. According to Fredrickson's 'build and broaden' theory, positive (pleasant) emotions are resources of agency. Emotions such as surprise, joy, interest and pride tend to broaden how individuals view the world and their opportunities to act within it, and build resources that they can draw on in future action (Fredrickson 2001, 2003; Fredrickson and Branigan 2005). They broaden the scope of our attention, cognition and action, and widen the array of precepts, thoughts and actions we think and consider. Furthermore, joy creates an urge to play, be creative and push existing limits. In sum, positive emotions augment agency.

Barbalet argues that confidence, trust and loyalty operate as silent background emotions that establish agency on personal, social and institutional levels (Barbalet 1996, 1998; see also Poder 2008). Confidence is fundamental to action: 'All action is ultimately founded on the actor's feeling of confidence in their capacities and the effectiveness of those capacities. The actor's confidence is a necessary source of action; without it, action simply would not occur' (Barbalet 1996:90). Confidence arises out of social relations in which the person is met with appreciation and granted access to the social and material resources relevant for the concerned future action (Barbalet 1998:86). Without access to resources, such as knowledge, tools and social support, the individual cannot sustain the feeling of being able to act on their own in relation to the unknowable future. This points to the fundamental temporal aspect of confidence as based on secured future access to resources. Thus, self-confidence is a genuinely social emotion in the sense that how we experience it depends on the social context of relevant resources in which the person concerned is inevitably enmeshed.

Trust is also a social emotion fundamental to cooperation; it is the belief that the actions of others will conform to expectations. Trust implies a feeling that one can rely on others' unknowable actions. The basis of trust cannot be knowledge or calculation but, instead, includes an affective or emotional acceptance of dependence on others (Barbalet 1996:78). While trust cannot be based on knowledge (as we never know what others will do), it is not constituted solely as an emotion. Trust is not blind – we trust each other because we know something about one another that makes trust possible. Knowledge and competence also contribute to generating trust. This emotional acceptance of dependence on others cannot be taken for granted, as it is achieved in interaction. Trust is a way of influencing others that creates greater understanding and less opposition than the more uneconomical means of coercion (Barbalet 1996:78). For Barbalet, the generation of trust is empowering, as it increases the capacity of others to interact.

According to Barbalet, 'loyalty is the emotion of confidence in organization' (1996:80). While trust concerns cooperation, loyalty is feeling the viability of the arrangement in which cooperation takes place. It is a feeling that the institutional context that extends beyond the immediate interaction will deliver what is expected. For example, while I might mistrust my bank manager, I can still feel assured that the bank will deliver the services it claims to provide. Loyalty is the source of fundamental social and political associations and is therefore of basic importance (Barbalet 1996:86).

Barbalet explains how emotions reside both in experiencing individuals and in their social relations. Both experiential and contextual elements of emotion are necessary in order to conceptualize emotion as a social phenomenon:

> What is important in an emotional experience is that it registers in the processes constitutive of the person, which is more than but includes the proposition that emotional experiences introduce physical and psychological changes in the subject of the experience.
>
> *(Barbalet 1998:80)*

Emotion is simultaneously a physical, psychological and social phenomenon. It cannot be reduced to its person-bound indicators when we realize that social context is a constitutive part of emotions. Consequently, emotions can be short-lived or last longer. They are not episodic *per se*: whether the emotional experience is long- or short-lived depends on the stability of the social context that forms the emotion (Barbalet 1998:80). It also depends on interpretation and remembrance. If one's interpretation of a situation remains the same, the remembrance can invoke the same emotions even after a long time. Consequently, emotions are not necessarily short-lived.

When we relate this point to self-confidence, we can stress that the constancy or longevity of the emotion depends on the actual character of the social context: as long as it is providing relevant resources for the persons concerned, they can feel self-confident. This emotion is not just dependent on how they are appraised by others and by themselves. While individuals can think of themselves as competent and be appreciated affirmatively by others, it is difficult to remain confident without access to resources. Subsequently, emotions can make their influence felt without subjects verbally articulating them or even being aware.

In summary, positive and background emotions contribute to the agency of people, both individually and as group members. Such emotions are stored both within individuals and within group symbols that energize them. In a nutshell, such emotions function as agency resources as their productive significance goes beyond their immediate presence. They are significant in order to understand what happens in the immediate situation but also for understanding what can happen next.

We now explore how particular kinds of interaction generate distinct agency dynamics that must be considered to grasp the course of events in conflicts.

Three forms of interaction in conflict

Group formation is simultaneously both a precondition *and* a product of conflict (Simmel [1908] 1955). Without internal solidarity, groups do not engage in conflicts with others (Collins 2005:41). At the same time, conflict generates and reinforces group solidarity. Consequently, we need to investigate how interactional dynamics engender group solidarity and EE, rather than looking for ancient hatred, trauma or underlying cultural influences. Parties do not actively pursue their goals and values without the EE of solidarity. Solidarity-oriented, cooperative interaction also engenders Fredrikson's positive emotions and Barbalet's background agency emotions, both of which augment agency (Figure 2.2).

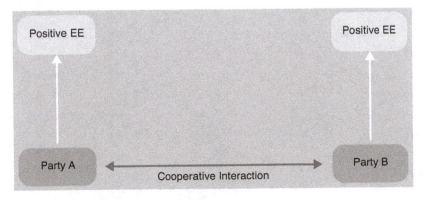

FIGURE 2.2 Cooperative Interaction (Bramsen & Poder 2018).

It is not a given fact, however, that social interaction always leads to higher EE for both parties. Collins theorizes power rituals where one party gets positive EE (confidence, pride), while the other party loses EE and becomes frightened or demoralized (shame, depression) (Figure 2.3). For example, while fear may be a dramatic emotion in response to shock, it also involves anticipation of an imminent threat, such as the possible eruption of a volcano. It is involved in constituting a situation with a particularly negative outlook, as when employees fear being fired because their company is operating unprofitably.

In their paper, "Negative Emotional Energy: A Theory of the 'Dark-Side' of Interaction Ritual Chains", David Boyns and Sarah Luery (2015:149) argue that it is too simplistic to think in terms of either energy or absence of energy: we must also think of energy involved in active enmity. While Collins's EE concept concerns positive energy that supports affiliation, Boyns and Luery contend that we also need to understand how negative emotions work as action-motivating energy. While Collins does not dismiss the role of negative emotions in conflict *per se*, he considers them as energizing action only insofar as negative emotions are transformed into solidarity through in-group interaction rituals. Regarding social movements, he suggests that 'shame is the initiating ingredient which becomes transformed, as in all social movements, into collective solidarity and hence energy for collective action' (Collins 2001:41).

Boyns and Leury suggest that shame and other negative emotions are products of interaction rituals, including conflictual interaction rituals. Negative EE as a general category refers to emotions such as avoidance, irritation, embarrassment, anger, shame, resentment, hatred, rage and fear (Boyns and Luery 2015:155). It is not the absence of EE but a category of emotions describing the emotionality of enmity. It contributes to the active opposing of and engaging with an enemy (as opposed to feeling indifferent) and to establishing a strong emotional bond between conflicting parties. While Collins argues that people are driven by their

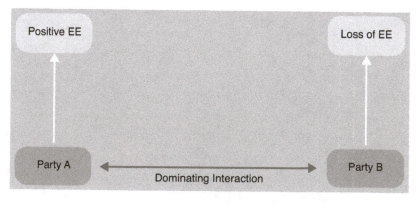

FIGURE 2.3 Dominating Interaction (Bramsen & Poder 2018).

will to maximize positive EE, Boyns and Luery describe how the main driver of negative EE is the need to get rid of uncomfortable emotions by, for example, punishing the enemy (Boyns and Luery 2015:160).

Conflicts, then, are not to be understood as merely broken rituals, as Collins (2005:110) suggests, but can be seen as rituals engendering negative EE. Emotions arising from situations of perceived misunderstanding, disrespect or interruptions are also significant drivers, as Boyns and Luery explain:

> EE+ is likely to emerge when the collective dynamics of social rituals are successful; EE− is likely to manifest when the social bases of EE+ are challenged, undermined, or unfulfilled. In short, EE− results as a consequence of failed or contentious social relationships and as a result of the attenuation or contravention of EE+.
>
> *(Boyns and Luery 2015:156)*

Interaction rituals, then, can fail to generate solidarity between parties. Boyns and Luery's crucial point is that unsuccessful interaction rituals do not necessarily lead to a lack of EE in Collins's positive sense. Loss of EE might be the outcome of, say, sitting in a boring meeting. However, the outcome can also be negative EE when interacting with others who, for example, do not accord another respect and recognition, which may lead one to feel offended or aggressive. Thus, interaction rituals can produce both positive EE and negative EE that can coexist as significant reserves of energy. The interaction ritual type we call conflictual interaction engenders negative EE in both the opposing parties (Figure 2.4).

For a conflict to continue, both positive and negative energies are necessary, for example, in both the hope that 'we will win' and anger towards the other. By specifying the respective contributions of positive and negative EEs, we can understand their mutual and intersecting influences on actions in conflicts.

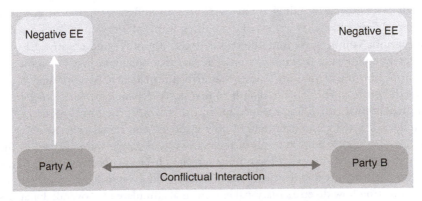

FIGURE 2.4 Conflictual Interaction (Bramsen & Poder 2018).

Boyns and Luery suggest that negative EE creates both an impetus and inertia for conflict. When negative EE increases, so does the potential for conflict.
When parties feel considerable animosity towards each other, there is a marked
indication of conflict (Boyns and Luery 2015:163). For the conflict to become
overt and for people to take conflictual action, there needs to be a certain, if not
high, level of group solidarity (Boyns and Luery 2015:163); you may well hate
your opponent intensely, but it is unlikely that you will engage in conflictual
action if your group is low on positive EE.

Negative EE can also serve as a thermostat for gauging conflict as it helps us
to understand the temperature, build-up and outbreak of antagonism (Boyns
and Luery 2015:163). This specification of negative and positive EEs more
fully appreciates the emotional nature of conflicts. Boyns and Luery suggest that the level of positive EE predicts the intensity of engagement but
not necessarily its destructiveness. They are correct: strong internal EE is a
precondition for a conflict to become overt, but whether it turns destructive
depends on other conditions, such as the chosen strategies of the involved
parties. Furthermore, both negative and positive EEs influence the intensity
of conflicts, since strong negative EE also intensifies conflicts. Moreover, if
Collins's basic assumption that human beings seek EE is valid, then engaging
in conflictual interaction can be an independent motive because it provides the
parties with EE. If engaging in conflict is the only way to be energized, then
we can explain attraction to such activity that by other accounts is deemed
destructive. The following figure summarizes the three forms of interaction
and emotional dynamics:

To summarize, the cooperative interaction follows Collins's interaction rituals
model in which a mutual focus of attention and a shared mood generate positive EE. Besides cooperative interaction rituals within each conflicting party,
conflict also involves conflictual interaction rituals that generate negative EE
and dominating interaction rituals that empty suppressed parties of EE when
they experience feelings such as hopelessness, humiliation and anxiety (Barbalet
1996:76). The three forms of interaction are basic, as they shape the course of all
kinds of conflicts, including latent/overt and asymmetric/symmetric conflicts.
Figure 2.5 provides an overview of these three forms of interaction. When assessing specific conflicts, we find different degrees of positive and negative EEs and
different combinations of interaction. The fact that one party may be dominated
in a specific interaction does not necessarily mean that it is suppressed in the
overall conflict. The actual strength of this party depends on what other kinds
of interactional rituals it is engaged in. In other words, the forms of interaction
framework provides an overview of how complex emotional experiences work
in three basic directions in terms of agency: while negative and positive EEs fuel
action, the loss of energy serves to limit action. This framework enable us to understand the nature and development of conflicts in greater depth and detail. By
investigating how diverse situational emotions accumulate into overall dynamics,
we are able to grasp how parties are socially constructed as active or passive.

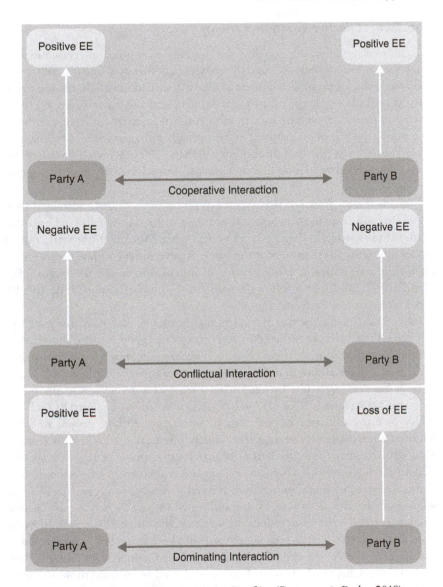

FIGURE 2.5 Three forms of interaction in Conflict (Bramsen & Poder 2018).

Emotional dynamics in the Arab uprisings

We have developed an analytical framework of three basic forms of interaction relevant to the different processes and developments of conflicts. To illustrate the applicability of this framework, we now discuss the Arab Spring as an example of how structural factors alone cannot explain conflict escalation, as emotional processes are crucial for enabling action.

Mobilizing collective emotional energy

In asymmetric conflict, the 'top dog' sustains the power position via dominating rituals such as random arrests, surveillance and raids that generate fear and suspicion among the suppressed (Pasquetti 2013). In domination rituals, the top dog is charged with EE, while the underdog is de-energized and thus passive. A crucial element of mobilization (and escalation of conflict) in an asymmetric conflict is overcoming the fear of punishment for revolting (Vinthagen 2006). Mobilization can be described as 'the mobilization of collective EE'; otherwise, de-energized people come together to mobilize enough energy and solidarity to challenge the top dogs (Collins 2005:133).

In many Arab countries, the regimes in power prior to 2011 sustained their power through fear: most people did not dare to be the first to challenge the regime by protesting on the streets. However, when Mohamed Bouazizi, a street vendor protesting his treatment at the hands of government authorities, set himself on fire in Tunisia in 2010, a wave of indignation broke the wall of fear (Castells 2012:20). In what follows, we discuss the mobilization of collective EE in Bahrain, Tunisia, Syria and Egypt.

In the Arab Spring, the fear of challenging the regime was overcome in at least four ways. First, activists[2] urged non-activists to courageously voice their dissent by modelling that courage themselves and encouraging anti-fear slogans such as 'We are no longer afraid' and 'No more fear after today' (Pearlman 2013:116). Second, fear was overcome by generating a sense of togetherness in the streets (Bramsen 2018; Castells 2012:21). Such togetherness can be explained by Collins's theory of how solidarity is generated in interaction rituals: people in street demonstrations generally stand together closely, often having direct body contact. With similar slogans and the rhythm of marching, a sphere of togetherness and solidarity is achieved that energizes people and enables them to overcome fear. Third, energized by moral indignation and righteous anger over regime killings, people once paralysed by fear were transformed into more active participants, which motivated even more to join the uprisings (Pearlman 2013:395). In Syria, protesters chanted, 'The Syrian people will not be humiliated', and refused to be stopped by the violent crackdown (World Affairs Council 2014 citing Robert Ford; see also Chapter 4). Fourth, humour was used to ridicule those in power and promote internal solidarity. For example, an Egyptian picture circulated in which a file called 'Freedom' was about to be installed on a server called 'Tunisia' before an error message stated, 'Please remove Mubarak and try again' (Popovic and Miller 2015).

These four methods of overcoming fear and fuelling action resonate with the mechanisms of positive and negative EEs. Following Collins's terminology, fear was overcome and action fuelled by different energizing emotions generated in specific situations, either mediated or face-to-face. Future research could investigate such emotional transformations in more micro-social detail than was performed in the above-mentioned studies. Applying the interaction ritual model would be fruitful because it specifies the processes and ingredients involved in transforming emotions and producing EE.

The positive and negative EEs that fuelled the Arab uprisings also emerged from online interaction. Previous theories of collective action argued that non-violent mobilization depended on charismatic leaders like Martin Luther King, Jr. or Gandhi (Bimber, Flanagin and Stohl 2005). Leaders whose rhetoric engenders courage can change the relative weight of fear in people. Today, social media provides new forms of mobilization that are less dependent on a single leader and can be described as a 'choreography of assembly' (Gerbaudo 2012:43). Choreographic leadership is a form of emotional leadership, where information and communication technologies (ICT) are used to evoke emotions, such as anger or enthusiasm, in order to set the scene for participation. Social media choreographers include Facebook page administrators and popular Twitter users who direct people towards specific protest events, guide the acts of the participants and sustain momentum. Thus, digitized social movements should not be seen as utterly spontaneous, unexpectedly emerging activity; in fact, they rely on emotional narration and scripting. Paulo Gerbaudo argues that ICTs are used to construct solidarity and consolidate emotions of anger, indignation and frustration, thereby turning individual sentiment into shared political passions (Gerbaudo 2012:161). Miriyam Arouragh and Anne Alexander reference an interview that demonstrates the role the Internet played in increasing people's anger leading up to the demonstrations in Egypt: 'When you asked people to go and demonstrate against the police, they were ready because you had already provided them with materials which made them angry' (2011:1348). Bahraini activist Zainab al Khawaja (Twitter name: Angry Arabia) wrote on Twitter, 'The first step is to forget your fear and realize that it is your right to be angry'. This statement justifies feeling a sense of anger and calls forth this emotion, which demonstrates the importance of negative EE in conflicts.

Following Meyrowitz's point that situations are defined by the flow of information, we suggest that emotional narration though ICTs can shape situations by, for example, expressing violent insults against the regime, which then generates anger, outrage and indignation. A particularly powerful message disseminated in the Egyptian revolution in 2011 was a video by Asmaa Mahfouz, a female activist. She incited (or perhaps even provoked) men to take to the streets by referring to their manhood: 'If you think yourself a man, come with me on 25 January. Whoever says women shouldn't go to protests because they will get beaten, let him have some honor and manhood and come with me on 25 January' (Gunning and Baron 2014:227). Mahfouz clearly framed the demonstrations as an opportunity or situation for a man to confirm his identity as a man.

Similarly, Wael Ghonim, the administrator of the central Egyptian Facebook page, 'We are all Kahlid Said', posted several messages about not acting in a cowardly manner and appealed to people's sense of pride on the revolution event page (Gerbaudo 2012:62). On 25 January, the first day of the revolution, the protesting crowd made contact with people who did not have access to the Internet through positive slogans like 'Bread, freedom and dignity', and invited them to join the demonstrations (Gerbaudo 2012:66).

Such choreography of assembly and emotional narration can be seen as 'situation making'; by instructing people to engage in non-violent behaviour and using certain slogans, the choreographers influence how events unfold. Before the 2011 demonstrations in Egypt, guidelines for non-violent resistance were distributed and suggested that the main protest slogan, 'The people want to overthrow the regime', be followed by 'Peaceful, peaceful' and 'Change does not mean extremism' (Azaz 2013). The choreographers also made people laugh. The April 6th Youth Movement, a prominent Egyptian activist group, attended a training course in non-violence in Serbia in 2009 where they learned about 'laughtivism'. This form of activism was invented by Otpor, a Serbian activist group, and is designed to make people laugh to overcome fear. Srdja Popovic, one of the Otpor leaders, has described how they toppled Milosevic in 2000 (in part) by creating situations that made people laugh. For example, Otpor released a turkey with a white flower on its head (the symbol of Milosevic's wife). Chasing and arresting the turkey, policemen made fools of themselves. This is a clear example of leadership constructing situations to generate certain emotions and, thus, certain actions or inactions.

Elite emotions and actions

Conflict escalation is an interactive process of action and reaction. While the outbreak of overt conflict depends on mobilization to challenge power relations, further escalation or de-escalation depends on the reaction of the counterpart, in this case the elites. Instrumentalist accounts of politics and emotions underline how elites are able to manipulate and subordinate people's emotions in order to promote their own interests. However, this does not mean that elite groups are unemotional, 'rational' decision makers. Socially created emotions are not exclusive to subordinate groups, as they can also be felt by superior groups when they perceive they are losing power (Barbalet 1998:161).

Barbalet argues that elite fear arises when power relationships are transformed in ways that threaten their position. Unlike depression, fear is not totally agency-depriving: 'Fear is a negative anticipation of what will happen, which assumes enough EE to take some initiative, or at least remain alert to situations that carry social dangers' (Collins 2005:129). Besides the strategies of flight or fight, Barbalet suggests containment as a third way of handling fear. During the First World War era, for example, the British elites were dealing with the rise of a discontented and restive working class. A climate of fear can be sensed in documents produced by the elite at the time and heard in ministers' speeches. This fear influenced the elite to take certain actions vis-à-vis the growing revolutionary forces. Their fear of the rising working class prompted them to incorporate the working class in a reformist manner, making it less threatening to their interests (Barbalet 2005: Chapter 7). Inspired by Barbalet's analysis, we might ask how elite fear plays a role in current conflicts and investigate the circumstances in which elites adopt a containment strategy.

Collins (2005:133) contends that revolutions succeed when a sufficient number of interaction rituals among elites fail, as when domination rituals that otherwise energize elites are not taken seriously by the people and subsequently fall apart. By contrast, Barbalet suggests that a containment strategy can help elites generate solidarity rituals among themselves and, through reform, transform dominating rituals to sustain power without upsetting the people.

By applying the framework of different interaction-forms, we can investigate how fear motivates elite actors. Due to the methodological difficulties mentioned, we can only speculate that containment strategies seem more likely if elites have relatively high levels of internal solidarity (positive EE). This strategy is less likely to succeed if elites have relatively low levels of internal solidarity, because containment strategies require that they coordinate their activities. While Barbalet is correct in suggesting containment as a strategy applicable to social threats, we must also recognize that there are situations wherein elites actually adopt responses oriented more towards destroying opponents than reforming the situation. For example, we have witnessed how the elites crushed opposition parties in authoritarian regimes in Syria and Bahrain.

Fear can also cause elites to flee the country. Former Tunisian President Ben Ali gave his last speech on 13 January 2011, the day before he fled the country. In his speech, Ali promised to meet most of the protesters' demands, including not running for election in the following autumn. Some protesters interpreted the speech as a sign of weakness and fear: 'Like look at him, he looks scared, he was shaking, he was sweating, he hit the mike twice, he was very like confused – you know like people felt it, they saw that – this is you know, we can't take steps back, we have to continue this, this is going somewhere' (Tunisian activist, interview by Isabel Bramsen, 7 April 2015). Further research should investigate how elites are influenced by fear emotions when making decisions that affect the course of conflicts; what influences a ruler to make reforms as in Jordan, crush an uprising as in Syria, or flee as in Tunisia?

Our challenge is to investigate the relationship and exchange between different emotional situations as conflicts emerge and escalate. How do mass demonstrations and popular uprisings influence the elite groups' emotions? What effects do such situations have on the elites? Elites often seem to present a calm public face or condemn the actions of protesting groups as illegal unrest and incivility. However, this kind of face work can exist alongside fear of losing their legitimacy and privileges when confronted with increasing popular protests. We need to investigate the interaction between different social situations.

Conclusion

In this analysis of the emotional complexities of conflicts, we suggest three superordinate categories. The first is positive EE, which is the sum of positive, agency-generating emotions such as group solidarity, hope and joy. The second is negative EE, which is the sum of negative emotions facilitating agency and binding the opponents to each other in a conflictual relationship. The third category features one party gaining EE and the other party becoming de-energized in ways that make it less capable of actions, such as through fear and hopelessness.

Whether and how a conflict escalates depends on the success of cooperative interaction rituals within the parties as well as depending on the intensity of conflictual interaction rituals between them. This involves the production of negative EE. In an asymmetric conflict where the 'top dog' has sustained its power through dominating rituals that de-energize the suppressed, the challenge for activists is to make cooperative interaction rituals among the people to generate sufficient EE for collective action.

As shown in the Arab Spring, mobilization is about *breaking the wall of fear* by energizing actors with both negative and positive EEs. Rather than playing on certain emotions, leaders can form situations that generate certain emotions, such as making people angry enough to overcome fear and engage in action. While the outbreak of overt conflict depends on the mobilization to change the status quo, further escalation or de-escalation depends on the reaction of the other party, which in the case of asymmetric conflicts is the 'top dog'.

In the Arab Spring, we saw very different responses to uprisings ranging from violent suppression to submission. We suggest that if the mobilization of protesters' EE is very high and the internal solidarity among politicians falls apart, changing power relations and potential regime change become apparent. Likewise, the ability of elites to either violently suppress or contain an uprising depends on its ability to sustain or transform dominating rituals and internal solidarity among the elite.

With the situational approach, we can appreciate how situations engender emotional transformations. These transformations provide different constellations and mixed emotions that, in turn, generate unexpected actions. We hope that the developed framework of emotional dynamics and forms of interaction in conflict will be a useful framework for approaching these exciting and demanding research challenges.

Notes

1 This chapter is a reworked and shortened version of a longer article by the authors (2014) published in *Peace Research: The Canadian Journal of Peace and Conflict Studies* 46 (2): 51–86 as 'Theorizing Three Basic Emotional Dynamics of Conflicts: A Situational Research Agenda'.

2 Here, the label 'activist' is used broadly to describe initiators of demonstrations and other kinds of activists, including, for example, lawyers, student activists and members of the Muslim brotherhood. The terms 'protester' and 'demonstrator', on the other hand, refer specifically to people participating in demonstrations on the streets.

References

Aouragh, Miriyam and Anne Alexander (2011) 'The Egyptian Experience: Sense and Nonsense of the Internet Revolution', *International Journal of Communication* 5: 1344–1358.

Azaz, Mahmoud (2013) *One Revolution but Two Languages: A Critical Political Discourse Analysis of Two Conflicting Discourses During the Egyptian Revolution.* www.utexas.edu/cola/depts/mes/events/conferences/jiljadid2013/jiljadid2013abstracts/Mahmoud AzazOneRevolutionTwoLanguages.pdf (accessed 25 May 2013).

Barbalet, Jack (1996) 'Social Emotions: Confidence, Trust and Loyalty', *International Journal of Sociology and Social Policy* 16 (9–10): 75–96.

Barbalet, Jack (1998) *Emotion, Social Theory and Social Structure: A Macrosocial Approach.* Cambridge: Cambridge University Press.

Bimber, Bruce, Andrew J. Flanagin and Cynthia Stohl (2005) 'Reconceptualizing Collective Action in the Contemporary Media Environment', *Communication Theory* 15 (4): 365–388.

Boyns, David and Sarah Luery (2015) 'Negative Emotional Energy: A Theory of the "Dark-Side" of Interaction Ritual Chains', *Social Sciences* 4 (1): 148–170.

Bramsen, Isabel (2018). How Civil Resistance Succeeds (or Not): Micro-Dynamics of Unity, Timing, and Escalatory Actions. *Peace & Change* 43: 61–89. doi:10.1111/pech.12274.

Bramsen, Isabel and Poul Poder (2018). *Emotional Dynamics in Conflict and Conflict Transformation.* Berghof Foundation. www.berghof-foundation.org/fileadmin/redaktion/Publications/Handbook/Articles/bramsen_poder_handbook.pdf (accessed 7 December 2018).

Castells, Manual (2012) *Networks of Outrage and Hope.* Cambridge: Polity Press.

Collins, Randall (1990) 'Stratification, Emotional Energy and the Transient Emotions', in Theodore Kemper (Ed.), *Research Agendas in the Sociology of Emotions* (27–57), Albany, NY: State University of New York Press.

Collins, Randall (2001) 'Social Movements and the Focus of Emotional Attention', in Jeff Goodwin, James M. Jasper and Francesca Polletta (Eds.), *Passionate Politics* (27–44), Chicago, IL: University of Chicago Press.

Collins, Randall (2005) *Interaction Ritual Chains.* Princeton, NJ: Princeton University Press.

Fredrickson, Barbara L. (2001) 'The Role of Positive Emotions in Positive Psychology: The Broaden-and-Build Theory of Positive Emotions', *American Psychologist* 56: 218–226.

Fredrickson, Barbara L. (2003) 'Positive Emotions and Upward Spirals in Organizational Settings', in Kim Cameron, Jane Dutton and Robert Quinn (Eds.), *Positive Organizational Scholarship: Foundations of a New Discipline*, San Francisco, CA: Berrett-Koehler: 163–175.

Fredrickson, Barbara L. and Christine Branigan (2005) 'Positive Emotions Broaden the Scope of Attention and Thought-Action Repertoires', *Cognition and Emotion* 19: 313–332.

Gerbaudo, Paulo (2012) *Tweets and the Streets: Social Media and Contemporary Activism.* London: Pluto.

Gunning, Jeroen and Ilan Zvi Baron (2014) *Why Occupy a Square? People, Protests and Movements in the Egyptian Revolution.* Oxford: Oxford University Press.

Kott, Sarah (2014) *Sveriges statsminister Frederik Reinfeldt i problemer efter Rusland kommentar.* http://jyllandsposten.dk/international/europa/ECE6530435/Sveriges+statsminister+-Fredrik+Reinfeldt+i+problemer+efter+Rusland-kommentar/ (accessed 20 June 2017).

Pasquetti, Silvia (2013) 'Legal Emotions: An Ethnography of Distrust and Fear in the Arab Districts of an Israeli City', *Law & Society Review* 47 (3): 461–492.

Pearlman, Wendy (2013) 'Emotions and the Microfoundations of the Arab Uprisings', *Perspectives on Politics* 11 (2): 387–409.

Pearlman, Wendy (2014) 'What do Affects Affect?: On Ross's Mixed Emotions', *Theory & Event* 17 (3). https://muse.jhu.edu/article/553388 (accessed 20 June 2017).

Poder, Poul (2008) 'The Sociology of Emotions: Managing, Exchanging and Generating Emotions in Everyday Life', in Michael Jacobsen (Ed.), *Sociologies of the Unnoticed* (299–352), London: Palgrave Macmillan.

Popovic, Srdja and Matthew Miller (2015) *Blueprint for Revolution: How to Use Rice Pudding, Lego Men, and Other Nonviolent Techniques to Galvanize Communities, Overthrow Dictators, or Simply Change the World*. New York: Random House.

Ross, Andrew A.G. (2014) *Mixed Emotions: Beyond Fear and Hatred in International Conflict*. Chicago, IL: The University of Chicago Press.

Simmel, Georg ([1908] 1955) *Conflict and the Web of Group-Affiliations*. Translated by Kurt H. Wolff and Reinhard Bendix. New York: Free Press.

World Affairs Council (2014) *Robert Ford on the War in Syria*. www.lawac.org/Events-and-Archives/Commentary/Post/471/Robert-Ford-on-the-War-in-Syria (accessed 20 June 2017).

3

ESCALATION OR DEMOBILIZATION?

Diverging dynamics of conflict displacement and violent repression in Bahrain and Syria

Isabel Bramsen

Introduction: micro-dynamics of escalation and demobilization in Syria and Bahrain

The relationship between repression and dissent is indeed ambiguous. Despite — or perhaps because of — many years of research on repression and dissent, there is no consensus on the 'repression/mobilization nexus' or 'repression popular protest paradox', that is, whether repression increases or decreases mobilization. Research has shown that repression increases dissent, reduces dissent as it raises the costs hereof, or that the relationship depends on time, the consistency of repression or the visibility hereof (Davenport 2007a; Davenport and Moore 2012; Lichbach 1987; Martin 2007; Tilly 1978). Zimmermann is often quoted for summing up how 'there are theoretical arguments for all conceivable basic relations between governmental coercion and rebellion except for no relationship' (Zimmermann 1980:181). Part of the problem is that repression is not one thing; it can vary in consistency, coerciveness and tactics and can occur in differing contexts.

The Syrian Civil War is often explained with reference to two factors: firstly, the sectarian composition of the society, with the majority Sunni population being ruled by the minority Alawite sect, often blaming the regime for 'playing the sectarian card', and secondly, the violent repression of dissent (see Hinnebusch, Imady and Zintl 2016; Leenders 2014, 2016). In Bahrain, the successful repression of protests is likewise explained with reference to sectarian tensions, the Sunni minority ruling a Shia minority and violent crackdown of dissent (see Fattahi 2012; Matthiesen 2013). Put bluntly, the same inputs of stirring up sectarian tensions and repressing mobilization are believed to explain civil war in one case and demobilization in another. This calls for the more in-depth exploration of *how* and *what type* of repression and sectarianism caused civil war in Syria and the silencing of the movement in Bahrain, respectively.

The chapter takes up this endeavour and analyses how the strategies of repression and increasing sectarian tensions applied by these two regimes assumed different forms and occurred in different environments, thereby shaping different outcomes in Bahrain and Syria. I argue that in both Bahrain and Syria, the regime violently repressed the opposition and displaced the lines of conflict from a conflict between the people and the regime to a sectarian one. But the scenario played out differently in the two countries (1) because the Bahraini regime was able to dominate the divided opposition, whereas the Syrian regime itself (the military, in particular) was divided and did not have the sufficient unity, material equipment or manpower to dominate the situation and (2) because the nature of repression differed in terms of *de-energizing repression* in Bahrain and *energizing repression* in Syria.

The argumentation is thus twofold. Firstly, I show how the strategy of *displacement of conflict lines* from a conflict between a state and its people to one between two sects in both Syria and Bahrain grew out of a deliberate regime strategy as well as everyday practices. Due to the composition of the security forces in Bahrain, with only Sunni and, to a large extent, foreign nationals, the displaced lines of conflict caused fragmentations within the movement but not the regime. In Syria, on the other hand, the displaced lines of conflict also caused fragmentation within the ranks of the regime itself, most notably the military, which also affected whether the regime was able to dominate the situation. Secondly, I analyse the similar ways that *energizing repression* fuelled further mobilization in Bahrain and Syria due to righteous anger motivating participation and the transformation of funerals into protest marches. In Syria, the increasingly lethal and visible *energizing repression* only fuelled further dissent. Conversely, the nature of repression in Bahrain changed over the course of the uprising – from lethal to more discrete violence with injuring and torture rather than direct killings – which I refer to as *de-energizing repression*. The chapter thus applies the theoretical framework suggested in Chapter 2 regarding how interaction rituals de-energize or energize individuals, thereby shaping further action or inaction.

The chapter builds on human rights reports, policy documents and 79 videos of demonstrations and repression,[1] together with 35 semi-structured interviews with 13 Bahraini and 22 Syrian activists,[2] opposition politicians and journalists as well as participation in a single Bahraini demonstration.[3] The interviews were conducted on a fieldtrip to Bahrain (February 2015) and Turkey (January 2016) as well as with refugees in Denmark and Sweden (2015–2016).

Large-N studies of the relationship between mobilization and regime repression or sectarian divisions cannot reveal the complex nature and effects of these dynamics. In in-depth, single-case studies of Syria and Bahrain, researchers analyse 'backwards' from the outcome of civil war and muted revolution, respectively, to repressive regime violence and 'playing the sectarian card', thereby missing the diverging dynamics hereof. By studying two comparable cases in which the outcomes have been explained by similar factors of regime brutality and sectarian tensions, I am able to show how the different contexts and the different kinds of repression had different outcomes.

The context of Bahrain

Before proceeding to analysing the differing dynamics of conflict displacement and violent repression, a brief introduction to the contexts of Bahrain and Syria is in order. Bahrain has been ruled by the Al Khalifa royal family since 1783 and was a British protectorate until 1971. The Al Khalifa family is Sunni, like 30% of the population, the majority (70%) of the population being Shia. The Bahraini military is composed of Sunnis of Bahraini origin and other nationalities, and most military personnel have good reasons – financial as well as identity-related – to remain loyal (Albrecht and Ohl 2016). The 2011 uprising in Bahrain has roots in a decades-long struggle for political rights and equality (Karolak 2012). Inspired by the then successful Arab Springs in Tunisia and Egypt, a group of Internet activists called for demonstrations in Bahrain on 14 March 2011 and occupied the central square, the Pearl Roundabout, in the capital Manama (BICI 2011). The Bahraini regime attempted to crack down on the revolution in mid-March, but a determined, outraged and peaceful crowd managed to reoccupy the roundabout the following day, aided by international pressure on the Bahraini government (Brownlee, Masoud and Reynolds 2015). This led to a month-long occupation of the Pearl Roundabout with massive demonstrations of up to 200,000 participants and little or no interference by the regime forces until the unity of the movement began deteriorating, revealing increasing internal divides and insecurity, enabling the Bahraini government to launch a crackdown at the roundabout. The symbolic statue of the Pearl Roundabout was destroyed, and a highway was established in its place that remains inaccessible to the public at the time of writing (Brownlee, Masoud and Reynolds 2015). Since then, sporadic demonstrations have taken place, in periods on a daily basis, but have been consistently repressed, although decreasingly with direct, lethal violence. While the movement has not been defeated once and for all, it has been significantly weakened, de-energized and demobilized.

The context of Syria

Syria has been ruled by the Baath Party since a coup in 1963 and the al-Assad family since 1970, at which time General Hafez al-Assad seized power. The majority of Syrians are Sunni (75%), while a minority are Alawite (part of Shia Islam), Christians, Kurds and others. Like many politicians in Syria, Bashar al-Assad is Alawite and self-identifies – and is perceived by many – as the protector of the remaining minorities. The Syrian military is structured so that roughly 90% of the officers are Alawite, while the majority of the military rank and file are Sunni (Nepstad 2013). The al-Assad family has intentionally hired trusted members of their own sect and family to secure the power of the regime.

Bashar al-Assad enjoyed relative legitimacy in large parts of the population, not least due to his foreign policy against Israel and the U.S. as well as the perception that it was the 'old guards' of the regime, and not Bashar, who stood in the way of change

(Yassin-Kassab and Al-Shami 2016:25). Many observers therefore did not expect the Arab Spring to reach Syria. The first demonstration was held in Damascus in January 2011, but the event that caused more people to take to the streets occurred in Dera'a, where a group of teenagers wrote 'the people want to topple the regime' on their school wall. Despite repressive efforts, al-Assad was unable to re-establish the 'silencing fear' that has long been an important pillar of the state's coercive authority, and the conflict escalated into a civil war (Pearlman 2016:24).

Displacement of conflict lines

Conflict is a process of conflictual interaction where tension, contradiction and counteractions, be they violent or non-violent, will challenge the parties and potentially change the status quo (see Chapter 1). Playing the 'sectarian card' can be seen as an act of displacement: changing the lines of conflict from those between the government and the protesters/people, to one between two or more groups. If the lines of conflict and contradiction can be displaced from being between the government and the people to be a conflict between two or more sects, the conflictual action will largely play out between these two groups and to a lesser degree be directed towards the regime. In other words, playing the 'sectarian card' would not only grant the government more legitimacy among the sect that it claims to represent and increase their fear of losing privileges, do-ing so would also displace the contradiction, tension and conflictual interaction from occurring between the government and the people to play out between two groups in society. Furthermore, the displacement of conflict lines will weaken the revolutionary movement, as the movement will no longer compromise 'the people' but rather a sectarian community. As Collins described, a movement can be divided and thus unsuccessful; 'Instead of one revolutionary collective con-sciousness sweeping up everyone, it split into rival identities, each with its own solidarity, its own emotional energy and moral righteousness' (2013:1).

In the following, I will show how it was a combination of the regimes' strat-egies and mundane causes that fuelled sectarian polarization of the societies in both Bahrain and Syria and contributed to the displacement of the conflict lines, but in two different ways. Hereafter, I will show how the killing of protesters in the beginning of the Bahraini uprising and throughout the non-violent phase of the Syrian revolution mobilized further demonstrations, funerals often turning into demonstrations.

Regime strategies of conflict displacement

Numerous steps were taken by the Bahraini and Syrian regimes so as to dis-place the conflict lines from a conflict between the protesters (or people) and the regime to the one between two sects. The Bahraini regime portrayed the revolutionary movement as exclusively Shia, supported or possibly even directed by Iran. It mobilized Sunni Islamists to stage public support for the regime in demonstrations (Abdo 2013; Fattahi 2012; ICG 2011a). One concrete attempt at conflict displacement in Bahrain occurred when the government suggested dialogue with the demonstrators. Rather than dialogue between the regime and the activists, they wanted the King to sit at the end of the table and representatives of the two sects to discuss the opposition's claims. The activists refused to engage in these talks for the very reason that doing so would turn the conflict into a sectarian dispute between two sects rather than a political conflict between the state and the people (L.E. Andersen 2011).

Many observers and activists have described how the Syrian regime intentionally fuelled sectarian tensions (see Hinnebusch, Imady and Zintl 2016; ICG 2011b; Yassin-Kassab and Al-Shami 2016). Yassin-Kassab and Al-Shami critically state that

> Assadist policy under father and son, at home and abroad, is to present itself as the essential solution to problems it had itself manufactured – a case of an arsonist dressing up as fireman. The double aim of the counter-revolutionary strategy was to frighten the secularists and religious minorities into loyally and the West into tolerance of the dictatorship's violence.
>
> *(2016:110)*

The regime used different strategies, perhaps not all of them intentionally, to promote sectarian tension. One aspect of the regime's repression that displaced the conflict lines to a conflict between two sects was indiscriminate violence against Sunnis. Yassin-Kassab and Al-Shami describe how, in addition to the protesters, the regime also targeted non-protesting Sunnis in villages in the beginning of the uprising (Yassin-Kassab and Al-Shanmi 2016). One activist told of how:

> after all the killing, people started seeing a pattern that if you're Sunni, you're getting your ass kicked just because you're Sunni. And this fear for your religion and fear for your belonging suddenly becomes, 'I belong to this, and then I'm threatened'.
>
> *(Interview 22)*

Moreover, the regime violence was often conducted by the Shabiha. The Shabiha are composed of thugs from various sectarian backgrounds, but in Homs, Hama and Lattakia, they are exclusively Alawi and Shia (Yassin-Kassab and Al-Shami 2016:112). Activists describe how it was the brutal violence perpetrated by the Shabiha that contributed to increasing sectarian tensions, as this paramilitary group was not seen as merely representing the regime but more so acting on their own orders 'with impunity' and in many regions representing the Alawite community. The Shabiha reportedly stormed houses and attacked demonstrations (Bartkowski and Kahf 2013). The regime's attacks on sacred Sunni sites and symbols further angered the Sunni community and turned the conflict into a sectarian rather than a political one (Yassin-Kassab and Al-Shami 2016). One activist described how the regime's strategy not only angered those who already identified with Sunni Islam but also activists who previously did not consider themselves religious: 'when they [the regime] played Shia songs at the check-points in all Sunni-neighbourhoods. Then my atheist friends began asserting their Sunnism' (Yassin-Kassab and Al-Shami 2016).

Mundane drivers of sectarianism

Part of the increasing sectarian tension was caused neither by the regime strategies nor by ancient hatred but instead by practical, mundane circumstances. These everyday situational dynamics are observable exactly with a micro-sociological analytical strategy. In Syria, as I have described, it was extremely difficult to gather and protest. The main opportunities to assemble were therefore either funerals or religious gatherings in the mosque. One activist described a gathering in the local mosque with thousands of attendees, where everyone was aware of the real purpose of gathering: 'the only reason they were in that mosque was not to pray, but to demonstrate. You could feel that vibe—just, you know, like a really tense, really excited vibe. And kind of anxious' (Interview 22). Although Christians, Kurds and other minorities did take part in demonstrations and attended the Friday prayers or waited outside the mosques until the prayers were over just to participate in the demonstration, the religious connotations, all things being equal, did scare away or simply not attract many minorities (Al Jazeera 2012; Pearlman 2017; Rosen 2011a, 2011b). In videos of demonstrations, protesters often chant or scream *'Allahu Akbar'* (God is great), and activists also sang this at night from their windows to increase solidarity and demonstrate their resistance. Demonstrators described how this phrase would empower them, boost morale and how it was as mundane as saying 'oh my God' in English; even in al-Assad's secular army, they were taught to shout *'Allahu Akbar'* before throwing a hand grenade (Interview 30, Interview 12). One citizen journalist explains how the religious slogans and rituals were used to create confidence and solidarity in life-threatening situations such as demonstrations:

> You're afraid. That's why you are shouting that [*Allahu Akbar*]. It gives strength. The underlying tone of shouting that in the beginning of the Syrian uprising was not sectarianism, it was fear: fear of prosecution, fear of oppression, fear of death. That's why people were praying in the streets and why people were doing all of these religious rituals – because of fear.
>
> *(Interview 23)*

However, some Christians felt alienated or even threatened by practices such as the shouting of *'Allahu Akbar'* out of the window at night (Wimmen 2014). Paradoxically, religious rituals energize participants and generate solidarity, which is crucial for further action, but at the same time, many of these religious rituals are exclusive and thus end up alienating potential followers from other sects and religions.

In Bahrain, the increasing sectarian tensions can also be ascribed to relatively mundane causes. Several Sunni activists apparently felt alienated by much of the rhetoric of the biggest opposition party, al-Wefaq (Abdo 2013). As in Syria, protesters sometimes used more religious slogans, such as 'With our soul, with our blood, we will defend you oh Hussein', which scared away many Sunnis (Matthiesen 2013:68). Again, the reason for using these slogans might be merely habitual – these are slogans that some Shias utter in tense situations. Moreover, as the demonstrations and occupation of the Pearl Roundabout continued in Bahrain, the interference with the daily traffic became increasingly annoying for those who continued to work. On 7 March 2011, protesters attempted to block the road to the financial harbour. A woman who tried to bypass the demonstration on her way to work was confronted by chanting activists who pounded on her car (Video 60). Demonstrators and police officers intervened to allow the car to pass, but it ran over one of the protesters while driving away. While it is unclear whether or not this was a deliberate act, according to the BICI report, the incident

> caused mass anger among the demonstrators who vowed to retaliate against the woman and her family. Later that evening, the woman's address was circulated via SMS messages and on internet social media platforms such as Twitter and Facebook, and there were calls for people to attack her residence.
>
> *(BICI 2011:114)*

To protect the woman, hundreds of Sunni men assembled outside the woman's house with knives, sticks and other weapons (BICI 2011:114). This exemplifies how an incident that was not initially sectarian in nature (the woman simply wanted to go to work) ended up further fuelling sectarian tensions.

De-energizing and energizing repression

The displacement of conflict lines played out differently in Bahrain and Syria and (more importantly) had very different consequences: demobilizing the movement in Bahrain and fuelling civil war in Syria. The regime's aim (to the extent that the sectarian tension can be considered a deliberate strategy) might have been similar in both cases: to displace the conflict lines and demobilize the movement. In Syria, however, the displacement of conflict lines also affected its own ranks, which created a situation wherein both parties were split and unable to dominate the situation.

Furthermore, the different outcomes can be explained by the nature of the repression that energized protesters in Syria and de-energized protesters in Bahrain. Attempts have been made to distinguish between, on the one hand, *low-intensity repression* (Levitsky and Way 2006), *channelling* (Earl 2003) and *civil liberties restrictions*, such as arrests, bans and curfews (Davenport 2007a) and, on the other hand, *high-intensity coercion* and *personal integrity violations* implying 'state or state-affiliated activities which target the integrity of the person (i.e., which directly threaten human life) such as torture and mass killing' (Davenport 2007b:487). Even this distinction is not sufficiently fine-grained, however, as the latter does not distinguish between torture and killings in the street since, although both are considered high-intensity repression, the effects on mobilization may vary. Interestingly, Bischof and Fink argue that, in the MENA region, 'moderate repression subdues political violence, low and high repression increase political violence' (2015:10). While insightful, this finding distinguishes between 'little repression' and 'large-scale repression' but does not distinguish between different forms of large-scale repression. Conversely, I propose that in Bahrain and Syria, direct killings in the streets amount to *energizing repression* that angered protesters and gave way for funerals that turned into demonstrations, whereas torture, imprisonment and injuring generally de-energized protesters, which will be unfolded in the following.

Energizing repression: killings, funerals and mobilization

A systematic pattern throughout the Arab Spring cases from Tunisia to Bahrain and Syria is that the killing of protesters further mobilized actors to take part in the revolutions (Andersen unpublished material; Fattahi 2012; Hinnebusch, Imady and Zintl 2016). The number of participants in Bahrain and Syria spiked significantly for every killing conducted by the regime. One activist from Homs told of how 'killings kept going. If today five people died, tomorrow eight will die. Because every time a person died, the number of demonstrations grew and, hence, the casualties grew as well' (Interview 17). Likewise, activists described how demonstrations

> made the regime grow more and more hateful, and resentful and revengeful towards us. And this caused them to start shooting more people, killing people with live rounds. And the more the death toll rose, the more the protests grew.
>
> *(Interview 19)*

This dynamic is partly because atrocities cause righteous anger within a group, which fuels further action (Collins 2011). As Pearlman (2013) has argued, the Syrian regime presumably meant to silence and scare away protesters by killing activists. However, it was exactly the moral indignation over violent atrocities that caused many Syrians to take to the streets. In line with Collins's theory, demonstrations can be understood as intense interaction rituals that generate group solidarity and emotional energy among the participants (Collins 2004). Videos of demonstrations reveal how participants rhythmically chant and march, generating solidarity by their bodily co-presence (Video 1-22NV). One Syrian activist precisely described this empowering dimension of demonstrating:

> When I was walking on the street with all these people, I felt so crazily empowered by the people standing next to me (…) suddenly, you stand in the middle of the city, in the middle of the capital, shouting. No matter what you shouted, you could shout 'apples and carrots!' – you would still feel so fucking empowered. I seriously can't describe it. I'm now getting back to that time (…) like when somebody supports you in an argument and you feel empowered – just multiply that by a thousand and add to that the fear. Oh my god, it was seriously incredible.
>
> *(Interview 22)*

Another, related reason for the link between killings and increasing mobilization is the mobilizing element of funerals. The difficulty of gathering made Friday prayers and funerals the main occasions of assembly in Bahrain and even more so in Syria. When a killing occurred, the ensuing funeral would therefore attract many people and facilitate powerful interaction rituals that would further energize actors. In Bahrain, the first funerals for fallen demonstrators were very intense, with relatives fainting out of grief (Al Jazeera 2011). At some point, the funerals turned into protest marches and headed towards the centre of Manama. As in Bahrain, Syrian funerals were powerful rituals that energized the participants with both positive and negative emotional energy and increased solidarity. It was not uncommon for funerals to turn into protest marches, sometimes spontaneously, sometimes more deliberately (Interview 22). One Syrian activist told of how he participated in a funeral in Damascus only because he knew it would turn into a protest march. When I asked at what point he knew that the funeral had turned into a demonstration, he explained how 'You could hear it, because of what people were saying. They didn't say anything about the dead guy – they were just saying stuff about the regime' (Interview 22). In Syria, the lethal repression of activists and demonstrators increased for every day of the uprising, with the death toll rising to 1,000 deaths by June 2011. Although the Syrian regime promised reforms, released political prisoners and enjoyed popularity among much of the population, the killings and humiliation that the security forces inflicted on the protesters continued to energize the movement despite the heightened costs of rebellion.

Visibility and mobilization

The mobilization of the revolutionary movement in Syria is closely related to the repressive lethal tactics of the regime and the fact that information about atrocities, unlike previously, had become visible and was disseminated via social media (Wessels, Chapter 5). The rural areas in Syria were relatively disconnected from the rest of the country. This may have convinced the regime that they could treat the incidents in Dera'a as relatively isolated, as they had succeeded in doing with revolts in Hama in 1982. Crushing the demonstrations in Dera'a could serve as a warning for others not to revolt. However, while the crackdown on demonstrators in Dera'a might have silenced the revolution temporarily (Holliday 2011), protesters from Idlib, Homs, Aleppo and Damascus describe how the army's actions in Dera'a were a large part of their motivation to take to the street. Many Syrians were discontent with the regime prior to 2011 given the severe oppression, humiliation and corruption that they experienced in their daily lives, but Bashar al-Assad was also a popular figure among many Syrians (Yassin-Kassab and Al-Shami 2016). Some of the activists with whom I spoke were in fact Assad supporters prior to 2011 and even took part in pro-Assad demonstrations in the beginning of the uprising. Upon hearing about the killings and humiliation in Dera'a, however, they joined the anti-Assad demonstrations instead. One activist from Homs described how, previously, 'we loved Bashar' and therefore initially 'went to demonstrations to support the regime' when hearing the news about demonstrations in Tunisia and Egypt (Interview 17). But in March 2011, he heard about the events in Dera'a, not through state television but through social media. He further investigated what occurred there. And then, "when we started seeing all of this footage, me and 20 young men from my neighbourhood started writing on the walls 'children from Dera'a, we are with you'" (Interview 17). Another activist from Idlib, studying in Aleppo in 2011, was part of a student council when the uprising started and took part in numerous pro-regime marches. At the end of April, one of his friends from Dera'a visited him and told him about the events there: 'how they're treating civilians, how they're killing people' (Interview 20). At first, he did not really believe his friend and continued to attend pro-regime marches. When his friend approached him again, he started changing his mind:

> the way he was crying made me question things. So I asked him if I could talk to anyone from his family in Dera'a. I spoke to his mom, who is in Dera'a, and she explained how they were breaking into houses, how they are detaining people, how they would shoot randomly at people and a kid got shot by mistake.
>
> *(Interview 20)*

In other words, had the news about what happened in Dera'a not been disseminated through new media and personal networks, the uprising would most likely have been silenced. Likewise, in Bahrain, the information about atrocities was disseminated via social media and, given the size of the country, the regime could neither isolate nor repress the revolution in one area without the remaining population knowing. Subsequently, the regime repression changed and became less visible in another way, namely via violent repression occurring increasingly behind bars rather than in the street, as discussed below.

De-energizing repression in Bahrain

Having unsuccessfully attempted to crack down on the movement in Bahrain when it had great momentum, the regime allowed activists to occupy the Pearl Roundabout (Bramsen 2018, 2019). They generally refrained from killing or targeting protesters. Since the crackdown in mid-March 2011, the regime systematically succeeded in de-energizing the movement. This was, for example, observable in a protest march in which I participated in 2015 in the village Bilal al-Qadeem. The protests were undoubtedly highly routinized: it followed the same route twice daily everyone knew where and when we would encounter the police. In this demonstration and in the videos from this period, the rhythm of chanting and marching is much slower than in videos from the beginning of the uprising (Video 1-10NV), indicating lower energy and intensity.

The movement has been demobilized through two forms of de-energizing repression. Firstly, through more indirect forms of repression corresponding what Davenport (2007a) coins 'civil liberties restrictions' or what Earl (2003) refers to as 'channelling strategies' through, for example, stripping activists of their national passports, and firing many of the people who participated in the uprising. The situation for the Shia community worsened considerably after 2011, protesters, opposition politicians and revolutionaries being imprisoned and many people losing their jobs (Interviews 1–10). One active member of the political party Wa'ad (National Democratic Action Society) described this 'de-energization' in the following way:

> In 4 years, I've aged maybe 40 years instead of only 4. Because every day you're facing an issue – how you're going to build your life because you're not allowed to work. You're not allowed to do anything. If they catch you at a checkpoint, you'll be humiliated. If they say that they will arrest you, they'll come to your house.
>
> *(Interview 6)*

Secondly, another de-energizing strategy by the regime implies that they refrain from killing protesters since 2011 directly in the streets, generally opting instead to injure, torture and humiliate them (Bramsen 2019). An activist, for example, explained how the riot police 'shoot people where you try not to kill them – injure them as much as you can, but not kill them' (Interview 1) and an opposition politician likewise described how,

> we don't have martyrs like we had before; every week, every week, every week people were on the streets and processions like that. But now they've told them, and I think they have new instructions to, like, do damage but not to kill. So, they shoot you in the face, you can lose an eye.
>
> *(Interview 6)*

This very brutal and still often lethal repression (dying of torture) corresponds with what Davenport (2007a) coins 'personal integrity violations'. Based on my observations from Bahrain and Syria, however, I would argue that killings openly in the streets have a very different impact on mobilization than injuring and torturing, albeit they both could be characterized as 'personal integrity violations'. The former generates moral outrage and anger and importantly brings people together at funerals, thus energizing them to further engage in protest activities. On the other hand, torture and injuring, although in many ways equally brutal and forceful, de-energize individuals by spreading fear and despair, thus shaping inaction rather than action. Therefore, it is important to draw more fine-grained distinctions between types of repression.

Martin (2007) argues that the mobilizing effects of repression, known as back-firing, are dependent on the visibility of repression and whether it is perceived as disproportionate and unjust. This in part explains why killings in the streets energized and mobilized activists – because it is more visible than torturing to death behind bars. But there is more to it I would argue. Mobilization is not merely a cognitive but also an emotional and social process requiring people to not only *know* about injustices but also being sufficiently *energized* to act upon this knowledge. Torture in Bahrain is not invisible as there is no shortage of documentation of torture in prisons which is provided, for example, by The Bahrain Centre for Human Rights and the Bahraini Independent Commission of Inquiry. This documentation neither lacks pictures or videos of tortured victims nor pictorial descriptions of the acts of torture. But there is a difference between *knowing* about a given atrocity and how this affects you *emotionally* in terms of promoting action or inaction. While pictures and/or descriptions of torture would often disgust and dishearten the viewer, directly observing the killing of protesters in the streets and gathering at funerals seems to enrage and energize participants.

Domination or escalation

Conflict involves the rejection of the other party's attempt at domination: a 'no' that follows another 'no' (Luhmann 1995). If one party significantly dominates the other (or if the parties find a solution through negotiations or change their relationship in another way), a conflict ends. If neither party is able to dominate the situation and they both have the material and motivational resources to continue the fight, the conflict will escalate (Collins 2011). In Bahrain, the regime's initial attempt at cracking down on the revolutionary momentum, when it was at its highest, failed. But when the uprising lost momentum after a month, the regime was able to sufficiently dominate and repress it. The Bahraini regime successfully displaced the conflict lines via sectarian strategies but also by ceasing to engage in overt conflict with the activists. As described, conflict produces negative emotional energy and in-group solidarity that energizes actors to act. When a government instead ceases to produce conflict by not attacking protesters and permitting their presence in the streets – or as they did at later stages, injuring, imprisoning and torturing activists – this potentially de-energizes or at least does not re-energize activists.

In Syria, on the other hand, neither the regime nor the opposition movement was able to dominate the situation and impose their will sufficiently. The lines of conflict were also displaced, but while the dispersion of protesters and suppression of the opposition might have been the aim of the Syrian regime as in Bahrain, the displacement of conflict lines from a struggle between the people and the regime to one between different sects caused fractions, both among activists *and* within the regime itself. This partly lies in the sectarian composition of the Syrian military, where especially many of the lower-ranking soldiers are Sunnis. The split, thus, also occurred in the regime's own ranks, with an increasing number of soldiers defecting throughout 2011 and 2012. The activists were able to destabilize the Syrian regime and challenge its organization, but the opposition likewise split, neither party therefore able to dominate the situation.

The inability of the regime and the revolutionary movement in Syria to dominate the situation also became evident in their inability to dominate physical space. Bahrain is a small island, which makes it easy to repress immediately, especially with assistance from Saudi Arabia and the Gulf Cooperation Council countries. Conversely, given the relatively larger size of Syria and the split in the military and the al-Assad regime's (well-based) mistrust in several of the forces, the regime was unable to repress all of the Syrian regions at once. In addition to apparently being short on teargas and riot police, the Syrian regime did not have the coercive apparatus – or at least not a sufficiently loyal one – to suppress all of the Syrian regions at once. The slow pace of the regime's actions is closely connected to the lack of sufficient resources compared to the relatively widespread uprising, as it was

> impossible for the regime's security forces to simultaneously garrison all of the country's key population centers and lines of communication. Therefore, the regime's strategy has been to maneuver elite clearance forces to key centers of unrest and conduct large scale cordon and search operations.
> *(Holliday 2011)*

Likewise, the Syrian opposition was unable to dominate the physical space sufficiently to challenge the regime. Unlike in Bahrain and other Arab uprisings, the Syrian protesters never managed to hold mass demonstrations in the capital, Damascus. Protesters described how they kept thinking that 'soon we will reach Damascus and then we'll win' (Interview 20). One activist from Damascus described how they kept trying to organize demonstrations but were forcefully dispersed every time by police with sticks who arrested several as well as by the Shabiha and pro-Assad protesters (Interview 16).

This inability of the regime to contain demonstrations once and for all, as the Bahraini regime more or less succeeded in doing, as well as the inability of the protesters to occupy central space in the capital, made up the contours of an escalatory situation in Syria. Neither party dominated the situation but kept escalating their actions to win. As illustrated in Table 3.1 below, the two mechanisms of repression and conflict displacement run in parallel, not sequentially.

TABLE 3.1 Diverging outcomes of violent repression and conflict displacement

	Violent repression	*Conflict displacement*	*Outcome*
Bahrain	De-energizing repression	Indivisible military and divisible movement	Demobilization
Syria	Energizing repression	Divisible military and divisible movement -> inability of both parties to dominate the situation	Escalation

Conclusion

How does sectarian tension and repression de-escalate or escalate conflict? I have shown how lethal violence initially amplified mobilization in both Bahrain and Syria. Over time, however, the Bahraini regime increasingly resorted to less lethal violence. The repression arguably continued to be equally forceful with the imprisoning, injuring and torturing of protesters, which I refer to as *de-energizing repression*, as this strategy discourages activists. In Syria, neither the regime nor the activists were able to dominate the situation, and the killings kept energizing the movement, with more people attending funerals that turned into protest marches, some also taking up arms in the name of revenge and protection. The displacement of conflict lines from a conflict between the state and the people to a sectarian one succeeds in destabilizing the opposition in both Bahrain and Syria, but in Syria this displacement also divided the regime, notably in terms of defecting soldiers. The combination of fractioning on both sides of the conflict in Syria as well as a continuous supply of positive and negative emotional energies provided the ingredients for an escalatory process: a process where no party in a conflict is able to dominate the situation – where localized protection and revenge keep fuelling anger and fear on both sides – appears to be a recipe for conflict escalation.

Showing how some forms of repression work better in terms of de-energizing and thus demobilizing activists can be seen as ethically problematic, as such information can inform authoritarian regimes (and their Western advisors) about how to improve their repression and consolidate their power. However, it is not normatively given whether a silenced revolution or 'tyrannical peace' (Davenport 2007b:485) is preferred over (violent) escalation and civil war. From a non-violent, activist perspective, the conclusions of the study might be used for activists to consider other ways of generating solidarity and energizing protesters in the absence of direct killings, as in Bahrain.

Notes

1 The video data sets are available online. Videos of violence (V): http://violence.ogtal. dk/. Videos of nonviolence (NV): https://violence.ogtal.dk/index2.php.
2 In this chapter, 'activists', 'demonstrators' and 'protesters' will be used interchangeably.
3 A list of the interviews is provided at the end of the chapter.

References

Abdo, Geneive (2013) 'The New Sectarianism: The Arab Uprisings and the Rebirth of the Shi'a-Sunni Divide', *Brookings Analysis Paper* 29. www.brookings.edu/wp-content/uploads/2016/06/sunni-shia-abdo.pdf (accessed 9 June 2017).

Al Jazeera (2011) *Shouting in the Dark*. www.youtube.com/watch?v=xaTKDMYOBOU (accessed 6 July 2016).

Al Jazeera (2012) *Q&A: Nir Rosen on Syrian sectarianism*. www.aljazeera.com/indepth/features/2012/02/2012218165546393720.html (accessed 9 June 2017).

Albrecht, Holger and Dorothy Ohl (2016) 'Exit, Resistance, Loyalty: Military Behavior During Unrest in Authoritarian Regimes', *Perspectives on Politics* 14 (1): 38–52.

Andersen, Lars Erslev (2011) 'Bahrain in the Shadow of the Libya War', *Democracy Now.* www.opendemocracy.net/lars-erslev-andersen/bahrain-in-shadow-of-libya-war (accessed 9 June 2017).

Andersen, Rasmus Fonnesbæk (unpublished material) *Secular Heroes, Islamist Free-Riders and the Military? The 2011 Egyptian Protests.* Copenhagen: Copenhagen University.

Bartkowski, Maciej and Mohja Kahf (2013) 'The Syrian Resistance: A Tale of Two Struggles', *Open Democracy.* www.opendemocracy.net/civilresistance/maciej-bartkowski-mohja-kahf/syrian-resistance-tale-of-two-struggles (accessed 9 June 2017).

Bramsen, Isabel (2018) 'How Civil Resistance Succeeds (or Not): Micro-Dynamics of Unity, Timing and Escalatory Actions', *Peace & Change* 43 (1): 61–89.

Bramsen, Isabel (2019). 'Micro-Sociological Dynamics of Repression: How Interactions between Protesters and Security Forces Shaped the Bahraini Uprising', *Scandinavian Journal of Military Studies* 2 (1): 9–19.

BICI (2011) *Report of the Bahrain Independent Commission of Inquiry*, Manama. www.bici.org.bh/BICIreportEN.pdf (accessed 6 July 2016).

Bischof, Daniel and Simon Fink (2015) 'Repression as a Double-Edged Sword: Resilient Monarchs, Repression and Revolution in the Arab World', *Swiss Political Science Review* 21 (3): 377–395.

Brownlee, Jason, Tarek E. Masoud and Andrew Reynolds (2015) *The Arab Spring: Pathways of Repression and Reform*, first edition. Oxford: Oxford University Press.

Collins, Randall (2004) *Interaction Ritual Chains: Princeton Studies in Cultural Sociology.* Princeton, NJ: Princeton University Press.

Collins, Randall (2011) 'C-Escalation and D-Escalation: A Theory of the Time-Dynamics of Conflict', *American Sociological Review* 77 (2012): 1–20.

Collins, Randall (2013) 'Tipping Point Revolutions and State Breakdown Revolutions: Why Revolutions Succeed or Fail', *The Sociological Eye.* http://sociological-eye.blog-spot.dk/2013/06/tipping-point-revolutions-and-state.html (accessed 6 July 2016).

Davenport, Christian (2007a) 'State Repression and Political Order', *Annual Review of Political Science* 10 (1): 101–123.

Davenport, Christian (2007b) 'State Repression and the Tyrannical Peace', *Journal of Peace Research* 44 (4): 485–504.

Davenport, Christian and Will H. Moore (2012) 'The Arab Spring, Winter, and Back Again? (Re)Introducing the Dissent-Repression Nexus with a Twist', *International Interactions* 38 (5): 704–713.

Earl, Jennifer (2003) 'Tanks, Tear Gas, and Taxes: Toward a Theory of Movement Repression', *Sociological Theory* 21 (1): 44–68.

Fattahi, Loghman (2012) 'Nonviolent Action Strategy: Lessons from Bahrain's Demonstration Movement', *Al Naklah, Online Journal on Southwest Asia and Islamic Civilization.* Spring 2012. The Fletcher School, Tufts University.

Hinnebusch, Raymond, Omar Imady and Tina Zintl (2016) 'Civil Resistance in the Syrian Uprising', in Adam Roberts, Michael J. Willis, Rory McCarthy and Timothy Garton Ash (Eds.), *Civil Resistance in the Arab Spring: Triumphs and Disasters* (223–247), Oxford: Oxford University Press.

Holliday, Joseph (2011) 'Middle East Security Report 2, The Struggle for Syria in 2011', *ISW.* www.understandingwar.org/sites/default/files/Struggle_For_Syria.pdf (accessed 9 June 2017).

ICG, International Crisis Group (2011a) 'Popular Protests in North Africa and the Middle East (III): The Bahrain Revolt', *Middle East/North Africa Report* No. 105. www.crisisgroup. org/middle-east-north-africa/gulf-and-arabian-peninsula/bahrain/popular-protests-north-africa-and-middle-east-iii-bahrain-revolt (accessed 9 June 2017).

ICG, International Crisis Group (2011b) 'Popular Protest in North Africa and the Middle East (VII): The Syrian Regime's Slow-Motion Suicide', *Middle East/North Africa Report* No. 109. https://www.crisisgroup.org/middle-east-north-africa/eastern-mediterranean/syria/popular-protest-north-africa-and-middle-east-vii-syrian-regime-s-slow-motion-suicide (accessed 9 June 2017).

Karolak, Magdalena (2012) 'Escalation of Social Conflict During Popular Upheavals: Evidence from Bahrain', *CEU Political Science Journal* 7 (2): 173–195.

Leenders, Reinoud (2014) 'Case Study: The Onset of the Syrian Uprising and the Origins of Violence in World', in Peter Burnell, Vicky Randall and Lise Rakner (Eds.), *Politics in the Developing World*, fourth edition, Oxford: Oxford University Press. http://global.oup. com/uk/orc/politics/countries/burnell4e/resources/cases/ (accessed 9 June 2017).

Leenders, Reinoud (2016) 'Master Frames of the Syrian Conflict: Early Violence and Sectarian Response Revisited', *POMPERS.* http://pomeps.org/2016/06/09/master-frames-of-the-syrian-conflict-early-violence-and-sectarian-response-revisited/ (accessed 9 June 2017).

Levitsky, Steven and Lucan Way (2006) 'The Dynamics of Autocratic Coercive Capacity after the Cold War', *Communist and Post-Communist Studies* 39 (3): 387–410.

Lichbach, Mark Irving (1987) 'Deterrence or Escalation? The Puzzle of Aggregate Studies of Repression and Dissent', *Journal of Conflict Resolution* 31: 266–297.

Luhmann, Niklas (1995) *Social Systems: Writing Science.* Stanford, CA: Stanford University Press.

Martin, Brian (2007) *Justice Ignited: The Dynamics of Backfire.* Lanham, MD: Rowman & Littlefield.

Matthiesen, Toby (2013) *Sectarian Gulf: Bahrain, Saudi Arabia, and the Arab Spring that Wasn't.* Stanford, CA: Stanford Briefs, an imprint of Stanford University Press.

Nepstad, Sharon E. (2013) 'Mutiny and Nonviolence in the Arab Spring: Exploring Military Defections and Loyalty in Egypt, Bahrain, and Syria', *Journal of Peace Research* 50 (3): 337–349.

Pearlman, Wendy (2013) 'Emotions and the Microfoundations of the Arab Uprisings', *Perspectives on Politics* 11(2): 387–409.

Pearlman, Wendy (2016) 'Narratives of Fear in Syria', *Perspectives on Politics* 14 (1): 21–37.

Pearlman, Wendy (2017) *We Crossed a Bridge and It Trembled: Syrian Chronicles.* New York: HarperCollins.

Rosen, Nir (2011a) 'A Tale of Two Villages', *Al Jazeera.* www.aljazeera.com/indepth/features/2011/10/2011102365913224161.html (accessed 9 June 2017).

Rosen, Nir (2011b) 'Ghosts in the Mosques'. *Al Jazeera.* www.aljazeera.com/indepth/features/2011/09/201193063322274258.html (accessed 9 June 2017).

Tilly, Charles (1978) *From Mobilization to Revolution.* New York: McGraw-Hill.

Wimmen, Heiko (2014) 'Divisive Rule: Sectarianism and Power Maintenance in the Arab Spring: Bahrain, Iraq, Lebanon and Syria'. *Stiftung Wissenschaft und Politik, Deutsches Institut für Internationale Politik und Sicherheit* (SWP Research Paper 4). http://nbn-resolving.de/urn:nbn:de:0168-ssoar-385599 (accessed 9 June 2017).

Yassin-Kassab, Robin and Leila Al-Sham (2016) *Burning Country: Syrians in Revolution and War.* London: Pluto Press.

Zimmermann, Ekkart (1980) 'Macro-Comparative Research on Political Protest', in Ted R. Gurr (Ed.), *Handbook of Political Conflict: Theory and Research* (167–237), New York: The Free Press.

Interviews

1. Bahraini activist
2. Bahraini activist
3. Bahraini journalist, including subsequent email correspondence
4. Bahraini opposition politician
5. 3 interviews with Bahraini opposition politician
6. Bahraini opposition politicians
7. Bahraini activists
8. Bahraini activist
9. Bahraini activist
10. 2 interviews with Bahraini activist
11. Syrian activist
12. Syrian activist
13. Syrian activist
14. Syrian activist
15. Syrian activist
16. Syrian activist
17. Syrian activist
18. Syrian activist
19. Syrian activists
20. Syrian activist
21. Defected officer
22. Syrian activist
23. Syrian journalist
24. Syrian activist
25. Syrian journalist
26. Syrian activist
27. Syrian activist
28. Syrian activist
29. Syrian activist
30. Syrian activist
31. Syrian defected journalist
32. Syrian activist
33. Bahraini activist

4

HUMILIATION DYNAMICS IN CONFLICTS IN OUR GLOBALIZED WORLD

Poul Poder

Introduction: mechanisms of humiliation and conflict

Humiliation involves putting down another party's sense of dignity, respect or self-worth (Lindner 2001). It can be defined as 'any sort of behaviour or condition that constitutes a sound reason for a person to consider his or her self-respect injured' (Margalit 1996:9). Humiliation refers to the perception of having one's self-respect or dignity injured, which also operates on the collective and cultural levels and not only among individuals (as Margalit's formulation might otherwise suggest). Humiliation is a normative experience of being treated unfairly and therefore motivates people to seek a re-establishing of justice, which is a basic reason for considering humiliation in the context of conflict (Barash and Lipton 2011; Scheff and Retzinger 1991). Fighting against humiliation is strong motivation for engaging in conflicts. Hitler mobilized political support by promising the Germans that he was the political leader who was able to bring Germany out of the humiliation suffered by the Versailles Treaty after the First World War (Scheff 2000). The word *Karama* (dignity) was central in Tunisia during the Arab Spring revolution, and the fight against humiliation also motivated Assad's opponents in Syria:

> We started the revolution because we wanted to be treated like humans, we are looking for our humanity… All my life I have been treated like an inferior, a human being of the 10th class, while Assad and his people controlled this country. We also have a right in this country.
>
> *(Syrian rebel cited in The Guardian 2011)*

In recent decades, the theme of humiliation has attracted significant attention in analyses of political and social conflicts in the contemporary, globalized world

(Fattah and Fierke 2009; Friedrichs 2016; Lindner 2006, 2007a, 2007b; Lukes 1997; Moïsi 2009; Smith 2006). One overall reason for this is the growing appreciation for how a perspective on emotions is important in understanding the conflict dynamic (Bramsen and Poder 2014). Humiliation is a particularly important case to this point, as I will demonstrate in this chapter. Firstly, I discuss how humiliation interacts with conflict to underline why humiliation is a latent motivation for engaging in conflict. Secondly, I review three diagnoses of humiliation pertaining to our globalized world: (a) Lindner's argument that humiliation is likely to proliferate in our globalized world, characterized by the ideology of human rights emphasizing the dignity of every human being and the material conditions that negate these promises for many people around the world (Lindner 2002a, 2002b, 2002c, 2006); (b) Friedrichs' (2016) exposition of culturally very distinct notions of what defines basic human self-worth and, consequently, distinct notions of what is actually humiliated when people fail to pay each other the appropriate form of respect and (c) Smith's (2006, 2008, 2017) diagnosis of humiliation as socially enforced displacement triggered by sociopolitical processes. Thirdly, I outline a framework of humiliation mechanisms in order to understand how contemporary humiliation issues are generated in various ways. Humiliation is often conceived in terms of interactional situations in which a perpetrator intentionally subjects a victim to degradation through actions or expressions (Klein 1991). However, humiliation does not depend on other actors' degradation and contempt, as feelings of humiliation can arise on the basis of the interpretations of persons or groups of particular conditions as degrading, which is an implication of understanding humiliation as 'any sort of behaviour or condition that constitutes a sound reason for a person to consider his or her self-respect injured' (Margalit 1996:9). To be well attuned to appreciate current humiliation issues, we must consider four other mechanisms: (1) symbolic humiliation, (2) representative humiliation, (3) humiliation qua non-recognition (when people are not accorded the respect they expect) and (4) self-perceived humiliation (when people without the action of a direct 'humiliator' interpret their conditions as humiliating). This chapter distils the significant mechanisms of humiliation and stresses how non-recognition and self-perceived humiliation are particularly crucial to consider thoroughly given the nature of contemporary humiliation issues. Understanding both the *what* and the *how* of the main contemporary humiliation issues is instrumental to anticipate the emerging potential conflicts, as humiliation often motivates people to engage in conflict. The challenge is to grasp less visible forms of humiliation compared to more direct and observable mechanisms as underlined in the conclusion, which deals with implications for research and conflict resolution practice.

How humiliation relates to conflict: a latent basis of mobilization

To understand the nature of humiliation, it must be differentiated from other emotions, such as shame and anger, which are close to but distinct from humiliation.

This implies a normative opposition and desire for restoring undermined self-respect and dignity. Humiliation is a particularly emotional experience, significant in understanding the emergence and escalation of conflict. It is a special motive for engaging in conflict as it concerns a desire for restoring dignity and appears to be more enduring than other emotional experiences, as will be explained.

The interactional nature of humiliation is often emphasized (see Klein 1991): humiliation is something that happens to one as somebody or something works to put one down. It can therefore be differentiated from shame, 'humiliation' referring to an outward anger towards the 'humiliator' or the humiliation itself, whereas shame refers to an inward feeling of devaluation, as shame often involves blaming oneself (Hartling and Luchetta 1999:6). While both shame and humiliation involve the devaluation of the self, there is a decisive difference in terms of how shame puts the person more on the defensive, whereas humiliation implies a normative opposition to a humiliating mistreatment or condition. Humiliation involves blaming others' perceived unfair actions or social conditions perceived as denigrating one's dignity. Humiliation shares characteristics with anger, shame and embarrassment but also differs from these emotions. Humiliation can involve anger, but anger is distinguishable from humiliation as it is not about feeling the devaluation of the self (Leidner, Sheikh and Ginges 2012). The emotion of humiliation 'arises from accepting a devaluation of the self, which, simultaneously, is appraised as unjust. Moreover, humiliation is associated with tendencies for approach and avoidance simultaneously' (Saulo, Saguy and Halperin 2015:976). While this definition captures some of the essential meaning, I suggest that the phrase 'accepting a devaluation of the self' should not be taken too literally, as humiliation is about experiences believed to be unjust. It is, therefore, about cognitively understanding something as entailing a devaluation of the self rather than accepting it normatively. Without such understanding, there is no experience of humiliation. If one interprets a remark said with the intent to humiliate you in a completely different way, feelings of humiliation will not arise. In contrast to humiliation, the experience of shame entails a normative acceptance of the devaluation of self, which is also why shame tends to pacify the concerned persons or groups (Barbalet 1998). In sum, humiliation is basically about the belittling of the self and a perception of such belittling as being unjust; it is not merely a psychologically unpleasant feeling but is about feeling unjustly devalued by others or by conditions.

The behavioural consequences of humiliation can take different routes. One position suggests that humiliation motivates payback responses, thereby escalating conflict. Hartling argues that the real pain of humiliation leads people to engage in destructive behaviours that devastate the lives of others and themselves (Hartling 2007:479). More recent research supports this idea, arguing that the pain a humiliated person feels can be released by acting violently towards the 'humiliator' or even a random third party (Barash and Lipton 2011). Moreover, Hartling and colleagues suggest that humiliating experiences might make the humiliated party more prone to engage in violence: the social pain following humiliation can lead people into a deconstructed state characterized by numbness or an inability to empathize with others (Hartling et al. 2013). Reducing the self-awareness of the suffering person in this manner makes it more likely that they have less self-regulation and will engage in self-defeating forms of behaviour; subsequently, they will feel less restricted as to engaging in violence. Humiliation can thereby serve as a precondition for violence, both in an immediate sense and it can lead people to harmful affiliations (e.g. gangs and extremist groups) that deliver payback responses in the more distant future (Hartling et al. 2013:65). Gingesa and Attran (2008) formulate an opposing position, arguing that humiliation produces a tendency towards the suppression of rebellious or violent action, which they call an 'inertia effect'. On the basis of studies measuring the humiliating experiences of Palestinians in the context of the Israeli occupation, the authors found that humiliation did not increase the propensity for violent reactions towards representatives of the Israeli occupation; rather, experiences of humiliation were generally negatively related to cognitive and emotional support for suicide attacks against Israelis (Gingesa and Atranb 2008:291). Similarly, Rothbart and Poder (2017) have argued that elites can dominate marginal groups by applying instruments of systemic humiliation, such as: (1) laws that unjustly favour social elites, (2) an ideology of supremacy that rationalizes such laws, (3) language that essentializes the degraded people, (4) images that reinforce such a status or (5) means to erase the achievements and capacities of these people. In societies with extreme social inequality, such instruments can help elites to control marginalized groups by damaging their self-worth and instilling a sense of being unworthy of the respect (dignity) of others (Rothbart and Poder 2017). A third argument suggests that humiliation does not necessarily lead to aggression nor passivity. From the history of non-violent resistance, we have examples of humiliated groups reacting with neither passivity nor violence. Mandela is a clear example, as he maintained his self-respect in the face of serial humiliation, as is Gandhi and his non-violent campaign against the British colonists and oppressors (Lindner 2006).

The essential defining feature of humiliation is normative opposition – a sense of non-acceptance of being treated unfairly. In terms of the action following from such opposition, one can distinguish between the following principled options: (1) direct and immediate aggression, (2) passivity/inertia (resignation or letting go) or (3) non-violent resistance or opposition. In what sense can we understand humiliation as motivating behaviour that establishes conflict when humiliation can lead to different types of action? The answer to this question resides in the fact that humiliation is a relatively durable experience (Otten and Jonas 2014) involving intense, other-directed outrage, low guilt and intense feelings of powerlessness (Leidner, Sheikh and Ginges 2012). Hartling and Luchetta argue that when people feel embarrassment, their discomfort stems from a particular aspect of their behaviour or persona. Humiliation is different in that it involves the whole self, which is not as easily changeable as making up for an embarrassing mistake (Hartling and Luchetta 1999:263). Since humiliation is about the devaluation of who you are, it is a more comprehensive experience that is not easily shrugged off. As the whole self is under attack in the process of humiliation, it is difficult merely to shrug off the experience of humiliation, which instils humiliation with an oft-noted longevity. The long-term memory of humiliation (Rioux and Redekop 2013) explains why it can operate as a latent basis for mobilization towards restoring justice and dignity. Some researchers have noted a 'rebound effect' associated with humiliation, which is to be explained by the fact that humiliation is not easily forgotten (Ginges and Attran 2008). The rebound effect refers to the circumstance where humiliated and dispirited people react in an immediate sense with violence in order to avenge the insult of their previously humiliated state as they subsequently become empowered through charismatic leaders of ideologies (Ginges and Attran 2008). Other conditions can also trigger such a rebound effect. A particularly humiliating example of such an event occurred when the street vendor Tarek el-Tayeb Mohamed Bouazizi set himself on fire on 17 December 2010, in response to the confiscation of his wares and the harassment and humiliation that he said were inflicted on him by a municipal official. This triggered feelings of righteous anger among the people of Tunis, who turned to the streets to rebel against the regime and the humiliation it had inflicted on them for decades (Bramsen 2018).

Summing up, humiliation implies a normative non-acceptance of the devaluation of the self of the humiliated party, which also explains why it can motivate humiliated parties to act in favour of rectifying the injustices. Compared to emotions of anger, rage, resentment or revenge, which seem stronger in an immediate sense, humiliation might seem a weaker motivation to engage in conflict behaviour. It is strong, however, as people seldom forget their painful humiliations (MacDonald and Leary 2005).

Current humiliation issues in our globalized world

This section presents three main arguments concerning how humiliation emerges as a socially and politically significant issue in our globalized world. Understanding humiliation issues is imperative in order to possibly anticipate where conflicts might emerge, as they can often be stirred by people feeling humiliated.

One significant diagnosis is Evelin Lindner's (2009) argument that 'dignity humiliation' – as distinct from humiliation of social honour – gains significance, as human rights come to form a normative framework increasingly adhered to globally. This development suggests revolutionary change in terms of how societies have been organized. Previously, humiliation was a steady part of how society was organized, and when subordinate groups revolted and sometimes succeeded in transforming the power balance, it was not unusual or considered illegitimate that previous power holders were then humiliated. Today, the human rights code delegitimatizes humiliation that undermines human dignity. Acts of degradations previously accepted as normal are now viewed as illegitimate. People realize themselves as *also* being members of a single in-group of humankind rather than exclusively defined in terms of nationalistic in-groups pitted against others (Lindner 2007a). The morality of human rights suggests an abandonment of cycles of act of humiliation. Humankind faces a truly historical challenge, that is, opportunity to change human history by adopting novel social practice that realizes the point 'that when humiliating people is no longer legitimate, humiliating humiliators is no longer legitimate either' (Lindner 2007b:30). As people increasingly believe in the notion of basic human dignity, we experience an increase in the significance of feelings of humiliation as compared to fear (Lindner 2007b:16).

The more people come to believe that they deserve a dignified life defined in terms of rights to freedom, safety, social security, education, food and shelter, etc., the more they can interpret their actual material living conditions as humiliating if they are seen as ruining dignified life. Feelings of 'dignity humiliation' can be felt by a growing number of people on our human rights-oriented planet as a consequence of the contrasts between the ideal of equal human dignity and the inequality in material living conditions. Such feelings of dignity humiliation are less a collective phenomenon prescribed within group relations but primarily salient and personal, that is, a latent reservoir of feelings to be mobilized for political action (Lindner 2007a:10). Lindner's thesis might seem paradoxical. On the one hand, she suggests that humiliation becomes illegitimate. Suppressed and humiliated people are no longer allowed to re-humiliate their suppressors, as the morality of human rights endorses that each and every human being has a sense of dignity requiring respect. On the other hand, she also contends that feelings of humiliation abound in the contemporary global condition. But should we not expect less humiliation as it becomes an illegitimate option and we have policies trying to secure the human rights and dignity of people? Lindner's thesis should be understood in dialectical terms. We have the transformation of institutional practices to secure people's dignity and we object against direct instances of humiliation (e.g. the torture and abuse of prisoners in Abu Ghraib). However, this does not entail that people cannot feel that their impoverished living conditions are an affront to their dignity in the normative light of human rights. Adhering to the ideas of life-enhancing rights is precisely what makes it possible to experience one's material living conditions as humiliating, since they do not substantiate these rights. Not understanding oneself as entitled to such dignified life, one will merely feel miserable rather than humiliated.

Lindner's thesis concerns a homogenization of outlooks on life in terms of increasing recognition of notions of human rights despite the enduring cultural, political and social differences between the countries around the world. However, main cultural differences still define what counts as humiliation, and it is important to reflect on what this means with increasing interaction among culturally different peoples. The next section therefore draws on Friedrichs' (2016) paper entitled 'An intercultural theory of international relations: how self-worth underlies politics among nations', which explains how humiliation relates to either honour, face or individual dignity.

A globalized world of increased intercultural interaction and friction also causes humiliation

Political scientist Jörg Friedrichs (2016) argues that self-worth is the ultimate human motivator, operating on individual and group levels alike. He is well aware that people are motivated by various concerns, such as power, wealth, knowledge and virtue. Ultimately, however, when people fight for power or wealth, they do so in order to be someone – a person of a certain value. In more specific terms, what defines this value differs according to three main cultures containing three distinct forms of self-worth: honour, face and dignity. Friedrichs provides a broad definition of humiliation, which can fit these cultural differences as to what counts as self-worth: 'Humiliation arises when an actor is unable to counteract misrecognition' (2016:73). Humiliation can therefore be understood as ways to negate self-worth. In honour cultures, people view social worth as internalized yet contestable when significant others fail to pay sufficient respect. In face cultures, social worth is determined by one's reference group and is therefore perceived as extrinsic and alienable. The contrast to this is that which Friedrichs refers to as the Western dignity culture in which people think of self-worth as intrinsic to the individual person and inalienable. The striving for social worth is equally strong among the main cultures, and the issue of humiliation is, therefore, a basic concern.

In other words, what people feel humiliated about depends on the culture to which they belong, and lack of understanding of basic cultural differences increases the likelihood of humiliating people. What plays out as misrecognition follows a different logic given the different cultures of self-worth. Humiliation concerns misrecognition, which relates to either group-oriented honour or face or to individual dignity. If people are unaware of how we operate along different lines of self-worth and how paying respect to a Westerner enmeshed in an individualistic notion of self-worth differs from paying respect to people who understand themselves in group terms of either honour or face, then they easily act in ways that will humiliate each other. Irrespective of the growing recognition of human rights, the main cultures are sticky frameworks that define how people pursue self-worth and what they can feel humiliated about. With growing interaction between cultures, there is more misunderstanding that inadvertently spells humiliation, as people often do not understand how they orient themselves differently in terms of self-worth.

Globalization leads to displacement of people, which is experienced as humiliation

Sociologist Dennis Smith defines humiliation as 'forced social displacement', which for those at the receiving end 'translates into shock, compounded by the victims' sense of helplessness' (2017:2). Such forced social displacement is often an effect of social and political crises, as when people flee from war zones. Humiliation is to be seen as a sociopolitical process that occurs as an overwhelming event or oppressive situation causing an unacceptable situation of degradation, which diminishes people in three ways: (1) subjection, a reduction in freedom and agency; (2) relegation, being pushed down the pecking order in terms of recognition; and (3) exclusion, being shut out of a group, institution, network or country with an inevitable loss of security (Smith 2017:1–2). Different sociopolitical dynamics characterizing our global condition generate humiliation. One of these dynamics is that which Smith refers to as the 'imperial impulse' (2006:54), that is, the determination of power holders to exercise absolute command and be prepared to humiliate others in order to get their way. One example of this is President Bush's address to the American people before the invasion of Iraq in March 2003 in which he made clear that the US can and will humiliate the enemy (Smith 2006:55). Another dynamic is the logic of the market. This logic places emphasis on providing everyone with the freedom of the market (the right to buy if people have money) rather than emphasis on giving the poor and weak security in terms of support and protection if they do not have effective market freedom (Smith 2006:83). The market logic defines the sociopolitical order as a set of mechanisms for encouraging agency by private individuals and companies rather than as an order providing the effective recognition of the social rights of marginalized persons (Smith 2006:83). A consequence of such thought is that the poor are pitied – and in that sense humiliated – but also feared (Smith 2006:83). Both of these systemic dynamics produce humiliation as an integral part of the parameters characterizing our current global condition.

Summing up, the morality of human rights suggests a complete no-go for humiliated parties to re-humiliate their oppressors should the opportunity present itself. Human rights push our development away from a historical past in which intentional humiliation on the part of power holders was an everyday occurrence (Smith 2006). However, such a development on a moral level does eliminate re-humiliating payback actions, which are a very deep-seated way of reacting to suffering for human beings (Barash and Lipton 2011). The historical limiting of intentional humiliation, however, does not necessarily eradicate humiliation. It is precisely the global distribution of basic human rights that makes it possible for people to increasingly interpret their living conditions as humiliating as they see them as shallow in the normative light of the human rights promise. Moreover, such a sense of living in humiliating conditions is easily aggregated by the fact that disprivileged people have become more exposed than ever qua global media to information about the living conditions of rich and secure privileged people who enjoy a dignified life with human rights. Differences in basic cultural notions of self-worth persist, and with increasing intercultural interaction and communications, people easily misrecognize each other in ways that will be perceived as humiliating. Forced social displacement is also a consequence of the global condition, and people will therefore continue to feel the discomfort of being taken out of their context.

To sum up, the current humiliation issues characterizing our global condition all illustrate how humiliation dynamics exceed a common-sense notion of humiliation as taking place between an intentional 'humiliator', a victim and often witnesses (Klein 1991). It is therefore relevant to reflect more thoroughly on how humiliation arises qua different mechanisms.

Four humiliation mechanisms: symbolic, representative, non-recognition and self-perceived

In this section, I discuss four significant ways humiliation emerges to achieve a comprehensive grasp of how humiliation comes about. All of these mechanisms differ from directly degrading actions or expression in concrete interaction between 'humiliator', victim and witnesses, thereby supplementing the usual understanding of humiliation as a very physical and interactional phenomenon. In the subsequent discussion, the mechanisms are applied to the understanding of the current humiliation issues discussed earlier.

Symbolic humiliation: violating group dignity

To understand what is violated in humiliation, it is insufficient to think only in terms of two different normative orientations: an honour code emphasizing, for example, the honour of the family, and a human rights code emphasizing the individual dignity of the person. We must also think in terms of social dignity, which relates to groups, as dignity is not merely linked to individual humans (Neuhäuser 2011). For example, we can think of the symbolic humiliation of groups as a form of collective humiliation that takes place as degrading action or attitudes target symbols of the concerned group rather than degradation of a particular member. Members feel humiliated when their cherished symbols are degraded, as illustrated by examples such as the vandalizing of Jewish cemeteries or degrading representations of homosexuals on TV. Symbolic humiliation was a significant mobilizing dynamic in the so-called Danish Cartoon Crisis in 2005–2006, which involved satirical drawings of the prophet Muhammed published in the Danish newspaper Jyllands-Posten. These drawings were then interpreted as humiliating all of the followers of Islam by Muslims in Denmark, but especially by large groups of people in the Middle East. This triggered mass demonstrations, the burning of the Danish flag and even the Danish embassies in Damascus and Beirut. As part of this conflict, representatives and leaders of Muslim communities in Denmark manipulated some of the drawings as part of a campaign to engender a further sense of humiliation among people in the Middle East. This case illustrates how people are engaged in terms of their social or collective dignity and how the engendering of humiliation is part of political mobilization, where political leaders can suggest themselves as a way of regaining lost dignity.

Representative humiliation

Another form of collective and symbolic humiliation is representative group humiliation, which occurs if one or more members of a group are being degraded. This form of collective humiliation is characterized by the following features:

(I) The humiliation of some members of a group is humiliating for the whole group, if: (II) the humiliation is directed against a collectively shared part of identity; (III) this shared part of identity is constitutive for the self-respect of the members of this group; (IV) the humiliation is sanctioned on a social level and/or no appropriate measures against it are taken.

(Neuhäuser 2011:30)

An illustrative example is the turmoil often caused by the mistreatment of individuals by the police. In 1992, the acquittal of four white policemen for having beaten Rodney King, a black man, triggered riots in Los Angeles. The riots did not start directly after King's beating became public but only when it became known that the policemen would not be convicted of anything. This can be seen as a response towards a social reactive attitude, which was experienced as a representative group humiliation. This is not to say that the riots were justified in any way; in fact, many serious crimes were committed; at least 53 persons were killed, many more injured and there was extensive damage to private and public properties. The judges, attorneys and members of the jury made two mistakes. First, they acquitted the four policemen despite their obviously having committed a serious crime. Second, they were unaware of the level of public scrutiny on the case. They did not foresee that many people would identify with King – not because he was a criminal but because he was black. They saw him as a black person mistreated by white policemen. In their eyes, this mistreatment was a humiliating act, because he was not treated as white criminals would have been. The acquittal of the policemen was tantamount to society sanctioning this humiliation, which became a case of representative group humiliation. Another example of representative group humiliation concerning the relationship between Western and Muslim countries involves the feelings of humiliation that developed in the context of the shocking and widely circulated images of American military personnel abusing prisoners in the Abu Ghraib Prison. This instance of the direct interactional humiliation of particular prisoners also led to feelings of humiliation among Muslims around the world, as they self-identified with the humiliated persons as Muslims (not prisoners) who were degraded by Westerners.

Both symbolic and representative humiliation are examples of how humiliation emerges because of some action taking place. As presented in the following, however, humiliation can also result from the failure to accord recognition.

Humiliation qua non-recognition

The notion of recognition is central to understanding one of the ways humiliation can occur: the accordance of respect affirms dignity. Showing respect affirms that people are seen as equally valuable (as possessing equal human dignity) despite their various differences. Such affirmation of dignity through the provision of respect can be negated in two different ways. Firstly, a person's sense of dignity is potentially undermined when they meet direct, denigrating and contemptuous behaviour that can often engender feelings of anger, shame and humiliation. Secondly, such feelings of disappointment and humiliation can also result from being subjected to non-recognition when ignored, overlooked and/or met with indifference (Heidegren 2010). Non-recognition is a less visible way of not being accorded respect than more direct forms of humiliation, such as direct interactional humiliation, the degradation of symbols or representative humiliation. In order to clarify what non-recognition implies, it is useful to distinguish between recognition in terms of respect and appreciation. Respect relates to equality and therefore concerns human dignity, whereas appreciation relates to difference and in this sense involves qualities such as prestige and status. The respect that is shown to us provides dignity, whereas the appreciation of our abilities engenders prestige. Respect concerns that which we share with or have in common with others (equality). One can respect all humans irrespective of their age, gender, etc. However, one cannot appreciate everybody to the same degree or for the same reasons. Appreciation relates to differences in terms of being better than or different from others (Heidegren 2010:52). Meeting people with respect does not imply that one has to appreciate them in their different individualities. Humiliation relates to a lack of respect – not an absence of appreciation. This point is important in order to avoid tallying all kinds of feelings of disappointment as humiliation. While one might feel disappointed about not being appreciated to the degree that one desires, this is different from the sense of humiliation resulting from not receiving the respect one deserves.

We have common expectations concerning the accordance of respect in certain situations, the discourse of human rights being one example of an increasing commonality. As an institution working to secure human rights, the United Nations is a positive example of according recognition in the form of respect for all humans. But expectations concerning the accordance of respect differ. It is not given that different groups of people have the same expectations concerning whom to (not) accord respect. One group can feel non-recognized vis-à-vis a certain other group that does not think of itself as being obligated to show respect to this particular group. This point underlines how dynamics of humiliation can establish themselves only with reference to the normative framework of a single group. In this sense, feelings of humiliation are in the eyes and mind of the beholder.

Self-perceived humiliation

The other dynamics all involve some form of interaction. This is not the case with self-perceived humiliation, as it refers to how people interpret their conditions as humiliating. A sense of humiliation can result without 'humiliators', which is why I describe this dynamic as self-perceived. People can interpret the conditions in which they are living as undermining their dignity and self-respect. When people think of themselves as enduring unfair conditions, a sense of humiliation can easily develop. People can, but do not have to, ascribe intentionality of humiliation to certain agents in order to feel humiliated. This mechanism is more subjective than others, but the term 'self-perceived' should not be taken too literally, as it relies on interpretations of external conditions meaningfully to be seen as detrimental to self-worth. When respect is perceived to be lacking, it is not important whether the factual backgrounds feeding feelings of humiliation are real or imagined (Lindner 2007a:3). Imagined factual backgrounds can make people feel just as humiliated as real ones. Self-perception can be mobilizing despite being very subjectivist. In order to gain support from other outside groups, however, it is important that the suffering party can align their interpretation with common normative standards. That is also why we often see the opponents in a conflict struggling to convince the rest of the world that they were the first party to be humiliated by the other (Sluzki 2013). With the self-perception notion, we are better suited to grasp how a humiliation dynamic can motivate conflict behaviour in unexpected situations, since we, as external observers, do not observe any interaction, expressions or behaviour that we would classify as humiliating.

Conclusion

In summary, then, humiliation is a particular emotional experience that serves as an enduring motivation for actions that can bring about conflict. The various sources explained earlier give rise to humiliation dynamics, which can motivate people to stand up for their dignity. The motivation of self-worth is a fundamental human one, but what defines self-worth varies culturally. Humiliation concerns different values, including face, honour, individual/personal dignity and social dignity. With the increasing interaction across different cultures, humiliation resulting from a lack of understanding is likely to result. Moreover, current sociopolitical crises (e.g. wars, catastrophes and hunger) and the deinstitutionalization effects of the market economy engender forced social displacement. While the increasing adherence to human rights contains an optimistic promise, the overall development is mixed. In the light of human rights ideals, the development of a sense of humiliation is to be expected as people have fewer normative reasons to believe that they deserve to live under conditions that do not come close to realizing fundamental human rights.

The exploration of current humiliation issues has shown that humiliation is often different from humiliation arising from a 'humiliator' acting in order to humiliate another party. On the basis of the elaborated framework, we can summarize how different mechanisms are involved in the humiliation issues diagnosed. Considering dignity humiliation, feelings of humiliation can result from several different mechanisms. An individual's sense of dignity can be undermined in direct interactional instances but also through various symbolic mechanisms, non-recognition and self-perceived humiliation. The latter two mechanisms in particular explain how dynamics of humiliation can motivate conflict behaviour in surprising ways, since they are less visible and audible than mechanisms initiated by observable actions of 'humiliators'. When humiliation results from parties not paying the appropriate form of respect due to a lack of awareness of the cultural codes of either face, honour or personal dignity, it is best understood in terms of non-recognition and self-perception. The other mechanisms presuppose some understanding of what one is going to degrade. Humiliation qua forced social displacement can intentionally be initiated by political powers seeking to humiliate particular groups in the population – but need not be so. When social displacement seems more the effect of anonymous social development, the mechanisms operating are best understood in terms of non-recognition and self-perception.

Conceptualizing conflict as a particular mode of interaction, it makes sense to distinguish analytically between the internal tensions within conflict parties and the relational tensions played out in the interaction between conflict parties and to suggest that the tension on one level does not necessarily correlate with the tension on another level (see the Introduction Chapter). One might therefore ask if humiliation is entirely an internal tension of inflicted suffering or whether it might also be a relational tension. How the inherent normative opposition in humiliation is actually realized (or not) depends on the actual situational dynamics and the broader cultural and normative framework of the concerned situations. Apparently, the aforementioned theorization of humiliation dynamics concerns the level of preconditions of conflict rather than conflict itself, as the SIT model conceptualizes it. Humiliation engenders an internal tension within the suffering parties in terms of a desire to have their self-respect or dignity re-established. However, this tension is not only internal when it motivates action leading to interaction with other parties in order to seek re-establishing of dignity. When humiliation is accompanied with anger and the blaming of the perpetrator, it enters into the relation to the opposing party in a conflict. Considering the different mechanisms, it becomes obvious to suggest that the more direct mechanisms containing intentional 'humiliators' will often cause anger, as a culpable perpetrator can be blamed, and it is therefore more likely that humiliation also emerges as a relational tension; whereas it is more likely that humiliation remains an internal tension considering the mechanisms of non-recognition and self-perception.

Humiliation dynamics vary considerably in the publicity they receive, which can be explained in terms of the framework of different mechanisms. Feelings generated by non-recognition and self-perception receive less public attention than direct humiliation or the degradation of collective symbols; think of the attention-grabbing images of the physical interactional humiliation in Abu Ghraib that the media circulated around the world. Both practically and in relation to research, it is significant to appreciate humiliation as an enduring motivation to become directly involved in a conflict. The challenge is therefore to become even more aware whether such motivation is lingering to foresee where conflicts might emerge. Conflict studies need to become more aware of not so easily observable humiliation mechanisms, which can motivate parties to engage in conflict actions that sometimes lead to payback responses if they appear as a viable option for humiliated parties. How can individual or private humiliation feelings be better explored? It is not necessarily easy to be aware of non-recognition and self-perception, as the task is to detect the less visible cues of feeling humiliated. Further research into such looming mechanisms will provide better opportunity to address them in terms of practical conflict resolution measures.

References

Barash, David P. and Judith E. Lipton (2011) *Payback: Why We Retaliate, Redirect Aggression and Take Revenge*. Oxford: Oxford University Press.

Barbalet, Jack (1998) *Emotion, Social Theory, and Social Structure: A Macrosociological Approach*. Cambridge: Cambridge University Press.

Bramsen, Isabel (2018) 'How Civil Resistance Succeeds (Or Not): Micro-dynamics of Unity, Timing, and Escalatory Actions', *Peace & Change: A Journal of Peace Research* 43(1): 61–89.

Bramsen, Isabel and Poul Poder (2014) 'Theorizing Three Basic Emotional Dynamics of Conflicts: A Situational Research Agenda', *Peace Research: The Canadian Journal of Peace and Conflict Studies* 46 (2): 51–86.

Fattah, Khaled and Karin M. Fierke (2009) 'A Clash of Emotions: The Politics of Humiliation and Political Violence in the Middle East', *European Journal of International Relations* 15 (1): 67–93.

Friedrichs, Jörg (2016) 'An Intercultural Theory of International Relations: How Self-Worth Underlies Politics among Nations', *International Theory* 8 (1): 63–96.

Gingesa, Jeremy and Scott Attran (2008) 'Humiliation and the Inertia Effect: Implications for Understanding Violence and Compromise in Intractable Intergroup Conflicts', *Journal of Cognition and Culture* 8: 281–294.

The Guardian (2011) *Inside Syria: The Rebel Call for Arms and Ammunition*. www.theguardian.com/world/2011/dec/11/inside-syria-rebels-call-arms (accessed 19 June 2017).

Hartling, Linda M. (2007) 'Humiliation: Real Pain, a Pathway to Violence', *Brazilian Journal of Sociology of Emotion* 6 (17): 466–479.

Hartling, Linda M., Evelyn G. Lindner, Uli Spalthoff and M. Britton (2013) 'Humiliation: The Nuclear Bomb of Emotions?', *Psicología Política* 46: 55–76.

Hartling, Linda M. and Tracy Luchetta (1999) 'Humiliation: Assessing the Impact of Derision, Degradation and Debasement', *The Journal of Primary Prevention* 19 (4): 259–278.

Heidegren, Carl-Göran (2010) *Anerkendelse: kort og godt* [Recognition: In Short]. Frederiksberg C: Samfundslitteratur.

Klein, Donald C. (1991) 'The Humiliation Dynamic: An Overview', *Journal of Primary Prevention* 12 (2): 93–121.

Leidner, Bernhard, Hammad Sheikh and Jeremy Ginges (2012) 'Affective Dimensions of Intergroup Humiliation', *PLoS ONE* 7 (9): e46375.

Lindner, Evelin G. (2001) *The Concept of Humiliation: Its Universal Core and Culture-Dependent Periphery*. Oslo: University of Oslo, unpublished manuscript.

Lindner, Evelin G. (2002a) 'Healing the Cycles of Humiliation: How to Attend to the Emotional Aspects of "Unsolvable" Conflicts and the Use of "Humiliation Entrepreneurship"', *Peace and Conflict: Journal of Peace Psychology* 8 (2): 125–138.

Lindner, Evelin G. (2002b) 'Human Rights and Humiliation', *Coexistence Chronicle* 2 (3): 2–6.

Lindner, Evelin G. (2002c) 'Gendercide and Humiliation in Honor and Human Rights', *Journal of Genocide Research* 4 (1): 137–155.

Lindner, Evelin G. (2006) *Making Enemies: Humiliation and International Conflict*. London: Preager.

Lindner, Evelin G. (2007a) 'In Times of Globalization and Human Rights: Does Humiliation Become the Most Disruptive Force?', *Journal of Human Dignity and Humiliation Studies* 1 (1). www.humiliationstudies.org/documents/evelin/HumiliationandFearin-GlobalizingWorldHumanDHSJournal.pdf (accessed 19 June 2017).

Lindner, Evelin G. (2007b) 'Dynamics of Humiliation in a Globalizing World', *International Journal on World Peace* 24 (3): 15–52.

Lindner, Evelin G. (2009) *Emotion and Conflict: How Human Rights Can Dignify Emotion and Help Us Wage Good Conflict.* London: Praeger.

Lukes, Steven (1997) 'Humiliation and Politics of Identity', *Social Research* 64 (1): 36–51.

MacDonald, Geoff and Mark R. Leary (2005) 'Why Does Social Exclusion Hurt? The Relationship between Social and Physical Pain', *Psychological Bulletin* 131 (2): 202–223.

Margalit, Avishai (1996) *The Decent Society.* Cambridge, MA: Harvard University Press.

Moïsi, Dominique (2009) *The Geopolitics of Emotion: How Cultures of Fear, Humiliation and Hope are Reshaping the World.* New York: Doubleday.

Neuhäuser, Christian (2011) 'Humiliation: The Collective Dimension', in Paulus Kaufmann, Hannes Kuch, Christian Neuhäuser and Elaine Webster (Eds.), *Humiliation, Degradation, Dehumanization: Human Dignity Violated* (21–36), Library of Ethics and Applied Philosophy 24. Berlin: Springer Science + Business Media B.V.

Otten, Marte and Kai J. Jonas (2014) 'Humiliation as an Intense Emotional Experience: Evidence from the Electro-Encephalogram', *Social Neuroscience* 9 (1): 23–35.

Rioux, Jean-Francois and Vern N. Redekop (2013) *Introduction to Conflict Studies: Empirical, Theoretical and Ethical Dimensions.* Oxford: Oxford University Press.

Rothbart, Daniel and Poul Poder (2017) 'Systemic Humiliation as Daily Social Suffering', in Ronald E. Anderson (Ed.), *Alleviating World Suffering: The Challenge of Negative Quality of Life* (35–48), New York: Springer International Publishing.

Saulo, Fernández, Tamar Saguy and Eran Halperin (2015) 'The Paradox of Humiliation: The Acceptance of an Unjust Devaluation of the Self', *Personality and Social Psychology Bulletin* 41 (7): 976–988.

Scheff, Thomas J. (2000) *Bloody Revenge: Emotions, Nationalism and War.* Lincoln, NE: iUniverse.

Scheff, Thomas J. and Suzanne Retzinger (1991) *Emotions and Violence: Shame and Rage in Destructive Conflicts.* Lexington, MA: Lexington Books.

Sluzki, Carlos E. (2013) 'Humiliation, Shame and Associated Social Emotions: A Systemic Approach and a Guide for its Transformation', in Carlos G. Bigliana, Rodolfo Moguillansky and Carlos E. Sluzki (Eds.), *Shame and Humiliation: A Dialogue between Psychoanalytic and Systemic Approaches* (57–102), London: Karnac Books.

Smith, Dennis (2006) *Globalization: The Hidden Agenda.* Oxford: Polity Press.

Smith, Dennis (2008) 'Globalization, Degradation and the Dynamics of Humiliation', *Current Sociology* 56 (3): 371–379.

Smith, Dennis (2017) *Exploring the Rocky Road: Getting from Humiliation to Conflict Transformation.* www.academia.edu/31583904/Exploring_The_Rocky_Road_Getting_From_Humiliation_To_Conflict_Transformation (accessed 19 June 2017).

5

SYRIA'S MOVING IMAGES

Moral outrage and the role of grassroots videos in conflict escalation

Josepha Ivanka Wessels[1]

Introduction: media access in Syria and the use of online media

The rapid spread of uploaded YouTube videos from parts of Syria that were inaccessible to Western media radically changed the audiovisual media landscape in Syria. In February 2011, the Syrian government decided to open public access to previously banned global digital platforms for image sharing, such as YouTube and Facebook. Syrian activists initially approached this new online universe with great caution. The Syrian President had previously been the head of the Syrian Computer Society (Stenberg and Salamandra 2015), and lifting the ban on YouTube in 2011 was a way to give people more (limited) freedom whilst at the same time also enabling the Syrian regime to monitor opposition activists online. Prior to 2011, in the first decade of the rule of Bashar al Assad, the majority of Syrians with access to Internet used proxies to use social media sites such as Facebook and YouTube. The use of these proxies also shielded people from being tracked online. With the ban lifted, proxies were not necessary anymore. Free access to new media, in the context of the Arab Spring, was seen as liberating by many Western analysts and therefore a major developer of positive change in the political landscape (Brownlee 2017). Although lifting the ban did little for establishing a more democratic society in Syria, the uncontrolled access to YouTube did illustrate the very personal and local experiences of Syrians going through revolutionary protests, grief and eventually war.

Since 2011, the velocity and visibility of audiovisual information about events on the Syrian streets increased rapidly, changing how Syrians communicate and share information over long distances. Where the national television networks and Arab satellite channels dominated the narratives and the airwaves prior to 2011, the uploading of over 400,000 video clips online from Syria challenged the hegemony of mass media TV Channels (Elias 2014; Halasa, Mahfoud and

Omareen 2014; Koettl 2014; Snowdon 2014; Wessels 2016). Many Syrians now get their information through social media accounts and YouTube channels, communicating with one another using a variety of applications like WhatsApp, Viber, Facebook and Skype, a situation unimaginable prior to 2011 (Wessels 2015, 2016).

This chapter focuses on the local experience of war (Jabri 2013; Mac Ginty 2014; Richmond and Mac Ginty 2015) as recorded on mobile phones and video cameras and the role of YouTube and audiovisual User-Generated Content in the escalation of conflict. The main question in this chapter is: What role did the emotions expressed in grassroots videos from Syria play in the conflict escalation in Syria? The chapter argues that the medium of video is not merely a technical tool but a powerful vehicle for expressing emotions, typically the emotion of moral outrage (Askanius 2012). Moral outrage is a specific type of anger that is expressed when a person observes a violation of norms, something that goes against the morals and beliefs of the observer. When observing a child being slapped by a parent, for example, the observer might become morally outraged if they are against the corporal punishment of children. Conversely, if the observer believes hitting children to be justifiable and an acceptable form of punishment, the observer does not become morally outraged. Moral outrage is therefore seen as an affective phenomenon, not as irrational but part of a rational action, influenced by cognitive processes, beliefs and moral values that are socially constructed and encoded within a set of specific circumstances (Jasper 2011). Jasper (2011) describes how activists use imagery that solicits 'moral shock' in order to gain political support or more members of activist collectives (Jasper 2011). Some of the content in the videos had a strong potential to provoke moral outrage in others who view the clips, and they have therefore triggered other events and actions elsewhere in the country.

Grassroots videos: violence and conflict theory

Instead of using conventional weapons, the grassroots video activists in Syria view their video cameras as alternative, non-violent weapons that give them power against state violence and repression. But what is this *power of the camera?* Is it really a *non-violent weapon?* Does the camera provide a false sense of protection (Askanius 2012; Jacobs 2013; Snowdon 2014)? After five years of misery and death in Syria, many young activists have reached the conclusion that the camera might not have been the effective weapon they believed it was. Despite the audiovisual documentation of hospital bombardments, aerial bombardments involving chemicals such as phosphorus and extreme violence, the camera has neither protected the people nor triggered the downfall of the Assad regime. However, the grassroots videos in Syria did seem to have a strong effect in conflict escalation.

If conflict is a special type of social relation and situation (Constantinou, Richmond and Watson 2008; Messmer 2003; Salice 2013) of varying intensity that does not necessarily have to lead to violence (see the Introduction Chapter) and different perspectives on the situation are important for how it escalates (Salice 2013; Schreuder 2014), then conflict can be seen as a specific form of communication. A conflict arises when two or more people have different perspectives and opinions on events, reality and 'truth'. Depending on the social relation(s) between those involved, the conflict is either resolved by listening to each other's different perspectives or it is increased when two parties refuse to listen and understand each other. How can we position Syrian grassroots videos within this frame of conflict escalation and communication? In many ways, video activism from Syria is a form of conflict communication. Grassroots videos record acts of violence and communicate emotional reactions towards a wider audience and, moreover, record the emotions and moral outrage of the victims who are directly affected. Through such audiovisual communication, the morally outraged are able to communicate with the perpetrators of the violence by shouting into the camera, speaking directly into the lens. In the next section, I will elaborate on and show how this expression of moral outrage and other emotions, recorded on digital video, impacted the escalation of the Syrian conflict.

Going through the wall of fear

The Syrian video activists I interviewed for this project often mentioned how they felt like they were passing through a 'wall of fear' together, which forms a central theme in the collective protests of the Arab uprisings in general. In her many interviews with Syrian refugees outside Syria, Pearlman finds the same centrality of collectively broken fear during pro-democracy demonstrations (Pearlman 2016; Wessels 2015). Despite serious dents being made in the wall of fear in the decade prior to 2011 (Stenberg and Salamandra 2015; Wessels 2015; Brownlee 2018), however, the wall of extreme fear in Syria was thought to be absolutely impenetrable in the beginning of the Syrian uprising. Syria was renowned for being the most repressive authoritarian state in the Arab world. Syrians going into the streets and openly protesting the Assad regime was unthinkable in 2010 until a small group of brave, non-violent protesters in Damascus started to organize peaceful vigils in the beginning of 2011. The seeds of the Syrian anti-regime protests had been planted over decades under the stress of a dictatorship. The Syrian regime was an absolute repressive state where people were suppressed into obedience (Brownlee 2018; Wedeen 1999; Wessels 2015). In 2000, the so-called 'Damascene Spring', which led to a hopeful opening up of the country, with promised reforms on the horizon, was reversed in a mere nine months (Brownlee 2018; George 2003; Stienen 2008). Developments like the Damascus Spring in 2000 (George 2003; Stienen 2008) and reformist non-violent advocacy movements in the years up to 2011 (Stenberg and Salamandra 2015) had gradually prepared Syrians that change was possible. Brownlee (2018) identified that Syria witnessed the emergence of a virtual form of civic resistance and mobilization in digital space that predates the 2011 uprising. Online news websites, using proxies, had been politically active, spreading petitions and discussing social issues online. Next to the younger urban, somewhat elitist, generation using online information and access to Internet cafes to exchange views, Syria also witnessed a growing discontent by people in the rural areas prior to the uprisings in 2011. Despite the government-controlled attempt to develop rural areas in Syria with the so-called GONGO such as the 'Syria Trust', a growing rural–urban divide and mass-mobility from the disenfranchised rural communities to the urban areas of Aleppo and Damascus had brought about an asymmetrical power relationship between the urban business elites and the poor Syrian rural population in the years 2000–2010. These developments were important preludes to the eventual public outburst of moral outrage on Syrian YouTube videos.

Grief, violence and funerals on YouTube

The first crucial trigger event in the Syrian uprisings through which grief, moral outrage and anger in online videos played a crucial role in terms of initiating reactionary protests was a video of the tortured body of a young child in Dera'a at his funeral. In January 2011, two women from Dera'a had talked about Hosni Mubarak's downfall in Egypt, speculating whether the Syrian regime would be next, which led to their arrest by the Syrian security forces (Wedeen 2013). Prompted by the women's arrest, school children in Dera'a wrote anti-regime slogans on a public wall in the city and were subsequently also arrested by Syrian security forces. The arrests of the children provoked demonstrations by citizens in the city streets demanding their immediate release. One of the arrested boys, a 13-year-old named Hamza Ali Al-Khateeb, was brutally tortured to death. His body was delivered to his parents as a warning message about preventing children from protesting (Sly 2011). Participants in Hamza's funeral uploaded mobile video recordings showing his extremely tortured body. According to Islamic custom, a body is to be buried within 24 hours. Video recordings of his funeral the next day circulated on YouTube and Facebook,[2] reinvigorating the protests. The amateur video showed the body of Hamza, covered in rose petals and with clear signs of torture.[3] In one YouTube video, the video is accompanied by the following introductory text:

> I am writing to you today, to tell you the story of a young boy. A boy whose story is not quite different from many boys like him who live in Syria. Hamza Al-Khatib, a child only 13 years old, was one like most his age.[4]

In the video, the voice of an unidentified man, possibly medical staff, describes in classical Arabic who the boy is and what happened. Wearing a plastic glove, his hand shows the torture marks on his body. The boy's neck had been broken, he had been tortured with cigarette butts and non-lethal bullets and his genitalia were cut off. The results are clearly visible in the video. The unidentified man explains:

> In the name of God the Merciful, you see here in front of us the latest freedom martyr [witness] from the city of Gizeh of the governorate of Dera'a. His name is Hamza Al-Khateeb, 13 years old. He was arrested and among the children who painted on the walls of Dera'a [...] here, you see how a bullet went through his arm from this side and into his body. It went into his belly. On the other side, we can see the marks of another gunshot that entered the other side of his body and eventually from above we see a gunshot mark in his front torso. When we look at his face, they broke his neck. Then we go to look at his legs and we see his knees are broken. His body is pummelled with bullets.[5]

The video ends with a photo of Hamza next to his coffin. Another Arabic voice, possibly one of the boy's relatives, states that "this is a boy who died because he wanted freedom. Because he was a 'terrorist'".

The following text appears in English subtitles to the video:

> Hamza Ali Alkhateeb. This boy has a story, which is very similar to many other boys like him live in Syria. He was only 13 years old when he was murdered by security forces in the Syrian regime. When the protests began in Syria, he was well aware of what is happening, the people want to live in freedom and dignity, so he decided to go out and participate in the protests. Unfortunately for him, he was arrested on April 29 during the crackdown of protests which was demanding for freedom and dignity, although he was not injured at the time of his arrest, he was returned dead to his family. There are clear signs of torture; the skin on his hands and feet is stripped, his neck is broken, tortured by non-lethal bullets, beaten, his genitalia cut off. Please keep in mind that this is a harmless child, only 13 years old. The story of Hamza is unfortunately one of many. There are many men, women and children, elderly who have yet to be returned to their families. The death toll in Syria since the beginning of these uprisings has exceeded 1000. Mass graves have been found in Dera'a. We demand the international community to take action against this. We demand UN and Amnesty to investigate the murder of this young child and many others like him. Syrian people deserve to live in freedom and dignity.

Whilst the Arabic voice graphically describes and shows the signs of torture on the body, the translation in the subtitles is explaining something entirely different. This would appear to indicate that the video activist who uploaded this clip was trying to inform two different audiences; (1) a non-Arabic language audience to demand that the international community take action and investigate the murder of this boy and (2) an Arabic-speaking audience to provide proof of the torture perpetrated by the regime and to stimulate moral outrage. The difference between the English subtitles and the spoken Arabic can thus be explained in terms of two different approaches to two distinctly different audiences; a Syrian Arabic-speaking audience addressed in Arabic, assuming that most Syrians would know this is perpetrated by the regime and that they are aware of the freedom protests. The visual information and guiding Arabic voice are providing evidence of what most Syrians already knew but had never actually seen on video. The voice is focused on sharing the sense of moral outrage. This moral outrage recorded on video, together with the graphic visuals, is intended to provoke fellow Syrians into action. The English text has a slightly different aim. It assumes that English-speaking viewers do not know the context in Syria, so the text gives a short background in terms of death toll numbers and a clear demand that the UN investigate and the international community take immediate action. Both messages are geared towards soliciting some kind of collective action. Whilst the reaction of the international community was limited, the Syrian audience reacted immediately to the video clip.

The video clip featuring Hamza Ali Al-Khateeb's body went viral among Syrians and provoked a public outcry and moral anger expressed collectively in the form of street protests. Shortly thereafter, the streets filled with angry anti-regime protests across the country, calling for the downfall of the regime. Most of these anti-regime protests still called for 'Salmiyyeh, Salmiyyeh' ('peaceful, peaceful' in Arabic). Hamza Ali Al-Khateeb became the first icon to motivate activists to organize demonstrations against the Assad regime.

The Hamza Ali Al-Khateeb video was the first in a long line of consecutive video clips, incessantly uploaded from Syria, to show demonstrations, grief, funerals, tortured bodies and regime violence (Halasa, Mahfoud and Omareen 2014; Wessels 2016). Syrian documentary filmmakers, amateur video-makers and citizens with mobile phones started uploading their own material to the Internet. These clips were instantaneously shared via social media, mainly Twitter and Facebook. The videos were a response to an urgent need, to record events as they were happening in front of their eyes (Elias 2014). Besides YouTube and Liveleaks, the live stream platform Bambuser was used extensively to live-stream the Friday demonstrations that spread like wildfire across Syria. Initially peaceful, these demonstrations gradually turned violent in response to the brutal crackdown by the Syrian security forces. Some demonstrations turned into funeral processions of martyrs, where the revolutionaries with mobile phones took the opportunity to document the events, usually holding a white sheet of paper with the name of the city and date (Elias 2014).

The two minutes of amateur video of Hamza Ali Al-Khateeb had an instant ripple effect on other video activists across Syria. The video had quickly reached even in places like Raqqa, 550 km north of Dera'a. A video activist form Raqqa described the process as follows:

On the 18th of March 2011, this was the start of the Syrian revolution in Raqqa. I began filming the street protests in April. The demonstrators were a group with people from all walks of life and it was peaceful. First, we heard about the arrests of the children in Dera'a on 15 March 2011 and then in May, we saw Hamza Khateeb's funeral on YouTube, so we became angry and really everybody got out on the streets (...) I worked with a video camera and a link to Al Jazeera Mubasher.[6] When we started to do the livefeeds, around 14 channels came to us for footage; CNN, BBC, France24 – they all took our footage from the demonstrations in Raqqa. We sent it to them through FTP and uploaded the footage. Then the army besieged Raqqa, we took the Assad statue from the roundabout and pulled it down. In one day, we had no martyrs. On 16 March 2013, the siege lasted for three days and we threw stones and they shot at us with AK 47 guns. We went out on the streets, we kept protesting. We were with 70 or 80 people in one room and for 72 hours I did not sleep at all. I have filmed everything. My people were being killed and I needed the world to know this.

(Raqqa based Syrian video activist)

The amount of user-generated video content uploaded on YouTube increased significantly after the establishment and further institutionalization of the Local Coordination Committees (LCCs), which emerged a few months after the first demonstrations hit the streets in Dera'a when civil society activists gathered in protest in front of the Ministry of Interior in Damascus on 15 March 2011 as a reaction to the arrests of the boys in Dera'a. According to Assaad al-Achi (Halasa, Mahfoud and Omareen 2014), who was initially involved in procuring technical equipment for citizen journalists of the LCCs, from spycams, phones, laptops and software, what began as a spontaneous popular movement gradually became organized with the involvement of the Syrian Center for Media and Freedom of Expression (SCM). With the organization also came a wider geographical reach throughout Syria.

The video of the funeral of Hamza Ali Al-Khateeb was a watershed moment in the Syrian uprisings. It led to bigger and more frequent protests, with protesters expressing their moral outrage and demanding the fall of the Syrian regime. In particular, the protests called for the dismissal of Bashar al-Assad, the president, who in their eyes had lost all legitimacy of being their president. The protests were subsequently cracked down with live fire by the Syrian security forces, which led to more funerals, more videos of funerals and a ripple effect that became unstoppable (Üngör 2013).

Using YouTube and video as a vehicle of expressing moral outrage and grief shows that Syrian YouTube videos can be seen as a special form of conflict communication that digitally archives the expressions (Askanius 2012; Schröter 2009). The Syrian state media and pro-Assad channels were quick to counter activist videos. Both parties, through their communication, do not communicate directly, but use video technology to express their claims and counterclaims on reality and truth.

The Syrian regime replied in several ways: (1) official television speeches by the President Bashar al-Assad (the first one broadcast on 30 March 2011) denying of the systematic nature of the violence and dismissing the protests as a foreign plot run by armed terrorist gangs – these speeches became more radical over time (Üngör 2013); (2) militarized propaganda videos, in which the Syrian Arab Army is admired as the defenders, laced with nationalist music and at the same time dehumanizing the opponents of Assad as 'vermin', 'cockroaches', 'beasts', 'savages', 'rats' and 'pigs'; and (3) Counter-narratives that screen forced confessions and doctors' statements justifying, and at the same time denying, regime torture and violence.

In the case of Hamza Ali al-Khateeb, the YouTube channel 'Truth Syria', which functions as a propaganda channel for the Syrian regime, uploaded an interview with a medical examiner who countered the video on 12 December 2011. The examiner states that the boy had not been killed through torture[7] and a confession by a so-called activist, Abdel Azeez from Dera'a, stated that Hamza Ali al-Khateeb had been part of a group of terrorists who committed violence against regime forces under the guidance of a Sunni *shaykh* who travelled to the United Arab Emirates frequently.[8]

There is a paradox in these counter-narratives by the regime; on the one hand, the doctor's interview denies any form of torture happened to Hamza Ali al-Khateeb's body and on the other hand, the confession by Abdel Azeez justifies the arrest, torture and death of Hamza Ali al-Khateeb because Hamza had supposedly been part of a terrorist group. Both narratives are without any proof of evidence, whilst the funeral video shows clear signs of torture on Hamza Ali al- Khateeb's body. It has not been proven that he was linked to any terrorist groups. He was just a child inspired by the Arab Spring, who wrote anti-regime slogans on a wall.

Government crackdown on protesters

When regime forces started targeting funeral processions, bakeries and using heavy artillery, these events were recorded and uploaded, causing a further upsurge in YouTube channels informing other Syrians. The counter-narrative by pro-regime YouTube channels became aggressive, depicting and sub-altering the protesters as terrorists, rats that should be exterminated. Via such enemy-labelling and othering processes towards the Syrian protesters, the pro-regime videos thus justified the extreme state violence and the killing of the protesters. In the meantime, the security forces arrested many media activists who disappeared without information of their whereabouts. Despite these dangers, video activists were determined to record the events.

The extraordinary events became ordinary, and the velocity and virality of the mobile phone videos became part of a non-linear, multidimensional entropic information flow on the spatial, temporal, aural and visual events picked up by the grassroots digital cameras. Through the increased interconnectivity, events on the ground could be followed in real time, and those who morally and empathically identified with the victims in the video reacted emotionally with more street demonstrations. Eventually, the regime changed from directly targeting group gatherings and demonstrations with live fire to aerial attacks and the deployment of tanks in residential areas to quell the uprisings.

For many street protesters, the widespread appearance of regime snipers and tanks in the streets after the crackdown in Hama at the end of 2011 was another watershed moment.[9] Now, their world had become a genuine war zone. Eventually, Syria was divided into four major regional territories, controlled at checkpoints by the various warring parties: (1) the area controlled by the Assad regime; (2) the areas controlled by the Free Syrian Army (FSA) and their affiliates; (3) the areas controlled by the Kurdish forces and (4) the areas controlled by ISIS.

In a ranking exercise with Syrian video activists, the areas under the control of the Kurdish and FSA-related forces were found to be the most free in terms of video recording: there is no censorship system and, except for certain military positions, video activists are free to film anywhere. They run the risk of being kidnapped by extremist Islamic groups such as Jabhat al-Nusra and, occasionally, Ahrar al-Sham. The areas under regime control are similar in terms of freedom as before the 2011 uprisings, although tighter control and prosecution have been put in place for those Syrian documentary filmmakers known to have been involved in anti-regime activities and demonstrations. The hardest area in Syria to conduct video activism is in the regions under the control of the ISIS; video activism is virtually impossible in the ISIS areas. A brave collective of young early revolutionaries called 'Raqqa is Being Slaughtered Silently (RBSS)' still operated undercover in Raqqa in 2014, to record daily life under ISIS and aerial bombardments by the international coalition air forces.

The power of mourning

FIGURE 5.1 Syrian Video Activist and His Family in Northern Syria, September 2014 © J.I. Wessels.

There is a strong emotional effect of seeing and hearing people cry and shout slogans of grief, moral outrage and despair. The power of mourning and violence as described by Butler (2004) resonates in Syrian grassroots videos and had an effect on those who identified with the victims. It is similar to the effect that the attacks of 9/11 had on Western audiences who immediately empathized with the victims portrayed in the television footage. There is a certain kind of selective empathy and social energy that is induced by watching videos of violence perpetrated to those one identifies with. It leads to large groups who feel directly hurt by the recorded event and express their moral outrage through demonstrations, demanding social justice and revenge. When Syrian security forces targeted the protesters directly in response to their demands, videos about these violent events started to appear on YouTube. In turn, this led to further protests organized by Syrians who were emotionally strongly affected and morally enraged after watching these YouTube videos. Thus, a cycle was formed whereby the activist videos, as means of conflict communication, provided the impetus for reactionary protests based on the shared moral outrage.

By 2014 and 2015, the content video activists were uploading from Syria changed from weekly Friday protests on the streets – with a sense of hope for reform and a new government – to the personal records and emotional experience of war and aerial bombardments. Syrian video activists gradually started organizing themselves in various networks and media collectives from their hometowns (see Figure 5.1). One such collective, the Nour Media Centre based in east Aleppo city, posted videos displaying a typical format and structure of violence. The duration of the videos of violence is typically between 2 and 4 minutes.

The video activists indicated that they often upload just a couple of minutes per day due to the poor Internet connection in their area but that they could upload 4 hours per day if the Internet connections were better. Their news videos have become increasingly sophisticated since 2013 and Nour Media Centre has a specific format for editing their videos. Their content contributes to the Aleppo-based news channel Aleppo Today providing daily news of the events in Syria, focused mainly on the Aleppo province but increasingly also covering areas beyond Aleppo. Nour Media Centre became famous among Syrians through their Miracle Baby Video Clip.[10] The bulk of their videos contain aerial bombardments, which usually start with a scene of the direct aftermath of an aerial bombardment featuring chaos, people in despair and an outcry. This is often followed by interviews with directly affected civilians, who use the camera as a testimonial tool to express their moral outrage over the bombardment that just happened. They speak directly to the camera, shouting their moral outrage and anger into the camera lens, gesturing, blaming either the regime or the Russians. The camera becomes an emotional outlet, a testimonial tool, to shout to the world outside, an unfortunate cry of despair in the dark, gesturing towards the camera, showing their children, or holding their heads, crying out.[11] In turn, these emotions then move others to go out and protest. The Nour Media channel also recorded street demonstrations that are organized and staged in reaction to the atrocities and bombardments. For example, protesters organized street protests to commemorate tragic events during the Syrian uprisings, such as the use of chemical weapons that took place in the Ghouta on 21 August 2013.[12]

The extraordinary in 2011 and 2012 became ordinary in 2014 and 2015. Yet, the video activists keep on filming their history, their world, their habitat, to share on YouTube (Elias 2014). The outside audiences were no longer shocked, and the brutal videos coming out of Syria have not become the agents of change that the video activists had hoped. Their YouTube videos led neither to democratization nor to a rush to aid and protect the Syrian people under duress. Instead of leading to a more concerned reaction, the overload of information generated fatigue and apathy in Western audiences. This outcome was deeply disappointing and created a deep sense of abandonment among those who had been video recording and protesting repression and dictatorships on the frontlines of popular uprisings. The thousands upon thousands of videos uploaded on YouTube by non-violent Syrian protestors failed to yield more and better political action to stop the war in Syria. This resonates with the remark of my Syrian friend early on in the uprisings about the use of YouTube: 'We used to be killed in the dark, now we're killed in the light'.

Conclusion

The main question in this chapter focused on which role emotions in the videos uploaded by Syrian video activists, emotions such as moral outrage, have played in conflict escalation in Syria. The chapter argues that the video medium provides a powerful conflict communication tool to express moral outrage travelling over long geographical distances. The videos document what Collins (2004, 2007) calls *social interaction rituals*. As indicated, the Syrian videos are a specific form of conflict communication, which can lead to further escalation (Messmer 2003; Prosser 1998; Salice 2013). In Chapter 1, Wæver and Bramsen refer to decisive watershed moments in conflict, situations in escalation and how they function as trigger events in conflict. These are the watershed moments that were recorded on digital video in Syria and consequently shared widely. The videos uploaded on YouTube from Syria are thus analysed as vehicles for communication to express strong emotions, such as moral outrage (Jasper 2011). Moral outrage is defined as a special type of anger over the observation of a violation of coded norms, beliefs and values.

The first videos from Syria displayed peaceful protests, which inspired others to take to the streets. They also recorded the moments when protesters broke through the often-mentioned 'wall of fear' together and filled up the existing media gaps on Syria. This had a ripple effect in that protesters elsewhere in Syria subsequently took to the streets, inspired by the first demonstrations. These videos were quickly followed by videos of the violent crackdown by the regime, which rapidly escalated the conflict further. Syrians who were not present watched the YouTube videos online and were so emotionally affected and morally outraged by the videos that they too took to the streets to protest. Specifically, the videos featuring the torture of children, the first being the aforementioned Hamza Ali al-Khateeb, were watershed moments. Hamza Ali al-Khateeb became a symbol of the Syrian uprising, and his image was found on a plethora of social media outlets. The perpetration of extreme violence against peaceful protesters is taken as a tipping point, where grassroots videos started playing a strong role in the communication and escalation of conflict. Grassroots videos spread information rapidly about crucial watershed moments in the Syrian revolution, triggering reactions on the ground, which led to a particular kind of conflict escalation.

The Assad regime reacted to the activist videos with their own videos to counterclaim the interpretation of reality and 'truth'. The conflict was further exacerbated by the reaction of the Syrian regime with more forceful violence to crush the uprising, which was consequently recorded on video and counter-narratives of denial on YouTube. The Assad regime consistently denied its use of barrel bombs; yet, countless videos document such bombings. The most recent denial from the regime top, by the President himself, is the accusation that the still image of an injured boy named Omran in an ambulance in Aleppo is staged and faked (Osborne 2016). The photo of Omran, which went viral worldwide on social media, was a video still from footage shot by an activist from the Aleppo Media Center (AMC) recording the aftermath of an aerial bombardment in eastern Aleppo city.[13] Expert analysis of the original video has determined that the sequence is neither faked nor staged.

Syrian publics were immediately morally outraged by the early video footage of the torture of Hamza Ali al-Khateeb, as publics that empathize with those who are culturally, religiously and ethnically close. The danger of selective moral outrage is that opposition activists in Syria are not regarded as equal humans by outsiders, certainly not if the Assad regime and Russia equate Syrian opposition activists with terrorists and ISIS in keeping with the consistent propaganda narrative by the regime (Prati 2015). The secular Assadist narrative of a *war on terror* is constructed to justify the regime's collective punishment, extreme violence against civilians (Abouzeid 2011) and the extermination of people. A prime watershed example of how the Russians have applied this *war on terror* narrative is seen in the 2016 siege of Aleppo, whereby Russian airplanes bomb and annihilate the rebel-controlled eastern parts of Aleppo city using barrel bombs and bunker busters. The Assad regime has denied these bombardments or justified them with reference to the security narrative of a so-called war on terrorism (Prati 2015; Wessels 2015). Herein, we see a convergence of American and Russian foreign policy narratives towards Syria, whereby ISIS is portrayed as the main enemy rather than the Assad regime, the lesser of two evils.

The international coalition bombings that started in Syria in 2014 are therefore also justified as part of a *global war on Islamic terror*. The international community would appear to have given Assad the green light to continue his brutal campaign against Syrian civilians that '*walk out of line*'. Until then, the protracted conflict in Syria seems only to deepen, with no end in sight and a continued refugee crisis.

In summary, grassroots YouTube videos in Syria indeed played an important triggering role in the escalation of conflict in Syria over long distances within the country. However, the moral outrage communicated in the videos only had an impact on specific audiences who identified personally with the pain and suffering of fellow Syrians recorded in the videos. These publics were notably first inside Syria, where the early videos featuring the torture of children by the regime led to further anti-regime protests in other parts of the country and rapidly spread throughout. With the upload of every recording of funerals, grief and violence, more and larger groups felt compelled to organize street protests. In other instances, the videos might have solicited a strong reaction from the viewers but did not necessarily lead to actions or more street protests. Specifically, the intended effect to impact audiences outside of Syria to take military action against the Assad regime and its international allies has not yet emerged as a crucial factor in the escalation of conflict in Syria at the international level.

Notes

1 Josepha Ivanka Wessels is a Visual Anthropologist/Human Geographer specialized in Syria where she worked and lived between 1997 and 2002 for her PhD (2008) dissertation. She carried out postdoctoral research at the University of Copenhagen for the Centre for Resolution of International Conflicts (CRIC) between 2014 and 2016. Her work focuses on audiovisual media and the role of YouTube videos in the Syrian uprisings. She carried out fieldwork in Turkey and northern Syria in 2014.
2 www.facebook.com/hamza.alshaheed/timeline.
3 YouTube الملف يفتر ةروس الشهداء (2011) 'Hamza Ali Alkhateeb 13 years old murdered by syrian security forces', *YouTube video clip uploaded 27 May 2011*, www.youtube. com/watch?v=WjwC_-bKGhs.
4 YouTube الملف يفتر ةروس الشهداء (2011) 'Hamza Ali Alkhateeb 13 years old murdered by syrian security forces', *YouTube video clip uploaded 27 May 2011*, www.youtube. com/watch?v=WjwC_-bKGhs.
5 YouTube الملف يفتر ةروس الشهداء (2011) 'Hamza Ali Alkhateeb 13 years old murdered by syrian security forces', *YouTube video clip uploaded 27 May 2011*, www.youtube. com/watch?v=WjwC_-bKGhs Unofficial translation from Arabic to English.
6 *Al Jazeera Mubasher* Al-'Amma (AJMG/ الجزيرة مباشر) was launched by the Al Jazeera Media Network in 2005 and provides 24-hour Arabic language news coverage using live streaming on YouTube. Available online at www.youtube.com/user/ aljazeeramubasher.
7 YouTube, an interview with Syrian Medical examiner by 'Truth Syria' on 12 December 2011, www.youtube.com/watch?v=7xlRDgVh6Dg&list=UUDrnROqHtRoes4MXz_ hsgTg&feature=plcp.
8 YouTube, an interview with Abdul Azeez al-Khateeb, confessing Hamza Ali al-Khateeb had been part of a terrorist group uploaded by 'Truth Syria' on 14 December 2011, www.youtube.com/watch?v=8C7qIL1M6lw.
9 Personal conversation with Syrian opposition activist in 2012.
10 YouTube, Aleppo Miracle Baby rescue effort, www.youtube.com/watch?v=vL1DX-tOZWtc; YouTube, Follow-up clip on the miracle baby from Aleppo, www.youtube. com/watch?v=pJr3QCfwC2g.
11 YouTube, Barrel bomb on Aleppo, www.youtube.com/watch?v=-0LVzCqP9lE; YouTube, Aerial bombardment Aleppo, www.youtube.com/watch?v=0w95f1km8Hk.
12 Commemoration in Aleppo of the 2013 Ghouta chemical attacks in the Ghouta, www.youtube.com/watch?v=eRyF5k-NEjE.
13 The Aleppo Media Centre video clip of Omran had over four million views. See original video clip online at www.youtube.com/watch?v=7cfBmRW3isc.

References

Abouzeid, Rania (2011) 'The Syrian Style of Repression: Thugs and Lectures', *Time Magazine*. http://content.time.com/time/world/article/0,8599,2055713,00.html (accessed July 2012).

Askanius, Tina (2012) 'DIY Dying: Video Activism as Archive, Commemoration and Evidence', *International Journal of E-Politics* 3 (1): 12–25.

Brownlee, Billie J. (2017) 'Media Development in Syria: The Janus-Faced Nature of Media Development Aid', *Third World Quarterly*, 38 (10): 2276–2294.

Brownlee, Billie J. (2018) 'Mediating the Syria Revolt: How New Media Technologies Change the Development of Social Movements and Conflicts', in Hinnebusch Raymond and Imady Omar (Eds.), *The Syrian Uprising 2011–2014: Roots and Trajectories* (188–206), Oxford: Routledge.

Butler, Judith (2004) *Precarious Life, the Powers of Mourning and Violence*, New York: Verso.

Collins, Randall (2004) *Interaction Ritual Chains*. Princeton, NJ: Princeton University Press.

Collins, Randall (2007) *Violence, a Micro-sociological Theory*. Princeton, NJ: Princeton University Press.

Constantinou, Costas M., Oliver P. Richmond and Alison Watson (Eds.) (2008) *Cultures and Politics of Global Communication*, Vol. 34: Review of International Studies. Cambridge: Cambridge University Press.

Elias, Chad (2014) 'Syria's Imperfect Cinema' in Malu Halasa, Nawara Mahfoud and Zaher Omareen (Eds.), *Syria Speaks: Art and Culture from the Frontline* (257–271), London: Saqi Books.

George, Alan (2003) *Syria: Neither Bread nor Freedom*. London: Zed Books.

Halasa, Malu, Nawara Mahfoud and Zaher Omareen (Eds.) (2014) *Syria Speaks: Art and Culture from the Frontline*. London: Saqi Books.

Jabri, Vivienne (2013) 'Peacebuilding, the Local and the International: A Colonial or a Postcolonial Rationality?', *Peacebuilding* 1 (1): 3–16.

Jacobs, Jessica (2013) 'Listen with Your Eyes: Towards a Filmic Geography', *Geography Compass* 7 (10): 714–728.

Jasper, James M. (2011) 'Emotions and Social Movements: Twenty Years of Theory and Research', *Annual Review of Sociology* 37 (1): 285–303.

Koettl, Christoph (2014) 'The YouTube War: Citizen Videos Revolutionize Human Rights Monitoring in Syria', *Media Shift*. http://mediashift.org/2014/02/the-youtube-war-citizen-videos-revolutionize-human-rights-monitoring-in-syria/ (accessed September 2014).

Mac Ginty, Roger M. (2014) 'Everyday Peace: Bottom-Up and Local Agency in Conflict-Affected Societies', *Security Dialogue* 45 (6): 548–564.

Messmer, Heinz (2003) *Der Soziale Konflikt: Kommunikative Emergenz und Systemische Reproduktion*. Stuttgart: Lucius Lucius.

Osborne, Samuel (2016) 'Omran Daqneesh: Assad Claims Pictures of Five-Year-Old Aleppo Boy Pulled from Rubble Were "Faked"', *The Independent*. www.independent.co.uk/news/world/middle-east/syria-assad-aleppo-boy-omran-daqneesh-photos-faked-forgery-a7371526.html (accessed January 2017).

Pearlman, Wendy (2016) 'Narratives of Fear in Syria', *Perspectives on Politics* 14 (1): 21–37.

Prati, Guilia (2015) 'Between Propaganda and Public Relations: An Analysis of the Bashar al-Assad's Digital Communications Campaign', *Journal of International Affairs Online*. https://jia.sipa.columbia.edu/online-articles/between-propaganda-and-public-relations-analysis-bashar-al-assad's-digital (accessed July 2016).

Prosser, Jon (Ed.) (1998) *Image-based Research: A Sourcebook for Qualitative Researchers*. London: Routledge Falmer Press, Taylor & Francis Group.

Richmond, Oliver P. and Roger Mac Ginty (2015) 'Where Now for the Critique of the Liberal Peace?', *Cooperation and Conflict* 50 (2): 171–189.

Salice, Alessandro (2013) 'Violence as a Social Fact', *Phenomenology and the Cognitive Sciences* 13 (1): 161–177.

Schreuder, Duco A. (2014) *Vision and Visual Perception: The Conscious Base of Seeing*. Bloomington, IN: Archway Publishing.

Schröter, Jens (2009) 'On the Logic of the Digital Archive', in Pelle Snickars and Patrick Vonderau (Eds.), *The YouTube Reader* (330–346), Stockholm: National Library of Sweden.

Sly, Liz (2011) 'Torture of Boy Reinvigorates Syria's Protest Movement', *The Washington Post*. www.washingtonpost.com/world/middle-east/torture-of-boy-reinvigorates-syrias-protest-movement/2011/05/29/AGPwIREH_story.html (accessed September 2014).

Snowdon, Peter (2014) 'The Revolution Will Be Uploaded: Vernacular Video and the Arab Spring', *Journal of Current Cultural Research* 6: 401–429.

Stenberg, Leif and Christa Salamandra (2015) 'Introduction: A Legacy of Raised Expectations', in Christa Salamandra and Leif Stenberg (Eds.), *Syria from Reform to Revolt, Volume 2: Culture, Society and Religion* (1–15), Syracuse, NY: Syracuse University Press.

Stienen, Petra (2008) *Dromen van een Arabische lente: Een Nederlandse diplomate in het Midden-Oosten*. Amsterdam: Nieuw Amsterdam.

Üngör, Uğur Ümit (2013) 'Mass Violence in Syria: A Preliminary Analysis', *New Middle Eastern Studies* 3: 1–22.

Wedeen, Lisa (1999) *Ambiguities of Domination: Politics, Rhetoric and Symbols in Contemporary Syria*. Chicago, IL: University of Chicago Press.

Wedeen, Lisa (2013) 'Ideology and Humor in Dark Times: Notes from Syria', *Critical Inquiry* 39 (4): 841–873.

Wessels, Josepha Ivanka (2015) 'Syrian Masquerades of War', in Christine Sylvester (Ed.), *Masquerades of War* (95–117), Abingdon, Oxon: Routledge.

Wessels, Josepha Ivanka (2016) 'YouTube and the Role of Digital Video for Transitional Justice in Syria', *Politik* 4 (19): 30–54.

6

CLERGY AND CONFLICT INTENSITY

The roles of the Sunni ulama in the
Syrian conflict

Jakob Skovgaard-Petersen

Introduction: the men of religion

Religion has come to the fore in numerous international conflicts and has, belatedly, been recognized as a significant independent element in conflict analysis. Thus far, however, this interest has concentrated on the obvious relevance of religious movements and ideologies with a propensity for violence, or, alternatively, on a comparison of foundational texts and an alleged 'ethos' in the various religions or on competing value systems inside them (Ramsbotham, Woodhouse and Miall 2011:349–346). Less attention has been paid to the role of the 'men of religion', the carrier group of religious authority in ordinary times, in Arabic known as the *'ulama* or the *shuyukh* (sheikhs). How do they respond to social and political tensions? What role do they play in inter-religious escalation? And what, in turn, might be their role and instruments in de-escalating the religious dimensions of violent conflict?

This paper proposes the examination of the Sunni Muslim scholars and preachers, the *ulama*, in Syria. The Sunni *ulama* are significant in that they represent the majority religion of the country but not the religion of the dominant figures of the ruling regime. Issues of regime legitimacy and, conversely, of the intensification of conflict and the mobilization of its actors are linked to the agency of the Sunni *ulama*, not least if we subscribe to the view presented in this book that conflict intensity is not solely reflected in actual violence.

Focusing on the Syrian conflict and the religious specialists of the majority Sunni confession, the *ulama*, this paper investigates the role of major *ulama* in 2011–2014, some loyal to the regime, some hesitantly abandoning it, some in exile and some calling for war and actually taking part in it. Drawing on Weberian perspectives on political legitimacy and religious authority, the paper analyses these *ulamas'* positions on the crucial issue of the Islamic legitimacy of rule and their actions in terms of organizational initiatives and religio-political communication (khutbas, fatwas). Demonstrating their various roles in conflict escalation, it surveys their marginalization in the phase of full-scale violent conflict and discusses their possible role in a later de-escalation phase.

Ulama in history and theory

In his groundbreaking study of the *ulama* in the Middle Ages, Ira M. Lapidus (1967) demonstrated that this status group was remarkably socially diverse, spanning members from elite families in control of significant estates to poor itinerant preachers. Defined through the training and systematic acquisition of the disciplines of scholarship (*'ilm*), the *ulama* were set apart by their social status, which allowed them to address the rulers on behalf of the population or, conversely, to convey the ruler's wishes to the believers. They were the glue of society, effectively helping its various estates to communicate and coexist (Lapidus 1967:107–130). This organicist and functionalist reading of the role of the *ulama* should be supplemented by more Weberian interpretations of the *ulama* as a carrier group of ideological change and renewal; in certain social conflicts, individual *ulama* were right at the centre, more as 'movers and shakers' than mediators. In 1099, for instance, the qadi of Jerusalem travelled to Baghdad not merely to inform the caliph about the loss of his city to the Franks but to shame him and the Muslims in Baghdad to mobilize and move to retake it. And as the Muslim campaign to evict the crusaders finally came to fruition 200 years later, famous Muslim scholars like ibn Qudama preached and fought in the successful siege of Tripoli. *Ulama*, in short, were drivers of political change. And they were not necessarily quietist.

Muhammad I Qasim Zaman's *The Ulama in Contemporary Islam: Custodians of Change* is a more recent and equally groundbreaking book on the *ulama*. The subtitle is a rebuttal to the identification of the *ulama* in modernization theory as the embodiment of the tradition that modernization would surely overcome (Zaman 2007). Despite losing their dominant position in education and the courts over the last 150 years, the *ulama* have been strikingly resilient, taking up modern forms of charity, social action, cultural life and media communication. To some degree, the popular revival of religion that has swept through the Muslim world since the 1970s, *al-sahwa*, has returned the role to them of conferring or withholding legitimacy to specific policies and even sometimes individual rulers, as when Islamist preacher Yusuf al-Qaradawi called for Libyans and Syrians to rise up against their rulers in 2011 on the Al Jazeera media network (Al-Qaradawi 2011, 2012). Now, however, they are up against other contenders for Islamic legitimacy, not least the Islamist movements. These movements have traditionally drawn their leadership from the modern professional classes and criticized the *ulama* for being old-fashioned or too subservient to power when it came to 'defending Islam' against the onslaught of secularization and Western culture.

The *ulama* are also internally divided, however, not only in terms of income and class, but also in terms of outlook and perceived social role. Some *ulama* are striving to uphold the social order, whereas others are working to change it. In *The Prophet's Pulpit*, Frank Gaffney (1994:35–37) proposes three ideal types of an *alim* in the modern age:

A   The preacher as a Sufi *wali*. This type bases his authority on his saintly cha-
     risma, *baraka*, and intimate knowledge of the esoteric world, *al-batin*. Sufi
     saints can be found throughout Syria, often combining their Sufism with a
     profound knowledge of law and theology.
B   The preacher as a scholar. Here, the authority is based on his learning, *'ilm*,
     and his ethical responsibility as a teacher and preacher in society. In a mod-
     ern state, this type represents a legal–ethical system that is parallel (and to a
     degree complementary) to that of the official state law. This would be the
     type educated in the Sharia faculties of Damascus and Aleppo and employed
     as preachers around the country.
C   The preacher as a warrior, *mujahid*. This type bases his authority on his will
     to fight and sacrifice together with his opposition to the powers that be. In
     Syria, this type was uncommon before 2011. If taken in the broader sense
     of preaching social change and protesting against the regime, some exiled
     ulama fit the description.

The *ulama* of Syria

Syria is a special case in several respects. In Syria, the dominant Islamist group, the Muslim Brotherhood, was actually founded and led by *ulama*. When Syria was unified with Egypt in 1958–1961, President Gamal Abdel Nasser proscribed the Muslim Brotherhood, as he had done in Egypt in 1954. But while Nasser's successor Anwar al-Sadat struck a deal with the leadership of the Brotherhood in Egypt, allowing the group to operate socially, albeit not politically, no such compromise was reached in Syria. On the contrary, President Hafez al-Assad weathered an attempt at an Islamist revolution in the years 1978 to 1982, which he brutally suppressed. Since then, the Brotherhood has been in exile. For dec-ades, the Sunni religious scene has been left to the *ulama*.

Syria is also different in other ways; however, its religious composition is an important feature: Syrian society is composed of numerous religious groups, both Christian and Muslim, which are spread unevenly throughout town and country. In contrast to neighbouring Lebanon and Iraq, however, one religious group holds the majority: the Sunnis. The power-sharing formulas making up Lebanon's history since the 1920s and recently having been incorporated into Iraq's post-2003 constitution were largely considered irrelevant in Syria. Instead, in its turbulent early post-independence history, various visions of Syrian and Arab nationalism contended for power, with the pan-Arabist Baath party emerg-ing victorious in 1963. Formally secularist, the Baath party was dominated by the religious minorities, with representatives of one of them the Alawites on top since 1966. While belonging in the Muslim camp, the Alawite religion has historically been considered by the Sunni *ulama* as an excessive theological aberration (*ghulw*). During the aborted attempt at an Islamic revolution in the late 1970s, the Alawites were denounced as a renegade sect. In modern Syria, the above-mentioned role of the Sunni *ulama* as custodians of Islamic political legitimacy thus has had a particularly precarious trajectory.

In yet another important monograph on *ulama*, Thomas Pierret (2011) demonstrates that Syrian *ulama* succeeded in winning over a significant group of young urban professionals to devote themselves to Sunni religious life. This group has striven to uphold a religious Sunni identity, having to confront not only ideological marginalization by the Baath party but also the Brotherhood's attempts at mobilizing this identity and ensuing stigmatization by the state security. Although divided over issues of theology, mysticism and practice, the Syrian *ulama* had survived by being flexible towards the state and its demands, by reaching out to this group of educated youth in state educational institutions, all the while maintaining their own private institutions and training (Pierret 2011:183–187). Some measure of autonomy from the state was reinforced by a good connection to significant parts of the Sunni upper classes, who supported the *ulama*'s social work and shared their religious outlook and social conservatism.

To answer the question of how the Sunni *ulama* in Syria have managed to coexist with a centralized, secularist regime dominated by Alawites, one must first understand the regime's policies. These have been characterized by centralization, surveillance, ideological instruction, co-optation and, when deemed necessary, violent suppression. Established as a French mandate after the First World War, the Syrian state inherited a tradition of a centralized *ulama* organization from its predecessor, the Ottoman Empire. The appointment of local judges, muftis and preachers was thus in the hands of the Hanafi Mufti of the capital who, in turn, was appointed by the ruler from among candidates nominated by the *ulama* themselves (Skovgaard-Petersen 2005). Certain grand *ulama* were rewarded by the regime for their loyalty and anti-Islamist stance. Invited to preach in major mosques and state media, they were allowed to establish significant educational institutions. A few who were known to be less loyal were still tolerated for their valuable social work (Pierret 2011:112–115). By the 1990s, satellite television and the Internet made it increasingly difficult for the regime to control and promote loyalist preachers and non-political interpretations of Islam. Next to the threat of Islamism, there was the more puritan and socially conservative Salafism emanating mainly from the Gulf States, but with a significant Syrian pedigree, particularly in Damascus. The rise of the jihadist threat in Lebanon (and especially in Iraq after 2003) and the international 'war on terrorism' after 2001 prompted the Syrian regime to mobilize against jihadism ideologically (if somewhat ambiguously in practice). Many *ulama* could support that stance (Pierret 2011:159–161).

There were, thus, alliances and flexibility, but also uneasiness and mutual suspicion, if no open conflict. And when a much more popular uprising finally came in 2011, not from the Islamists but largely from the underprivileged segments of the Sunni population, the preachers were caught in a dilemma: between, on the one hand, their protector (the state) and economic benefactors (the Sunni bourgeoisie), and, on the other hand, the bulk of the believers. It is therefore no wonder that the Sunni *ulama*, like much of the rest of the population, were divided.

Conflict intensification

The protests in Syria cannot be said to have been fomented by *ulama*. Most importantly, by going about their daily chores and preaching on non-controversial subjects, the vast majority of the *ulama* were passively supporting a regime in a state that provided their livelihood. There were, however, exceptions to this rule. The Internet allowed a few *ulama* to reside in the Gulf but communicate into Syria. One organization with Islamist leanings, the League of Syrian Ulama (*Rabitat al-ulama al-suriyin*), organized *ulama* who for the most part had been exiled since the uprising in the 1980s. More immediately worrying for the regime was probably the support given by pan-Arab media to the uprisings in Tunisia and Syria, not least Al Jazeera, whose star *'alim*, the Egyptian Yusuf al-Qaradawi, was also much admired in Syria. Al-Qaradawi had been exiled from Egypt but returned triumphantly on February 18 to deliver the first post-Mubarak sermon at Tahrir Square in front of more than one million Muslims. Al Jazeera broadcast his praise for the Egyptian people, who had at long last brought down the 'tyrant'. The Syrian regime was obviously nervous and tightened its control over the Sunni mosques. I was briefly in Syria in early 2011 and visited a mosque of a well-known sheikh who read the Friday sermon aloud from a paper to make clear to the believers that, on that day, the *khutba* was not of his own making but distributed by the Ministry of Religious Endowments. It was about foreign hands sowing enmity between Muslims and Christians, as had been evidenced in the secession of South Sudan and its proclamation as a state.

As is well known, protests began in the southern city of Dera'a in response to the Syrian authorities' maltreatment of a group of children who had written 'the people want the fall of the regime' on a wall. The protests did not call for the downfall of the regime but rather an end to impunity and excessive police and security force violence. As it became clear that the regime prioritized its security forces over the people, protests spread to other cities. While clergy were not at the forefront of this early wave of protests, it soon became clear that they could hardly stand by. As protests intensified and the authorities tried to quell them with arrests and snipers, the protesters began their protests by congregating in mosques to reach critical mass. After the Friday sermon, they would then march out of the mosque, knowing full well that they might be met with bullets. This would be difficult to ignore and put the individual preacher in a dilemma, as any open support for the protesters would likely be reported to the intelligence services. Similarly, as protests intensified, the funerals of slain protesters became the catalysts for new demonstrations, the local 'alim again finding himself between a rock and a hard place.

One particular problem for the preacher would be the benediction of the ruler traditionally inserted in the *khutba* (sermon). Historically, this has been a loyalty test for the individual preacher in times of turmoil. More generally, an Islamic *khutba* is not given over a specific text, and there is a long tradition for political sermons. Major *ulama* were thus expected to comment on the situation by their flock – who would inevitably include security service spies. Here, a number of well-known *ulama* in Damascus known for their independence of the regime resorted to a special type of sermon, the 'advice' (*nasiha*), berating the ruler to listen to and be lenient towards the people. Giving advice to the ruler takes courage, even if implicitly affirming that the preacher stands by him and underwrites his legitimacy. Not responding at all to what was going on, however, might also alienate the preacher's constituency. They were walking a fine line.

Traditionally, the preachers had yet another weapon in their arsenal: formally denouncing the ruler in a sermon known as *kalimat al-haqq* ('a word of truth'). As regime violence escalated, some of the preachers who had 'advised' al-Assad gave such sermons. The elderly Karim al-Rajih in the popular district of al-Midan, who had given a *nasiha* on the first of April, resorted to a complete denunciation of the regime on July 11. Among the most influential *ulama* in Damascus were the brothers Osama and Saraya al-Rifai, who were known for their independence from the regime and had been in exile for many years. They ran a significant charity, Zayd, in another popular district. During the initial phase, they had been sent by the regime to talk to the protesters and returned with their demands. The regime ignored these demands, proceeding to kill 40 people in Dera'a two days later. In a sermon aired on Al Jazeera on June 17, Osama also harshly criticized the regime, but regime thugs attacked his mosque on August 28, killing one person and beating up the octogenarian sheikh. By then, Ramadan had come, and with it a more intense military response from the regime. On August 1, a greater number of *ulama* had signed a last collective statement placing the blame on the regime (Pierret 2013:228). These sheikhs were forced to leave Syria and settled in Arab capitals or Turkey. In an interview in Al Jazeera in the summer of 2012, Saraya al-Rifa'i claimed that more than 50 *ulama* had denounced the regime and were now in exile or imprisoned (Al-Rifa'i 2012).

Regime mobilization

The Syrian state also mobilized its *ulama*. This was not the regime's primary strategy, which mainly sought to suppress the protests by force and denounce the protesters as foreign agents. Regime media depicted President Assad as a magnanimous father who would forgive his children while defending the country against foreign interference, largely identified as pro-Israeli Western forces. The Sunni dimension to the uprising could not be ignored, however, and allowed the regime to play to the fear of non-Sunni minorities. But it would also need a strategy towards the Sunnis themselves, approximately 70% of the population. Naturally, the regime turned to its top *ulama*, namely the Minister of Religious Endowments and the Mufti of the Republic, who, apart from having demonstrated loyalty over the years, were known for their anti-Islamist and anti-Salafi convictions. The ministry organized a conference for *ulama* from all over Syria, which issued a statement in support of the legitimate government.

The most important *'alim* on the regime side was the frail, ageing, but nevertheless impressive Said Ramadan al-Buti (1929–2013). Educated at the prestigious al-Azhar in Cairo, he had published studies for 50 years defending the classical legal schools against modernist reformers and puritan Salafis who, each from their own angles, had called for a dismissal of this huge theological and legal tradition and a renewed interpretation of the Qur'an and Hadith. His criticism of reformism – as represented by the Muslim Brotherhood and puritan Salafism as sponsored by Saudi Arabia – was known far beyond Syria's borders (Christmann 1998). Al-Buti and like-minded scholars dominated the Sharia Faculty of Damascus University, for decades the only formal *'alim* education in the country. Moreover, al-Buti had demonstrated his loyalty to the regime during the Islamist uprising in 1978–1982, and Hafez al-Assad, the former president, had shown him much respect (Pierret 2011, 2016). Hafez' son Bashar had less cordial relations to al-Buti, as he was pursuing a culturally more liberal agenda than al-Buti could endorse. In 2010, al-Buti attacked a highly popular television drama with a clear message of female emancipation. Bashar and his wife Asma came out in support of it. Still, he accepted the legitimacy of the Syrian regime and concentrated his criticism on specific moral issues. In turn, the regime allowed him to run a programme on Syrian television. Among other top ulama, al-Buti's sermons and fatwas were published on a weekly basis on the Naseem al-Sham website.

When the uprising broke out in 2011, the regime realized that it needed al-Buti more than ever, but he now had specific demands: an umbrella organization for the *ulama* was set up with himself as the president and the *Nur al-Sham* Islamic television station was established. Broadcasting from the summer of 2011, it was meant to counter the harshly anti-regime propaganda now beaming in from Salafi and Islamist preachers abroad. As many of the major *ulama* began to defect, others were promoted to fill the void. On the Nasseem al-Sham website, al-Buti's fatwas and sermons were by far the most downloaded, and they were gradually marked by a far more uncompromising pro-regime position (Skovgaard-Petersen 2013).

On June 11, 2011, an ordinary Syrian believer asked al-Buti which sheikh to follow in a situation where some sheikhs supported the government and others were against it. Al-Buti replied in a fatwa that in such a situation, the believer must concentrate on not committing major sins, which would mean opposing provocative acts. This is established in religion and ought to be clear to all. Hence, he should follow one of the sheikhs who were not engaged in fomenting uproar against the authorities (Al-Buti 2011a).

The following week, al-Buti was consulted on the same issue by an inhabitant from the poor Damascene suburb al-Duma, which had staged a complete insurrection with the support of its *ulama*. Al-Buti answered that if the prophet Muhammad returned to this earth and spoke, these preachers would consider him part of the regime (Al-Buti 2011b). On the same day, he was also asked by a soldier who had acted on orders to shoot into the demonstrating crowds and now felt remorse about what kind of atonement Islam prescribed. Al-Buti did not condemn the procedure but told him that he was no criminal and that he should pray for the people he might have killed. If it was established that he had killed a specific person, he should pay blood money (*diyya*) and fast for two months (Al-Buti 2011c). On July 7, he was consulted about an incident where pro-regime fighters (*shabbiha*) had ordered detained demonstrators to prostrate before a picture of al-Assad instead of God. Al-Buti did not doubt the practice, but retorted that he should be asked about why such practices now occurred, and proceeded to condemn the demonstrations (Al-Buti 2011d).

Next to the fatwas, al-Buti was also preaching in support of the regime, often from Syria's most prestigious pulpit, that of the Umayyad Mosque, and broadcast on Syrian TV. His sermons were typically more political and polemic; he referred to President Bashar al-Assad as the Saladin of our time; for as in the age of the crusades, Syria was the coveted prize of the West. The pliant Gulf States were the new tool of the crusaders. But all of this was God's trial (*mihna*), and it was up to the Syrian believers to endure. On the very day of this sermon (February 17, 2012), his arch rival, the Islamist Yusuf al-Qaradawi, expressed the pious wish in a mosque in Qatar that he himself would soon be preaching in the Umayyad mosque. In several sermons, al-Qaradawi addressed al-Buti directly, calling him to leave the 'tyrant' and support the 'Muslims' (Al-Qaradawi 2011, 2012). Al-Buti and his supporters gave back in kind.

To sum up, for the Syrian Sunni *ulama*, conflict intensification made an already tenuous situation untenable. Their 'medieval' role of upholding a moral status quo and a durable balance between ruler and ruled could no longer be upheld, and they were forced to take sides in a conflict that also had dimensions of identity and religious sanction. The group of *ulama* was polarized between a smaller group of regime supporters (whose significance to the powers increased sharply) and a group of sheikhs with a significant following who supported the uprising and tried for a while to appeal to the regime for concessions but later had to flee. Due to their capacity to bestow or withhold religious legitimacy, at this stage, the *ulama* were significant actors whose choices fed into the conflict and ultimately furthered its escalation.

Further escalation: the inter-sectarian dimension

Early in 2012, the conflict quickly took international dimensions. Early attempts by the Arab League to intervene with observing soldiers failed. In September 2011, Russia and China had blocked attempts by the US and its allies to obtain the Security Council's endorsement for an intervention under the clause of responsibility to protect civilian life. Instead, in early 2012, a string of UN appointed officials began working to present a peace plan that would be acceptable for all parties. Negotiations were initiated in Geneva after the United States and Russia reached agreement, but to no avail. 'The Friends of Syria', a US-led coalition of Western and Arab countries, sought to unify and empower an alternative Syrian government and delivered weapons to assorted rebel groups. Russia and Iran provided financial and military aid to the Syrian regime, which, short of manpower, invited Shia militias from Lebanon and Iraq in to fight alongside its regular and irregular forces. The fighting spread to almost all parts of the country, but as the rebels lacked airpower and even anti-air missiles, the rebel-held areas were pummelled from the air and the cities and districts they controlled were reduced to rubble. Six years later, the fighting continues.

The *ulama* have been a part in this intensified phase, but not a decisive part. Except in one respect, the conflict with the regime gradually turned into an intra-sectarian conflict, pitting the Sunnis against the religious minorities. And some oppositional *ulama* were at least instrumental in this. Neither the minority group religious leaders nor the regime was exempted from blame, the latter clearly interested in divesting the focus of the conflict from a protest against its own corruption and brutality and towards a conflict between religious identities, thus shoring up the support of anxious members of the religious minority groups. In several places, agents of the regime actively provoked tensions between the Sunni population and other groups; all the while, the regime promised to protect all Syrians against *fitna ta'ifiyya*: inter-religious strife.

The political opposition also went out of its way to reassure the population and foreign observers that it had a vision of an inclusive Syria based on the equality of all citizens. The centrepiece in the peaceful strategy of the first months, the Friday demonstrations, was given names, some referring specifically to other religious groups – the Christians, the Alawites – to underline their inclusion, even if the demonstrations would be setting out from the mosques after the Friday prayer.

Despite these reassurances, inter-sectarian tensions increased immediately, even if they were actively confronted by decisive action in some areas (Wimmen 2016). Moreover, important groups within the uprising, the Salafis and at least some Islamists, did not subscribe to full religious equality, instead envisioning Syria as an Islamic State (IS) with Sunni Muslim pre-eminence. Not well established on the ground but strong in the political opposition, the Muslim Brotherhood officially came out in 2012 for a democratic and religiously inclusive Syria, where it would merely be one party among others (Ikhwan 2012). That was a political statement, however, and would unlikely receive support from all its members. And certainly not from all of the *ulama,* some of whom considered Syria an IS, with other religious groups under 'protection'. Some preachers openly called for a jihad against Alawite unbelievers. During the first year, the most vocal sheikh condemning the Alawites (instead of the regime) was the exiled sheikh 'Adnan al-'Ar'ur, who was active on the Salafi TV channel al-Safa and Twitter (The Economist 2012). His rants against the Alawites found eager listeners among a rapidly growing Salafi current as well as among many of those who now took up arms. Confirming the fears of other sects, militias with distinctly Islamic names sprang up around the country, some beholden to a particular sheikh.

High conflict intensification

The role of preachers changed after the escalation of violence in 2012, decreasing for many. Like the rest of the population, *ulama* were arrested and imprisoned, forced into exile, internally displaced or simply killed.

On the regime side, the most important casualty was undoubtedly Said Ramadan al-Buti, who was killed whilst teaching in a mosque on 21 March 2013. Confusion reigned over his death, as the regime's footage seemed to be fabricated, although it was difficult to see why the regime itself would in any way benefit from his death. While preachers have continued to work in regime-controlled areas, apart from upholding a veneer of normalcy, these preachers – some with little training – are not part of a more elaborate strategy of regime legitimation. The centrepiece of the latter is now the Mufti of the Republic, Ahmad Hassoun, who appears frequently in government media. He is also the head of the High Council for Ifta, the regime's main Sunni religious body, which was practically unknown before the war. A week before Buti's death, the High Council for Ifta issued a declaration of jihad as a duty for all Syrians and called on Iran and other Muslim countries to come to the aid of the Syrian government and army (Al-Tamimi 2013).

The preachers were under surveillance in regime-controlled areas, whereas they were expected to preach against the regime in the so-called liberated areas. Many did. And in some areas, *ulama* were also involved in setting up the so-called Sharia courts, thus moving into their classical field of administering the law.

Major oppositional *ulama* went into exile. In Turkey in particular, new *ulama* organizations were set up, which merged in 2014 to form the Council of Syrian *Ulama*. The old Damascene preacher Osama al-Rifa'i was its president. Comprising many of the well-known *ulama*, also in the rebel-held parts of the country, the *Majlis al-Ulama* acts as a counterweight not just to the regime but also to the Jihadi and Salafi *ulama*, who dominate in many of these territories (Pierret 2014). Most controversial has been its neglect of the above-mentioned Salafi sheikh Adnan al-'Ar'ur, who has condemned the Council and thereby weakened its influence on the Islamic courts in the rebel-held area (al-Arabi 2016).

Another council of ulama emerged in 2015, representing the more radical and jihadist factions. Entitled the League of People of Scholarship in Syria (*Rabitat ahl al-'ilm fi 'l-Sham*), it has issued statements on political developments, labelling all other groups unbelievers (*kuffar*) (Rabitat ahl al-'ilm fi al-Sham 2015). While the

Islamic Council comprises a council of 128 delegates, this group signed its most important document, a call for a general mobilization of the Muslims in Syria, with the names of 36 sheikhs (Rabitat ahl al-ʻilm fi al-Sham 2015).

The latter group can be considered a prime example of Gaffney's third category of preachers, the *ulama mujahidun,* some of whom have taken up arms themselves. These are generally connected to the jihadist group, Jabhat al-Nosra, from 2016 forming part of the broader 'Conquest of Syria' alliance.

Finally, there is the new IS, proclaimed as a caliphate in July 2014. Controlling at the pinnacle of its power, a vast territory in Eastern Syria and Western Iraq with some eight million inhabitants, IS set up ministries and other state-like structures, including a complete religious administration and a sprawling school system. *Ulama* are thus essential to the functioning of the IS, but also to its legitimacy. These are a different breed of *ulama.* Local *ulama* in the area have been vetted, and those considered acceptable have been retrained. In the capital city of Raqqa, top *ulama* known to have defended the Assad regime were executed or fled, and few have embraced their new rulers (Eissa[1], Hussam (2016). Personal communication, 26 November).

The true IS *ulama* are certainly *ulama* mujahidin and strongly condemning all other *ulama.* The caliph was appointed by a council of *ulama* and proclaimed by their spokesman, Muhammad al-ʻAdnani (who was killed in 2016). The caliph, with the adopted name Abu Bakr al-Baghdadi, received his formal Islamic education in Baghdad. Still, neither he nor al-ʻAdnani owed their position to their scholarly achievements, but to their service to the jihadi cause since the American invasion in Iraq in 2003. Another scholarly authority without this jihadi pedigree was Turki Binʻali, who along with al-ʻAdnani came to represent the ideological line of IS. Born in 1984 in Bahrain, Binʻali was a student with various Salafi sheikhs in Saudi Arabia, and like al-ʻAdnani had been influenced by the Jordanian Salafi sheikh Muhammad al-Maqdisi, whom they now both decried in a major ideological contest with the supporters of al-Qaeda.

De-escalation

During this phase of high conflict intensification, the polarization of the *ulama* was never complete. There were *ulama* who rejected violence on both sides, and there were *ulama* who worked to reunite the Syrian population irrespective of sect and to begin serious negotiations over a possible political transition.

An outstanding example of the former is Jawdat al-Said, the 'Ghandi of Syria', whose antimilitarism dates back to the 1960s and has been laid out in a number of books, presenting his own interpretation of the Qur'an and the early life of the Muslim community. Residing in Damascus and his native village in the Golan, Jawdat al-Said had an intellectual following and was one of the signatories to the 'Damascus Declaration' of 2005, calling for democratic reforms (Pierret 2011:171). When the demonstrations broke out, Said exhorted them to remain peaceful even in the face of regime violence (Said 2011).

The most important example of the latter is Muez al-Khatib, an engineer turned *alim* with a long preaching career in Damascus, who is another Damascus Declaration signatory (Pierret 2011:173). An outspoken regime critic, al-Khatib went into exile in 2012 and was appointed the president of the main opposition organization, the Syrian National Coalition of Oppositional and Resistance Forces, an American-initiated attempt at unifying the opposition and marginalizing the Islamists within it. Despite claims to the contrary by regime supporters, al-Khatib saw his role as bridging the religious divides between the Syrians, drawing on his standing as a Sunni *alim* to reach out to the other religious communities (Harding and Chulov 2012). Although inspiring confidence, al-Khatib withdrew from the presidency in 2013, complaining about interference from donor countries.

Since 2013, several small initiatives have been made to gather Syrian religious leaders abroad to affirm that they can work for a unified Syria, combat hate speech and reject jihadism. Well-known Syrian preachers, such as Muhammad al-Yacoubi, Muhammad al-Habash and his wife Amina Koftaro, have taken part in these. Inside Syria, the regime has also hosted conferences on inter-religious understanding. The issue of religious diversity, for decades a taboo due to the Alawite control of power, is now a selling point for the Syrian regime, which casts itself as the protector of a multireligious Syria. While the messages may sound strikingly similar, the context is still polarized over whether Syria shall move towards a political transition or if the regime shall simply reinstate itself as the only powerholder in the country. As long as the Geneva high-level negotiations over a political transition are stuck, any *ulama* involvement in mediation is on standby.

Conclusion

Scott Appleby identifies three roles of religious agents in conflict transformation. In early phases, they can act as social critics, opposing injustice and speaking up for the oppressed. In a violent phase, they can use their good offices and mediate between warring parties. And in post-conflict, they can help to heal wounds and work for social reconstruction (Appleby 2000:213–221). The Sunni *ulama* of Syria are, of course, a particular variety of religious actors. Neither affiliated to a hierarchical and powerful church nor holding the authority of top Shia *ulama*, they have nevertheless been in a key position as the religious representatives of the majority population in a country where political actors independent of the regime (including Sunni religio-political actors) had been suppressed. They were present at the local level and represented the religion of an oft-devoted constituency. Moreover, Islamic tradition gave them a special role as mediators to power and as stewards of a religio-political legitimacy that they could potentially withdraw from the ruler.

In the Syrian case, the Sunni *ulama* easily lived up to Appleby's first role. For years, they represented their respective flocks and raised social and moral concerns while preaching obedience to the regime. When the uprising began, they were divided; many top *ulama* like al-Buti remained loyal and, in line with a dominant tradition of the Sunni *ulama*, they stressed the duty of obedience to the ruler, the *wali al-amr*. Other *ulama* went along with the uprising, but only judiciously so and only after repeated appeals to the ruler to address the people's legitimate demands.

Other *ulama* were definitely not concerned with upholding social peace. Theirs was a vision of social and political transformation towards the establishment of an IS. They were moving and leading, not least in the denunciation of Alawites as heretics. And later, the jihadi militias appeared with their own anticlerical *ulama mujahidun*. In the long period of intensified and violent conflict, however, some *ulama* also reached out to religious leaders from the other sects and considered it a religious duty to steer Syrian society towards a transformation of the conflict. Can they also work to heal the wounds and work for social reconstruction? Definitely. Syrians share much in common across their sectarian divisions, and there is a deeply felt interest on all sides to end the fighting. But with *ulama* in every camp, the conflict has demonstrated that the instrumentalization of the *ulama* is a coveted tool of political mobilization. It is unlikely that competing factions in a post-war Syria will live without it.

In terms of impacting the dynamics of conflict, the contribution of the *ulama* appears to be shaped and propelled by the overall conflict, but the peculiar nature of their authority, in turn, gives a specific bearing on the conflict. This is due to several factors related to the complex social and intellectual sources of their social and political influences on parts of the population together with their tenuous relationships to the political actors. In the Syrian context – with an Alawite-dominated regime, a Sunni majority population and a lengthy history of suppression of Islamist political actors – the 'men of religion' were drawn into the conflict in a specific way, quite different from other actors. In a society bereft of independent political actors, the religious leaders were well-known figures to whom people could turn and from whom they expected guidance. The individual sheikhs, then, were among the first to register and experience the escalating conflict. To some, this offered opportunity; to all, it imposed hard choices.

When political conflict intensifies in religiously divided and somewhat depoliticized societies, 'men of religion' can suddenly find themselves to be significant political actors. Defined by Max Weber as holders of the 'goods of salvation', this should not only be understood in the other-worldly sense. In periods of conflict escalation and de-escalation, these goods of salvation can refer to political legitimacy, group representation and, ultimately, social peace and reintegration. Policymakers and scholars would be well advised to note that, in the pursuit of durable peaceful settlements in the Muslim tradition – Shia and Sunni alike – the *ulama* should be observed, consulted and sometimes engaged. But never ignored.

Note

1 Hussam Eissa is among the founders of the reporting group 'Raqqa is silently slaughtered'.

References

al-Arabi (2016) *Al-Majlis al-Islami al-Suri – Mamnu' dukhul al-'Ar'ur wa al-'Allush.* http://3arabionline.com/?page=article&id=15154 (accessed 28 November 2016).

Al-Buti, Said Ramadan (2011a) *Fatwa 14/6.* www.naseemalsham.com/ar/Pages. php?page=readFatwa&pg_id=13748&back=1986 (accessed 24 November 2016).

Al-Buti, Said Ramadan (2011b) *Fatwa 23/6.* www.naseemalsham.com/ar/Pages. php?page=readFatwa&pg_id=14317&back=8913 (accessed 24 November 2016).

Al-Buti, Said Ramadan (2011c) *Fatwa 23/6.* www.naseemalsham.com/ar/Pages. php?page=readFatwa&pg_id=14375&back=8913 (accessed 24 November 2016).

Al-Buti, Said Ramadan (2011d) *Fatwa 7/7.* www.naseemalsham.com/ar/Pages. php?page=readFatwa&pg_id=14658&back=8928 (accessed 24 November 2016).

Al-Qaradawi, Yusuf (2011) *Sermon in Doha in December: It Is not Allowed for a Scholar to Support a Tyrant.* www.qaradawi.net/new/Articles-5503 (accessed 24 November 2016).

Al-Qaradawi, Yusuf (2012) *Sermon in Doha in June: You Are Committing Haram by Supporting the Tyrant.* www.qaradawi.net/new/Articles-1185 (accessed 24 November 2016).

Al-Rifa'i, Saraya (2012) 'Dur al-ulama fi 'l-mujtama'', *Al-Jazeera,* 15 July 2012. www. aljazeera.net/programs/religionandlife/2012/7/19/%D8%AF%D9%88%D8%B1-%D 8%A7%D9%84%D8%B9%D9%84%D9%85%D8%A7%D8%A1-%D9%81%D9%8A- %D8%A7%D9%84%D9%85%D8%AC%D8%AA%D9%85%D8%B9-%D9%88%D8% A7%D9%84%D8%AF%D9%88%D9%84%D8%A9 (accessed 24 November 2016).

Al-Tamimi, Ayman (2013) 'Jihad in Syria (Part 2): The Regime Perspective', *Syria Comment,* 25 March 2013. www.joshualandis.com/blog/jihad-in-syria-part-ii-the-assad-regime- perspective-by-aymenn-jawad-al-tamimi/?utm_source=feedburner&utm_medium= email&utm_campaign=Feed%3A%20Syriacomment%20%28Syria%20Comment%29 (accessed 24 November 2016).

Appleby, Scott (2000) *The Ambivalence of the Sacred.* Lanham, MD: Rowman and Littlefield.

Christmann, Andreas (1998) 'Islamic Scholar and Religious Leader: A Portrait of Shaikh Sa'id Ramadan al-Buti', *Islam and Christian-Muslim Relations* 9 (2): 149–169.

Gaffney, Frank (1994) *The Prophet's Pulpit.* Berkeley: UCLA Press.

Harding, Luke and Martin Chulov (2012) 'Moaz al-Khatib: Ex-imam Charged with Uniting Syria's Opposition', *The Guardian,* 12 November 2012. www.theguardian.com/ world/2012/nov/12/moaz-al-khatib-syria-opposition (accessed 29 November 2016).

Ikhwan (2012). 'Wathiqat 'ahd wa mithaq ikhwan Suriya', *Al-Jazeera,* 26 March 2012. www.aljazeera.net/news/arabic/2012/3/26/%D9%88%D8%AB%D9%8A%D9%82 %D8%A9-%D8%B9%D9%87%D8%AF-%D9%88%D9%85%D9%8A%D8%AB%D 8%A7%D9%82-%D8%A5%D8%AE%D9%88%D8%A7%D9%86-%D8%B3%D9%- 88%D8%B1%D9%8A%D8%A7 (accessed 24 November 2016).

Lapidus, Ira M. (1967) *Muslim Cities in the Later Middle Ages.* Cambridge, MA: Harvard University Press.

Pierret, Thomas (2011) *Baath et islam en Syrie.* Paris: PUF.

Pierret, Thomas (2013) *Religion and State in Syria: The Sunni Ulama from Coup to Revolution.* Cambridge: Cambridge University Press.

Pierret, Thomas (2014) *The Islamic Council of Syria.* http://carnegie-mec.org/diwan /55580?lang=en (accessed 26 November 2016).

Pierret, Thomas (2016) *al-Buti, Muhammad Said Ramadan. Encyclopedia of Islam 3* (54–57). Leiden: Brill.

Rabitat ahl al-'ilm fi al-Sham (2015) *Bayan istinfar 'am.* 28 December 2015. https://azelin. files.wordpress.com/2016/01/racc84bitcca3at-ahl-al-e28098ilm-ficc84-al-shacc84m- 22ruling-of-jihacc84d-in-bilacc84d-al-shacc84m22.pdf (accessed 28 November 2016).

Ramsbotham, Oliver, Tom Woodhouse and Hugh Miall (2011) *Contemporary Conflict Resolution*, 3rd ed. London: Wiley.

Said, Jawdat (2011) *Khutbat al-juma'a al- 'azima 22/4*. www.jawdatsaid.net/index.php?titl e=%D8%A7%D9%84%D8%B5%D9%81%D8%AD%D8%A9_%D8%A7%D9%84%D 8%B1%D8%A6%D9%8A%D8%B3%D9%8A%D8%A9 (accessed 29 November 2016).

Skovgaard-Petersen, Jakob (2005) 'Levantine State Muftis: An Ottoman Legacy?', in Elizabeth Özdalga (Ed.), *Late Ottoman Society. The Intellectual Legacy* (274–288), London and New York: RoutledgeCurzon.

Skovgaard-Petersen, Jakob (2013) 'Syriens kendteste TV-shaykh bakker stædigt op bag styret. Hvorfor?', *Tidsskrift for Islamforskning* 7 (1):69–87.

The Economist (2012) *The Charm of Telesalafism*. www.economist.com/news/middle-east-and-africa/21564913-influential-rebel-preacher-who-needs-tone-things-down (accessed 24 November 2016).

Wimmen, Heiko (2016) *Syria's Path from Civic Uprising to Civil War*. Washington, DC: Carnegie.

Zaman, Muhammad Qasem (2002) *The Ulama in Conpemporary Islam: Custodians of Change*. Princeton, NJ: Princeton University Press.

7

FOREIGN FIGHTERS

Violence and modern subjectivity[1]

Dietrich Jung

Introduction: violence in the formation of modern subjects

In October 2016, the Danish daily *Politiken* featured the story of Rawand Taher, a young Dane with a Kurdish background. Taher was among the approximately 135 Danish foreign fighters who have travelled to Syria and Iraq since 2012. The article described how Taher transformed from a role model of Danish integration into a leading Jihadist in the ranks of the Islamic State in just a few years. On 7 December 2015, a US missile hit his car in the Syrian town of Raqqa, killing him and another Dane instantly. In the newspaper article, former friends, teachers and employers described him as a handsome, intelligent and resourceful young man who once even volunteered as a mentor for the labour-market integration of Danish youngsters with an immigrant background (Sheikh 2016). How could this young and well-integrated Danish Muslim become a member of the most brutal Jihadist organization that has been operating in Syria and Iraq?

The Politiken article described Rawand Taher's path from a Danish role model to a foreign fighter for the Islamic State along the lines of a gradual radicalization process. In this process, grievances, social networks, ideological framings and specific support structures facilitated his path to volunteering in the war. This storyline is consistent with the dominant narrative in public and academic debates in understanding the current foreign fighter phenomenon (Hafez and Mullins 2015). According to this narrative, the decision to join Jihadist militias is at the end of an individual process of cognitive and/or behavioural radicalization. While the first concept focuses on individuals adopting extremist beliefs, the second addresses individuals who decide to take up violent means (Neumann 2013). In both concepts, violence appears as the ultimate consequence of a social process in which individuals deviate from the unquestioned normality of social coexistence in a peaceful manner. The two conceptual approaches differ only in how they give practical advice, that is, how they suggest preventing individuals from taking this deviant path. Their dispute is about the question of whether we should attempt to control thoughts or social actions.

This chapter takes a different approach. Contrary to the dominant narrative of individual radicalization, violence is an independent variable in my enquiry.[2] This change of perspective wants to contribute to our understanding of both dynamics of conflicts and their violent escalation. In the following pages, I therefore do not treat foreign fighters in 'pathological terms', taking them instead as examples for an alternative way in the construction of meaningful modern selfhoods. To be sure, research in processes of radicalization and its prevention is not without merits. On the contrary, the individual paths to becoming foreign fighters deserve our attention. Yet with this chapter, I pursue different aims. In taking up the current foreign fighter phenomenon, I want to address the relative exclusion of the role of violence in scholarly approaches to modern subjectivity formation. The chapter suggests adding violence as a core variable in the formation of modern subjects. The formation of modern subjectivities is related to socially accepted representations of meaningful selfhoods. These social imaginaries serve as points of reference for individual identity constructions. According to the hegemonic liberal imaginary of the emancipation of a reflexive, rational, self-interested and expressive modern individual, subjectivity formation is supposed to take place in a pacified world. Yet, the twentieth century witnessed a continuing series of wars and violent conflicts that do not correspond to this liberal imaginary. My starting point is therefore the recognition 'that modernity can exist with extreme violence' (Reemtsma 2012:7). War and conflict represent transformative stages for the construction of individual and collective identities. The Rawand Taher example is merely a single case in point. Why this neglect of violence in modern subjectivity formation? Do foreign fighters represent an alternative type of specifically violent modern subjectivities?[3]

The chapter answers these questions in four steps. The first section presents the findings of a comparison of the profiles of current Jihadists in the wars in Syria and Iraq with foreign fighters who joined republican forces in the Spanish Civil War. This comparison positions the phenomenon of contemporary Jihadist foreign fighters in a longer tradition of foreign war volunteers in modern violent conflicts. The section argues that becoming a war volunteer seemingly has not only historical roots but also a transcultural face. These findings lead directly to a brief, fragmented, but nevertheless critical review of the role of war and violence in social theory. The argument in this second part of the chapter is the need to consider violent action as a constant option in modern social life. From this perspective, foreign fighters may represent an alternative type of modern subjectivities – 'violent subjects' – deviating from the hegemonic models that the narrative of liberalism provides. In the third part, I will empirically underpin this thesis of an alternative type of modern subjectivity formation with respect to the recruitment processes of foreign fighters, which is a crucial element in the escalation of local conflicts. The conclusion, then, will sum up the argument and briefly point to consequences of my approach for issues of conflict escalation and conflict resolution.

Foreign fighters in Syria and Spain

Rawand Taher was one of the estimated 20,000 to 30,000 foreign fighters who have joined the civil wars in Syria and Iraq since early 2012.[4] While most of these war volunteers come from Arab countries, in particular from Saudi Arabia, Tunisia, Libya and Morocco, some 3,400 of them have originated from Australia, the United States or countries in Western Europe (Byman 2015:582; Masbah 2015). This increasing number of foreign fighters who grew up in Western democracies marks a stark difference to previous wars, such as those in Afghanistan, Chechnya, Iraq or the former Yugoslavia, in which Muslim foreign fighters took part.[5] While the majority of foreigners fighting in these countries have their national background in regional Middle Eastern states, the number of young Western Muslims travelling to Syria and Iraq has assumed previously unknown heights. This significant change in the origin of Muslim foreign fighters with respect to the current civil wars in Syria and Iraq has been a major concern of Western governments.

To be cautious, we currently have rather weak data on these foreign fighters, resulting from open sources such as disclosed intelligence reports, journalistic accounts and often quite questionable Internet platforms. While our knowledge of foreign fighters remains imprecise in terms of quantitative data, we know something more about some personal profiles, that is, about the individual backgrounds of some of those who went (Roy 2015:3). In 2014, the Australian Security Intelligence Organization estimated that roughly 60 Australians had been fighting in Syria and Iraq, of which 15 were killed on the battlefield. Based on the very small number of those killed in battle, the typical Australian foreign fighter was under 30 years old, predominantly male and of Lebanese- or Turkish-Australian background; of these, some had family, while others were single men, and most of them had a criminal record with the Australian security authorities (Zammit 2014:6).

The general image of Western foreign fighters in Syria and Iraq partly confirms this profile of the Australian volunteers in terms of age, gender and social background. A study of the small group of Belgian and French foreign fighters who joined al-Qaida in Iraq concluded that they represented a small group of mostly single young males from rather modest socio-economic backgrounds who were connected through local friendship and kinship ties (Holman 2015:615). Olivier Roy (2015) described French war volunteers as young people of mixed social backgrounds and often with a past of petty delinquency. The majority of them represent second-generation Muslim immigrants, although there are also a significant number of converts among them. Beyond these rather broad patterns, it is still very difficult to generalize more with respect to socio-economic status, the political and religious attitudes or the educational backgrounds of Western foreign fighters (Stern and Berger 2015). In short, these young Muslims leaving the West to fight in the Middle East make up a very mixed group of individuals with very different personal backgrounds.

These attempts to generalize with respect to foreign fighters become even more elusive when considering their motivational background. In an interview with the Carnegie Council for Ethics in International Affairs, for instance, Richard Barrett (2014) gave a very tentative account of the motivations of foreign fighters in Syria. According to him, we can only discern some common themes among these volunteers, such as a general disillusionment with national and international politics, a lack of social belonging, a desire for respect and recognition, a search for religious spirituality and the conviction to live in times of an Islam in defence. This description fits well with the observations of other authors. Mario Van San, for instance, discerned among young Belgian and Dutch supporters of the transnational Jihad that they had a 'highly romanticized image of what it meant to actually participate in armed combat'. These Muslim youngsters perceived the world as being divided into victims and oppressors in a war against Islam (Van San 2015:331–340).

When it comes to religion, this perception of 'Islam in defence' is often accompanied by a remarkable ignorance of the teachings of Islam and the local conditions in Syria. In his analysis of the Jihadist scene in France, for example, Olivier Roy stated that the religious knowledge of French Jihadists is low. According to him, the rigid ideology of jihadist Salafism provides a religion for 'disenfranchised youngsters', representing a specific kind of radicalized youth movement (Roy 2015). Generally speaking, the motivation to go to war seems to vary extremely from individual to individual. While a broad range of individual grievances may play a role, these grievances are neither specific to foreign fighters nor are all of them necessarily mutually shared. Rather than discerning clear general patterns of individual motivations, we observe certain ideological Islamist templates at work that are able to turn complex patterns of individual grievances into more common push factors to go (Barrett 2014). Furthermore, potential foreign fighters share an attraction to violence and war.

These admittedly very vague findings regarding the profile of contemporary Muslim foreign fighters show striking parallels to the war volunteers who went to the battlefields of the civil war in Spain (1936–1938). This particularly applies to the foreign fighters who joined the ranks of the 'republican' International Brigades, whose ranks were filled by the systematic recruitment efforts of Comintern, the Communist International Organization founded in 1915. From their formation in late October 1936 until February 1937, the International Brigades were able to recruit some 25,000 foreign fighters (Richardson 1976:11). This number increased to approximately 41,000 volunteers from 50 different countries during the year 1937.[6] In his studies of the roughly 3,000 Americans who crossed the Atlantic to fight with the International Brigades in Spain, Robert Rosenstone painted a similarly complex picture regarding the origins and motivational backgrounds of the volunteers in the 'Abraham

Lincoln Battalion' (Rosenstone 1967, 1969). The majority of these American volunteers were males under age 30 with an urban background (Rosenstone 1969:104). They were convinced that 'Fascism had to be defeated in all its manifestations throughout the world' (Rosenstone 1969:258). The American foreign fighters represented a broad variety of occupational backgrounds, however, with a relative majority coming from two specific groups: the working class and students (Rosenstone 1969:94). In their ethnic and religious composition, the Brigadists were very heterogeneous; yet, many of them were born abroad or were first-generation immigrants to the United States (Rosenstone 1967:329 and 331, 1969:109–110).

The common themes of these American war volunteers were related to a rather small group of people in the United States, whose political narratives emerged during the Great Depression and the rise of Fascism in Europe. The typical American foreign fighter took his decision to leave for an unknown war in the atmosphere of a 'world in crisis'. Most were guided by an unspecific amalgam of left-wing feelings, socialist ideals, theories and beliefs, which seemed to offer a solution to this global crisis (Rosenstone 1969: Chapter 2). In Spain, American and European Brigadists were collectively 'defending civilization against fascism', but they did so with very different individual attitudes, motivations and personal backgrounds (Richardson 1976:9). While international communism and the Soviet Union were in fact behind the organization of the brigades, many of the volunteers did not have a doctrinal approach to communist ideology. In the American case, very few foreign fighters had ever read Marxist literature, many adopting their leftist attitudes only recently or even developing them as late as in the context of the Spanish Civil War itself (Rosenstone 1967:337).

In summary, then, the current foreign fighter phenomenon is not unique; foreign fighters have been a recurring phenomenon in modern wars (Bakke 2014:155). At least on a very general level, the foreign fighters in Syria and Iraq share a number of traits with their predecessors who enlisted voluntarily in the International Brigades in Spain: they are young, male,[7] of mixed socio-economic status, and of a recent immigration background. The war volunteers in Syria and Spain seem to represent a generation that has grown up in a certain atmosphere of crisis, whose alleged or real threats they apprehend with reference to broader, globally relevant ideologies. In both cases, a 'defensive messaging' speaks to individuals' very particular fears and grievances. They are mobilizing emotions in framing a distant war as an existential threat to an imagined transnational identity group (cf. Malet 2010:99–101). The theoretical and/or theological underpinnings of these ideological frameworks, however, are to a large extent far from their comprehension. Furthermore, foreign fighters travel to war zones about which they often have no deeper knowledge. Yet while these predominantly young men have very different personal and motivational backgrounds, they share one central feature: violence and war seemingly exert a major attraction on them. Apparently, violent fantasies and war romanticism represent core elements in their identity constructions, rather than being mere consequences of individual paths of radicalization. How to explain this phenomenon? How to understand the convergence of the utterly different life trajectories of these young men in becoming foreign fighters? Does social theory provide us with conceptual tools to analyse the emergence of these violent subjects?

Modernity and barbarity

In a seminal book on modern subjectivity formation, German sociologist Andreas Reckwitz synthesized a vast amount of sociological literature about the modern subject. Following Michel Foucault, Reckwitz understands modern subjectivity formation as a complex process of the elaboration of oneself in everyday life. The modern subject represents a paradox result of both self-elaboration and subjugation to structural constraints with respect to three distinct complexes of social practices: as working subject, as subject of private and intimate relations (intimacy), and as subject of technologies of the self. Each field is characterized by networks of collectively acknowledged discourses and social practices that offer modern individuals various dispositions of institutionalized modes of behaviour and symbolic orientation for the interpretative construction of their identities. In drawing from the history of Europe and North America, Reckwitz (2006) constructed three types of subject cultures – the classical bourgeois, the salaried masses, and the creative worker and entrepreneur – that have subsequently dominated the modern epoch. War and violence, however, play no role in Reckwitz's typology of modern subject cultures; violence would appear to be absent from the social practices of modern everyday life.

With its blind eye to violence, Reckwitz's theory of modern subjectivity formation fits into the mainstream of sociological theory. There has been a strong tendency in social theory to treat violence and war as mere 'accidents of civilization' (Nedelmann 1997:64; cf. Joas and Knöbl 2008). In the designs of major sociologies of modernity, violence does not play the role of an independent theoretical element; on the contrary, violence often appears to be the 'other' of modernity and represents a 'barbarian relict' of premodern times. Consequently, social theory has often dealt with violence as an atavistic problem rather than a social phenomenon, which should be understood on its own terms (Beck and Schlichte 2014:23). In line with the liberal worldview, mainstream social sciences have tended to reduce violence to its causes, expecting its disappearance along with increasing modern social differentiation (Trotha 1997:11). The current discourse on radicalization is firmly embedded in this stream of thought. Building on a dichotomy between modernity and violence, this discourse constructs foreign fighters as deviant modern subjects. The move of individuals towards violent thought and action is explained by social inequalities, disappointment with the promises of Western liberalism or ideological indoctrinations. Yet, the very different profiles of foreign fighters in Syria and Spain raised questions about these assumptions. These profiles only converge in constructing themselves as violent subjects; the role of violence in individual identity constructions is their common denominator. The historical comparison of foreign fighters suggests viewing violence not as the late result of individual transformation processes but to take it seriously as a core feature in the identity constructions of these war volunteers. Moreover, the hegemonic narrative of defiance fails to explain the mere fact that millions of people (fortunately) do not want to compensate for individual grievances and social deprivations on the killing fields of what are for them, in principle, unknown wars.

The dichotomy between modernity and violence stands in stark contrast to the historical experience of violence in the twentieth century. This century was an epoch of exceptionally destructive wars and mass violence (Behrends 2013:39). The Holocaust in particular led many social theorists to fundamentally question the liberal presumption of the inherently peaceful character of modernity. From different theoretical angles, scholars such as Theodor W. Adorno and Max Horkheimer (1989), Hannah Arendt (1963, 1967), Zygmunt Baumann (1989) and Wolfgang Sofsky (1996) have criticized the liberal narrative of a progressively peaceful modernization process. Some, such as Wolfgang Sofsky, even declared modernity synonymous with barbarity, making violence the hidden but fundamental principle of modernity rather than its traditional predecessor. But this equation of modernity with mass violence tends to dismiss another significant historical experience of the twentieth century: the increasing delegitimation of violence by international law. In the rise of modernity, the establishment of non-violence as an international norm has gone along with the simultaneous occurrence of mass violence (Beck and Werron 2013).

I consider this ambiguity in the relationship of modernity and violence to be a key for understanding the current foreign fighter phenomenon and the dynamic escalation of contemporary conflicts. On the one hand, we can read modernization in Norbert Elias's terms as a 'civilizing process'. Elias defined this process as a transformation of both forms of social organization and modes of individual behaviour. Increasing social complexity and dependency on the macro-level is reflected in a more differentiated and stabilized self-control of the individual (Elias 1994:443). In modern times, violence has been under increasing social and individual control. In the course of the civilizing process, the renouncement of violence achieved the status of a universalistic modern norm. In light of this hegemony of non-violence, violent action became a 'scandal' (Beck and Werron 2013:1). This scandalization of violence in modern history has been reflected in the aforementioned relative absence from the mainstream of sociological thought. Conversely, a minority of scholars (e.g. Randal Collins, Heinrich Popitz and Trutz von Trotha) emphasized the fundamental role of violence as, in principle, an ubiquitous resource in everyday life (Behrends 2013:41), understanding violence as a relational social phenomenon resulting from a triangular structure between perpetrators, victims and observers (Beck and Werron 2013:14; Nedelmann 1997:67). Violence is, then, both a means of social action aimed at the humiliation of the body and a means of communication establishing contextual spaces of violence in which the boundaries among perpetrators, victims and observers often become blurred. It is this body of literature based on phenomenological and relational theories of violence that suggests considering war and violence as an alternative complex of social practices in the formation of modern subjectivities.

According to Heinrich Popitz, violence is a form of power (*Aktionsmacht*) that puts the human body in the centre of social action. As the most direct and ultimate form of existential social power relations, Popitz (1986:68–106) declares violence to be an 'anthropological fact'. From this perspective, both the use of violence and its domestication are constitutive processes in the formation of modern social orders. Violence is therefore obsessive, and wars and armed conflicts become core features in the collective memories of groups (Trotha 1997). Similar to Popitz and Trotha, Collins (2008:2) argues for an anthropological understanding of violence in intertwining 'human emotions of fear, anger and excitement'. In aiming at a general theory of violence, however, Collins takes his point of departure not in anthropological predispositions but in the relational structures of violent situations. For him, violence is a constant option in human behaviour, but not an easy one. On the contrary, Collins sees violent interaction as the exception, not the rule. Violent actors must overcome a threshold of confrontational tension and fear, which makes violence self-limiting and dependent on the escalation in situations characterized by the triggering actions of the 'violent few' (Collins 2009). Despite their conceptual differences, however, these three authors share the position to see violence as, in principle, a constantly available and meaningful element of social action. Their theories make us aware of the organizational, institutional and situational contexts in which violent actions occur. The following section will show how this central role of violence as a social phenomenon becomes observable in the recruitment of foreign fighters. Social structures and individual identity constructions intersect in this recruitment process. Instead of an individual radicalization process, I suggest understanding the path to becoming a foreign fighter as the formation of an alternative type of modern subjectivity. Let us put violent practices in the centre of this type of subjectivity, replacing Reckwitz's core feature of the working subject. Foreign fighters, then, do not construct meaningful selfhoods through work but through violence. Moreover, the structural context offers both militarized forms of intimacy and violent technologies of the self for their individual identity constructions.

Recruitment of foreign fighters and the formation of violent subjects

On the basis of the individual fascination of foreign fighters with violence, the formation of violent subjectivities depends on an enabling structural context. These enabling structures are observable in the recruitment processes of foreign fighters. Thomas Hegghammer convincingly argued that in the case of foreign fighters, this macro-sociological context has two crucial components. Firstly, the transformation of individuals into foreign fighters relies on a strong and convincing ideological framework attaching emotions and meaning to violence. The recruitment of foreign fighters therefore works through the justification of violent action in the name of solidarity within an imagined transnational community under existential threat. Second, there must be a 'strong cadre of transnationalist activists' that is able to mobilize volunteers and to facilitate their move to the battlefield. These organizational cadres play the role of the 'violent few', and they act in relative autonomy from direct state control. At the same time, however, they have 'access to state-like resources and privileges' (Hegghammer 2010/2011:90). Ideological and organizational structures hereby extend violent spaces beyond the concrete zones of war, which serve as recruiting milieus for prospective foreign fighters.

When it comes to the first component, ideological frameworks, we can clearly discern globally relevant dichotomies of mobilizing ideologies at work in Syria and Spain. In both cases, global discourses construct local conflicts in terms of existential struggles between good and evil, inviting people to participate in a moment of history (see Barrett 2014). The global battle against Fascism and the transnational Jihad for an Islamic Caliphate share this character of being staged by their protagonists as emotional world historical moments transcending the geographical limits of the factual zones of conflict. These ideological frameworks add meaning to violence and shape new violent conflict dynamics. Despite their differences in values and worldviews, the International Brigades and Islamic State militias provide war volunteers with opportunity structures to make their violent fantasies true and take part in an existential confrontation. They facilitated the escalation of local conflicts into instances of a 'global civil war'. The battlefields in Spain and Syria offer violent spaces for the construction of meaningful selfhoods as violent subjects. In addition, the transnationalist communist and Islamist ideologies at work provide violent templates that give meaning to a complex variety of individual grievances, personal circumstances and national particularities, channelling them towards a common course of action. In being part of such an existential struggle, foreign fighters turn from 'victims' into perpetrators and make a previously unknown war into a meaningful struggle of their own.

Looking at Hegghammer's second component behind the foreign fighter phenomenon, the organizational features, transnational networks and strong states have been involved in the mobilization of foreign war recruits in Syria, just as they were in Spain. In Spain, this was Comintern and the Soviet Union. The International Brigades 'had their own officers, mostly Communists, and at first the top commanders were Red Army or Soviet military intelligence officers of non-Russian nationality' (Payne 2012:153). In the United States, cadres of the American Communist Party recruited volunteers for the Lincoln Battalion (Rosenstone 1969). For Dan Richardson, the International Brigades in Spain always represented a Comintern-controlled force whose military and organizational strength built entirely on the experience of Red Army officers and Soviet advisers (Richardson 1982:178). Without these organizational structures, the formation of individual foreign fighter identities would not be possible. Moreover, they provided social environments for the establishment of new forms of intimacy and the acquisition of violent technologies of the self.

Returning to the present, the recent mobilization of foreign fighters in Syria has been facilitated by transnational Jihadist networks and influential Sunni Muslim states, such as Turkey, Saudi Arabia and Qatar. From a historical perspective, the role of Saudi Arabia has been particularly instrumental in the development and dissemination of the necessary ideological preconditions for the rise of the Muslim foreign fighter phenomenon. Since the 1960s, the Saudi state has provided the institutions, resources and ideological underpinnings for the emergence of a new pan-Islamic movement, making the Saudi region of the Hejaz into 'a melting pot of international Islamists'. These pan-Islamic activists have created an 'alarmist, self-victimizing, conspiratorial, and xenophobic' identity discourse of Muslim unity that has been disseminated around the world (Hegghammer 2010/2011:81–83). They have spread a discourse of Islam in defence that has established a transnational violent space transcending, amalgamating and escalating various armed conflicts in the Muslim world.[8] The propaganda of the Islamic State is a clear extension of this discourse. Moreover, the involvement of previous Baath officers and Iraqi security personnel in the military structure of Islamic State (Lister 2015:90) echoes the role of security personnel in the International Brigades in Spain, who received their military training from Soviet state institutions.

This brief comparison of the structural context of the foreign fighter phenomenon in Spain and Syria shows significant parallels between the two cases regarding factors such as ideology, resources, transnational networks, indirect state support and recruitment infrastructure. The emergence of the foreign fighter phenomenon relies on a necessary support structure in ideological, material and communicational terms. Without this support structure, it would be impossible for the phenomenon to appear in this magnitude. Understanding the micro-level of the phenomenon is more difficult, that is, the individual reasons that eventually make these young men go. Support structures facilitate the recruitment of foreign fighters, but they do not make recruits. While ideological and organizational structures are necessary to explain the collective nature of the phenomenon, they are by no means sufficient; they can provide violent social imaginaries but cannot cause individuals to adopt them in their own identity constructions. Why do groups of predominantly young men with very different historical, cultural, socio-economic and religious backgrounds find it attractive to join foreign militias and fight their wars? Why do they want to take part and even die in a local war imagined as an existential struggle of humankind?

These questions bring me back to the relative neglect of violence as an independent variable in social theory. Contrary to this neglect, Robert Rosenstone emphasized that for most of the volunteers in the Lincoln Battalion, the search for war adventures in combination with the mutually reinforcing power of friendship played an important role in the decision to go. For many of them, violence came first. Moreover, some of the American war volunteers had experienced violence in the course of demonstrations during the Great Depression. On the individual level, the driving force behind joining the International Brigades in Spain was a more general fascination with collective violence committed in the name of a just cause (Rosenstone 1967:337). 'The violence of war fascinates, the more so since war glorifies violence' (Trotha 1999:73). This autonomous role of violence in the subjectivity formation of foreign fighters also applies to the current situation in Syria and Iraq. The enticement strategies of Islamic State propaganda videos build on this fascination with war and violent action. As a core feature of global communication structures, digital media thus have a strong impact on the escalation and perpetuation of violent conflicts.

While the previous criminal records of foreign fighters indicate a central role of violence in their individual identity constructions, Islamic State propaganda has been increasingly characterized by its emphasis on friendship, brotherhood and family life. Becoming a foreign fighter is therefore also envisioned as a kind of 'lifestyle decision' (Klausen 2015:10, 17). Appealing to the desire for violent action, Islamic State media outlets construct foreign fighters as complete modern subjects embedded in a new environment of social intimacy inseparably linked to the conduct of violence. Whatever this actually means for the respective individual, many Western foreign fighters have possibly been motivated by a combination of both violence and social inclusion;[9] that which the mainstream literature on foreign fighters labels a process of radicalization could be considered a form of modern subjectivity formation revolving around violence.

Our attempts at comprehending the foreign fighter phenomenon should take these indications of a more general fascination with violent conflict seriously. War seems to hold an attraction, not only for those who fight but also for the spectator. In Spain, for instance, the nationalist side invited European tourists to visit the country in the midst of war. Thousands of Europeans participated in organized bus tours, which staged human suffering as tourist spectacles and served the nationalist camp as a means of sacralizing both 'the battle sites and the Nationalist soldiers who had conquered the land' (Holguín 2005:1400). Today, digital media are inviting a global audience to take part in local wars and Islamic State media outlets have intensively addressed this global public. These examples perfectly illustrate the triangular interlacement of perpetrators, victims and observers. The propaganda videos of Islamic State have not only delivered social imaginaries for violent subjects, but with its ostensive violation of the norms of non-violence, the Islamic State has engaged in a global competition for attention and legitimacy (*cf.* Beck and Werron 2013:22). In dismissing war as a mere pathology of modernity, we too easily endorse uncritically peaceful narratives of modernization. The foreign fighter phenomenon indicates the existence of types of modern subjectivity formation beyond those of the sovereign bourgeois, the salaried masses or the creative entrepreneur. The civil wars in Spain and Syria became stages for the formation of modern violent subjects. On those battlefields, foreign fighters have constructed meaningful selfhoods in contradistinction to the liberal narrative of the ever-increasingly peaceful nature of modern life.

Conclusion

This chapter began by addressing the question of the transformation of Rawand Taher from a well-integrated Danish Muslim to a Jihadist fighter in the ranks of the Islamic State. Contrary to the standard narrative of a gradual radicalization of individuals, it explained his path to Islamic State in terms of an alternative formation of modern subjectivities. From this perspective, Rawand Taher constructed himself anew according to the social imaginary of a 'violent subject'. I argue that extremist ideologies and personal grievances might not be the primary causes for becoming a foreign fighter. Examples from the civil wars in Spain and Syria suggest that the attraction of violent action in itself might be the decisive driving force behind joining foreign militias. In order to understand the war-prone history of modernity and the continuing violent escalation of conflicts, we must add the idea of the construction of meaningful violent selfhoods to Reckwitz's typology of modern subjectivities. Foreign fighters such as Rawand Taher may, thus, represent examples of an alternative type of modern violent subjectivity that has appeared throughout the history of modernity in different forms. War volunteers search for meaning in war.

When it comes to the dynamics of conflict and issues of conflict resolution, this finding implies an understanding of violence as cause – not only as effect. The mobilizing presence of 'violent few' and violence as a meaningful form of social action in individual identity constructions should inform our analysis of contemporary wars. The foreign fighter is not necessarily engaged in a specific conflict in his search for violent action. Phenomenological and relational approaches to violence provide conceptual means to take violence into analytical consideration as a complex of social practices independent of conflict. In this sense, this chapter underpins the argument of Ole Wæver and Isabel Bramsen in Chapter 1 of this book that there is no intrinsic or even linear relationship between conflict intensity and violence. In practical terms, this finding suggests no longer treating violence as a 'scandal of modernity'. On the one hand, violence is a constant option in social relations: it remains both a means and an end of individual and collective action to be put under mechanisms of personal and institutional control. On the other hand, violence represents a means of communication with enormous discursive power that has been amplified by the global and instant reach of digital media. Due to the dialectical relationship between norms of non-violence and the factual ubiquitous presence of violence as a social phenomenon, we can observe often contradicting communicative dynamics in the competition for global attention and legitimacy. While social actors might seek legitimacy for their cause via the ostensive renunciation of violence, other actors try to gain attention through deliberate violations of the international norms of non-violence. The lessons for attempts at conflict resolution are that violence can come first in both cases. Consequently, violent conflicts not only exist despite the ideal of non-violence, the latter can also play a part in the violent escalation of conflicts due to the communicative power of violence as a scandal (Beck and Werron 2013:24).

Notes

1 The empirical sections of this chapter are based on two previously published working papers: 'Foreign Fighters: Comparative Reflections on Syria and Spain' Middle East Insight 132, Singapore (2015) and 'The Search for Meaning in War: Foreign Fighters in a Comparative Perspective', IAI Working Paper 16/02, Rome, New Med research network (2016). In addition, I was grateful to be able to present my thoughts on this issue at the New Med Conference 'Radicalization in the Mediterranean Region: Old and New Drivers', in Ankara, 14 December 2015.

2 In this sense, my approach is sympathetic with Mani Crone's suggestion to understand homegrown terrorism in considering 'violence as a precondition for engaging with extremist ideology' (Crone 2016:592).

3 In this chapter, I define the term foreign fighter distinct from other types of foreign combatants. With reference to the definition by Thomas Hegghammer (2010/2011:58), I designate foreign fighters as those war volunteers who deliberately join an insurgency, who are not linked to the warring factions by citizenship or kinship ties, who are not part of an official military organization and who do not receive payment like mercenaries.

4 It is difficult to present accurate figures regarding the number of foreign fighters who have travelled to Syria and Iraq. In September 2014, the US administration estimated that 12,000–15,000 foreign fighters from approximately 80 different countries had joined the civil war in Syria since early 2012 (Byman and Shapiro 2014:9). In February 2015, these estimates were raised to more than 20,000. Most of them joined radical Jihadist militias such as the Islamic State. In 2016, the number of foreign fighters travelling to the war zones in Syria and Iraq declined drastically. The German daily *Süddeutsche Zeitung*, for instance, published German intelligence figures according to which the highest estimated number of German foreign fighters leaving the country was about 100 volunteers per month but that this figure had dropped to less than five in 2016 (Mascolo 2016).

5 For literature on these wars, see Felter and Fishman (2007), Holman (2015), Kohlmann and Alkhouri (2014), and Moore and Tumelty (2008).

6 When applying the definition of a foreign fighter presented in the introduction to this chapter, the contingent of the republican side exceeded by far the 1,500–3,000 volunteers who deliberately joined General Franco's nationalists (Jackson 2001:vi; Keen 2001; Othen 2013:4). In total numbers of foreign combatants, however, international support for Franco's troops was actually much higher. In the course of the war, the nationalist side enlisted some 78,000 soldiers from Morocco and about 8,000 fighters from Portugal, while the fascist regimes of Germany and Italy supported the Spanish nationalist cause with some 35,000 and 80,000, troops, respectively (Othen 2013:4).

7 It should be mentioned that, as was the case in Spain, women have also joined the warring groups in Syria. In both cases, however, women join the armed groups in much fewer numbers than men and mostly not as combatants. In Spain, the republican side mobilized women in emancipative terms, while the Nationalists emphasized their traditional roles, using them in various social, economic and medical activities (Payne 2012:128). In the war in Syria, women play an important role as disseminators in the media (Klausen 2015:15–16). It is estimated that roughly 10% of Western foreigners who have joined the Islamic State are women. These women are predominantly envisaged in patriarchal terms and have non-combat roles (Peresin and Cervone 2015:499).

8 In the Lebanese Palestinian camp of Ain al-Helweh, for instance, French scholar Bernard Rougier observed young Palestinians entertaining themselves by watching the war adventures of 'Commander Khattab' in Afghanistan and Chechnya, who was fighting a technologically dominant enemy with the moral power of his Islamic faith (Rougier 2004). Young Muslims hereby consume the products of a politically interested 'cultural industry' that contributes considerably to disseminating the ideological narrative of an Islam in defence.

9 This combination of the defence of Islam with a desire for social inclusion is also a common theme in the biographies of the young Danes who have been described in a recent book by Danish journalist Jakob Sheikh (2015).

References

Adorno, Theodor W. and Max Horkheimer (1989) *Dialectic of Enlightenment*. London: Verso.

Arendt, Hannah (1963) *Eichmann in Jerusalem: A Report on the Banality of Evil*. New York: The Viking Press.

Arendt, Hannah (1967) *The Origins of Totalitarianism*, third edition. London: Allen and Unwin.

Bakke, Kristin M. (2014) 'Help Wanted? The Mixed Record of Foreign Fighters in Domestic Insurgencies', *International Security* 38 (4): 150–187.

Barrett, Richard (2014) *Foreign Fighters in Syria*. https://www.carnegiecouncil.org/studio/multimedia/20140923-foreign-fighters-in-syria (accessed 12 June 2017).

Baumann, Zygmunt (1989) *Modernity and the Holocaust*. Ithaca, NY: Cornell University Press.

Beck, Teresa Koloma and Klaus Schlichte (2014) *Theorien der Gewalt*. Hamburg: Junius Verlag.

Beck, Teresa Koloma and Tobias Werron (2013) 'Gewaltwettbewerbe. Gewalt in globalen Konkurrenzen um Aufmerksamkeit und Legitimität', *Leviathan* 27: 249–277.

Behrends, Jan C. (2013) 'Gewalt und Staatlichkeit im 20. Jahrhundert. Einige Tendenzen zeithistorischer Forschung', *Neue Politische Literatur* 58 (1): 39–58.

Byman, Daniel (2015) 'The Homecomings: What Happens When Arab Foreign Fighters in Iraq and Syria Return?' *Studies in Conflict & Terrorism* 38 (8): 581–602.

Byman, Daniel and Jeremy Shapiro (2014) 'Be Afraid. Be A Little Afraid: The Threat of Terrorism from Western Foreign Fighters in Syria and Iraq', *Policy Paper* 34 (November 2014). Washington, DC: Brookings.

Collins, Randall (2008) *Violence: A Micro-Sociological Theory*. Princeton, NJ: Princeton University Press.

Collins, Randall (2009) 'Micro and Macro Causes of Violence', *International Journal of Conflict and Violence* 3 (1): 9–22.

Crone, Mani (2016) 'Radicalization Revisited: Violence, Politics and the Skills of the Body', *International Affairs* 92 (3): 587–604.

Elias, Norbert (1994) *The Civilizing Process: The History of Manners and State Formation and Civilization*. Oxford: Basil Blackwell.

Felter, Joseph and Brian Fishman (2007) *Al-Qa'ida's Foreign Fighters in Iraq: A First Look at the Sinjar Records*. West Point, NY: Combating Terrorism Center.

Hafez, Mohammed and Creighton Mullins (2015) 'The Radicalization Puzzle: A Theoretical Synthesis of Empirical Approaches to Homegrown Extremism', *Studies in Conflict & Terrorism* 38: 958–975.

Hegghammer, Thomas (2010/2011) 'The Rise of Muslim Foreign Fighters: Islam and the Globalization of Jihad', *International Security* 35 (3): 53–94.

Holguín, Sandie (2005) '"National Spain Invites You": Battlefield Tourism During the Spanish Civil War', *American Historical Review* 110 (5): 1399–1426.

Holman, Timothy (2015) 'Belgian and French Foreign Fighters in Iraq 2003–2005: A Comparative Case Study', *Studies in Conflict & Terrorism* 38 (8): 603–621.

Jackson, Gabriel (2001) 'Foreword', in Judith Keen (Ed.), *Fighting for Franco: International Volunteers in Nationalist Spain During the Spanish Civil War, 1936–39* (vi–vii), London and New York: Leicester University Press.

Joas, Hans and Wolfgang Knöbl (2008) *Kriegsverdrängung: Ein Problem in der Geschichte der Sozialtheorie*. Frankfurt am Main: Suhrkamp.

Keen, Judith (2001) *Fighting for Franco: International Volunteers in Nationalist Spain During the Spanish Civil War, 1936–39*. London and New York: Leicester University Press.

Klausen, Jytte (2015) 'Tweeting the Jihad: Social Media Networks of Western Foreign Fighters in Syria and Iraq', *Studies in Conflict & Terrorism* 38 (1): 1–22.

Kohlmann, Evan and Laith Alkhouri (2014) 'Profiles of Foreign Fighters in Syria and Iraq', *CTC Sentinel* 7 (9): 1–5.

Lister, Charles R. (2015) *The Syrian Jihad: Al-Qaida, the Islamic State and the Evolution of an Insurgency*. Oxford: Oxford University Press.

Malet, David (2010) 'Why Foreign Fighters? Historical Perspectives and Solutions', *Orbis* 54 (1): 97–114.

Masbah, Mohammed (2015) 'Moroccan Foreign Fighters: Evolution of the Phenomenon, Promotive Factors, and the Limits of Hardline Policies', *SWP Comments* 46. Berlin: German Institute for International and Security Studies.

Mascolo, Georg (2016) *Aus Deutschland zieht es nur noch wenige zum IS*. www.sueddeutsche.de/politik/islamismus-aus-deutschland-zieht-es-nur-noch-wenige-zum-is-1.3252194#re-directedFromLandingpage (accessed 12 June 2017).

Moore, Cerwyn and Paul Tumelty (2008) 'Foreign Fighters and the Case of Chechnya: A Critical Assessment', *Studies in Conflict & Terrorism* 31 (5): 412–433.

Nedelmann, Birgitta (1997) 'Gewaltsoziologie am Scheideweg: Die Auseinandersetzung in der gegenwärtigen und Wege der künftigen Gewaltforschung', *Kölner Zeitschrift für Soziologie und Sozialpsychologie, Sonderheft* 37: 59–85.

Neumann, Peter R. (2013) 'The Trouble with Radicalization', *International Affairs* 89 (4): 873–893.

Othen, Christopher (2013) *Franco's International Brigades: Adventurers, Fascists, and Christian Crusaders in the Spanish Civil War*. London: Hurst.

Payne, Stanley G. (2012) *The Spanish Civil War*. Cambridge: Cambridge University Press

Peresin, Anita and Albert Cevone (2015) 'The Western Muhajirat of ISIS', *Studies in Conflict & Terrorism* 38 (7): 495–509.

Popitz, Heinrich (1986) *Phänomen der Macht. Autorität – Herrschaft – Gewalt – Technik*. Tübingen: J.C.B. Mohr (Paul Siebeck).

Reckwitz, Andreas (2006) *Das hybride Subject: Eine Theorie der Subjektkulturen von der bürgerlichen Moderne zur Postmoderne*. Weilerswist: Velbrück Wissenschaft.

Reemtsma, Jan Phillip (2012) *Trust and Violence: An Essay on a Modern Relationship*. Princeton, NJ: Princeton University Press.

Richardson, R. Dan (1976) 'Foreign Fighters in Spanish Militias: The Spanish Civil War 1936–1939', *Military Affairs* 40 (1): 7–11.

Richardson, R. Dan (1982) *Comintern Army: The International Brigades and the Spanish Civil War*. Lexington: The University of Kentucky Press.

Rosenstone, Robert A. (1967) 'The Men of the Abraham Lincoln Battalion', *The Journal of American History* 54 (2): 327–338.

Rosenstone, Robert A. (1969) *Crusade of the Left: The Lincoln Battalion in the Spanish Civil War*. New York: Pegasus.

Rougier, Bernard (2004) 'Religious Mobilization in Palestinian Refugee Camps in Lebanon: The Case of Ain al-Helweh', in Dietrich Jung (Ed.), *The Middle East and Palestine: Global Politics and Regional Conflict* (151–182), New York: Palgrave Macmillan.

Roy, Olivier (2015) *What is the Driving Force behind Jihadist Terrorism? A Scientific Perspective on the Causes/Circumstances of Joining the Scene*. Speech at the BKA Autumn

Conference International Terrorism: How Can Prevention and Repression Keep Pace? 18–19 November 2015, Bundeskriminalamt, Mainz, Germany.

Sheikh, Jakob (2015) *Danmarks børn i hellig krig.* Copenhagen: Lindhardt og Ringhof Forlag.

Sheikh, Jakob (2016) *Sådan endte en student fra Frederiksberg i toppen af Islamisk Stat.* http://politiken.dk/indland/art5648737/Sådan-endte-en-student-fra-Frederiksberg-i-toppen-af-Islamisk-Stat (accessed 12 June 2017).

Stern, Jessica and John M. Berger (2015) *ISIS and the Foreign-Fighter Phenomenon.* www.theatlantic.com/international/archive/2015/03/isis-and-the-foreign-fighter-problem/387166/ (accessed 12 June 2017).

Sofsky, Wolfgang (1996) *Traktat über die Gewalt.* Frankfurt am Main: Fischer.

Trotha, Trutz von (1997) 'Zur Soziologie der Gewalt', *Kölner Zeitschrift für Soziologie und Sozialpsychologie, Sonderheft* 37: 9–58.

Trotha, Trutz von (1999) 'Formen des Krieges. Zur Typologie kriegerischer Aktionsmacht', in Sighard Neckel and Michael Schwab-Trapp (Eds.), *Ordnungen der Gewalt. Beiträge zu einer politischen Soziologie der Gewalt und des Krieges* (71–95), Opladen: Leske und Budrich.

Van San, Mario (2015) 'Striving in the Way of God: Justifying Jihad by Young Belgian and Dutch Muslims', *Studies in Conflict & Terrorism* 38 (5): 328–342.

Zammit, Andrew (2014) 'New Developments in Australian Foreign Fighter Activity', *CTC Sentinel* 7 (9): 5–8.

8

PREVENTING ESCALATION

The international pursuit of conflict transformation in Burundi

Troels Gauslå Engell and Katja Lindskov Jacobsen

Introduction: the international community, the primacy of politics and a crisis in Burundi

The international community has been heavily involved in the political crisis in Burundi, which began in the spring of 2015 when the sitting president, Pierre Nkurunziza, announced that he would run for another term in office. When the opposition started protesting Nkurunziza's candidature and the security forces responded by cracking down on demonstrators, the preventive diplomacy machinery of the international community was set in full motion. Fears had mounted that the crisis and violence would escalate, possibly into an open conflict along ethnic lines, or even into another genocide in the worst-case scenario. Indeed, the conflict in Burundi 'has alarmed a region where memories of the Rwanda's 1994 genocide remain raw' (Reuters 2016) – an important factor to bear in mind when seeking to explain the international community's involvement in conflict prevention in Burundi.[1]

To prevent worst-case scenarios from materializing, the international community, not least the United Nations (UN), sent numerous mediators to Burundi to call upon the parties to show restraint and engage in political dialogue rather than violent confrontations. As a case in point, the UN Security Council went on two visiting missions to Burundi in 2015–2016. The Security Council adopted three resolutions and three Presidential Statements in this same period, and the UN Secretary-General visited Burundi and appointed a succession of special envoys to mediate on his behalf.

All of these initiatives focused on enabling a political dialogue, the aim of which was to assist the parties to the conflict in finding a peaceful solution to the crisis. The UN's prioritization of political dialogue for its engagement in the crisis in Burundi can be understood with reference to a number of recommendations made by the High-Level Independent Panel on Peace Operations in its 2015 report, which occasioned discussions in the UN system about reforms of UN peace operations. Central among the reform themes was a focus on political solutions, conflict prevention and partnerships. These discussions were current at the exact time of the outbreak of the political crisis in Burundi, and in some sense responding to the crisis in Burundi came to be regarded as an opportunity to experiment with the UN's new approach to conflict prevention (Jacobsen and Engell 2017). Conflict prevention has been a long-standing UN ambition, an ambition that has received renewed attention with the HIPPO report and the Peacebuilding Commission (PBC) report on sustaining peace (Advisory Group of Experts 2015). More recently, newly appointed Secretary-General Antonio Guterres made conflict prevention his first priority. The issue of conflict prevention was, for example, the main theme of Guterres' first address to the UN Security Council in an open debate on 10 January 2017 UN Security Council (2017).

To engage in conflict prevention, the thinking in the UN is also that partnerships are central – and in the case of Burundi, both the African Union (AU) and the East African Community (EAC) were involved in various conflict prevention measures alongside the UN. As an example, the AU responded to the situation with an effort to find 'a lasting solution to the crisis in Burundi', which meant that the AU decided – in January 2016 – to send a high-level delegation to Burundi 'to consult with the Government, as well as with other Burundian actors, on the inclusive dialogue' (African Union 2016). Reflecting the composition of the AU, this delegation consisted of representatives from each of the five sub-regions of Africa: Mauritania for North Africa, South Africa for Southern Africa, Senegal for West Africa, Gabon for Central Africa and Ethiopia for Eastern Africa. Furthermore, the EAC, which is the regional organization of which Burundi is a member (together with Kenya, Rwanda, South Sudan, Tanzania and Uganda), appointed a Mediator, who was later supplemented by a 'facilitator of peace talks between rival factions in volatile Burundi' (Africanews 2016). These peace talks are also referred to as the intra-Burundian dialogue. This was 'the first time, the EAC took upon itself the mantle of leadership in a crisis affecting one of its member states' (Institute for Security Studies 2016). This chapter offers an analysis of some of the initiatives taken by the UN, AU, EAC and the EU during the crisis in Burundi to prevent an escalation of violence.

The various efforts undertaken by this composition of global, regional and sub-regional external actors can be seen as attempts at conflict transformation as defined by Wæver and Bramsen in Chapter 1. Indeed, a key objective with reference to which each of these institutional actors legitimized their preventive endeavours was transforming the conflict from low-intensity violence and the open contestation of the president's legitimacy to an inclusive political dialogue. Wæver and Bramsen understand conflict transformation as having three components: changing the situation, changing the interaction and changing the level of tension. We use this understanding of conflict transformation to frame our analysis of how preventive diplomacy was carried out in Burundi during

2015–2016 – primarily by the UN, but also by the AU and the EAC. As such, each of the following three sections begins with a brief recap of how Bramsen, Poder and Wæver define transformation in relation to each of these three components. We then discuss some of the specific efforts that fall under each heading. Our analysis is based on interviews with various Burundian actors as well as with UN offices in Bujumbura carried out in June 2016 together with subsequent interviews in New York.[2] Our account is also based on available reports and official statements from each organization, on regional and international news sources, as well as on think tank/advocacy reports and academic literature. Importantly, the aim of this analysis is not to explain the entire crisis in Burundi. Instead, the analysis highlights a number of elements that have been characteristic of international, regional and sub-regional efforts aimed at conflict transformation in Burundi during the period 2015–2016.

Changing the situation

As defined by Wæver and Bramsen in Chapter 1, changing the situation means to:

> change the structure of the situation i.e. the opposing positioning of the parties. The structure of a conflict situation need not be destructive with mutually exclusive identities and thus, a conflict should not necessarily be turned into collaboration but also to other types of 'conflict modes' e.g. from antagonism (where the other is non-recognized and ultimately to be eradicated) to agonism (as a legitimate opponent).

When it comes to the involvement of the UN in the situation in Burundi, this focus on changing the structure of the situation is very much in line with the UN's overall ambition to turn the conflict away from low-intensity violence in the streets of Bujumbura and the surrounding hills, towards a political dialogue aimed at finding a peaceful solution. Where parties to the conflict have seen themselves as antagonists with mutually exclusive goals – not least concerning the question of whether Nkurunziza could continue as the president – the UN wanted to bring the parties together around the negotiation table and to have them recognize each other as legitimate political opponents. As we shall now see, however, mediation efforts have thus far turned out differently from the UN's envisioned focus on inclusivity.

First, the Government of Burundi (GoB) has been extremely reluctant to allow for the involvement of external actors in the crisis, which it regards as an internal Burundian matter. As the most poignant in a series of examples of how the GoB has denied the international community access, it decided in October 2016 to stop cooperating with the Office of the UN High Commissioner for Human Rights, decided to leave the International Criminal Court and declared critical UN experts for *persona non grata* (Government of Burundi 2016). These examples also illustrate how the GoB's reluctance to allow an international presence has not been limited to the mediation process, as it has also included a wide range of activities undertaken by the international community. With respect to the issue of mediation and political dialogue, however, the government's distrust of the UN meant that it found the involvement of EAC to be more acceptable, as the EAC was seen as having closer ties to Burundi.

EAC and regional mediation

At the request of the GoB, the EAC was designated as the official mediator, and Ugandan president Museveni was appointed to act on the organization's behalf. In December 2015, Museveni led a first round of negotiations at Entebbe State House in Uganda. Rather than playing a key role in the talks in Kampala, a UN representative merely 'attended the talks', as did a small number of Western donors (Reuters 2016). Now, this first round of negotiations reached a stalemate due to opposing positions on which 'identities' to include in the negotiations. Although much criticized for not being able to move the political dialogue forward, Museveni had made attempts at restructuring the situation towards agonism rather than antagonism by inviting a broad spectrum of stakeholders to the dialogue. Specifically, Museveni had called upon the Nkurunziza government to grant temporary amnesty to members of the CNARED-opposition (National Council for the Restoration of Arusha Agreement and Rule of Law) who were allegedly implicated in the attempted military coup in May 2015 (Vandeginste 2016:517).

The GoB, however, had issued arrest warrants and extradition requests on several of the same opposition leaders living in exile, and so they rejected Museveni's suggestion: 'If the people we have evidence against [for] participating in the coup show up in the [negotiating] room, we get out. It's a simple as that', Alain Aimé Nyamitwe, Burundi's foreign minister and the head of the government delegation, was quoted as saying (IRIN 2016). In fact, the actual meetings never even started negotiating a political solution because there was disagreement over who should be represented at the table. For its part, much of the opposition insisted that Nkurunziza should step down before they would participate. Some of the exiled opposition members expressed that they were willing to negotiate with the Government, but only on the condition that Nkurunziza would step down as the president: "We shall negotiate with the enemy. But he [Nkurunziza] can't say, 'Give me five [more] years' ... He must go" (IRIN 2016).

We therefore have a case of 'mutually exclusive identities', and although the EAC, represented by Museveni, attempted to change the situation as part of an effort to find a lasting political solution to the conflict, this attempt did not succeed in changing the parties' positions. Rather, it resulted in a stalemate and in peace talks that concluded without having made any serious headway towards finding a solution to the conflict in Burundi, which continued to unfold (IRIN 2016). It was often added in our interviews that Museveni and the EAC might not have been entirely genuine in their efforts to bring the opposition into the formal process, especially in light of the fact that several of the heads of state of EAC member countries have held the presidency for more terms than Nkurunziza.

The question of who should be included as 'legitimate opponents' in the political dialogue continued to stall the EAC mediation efforts. For example, in January 2016 when talks were scheduled to resume in Arusha, Tanzania, and the EAC process had been reinforced by appointing the former Tanzanian President Benjamin Mkapa as a facilitator,[3] the deadlock continued. The peace talks were postponed once again due to disagreements over whom to (not) invite (VOA News 2016). The government representatives that we interviewed repeatedly referred to UN Security Council Resolution 2248 (2015) to legitimize their position that those involved in the coup should not be included. Since this resolution states that only 'peaceful stakeholders' should be involved in the dialogue, they used that as a reference in their argumentation. In one such interview with a high-ranking civil servant, it was clearly stated that the GoB would 'not negotiate with people with blood on their hands'. With this deadlock in mind, the Security Council changed the language of its subsequent resolution 2279 (2016a) to be forward-looking, rather than excluding anyone who had hitherto been not peaceful (authors' interviews with UNSC diplomats). In the second resolution from April 2016, the wording was about actors 'committed to a peaceful solution' instead, opening for an interpretation that those involved in the coup could be included if they were now committed to negotiations (UN Security Council 2016b). In these ways, the UN sought to avoid obstructing progress in the negotiations. However, the following round of negotiations in Arusha nevertheless also ended in June 2016 without ever getting to the substantial negotiations.

Summary: risks of perpetuating violence and becoming irrelevant

Zooming out again on the broader mediation context, the UN continues to call for an inclusive political dialogue with the broad participation of opposition parties. At the same time, the UN's role in the actual negotiations was reduced to offering support and advice to the EAC. Whether promoted by the UN or the EAC – although in different ways – the idea that it would be possible to arrive at a situation where exiled opposition leaders were accepted as legitimate opponents is yet to materialize. In fact, there seems to be at least one notable trade-off between the long-term efforts focused on this aim of changing the situation into one of agonism and the more immediate goal of ending violence in Burundi: as long as there was a stalemate, the crisis in Burundi – including the disappearances, assassinations, continued refugee movements and more – could continue. In short, while disagreement over whom to consider a legitimate opponent has obstructed the political process since late 2015 – with no considerable progress in changing the situation from non-recognition to recognition – violence in Burundi continued all along. Indeed, in February 2017, Antonio Guterres warned that forced disappearances, killings and the discovery of dead bodies continued at an increasing rate (UN Secretary-General 2017). We shall return to the issue of how the level of tension has changed. The point to stress here is that when attempts at changing the situation drag out, there is a trade-off that must be considered between this strategy and the risks posed by the continuous pursuit of low-level violence.

The EAC was conducting a careful balancing act (e.g. in the form of Museveni's calls for temporary immunity to exiled members of the opposition). If it pushed too hard, the EAC would risk becoming irrelevant as a result of the GoB trying to circumvent the EAC, thereby cutting off its influence. This would be a parallel to how the GoB has sidelined the UN in the peace process with reference to the EAC having the role as a mediator and facilitator. Indeed, Burundi recently applied to become a member of the South African Development Community (SADC), highlighting that the risk of sidelining is very real, as membership in SADC would allow the GoB to expand its forum-shopping. Geographically, Burundi's three neighbouring countries have different institutional profiles in this regard: Tanzania is both a member of EAC and SADC, Rwanda is only a member of EAC, while the Democratic Republic of Congo is only a member of SADC. However, it is interesting to note how, after 10 years of EAC membership (since 2007), Burundi's application to SADC coincides with a moment in which the EAC is seen as pushing harder to make the GoB engage in inclusive peace talks. Specifically, Mkapa stressed in February 2017 that in order to boost the political dialogue, it was 'imperative to convene an extraordinary summit of Heads of East African Community states' (IWACU 2017). Conversely, SADC does not have a track record of interfering in its member states to prevent tense situations from escalating. Most recently, despite various organizations calling for its involvement (Human Rights Watch 2016; van Staden 2016:9; see also the final report of the UN's Independent Investigation in Burundi (UNIIB 2016)), SADC has not interfered in the Mozambique conflict. Adding to this, current SADC member states such as Swaziland and Zimbabwe arguably also 'systematically violate the club's ostensible rules, regarding respect for democracy' and do so 'without evident fear of expulsion' from this regional institution (Fabricius 2017). As such, changing institutional membership thus also means turning to an organization with a different position on the legitimacy of preventive interference. Thus, in applying to the SADC, the GoB strongly signals its discontentment with EAC's involvement in what it sees as internal Burundian affairs. Furthermore, this example illustrates how efforts aimed at changing the situation entail a delicate balancing act: pushing too much, the EAC risks deselection.

Changing the interaction

Besides influencing conflict dynamics by aiming for changes at the level of identity – from antagonist identity positions towards recognition of opponents as legitimate – external actors can also aim at changing the conflict through efforts that aim to 'create a platform for handling conflict by nonviolent and political means' as Wæver and Bramsen writes in Chapter 1.

Withdrawal of election support

One such potential platform for handling conflict was the election process. The conflict had already started before the re-election of Nkurunziza in July 2016. From April 2015, when it was announced that Nkurunziza would run for a third term in the 2015 presidential election, protests started immediately by those opposed to his candidature (UN Secretary-General 2015b:2). The attempted coup on 5 May was also part of the pre-election violence. Considering this pre-election violence, and numerous reports of the GoB repressing freedom of expression, a number of international actors decided to withdraw their elections support. Specifically, the UN, which was mandated to support the GoB in holding free and fair elections,[4] decided to withdraw its election support at the last moment (authors' interviews with the UN official). Other donors, including the EU and the AU, had made similar decisions.[5]

Insofar as the aim was to call upon the GoB to delay elections and to ensure a conducive environment for free and fair elections, the decision to withdraw election support was arguably made on the assumption that the government could be pushed to change behaviour, and that it would result in an election process that could serve as a platform through which the conflict could be handled by political means (i.e. voting). However, elections went ahead despite international donors' withdrawal of support, and the UN election monitoring body in Burundi, MENUB (United Nations Electoral Observation Mission in Burundi), concluded that 'the overall environment was not conducive for an inclusive, free and credible electoral process' (MENUB 2015:2). As such, the withdrawal of support did not result in the creation of an elections platform for handling the conflict. To the contrary, conflict dynamics intensified in the wake of the much-contested election on 21 July 2015. This is not to say that these efforts at changing the interaction had no effect on conflict dynamics. It is merely to say that they did not have the intended effects. Rather than pushing the government to ensure a more conducive election environment, the withdrawal of election support ended up being used by the government as part of a story about how committed the population of Burundi was to the process – and hence to the legitimacy of the election. As one of our informants put it, referring to a popular fundraising effort in favour of holding the elections without international support 'the people of Burundi have shown that they are willing to pay for the election themselves – also in 2020', which he found to be a proof that the people were with the GoB and not the opposition. The alternative of supporting the elections, though, could have proven even easier for the GoB to turn to its advantage. The international community was therefore in a difficult position insofar as they were presented with two choices – none of which were ideal from a conflict prevention perspective. Confronted with this difficulty, the UN, EU and AU all decided not to be complicit in legitimizing human rights violations in relation to the election process. An approach that, however, did not succeed in creating a platform for peaceful change.

Aid and sanctions

Changing interactions between parties 'from violent to non-violent' in a conflict can also be pursued through other types of engagements, as Wæver and Bramsen write in Chapter 1. We can regard the EU's withdrawal of development aid as a decision aimed at changing the interaction by way of pushing the Nkurunziza government to reduce levels of violence and to engage more in the political negotiations. This would be a 'punitive incentive strategy' using the terms from Nikolas Emmanuel in Chapter 11. In March 2016, the EU imposed aid sanctions on Burundi, stopping direct funding to the Government by invoking article 96 of the ACP-EU Cotonou partnership agreement, which stipulates that 'human rights, democratic principles, and the rule of law are essential elements of their partnership and key pillars for long-term development', and that non-compliance is a reason to suspend development assistance (European Council 2016). The commitments and actions that the EU required on the part of the GoB in order for these sanctions to be eased included (a) an improved human rights situation and (b) the Nkurunziza government's participation in an internationally mediated dialogue. Put differently, the EU – whilst not engaged directly in debates about whom to accept as a legitimate opponent – nonetheless sought to change the interaction, notably the Burundian government's engagement in the political dialogue. By withholding aid, the EU sought to pressure the government to do more to end the conflict in Burundi (Guardian 2016). As an interviewee working in an international organization put it: 'the EU is using carrot and stick', a metaphor that conveys the sense in which aid sanctions were intended as a strategy through which to push the GoB to 'do more human rights' in order to 'get back its aid'). As further evidence of this use of aid sanctions to push the government to engage more actively in finding a solution to the conflict, another interviewee noted about these measures that: 'further deterioration of the economic situation, especially lack of foreign currency, could make them change their minds' (authors' interview with member of the diplomatic corps in Bujumbura).

Yet, the extent to which the use of development assistance and sanctions can help change the interaction in a given conflict situation is extremely context dependent. In Burundi, the EU's use of article 96 has certainly hampered the economy, especially the private sector. However, according to an international observer, 'only 10% of the population is affected by the economic situation because the majority are farmers and will not be affected by sanctions' and 'the current political elite does not mind because Bujumbura is the seat of the ancient elite and of resistance to the President' (authors' interview). Thus, contrary to having succeeded in pushing the government to ensure a platform for handling conflict peacefully, observers from the international community in Burundi instead pointed out that the sanctions had contributed to hardening the government's position. This viewpoint was also articulated by pro-government sources: 'Your brothers, the EU, pulled its support and now we see that some of the coup-makers are walking around freely in your countries' (authors' interview). It was made with reference to a recurring theme among Nkurunziza supporters, which would have it that Belgium was hosting people that were under arrest orders in Burundi. Deciding to withdraw aid thus became part of a broader narrative about the international community being in support of the opposition, and thus contributing to hardening the position of the government vis-à-vis external actors in what it considered an internal Burundian matter. What must also be said is that, again, inter-institutional dynamics meant that the EU's decision to withdraw aid also affected other external actors' preventive efforts. Likewise, the EU relied on UN reporting about the situation to evaluate progress or setbacks. In a number of interviews in Bujumbura, the EU's role in the conflict (including its decision to withdraw aid) was narrated as part of a broader government-narrative that delegitimized the AU. As one source close to the regime phrased it, 'the EU funds the AU, so the AU is under influence from the EU. The EU was the first to make sanctions against Burundi. There is deep concern about what the AU is doing' (authors' interview). Economic sanctions did not have the intended effects of pushing the government to reduce violence and increase its willingness to engage in inclusive political dialogue. The sanctions contributed to delegitimizing the EU and the AU from the perspective of the GoB. As with the election support, however, it is difficult to see what other options were available to the EU and AU if they were to remain true to their stated values.

Summary: no need to compromise

On the one hand, the international community has sought to change the interaction in at least two ways: (1) by imposing aid sanctions in an attempt to push the Nkurunziza government to reduce levels of violence and to move the negotiations forward and (2) by withdrawing election support in an attempt to push the government to ensure conditions for a more 'inclusive, free and credible electoral process' (MENUB 2015:2) and as such a platform for handling conflict. Yet, on the other hand, the result of these attempts is that sanctions have contributed to a hardening of the GoB's position and elections have been turned into a story about the Burundian people's self-reliance and defence of their sovereignty. As such, these attempts have unintentionally contributed to a situation where the 'government feels it is winning, so it has no need to compromise' (authors' interview with a member of the diplomatic corps in Bujumbura). This, in turn, reflected back on the peace talks, and it likely contributed to the making of antagonistic rather than agonistic positions – thus working against the aim of changing the situation as described earlier.

Changing the level of tension

According to Wæver and Bramsen in Chapter 1:

> the objective should not necessarily be 'to remove tensions as to direct them into useful channels and to turn them to constructive social ends' (UNESCO tension project). In some cases, the most constructive approach may even be to increase tensions. As argued by Jabri (1996), Dudouet (2008) and others, conflicts may not always be ripe for resolution.

We see at least three ways in which changing the level of tension is relevant when describing the international community's engagement in Burundi: unheard attempts at transformation, unspoken ideas of transformation and unintended consequences of attempts at transformation.

Unheard attempts at transformation: calls for restraint

Besides the political dialogue track of international involvement in the Burundi crisis, the manifold organizations also kept calling for the parties to show restraint and to refrain from violence. The UN did so through reports and statements. Outside of the formal EAC-led, peace talks, the UN Secretary-General, for example, sent out a statement saying that: 'The Secretary-General reiterates his calls for calm and restraint', and continued to say that he 'calls the parties to the consultative political dialogue not to be deterred by those who, through violence, seek to prevent the creation of an environment conducive to peaceful, credible and inclusive elections in Burundi' (UN Secretary-General 2015a). The Security Council, likewise, resolved that it:

> *Strongly urges* the Government of Burundi and all parties to cease and reject any kind of violence and condemn any public statement inciting violence or hatred, and *demands* that all sides in Burundi refrain from any action that would threaten peace and stability in the country or undermine the inter-Burundian dialogue.
>
> *(UN Security Council 2016b:3; emphasis in original)*

While the UN has not been able to play a central role in the actual peace talks – as only EAC was accepted by the GoB – the UN undertook various other conflict prevention endeavours. Besides the calls for restraint, this included reporting on human rights violations, which became a central contribution to its preventive diplomacy. A main aim of both endeavours was to lower the level of tension. Indeed, a senior UN official told us that if the UN has not been observing and reporting on the level of violence and tension in Burundi, the situation would have been much worse. Several UN officials went as far as to say that genocide had been likely in Burundi if it had not been for the monitoring and diplomatic pressure that the organization provided (authors' interviews in New York).

Unspoken ideas of transformation: do things need to get worse before they get better?

The UN's logic behind its prevention work is that it finds that tensions need to be lowered in order to create a conducive space for political dialogue. As intuitive as it may seem, this position constrains the UN from considering the alternative that Bramsen, Poder and Wæver describe, namely that in some cases, a temporary rise in tensions might be beneficial. As Bramsen, Poder and Wæver describe this dynamic, 'conflicts may not always be ripe for resolution'. This could, for example, be the case if 'power relations need to be challenged'. Some of our interviewees in Burundi articulated a similar view. Representatives from the diplomatic community saw a situation in Burundi where the government had no incentive to negotiate in good faith. Crucially, this analysis, which differed starkly from the official approach, should be seen in light of the stalemate in peace negotiations, which made this otherwise silenced possibility attractive. One interviewee told us directly that 'some say things need to get worse before they get better' (authors' interview with a member of the diplomatic corps in Bujumbura). The crisis in Burundi can be considered a situation of asymmetric power relations insofar as the main fault line was between the opposition and the government, and the latter controlled the security forces and a paramilitary youth wing of the ruling party called the *Imbonerakure*. Therefore, if the opposition was to gain any leverage in the negotiations, they probably needed an increase in tensions and a challenge to existing power relations. Arguably, this is why they started demonstrating against the president's candidature in the first place. They speculated that maybe a worsening of the situation would be enough to push the government to the negation table. In other words, some followed the logic that increasing tensions may be constructive if they want power relations to change. This is obviously a risky strategy, especially if the warnings from UN sources were correct that escalation could lead to ethnic conflict (see OHCHR 2016). Such a risk would be unacceptable to the international organizations, and even the remotest risk conjures the spectre of the Rwandan genocide, which remains a trauma for the international community when dealing with the Great Lakes region.

Unintended consequences of attempts at transformation: from overt to covert violence

External actors' involvement with the conflict may have contributed to shifting the patterns of violence rather than doing away with them. The starting point for the international community's attempts at conflict prevention was a situation of manifest violence in the streets of Bujumbura, an attempted military coup and government crackdowns on opposition neighbourhoods and the freedom of expression. This picture has changed over the course of 2015–2016. The situation is not one where tensions have been removed and patterns of violence disappeared in favour of more 'constructive social ends', as Bramsen, Poder and Wæver call them. What we see instead is that violence has moved from overt to covert. Violence increasingly takes the form of arbitrary arrests and abductions of people who are then taken to unknown destinations, where they are sometimes allegedly executed in secret (Atrocities Watch – Africa 2017; FIDH

2016:51). The overt violence that remains has taken the form of an increase in targeted killings, including assassination of high-ranking officers as well as relatives of CNDD-FDD members. So when asked about the security situation in the country, one of the Burundian officials we interviewed exclaimed: 'just look out of the window. You see! Our country is safe'. The following day, Burundi's representative in the East African Legislative Assembly, Hafsa Mossi, was assassinated in the streets of Bujumbura (BBC 2016), presumably by opponents of the GoB.

While international efforts have been made to limit pre- and post-election violence in Burundi, it nonetheless continued throughout the period. What does, however, seem to be an unintended result of some of these endeavours – notably the presence of international observers – is that the GoB's application of violence has shifted to more covert forms that international monitors are ill equipped to report about, let alone to transform or predict a possible intensification of. It is much easier to verify violence in public spaces than in secret detention centres. In addition, after October 2016, the UN and AU observers did not have their safety guaranteed, so they were severely limited in moving around to collect information, which meant that they were effectively obstructed from providing the monitoring and reporting they were mandated to do, allowing the GoB to continue its violent policies with impunity.

So at the level of intensity of the violence, it is perhaps more correct to say that it has shifted rather than decreased; from being directed at large groups of demonstrators in the streets of Bujumbura, violence is now targeted at fewer individuals, but arguably in a more intense manner. The fear remains, of course, that the violence – which is now primarily directed at political figures on both sides – will turn ethnic and intensify both in terms of severity and number of victims. It is difficult to know if the situation would have been worse, or even different, without the outside involvement, but it is clear that all the consequences of engaging with the conflict had not been considered by the international community in advance.

Conclusion

This chapter has assessed the role of the international community in transforming the conflict in Burundi in 2015–2016. Mainly, the international community attempted to change the conflict situation by calling for political dialogue. In this process, the UN was sidelined in favour of granting a more prominent role to the EAC in the facilitation of a political dialogue. However, peace talks did not make any headway. The international organizations then attempted to change the interaction by insisting on making the political dialogue inclusive, in the sense that they requested the GoB to negotiate with the full spectrum of the opposition, which the government refused. Finally, the UN aimed to lower the level of tensions from the outset of the crisis. However, the result was not the emergence of a situation of less violence – in a certain sense, patterns of violence had shifted rather than lessened as violence continued albeit in other, less overt, forms. In short, the different international actors can be said to have acted in ways that aimed at producing the three effects recommended by Bramsen, Poder and Wæver in order to transform the conflict in Burundi.

The account offered in this chapter does not claim to provide an exhaustive overview of the international engagement in the crisis. Having addressed key efforts under the three headings of 'changing the situation', 'changing the interaction' and 'changing the level of tension', the chapter illustrated the difficulties that external actors faced when trying to pursue different strategies towards each of these dimensions of conflict transformation.

Although neither the UN nor any other external actors succeeded in resolving the conflict in the period analysed in this chapter, the conflict did nonetheless 'transform' – albeit not towards resolution and peaceful settlement. Instead, the transformations that we saw were that conflict shifted from public violence and open contestation and back to an uneasy and superficial calm, where violence was hidden away or took the form of political assassinations.

By early 2017, most of the international community had de facto resigned itself to acceptance of Nkurunziza's presidency, at least until 2020 when the next elections are scheduled. Then, to the surprise of observers and many UN officials, the latest UN envoy, Mr. Jamal Benomar as the Special Advisor of the Secretary-General for conflict prevention, including in Burundi, drafted a report on behalf of the Secretary-General that rekindled criticism of Nkurunziza. The report describes, for the first time in official UN documents, the presidency as a 'third term', which reflects the opposition's view that the presidency is unconstitutional. The report adds a warning about the danger of a possible 'fourth term' in the 2020 elections in case Nkurunziza succeeds in changing the constitutional term limit before that time (UN Secretary-General 2017). As could be expected, official reactions from the GoB were swift and sharp. Moreover, the constitution was changed by a referendum in May 2018, effectively opening an avenue for Nkurunziza to run again in 2020 and then for a term of seven years (Moore 2018).

This goes to show that the mixed results of UN preventive diplomacy, when seen as attempts at conflict transformation, left the UN unresolved about its own role. There was never full agreement on how to approach the crisis in Burundi among the various departments, funds and agencies, and the lack of clear failure or success exacerbated those internal divisions of the UN. The question of whether the engagement in Burundi represents a failure or success for prevention is still a question that excites debate inside the UN system. Some UN officials would say that the UN has failed because the underlying disagreements are still in place and the parties have not moved from antagonist to agonist positions. Others would say that the engagement has prevented the conflict from escalating even further, possibly into armed conflict along ethnic lines or even genocide. The latter argument suffers from the perpetual problem with ascertaining the effects of prevention, which is that any claim to success has to rest on counter-factual assertions. A conclusion is not likely to be reached, allowing the politicking to continue over which approach to conflict transformation the UN should pursue in Burundi, and possibly also vis-à-vis other conflict situations.

What can be said, however, is that if the international community had understood conflict prevention as a type of intervention – rather than as a neutral act of observation – this would have made it possible to plan attempts at conflict transformation that factored in the responses from the GoB.

Notes

1 The international community, including the UN, has been present in Burundi for decades. Moreover, our Burundian interviewees from both the government and opposition sides emphasize the importance of Burundi's history in understanding conflict dynamics in the country. This chapter, however, limits its scope to the crisis in 2015–2016 related to the presidential term, which has some distinct features, including a reconfigured international presence after the withdrawal of the UN peacekeeping operations (BNUB) at the end of 2014.

2 As the situation in Burundi remains tense at the time of writing, all interviewees are anonymized to minimize risks of reprisals.

3 In March 2016, EAC appointed Benjamin Mkapa 'to assist and facilitate the mediation led by Musenevi' (Vandeginste 2016:518).

4 Until 31 December 2014, the election support was part of the mandate of the United Nations Office in Burundi (BNUB). From 1 January 2015, the role was transferred to the United Nations Electoral Observation Mission in Burundi (MENUB).

5

> On 28 May, following an assessment of the electoral environment, EU announced that it had suspended its electoral observation mission to Burundi until the conditions for credible elections were met (...) on 7 May, the Chair of the African Union Commission, Nkosazana Dlamini-Zuma, stated that the prevailing situation in Burundi was not conducive to the holding of elections.
>
> *(MENUB 2015:14)*

References

Advisory Group of Experts (2015) *The Challenge of Sustaining Peace*. New York: United Nations.

Africanews (2016) *East African Community Appoints Mkapa as Mediator for Peace Talks in Burundi*. www.africanews.com/2016/03/03/east-african-community-appoints-mkapa-as-mediator-for-peace-talks-in-burundi// (accessed 11 May 2017).

African Union (2016) *Communique of the Visit of the African Union High Level Delegation to Burundi*. www.peaceau.org/uploads/com.burundi-25-26-02-2016.pdf (accessed 10 May 2017).

Atrocities Watch – Africa (2017) *Update 58 on Burundi*. www.atrocitieswatch.org/statements/168-update-58-on-burundi (accessed 11 May 2017).

BBC (2016) *Burundi Crisis: MP Hafsa Mossi Shot Dead in Bujumbura*. www.bbc.com/news/world-africa-36783069 (accessed 11 May 2017).

European Council (2016) *Article 96 of the Cotonou Agreement: Consultation Procedure*. www.consilium.europa.eu/en/policies/eu-africa/article-96-cotonou-agreement/ (accessed 11 May 2017).

Fabricius, Peter (2017) *Burundi Keeps Knocking at SADC's Door.* https://issafrica.org/iss-today/burundi-keeps-knocking-at-sadcs-door?utm_source=BenchmarkEmail&utm_campaign=ISS+Weekly&utm_medium=email (accessed 11 May 2017).

FIDH (2016) *Repression and Genocidal Dynamics in Burundi.* www.fidh.org/IMG/pdf/burundi_report_english-2.pdf (accessed 16 December 2016).

Government of Burundi (2016) *Declaration du Gouvernement Burundais sur la Collaboration et la Cooperation avec L'office du Haut Commissariat Des Droits de L'homme au Burundi.* www.burundi.gov.bi/spip.php?article1538 (accessed 10 May 2017).

Guardian (2016) *EU Suspends Aid to Burundi's Government.* www.theguardian.com/global-development/2016/mar/15/eu-suspends-aid-to-burundi-government (accessed 11 May 2017).

Human Rights Watch (2016) *SADC: Reverse Downward Slide on Rights.* www.hrw.org/news/2016/08/30/sadc-reverse-downward-slide-rights (accessed 15 May 2017).

Institute for Security Studies (2016) *Central Africa Report: The East African Community Takes on the Burundi Crisis.* https://issafrica.s3.amazonaws.com/site/uploads/car8-v2.pdf (accessed 15 May 2017).

IRIN (2016) *Briefing: What Next for the Burundi Peace Process?* www.irinnews.org/analysis/2016/01/04/briefing-what-next-burundi-peace-process (accessed 11 May 2017).

IWACU (2017) *Mkapa Calls for Extraordinary EAC Summit to Boost Inter-Burundian Dialogue.* www.iwacu-burundi.org/englishnews/mkapa-calls-for-extraordinary-eac-summit-to-boost-inter-burundian-dialogue/ (accessed 11 May 2017).

Jacobsen, Katja L. and Troels G. Engell (2017) *Strengthening and Renewing UN Peace Operations: Political and Practical Challenges Towards a Stronger UN.* Centre for Military Studies, University of Copenhagen. http://cms.polsci.ku.dk/english/publications/strengthening-and-renewing-un-peace-operations/CMS_Rapport_2017_Strengthening_and_renewing_UN_peace_operations.pdf (accessed 6 June 2017).

MENUB (2015) *Preliminary Statement on the Presidential Elections.* https://menub.unmissions.org/sites/default/files/francee.pdf (accessed 11 May 2017).

Moore, Jina (2018) *Burundi Voters Back Constitution Extending Presidential Term.* www.nytimes.com/2018/05/18/world/africa/burundi-constitution-referendum.html (accessed 20 June 2018)

OHCHR (2016) *Statement by Zeid Ra'ad Al Hussein, United Nations High Commissioner for Human Rights, on the Situation in Burundi.* www.ohchr.org/EN/NewsEvents/Pages/DisplayNews.aspx?NewsID=20215 (accessed 11 May 2017).

Reuters (2016) *Burundi Peace Talks Open in Tanzania with Opposition Criticism.* http://af.reuters.com/article/topNews/idAFKCN0YD08E (accessed 10 May 2017).

UNIIB (2016) *Final Report of the Mission of Independent Experts to Burundi,* A/HRC/33/37. www.ohchr.org/EN/HRBodies/HRC/RegularSessions/Session33/Pages/ListReports.aspx (accessed 16 May 2017).

UN Secretary-General (2015a) *Statement Attributable to the Spokesperson for the Secretary-General on Burundi.* www.un.org/sg/en/content/sg/statement/2015-05-23/statement-attributable-spokesperson-secretary-general-burundi-scroll (accessed 11 May 2017).

UN Secretary-General (2015b) *Report of the Secretary-General on the United Nations Electoral Observation Mission in Burundi.* S/2015/510.

UN Secretary-General (2017) *Report of the Secretary-General on Burundi.* S/2017/165.

UN Security Council (2015) *Security Council Resolution 2248 (2015).* S/RES/2248.

UN Security Council (2016a) *Security Council Resolution 2279 (2016).* S/RES/2279.

UN Security Council (2016b) *Security Council Resolution 2303 (2016).* S/RES/2303.

UN Security Council (2017) *7857th meeting.* S/PV.7857.

Vandeginste, Stef (2016) 'Museveni, Burundi and the Perversity of Immunite Provisoire', *International Journal of Transitional Justice* 10 (3): 516–526.

van Staden, Gary (2016) *SADC Intervention Needed in Mozambique*. www.cnbcafrica.com/news/southern-africa/2016/05/23/mozambique-regional-intervention-required/ (accessed 14 May 2017).

VOA News (2016) *Burundi Peace Talks Postponed*. www.voanews.com/a/burundi-peace-talks-repostponed/3131978.html (accessed 9 May 2017).

9

'NOTHING IS AGREED UNTIL EVERYTHING IS AGREED'

Institutionalizing *radical disagreement* and dealing with the past in Northern Ireland

Sara Dybris McQuaid

Introduction: the 'Northern Ireland model' of dealing with the past

In the early 1990s, Northern Ireland embarked on a peace process that would see it transition slowly from a society embroiled in protracted violent conflict to a conflict society emerging from violence. The political peace agreement that was finally reached in 1998 (Northern Ireland Office UK) after three decades of violence was the result of a negotiated compromise between the outwardly incommensurable positions of unionism and nationalism. This particular political transition is an example of how 'radical disagreement' (Ramsbotham 2010) has been institutionalized by enshrining both power sharing (between the main conflict parties) and guaranteeing future (diverging) constitutional aspirations. Both the key conflict parties and the key contradiction of the conflict have, thus, been locked in place to discontinue violence. The ongoing transition since 1998 has been fundamentally shaped by the order of this compromise.

In societies transitioning from conflict, the past is often an important source of continuing antagonism, although it can also be harnessed to form part of conflict transformation and reconciliation. In Northern Ireland, while a political constitutional compromise was reached 19 years ago, the government is yet to agree *and* implement a coordinated policy on dealing with the legacy of conflict, as the contested past continues to be a crucial reservoir for the formation of politico-cultural identities and ideologies for the future. Nevertheless, numerous initiatives have attempted to deal with Northern Ireland's past. Indeed, this chapter argues that a peculiar 'Northern Ireland model' of dealing with a violent past is emerging: a model of fits and starts in which institutionalized conflict is both shaped by and giving shape to piecemeal interventions. Rather than the result of consistent strategy or premeditated design, the model is pluralistic, complex, at times contradictory and appearing through accumulated, disparate attempts at dealing with the past.

The chapter starts by laying out Oliver Ramsbotham's (2010) notion of radical disagreement and the associated concept of agonistic dialogue as theoretical perspectives on the Northern Ireland case. The chapter then argues that the transitional status of Northern Ireland is fundamentally ambiguous: it is effectively still 'in process'. This process is impacted by shifting political landscapes (local and national) of the past 20 years together with the changing norms of international peacebuilding aimed at conflict transformation and reconciliation. It is argued that the paradigm clash of these terms, radical disagreement and ambiguous transition fundamentally shape political developments and dialogues in Northern Ireland and not least its initiatives for dealing with the past.

The following section turns to the question of dealing with the past in the context of a radical disagreement and policy vacuum like Northern Ireland. It discusses a few of the various initiatives that look to do so in part through the *kinds* of truth they aim to uncover and the justice to which they hope to aspire. It draws on two emblematic cases of dealing with the past in Northern Ireland, the Belfast Project at Boston College and the Bloody Sunday Inquiry, to illustrate how radical disagreement and ambiguous transition shape the opportunities for dealing with the past as well as how these initiatives themselves shape future policies for the past. The chapter proceeds to reflect on the dialogues between existing initiatives and policy. These dialogues increasingly also take place between 'track 1' and 'track 2', as official policy discourses and societal initiatives bump and blend in the contradictions between radical disagreement and transformative and reconciliatory discourses. Finally, I gather these points in a discussion of the Northern Ireland model, suggesting its possibilities and limitations for the promotion of reconciliation.

Radical disagreement and agonistic dialogue

The following section draws on Oliver Ramsbotham's (2010) definition of radical disagreement, and I forward the peace agreement of 1998 in Northern Ireland as an example of the institutionalization of what has long been considered to be the radical disagreement there. According to Ramsbotham (2010:166), a radical disagreement occurs when parties refuse to distinguish positions from interests and needs; when they object to reframing competition into shared problem-solving or reshape adversarial debate into constructive controversy; in short, when there is no conceptual or emotional capacity for mutual understanding or fusion of horizons. As in other conflicts, this is referred to in Northern Ireland as a zero-sum game. While much research in the conflict resolution field tries to shift or overcome radical disagreement, Ramsbotham suggests that we linger with it as the object to explore, understand and manage.

The conflict in and over Northern Ireland has long been understood to centre around questions of identity (ethnic and national) and allegiance (ethnic and national), that is, in constitutional terms whether Northern Ireland, and the people living there, should (legitimately) be recognized as British or Irish. The peace agreement of 1998 recognized and gave credence to this key radical disagreement by enshrining the right to pursue diverging national aspirations based on the principle of democratic consent (Northern Ireland Office UK 1998: Constitutional Issues).

Enshrining radical disagreement on constitutional futures has been accompanied by what we may call the institutionalization of *agonistic dualism*. I develop the term from Mouffe's (1999) notion of 'agonistic pluralism', which she coined as an alternative to ideas of 'deliberative democracy'. Agonistic pluralism could transform 'enemies' into 'adversaries' without eliminating antagonism. As such, the primary task of democratic politics is not to eliminate passions but to mobilize them towards the promotion of democratic designs (Mouffe 1999:755-756). In Northern Ireland, agonistic dualism was entrenched in power-sharing institutions but without the pluralism Mouffe conceived. Rather, only two political positions count, as exemplified in how assembly members are required to designate their political identities as either 'unionist, nationalist or other'. This principle of designation underlies safeguards such as parallel consent, weighted majorities and cross-community support for policymaking (where 'others' do not enjoy any of the minority safeguards). The system of designated power sharing therefore goes beyond acknowledging the dimensions of power and antagonism in Northern Ireland (as agonistic pluralism would) to privileging two positions and their accompanying discourses constitutionally, thus removing them from the political by enshrining their politics.

In effect, this means that radical disagreement on ends persists, while agreement on means (democracy and non-violence) has been reached. This is what Ramsbotham (2010:165) calls 'extremism of ends rather than means'. In the framework of this book, one might argue that the interaction has shifted from violent to non-violent or political, while the situation of contradiction and tension remains. Although these elements of radical disagreement were essential to the compromise reached in 1998, taken together they obviously give rise to a number of challenges for would-be policy- and history-makers, as the present status quo is accepted at once as threshold and steady state and partisan perspectives are locked into power. Furthermore, in terms of dealing with the past, there is little consensus on the causes and drivers of conflict. In order to grapple further with understanding the difficulties of coming to terms with the past, we might consider a slightly different conceptualization of agonism by Ramsbotham to think about the status quo ante (as before the peace agreement). While Mouffe's conception of agonism sees violent antagonism 'domesticated' within the democratic agon, Ramsbotham (2010:94) suggests that 'agonistic dialogue' is the dialogue of intense political struggle without trying to distinguish from the outset between domesticated (non-violent) and undomesticated (violent) varieties. One of the main difficulties in attempts to deal with the past in Northern Ireland, before political agreement, is considering the status of violence and victims of violence without making this distinction. Peace thus remains fragile, perched on a certain bracketing of the past and future, with severe consequences for policy and reconciliation processes.

Ambiguous transition towards reconciliation

A basic observation is that any political peace agreement is only ever a starting point for an equally difficult transitional process of reconciliation in which the past looms large. The Agreement has reordered the Northern Irish political, but the parameters of politics have also been reconstructed by the ongoing transition. As we return to below, the navigation of forms of truth and justice is essential to the Northern Ireland model of dealing with the past. As Teitel suggests, 'the conception of justice in periods of political change is extraordinary and constructivist' (2000:6), both constituted by and constitutive of transition. The constructivism of the transition often flows uneasily against the fixtures of the Agreement.

The status of Northern Ireland as a transitional society is ambiguous. Is the country transitioning from war to peace? From dictatorship to democracy? From anarchy to rule of law? Different transitions obviously promote different approaches to dealing with the past and constructing the future. In the case of Northern Ireland, the answers to these questions are 'both and', 'not quite' and 'in a manner of speaking': it is not a 'paradigmatic transition' (Campbell and Ni Aolain 2005). The Northern Ireland conflict has been more of a low-intensity conflict than a war. There was no real dictatorship, although the unionist hegemony (1920–1972) and British Direct Rule (1972–1998) certainly had a heavy democratic deficit. Nor was it total anarchy, even if the monopoly on violence was breached throughout. This ambiguous state of affairs complicates the choice of appropriate measures, and the settlement of the conflict by compromise compounds the dilemma. Furthermore, the period of transition is not defined in temporal terms (i.e. a number of years) or in a particular moment of completion (as some issues were left outstanding and extremism of ends persists). In effect, this means that 20 years after the Agreement, Northern Ireland is still 'in progress'. During those 20 years, however, the political landscape in which the Agreement originally stood has shifted radically. This is true in terms of the 'internal' power balances in which Sinn Féin (SF) and the Democratic Unionist Party (DUP) have emerged as the largest parties as well as in terms of national developments in the UK and Ireland, where the DUP and SF have become important players in much more fragmented political cultures. International norms regarding peacebuilding have also changed since the Agreement was reached in 1998, including a sharpened focus on transitional justice (Teitel 2008), 'the local' (Mac Ginty and Richmond 2013), women in peacebuilding (UN 2000, S/RES/1325) and a focus on memorialization and inclusive historical dialogues (Barsalou 2014; Barsalou and Baxter 2007; UN Human Rights Council 2014, A/HRC/28/36).

Following Vandeginste and Sriram (2011), Northern Ireland might be said to have come to epitomize a clash of paradigms, that is, a guiding principle from the early part of the peace process in Northern Ireland has focused on ending violence by giving power-sharing incentives to warring parties in institutionalizing radical disagreement. At the same time, the shifting political and peacebuilding contexts and norms outlined earlier at once attend to and challenge this principle. In line with normative developments in global human rights discourses, for example, internationally brokered peace processes often incorporate mechanisms for dealing with past abuses as a path towards reconciliation. Forms of transitional justice have thus become a steadily more critical framework for post-conflict processes. As Teitel goes on to suggest, 'its normative effects are now seen as having the potential of fostering the rule of law and security on the ground' (2008:3). However, these effects may easily come in to conflict with the structures of radical disagreement. Indeed, the growing tensions between these two paradigms of radical disagreement and ambiguous transition are unsettling the shift from low-intensity war to precarious peace and have come to characterize what I call the 'Northern Ireland model'.

This clash of paradigms operates on different scales. In crude terms, we might claim that the principles of power sharing, radical disagreement and agonism have guided the political agreements and interactions in 'track 1' negotiations, while ideas derived from a developing paradigm of transitional justice have increasingly guided the processes of societal reconstruction and reconciliation in 'track 2' diplomacy at the societal level (Mapendere 2005). As presented in the next section, trying to avoid the clash – or obvious incongruence – between these two paradigms has involved trying to distinguish between different kinds of truth and justice in dealing with the past.

Dealing with the past in Northern Ireland

The 1998 peace agreement was preceded and shaped by a number of failed or partial agreements over a 30-year period (McQuaid 2009). Questions of the past (understood as root causes of conflict) echoed throughout this period. Indeed, the institutionalization of radical disagreement in Northern Ireland precisely seeks to tether these issues rather than resolve them within an overarching framework. Partly therefore, coming to terms with the past is also becoming an accumulated process of partially (or yet to be) implemented policy proposals. A number of comprehensive 'legacy architectures' have been proposed (The Consultative Group on the Past 2009; Haass and O'Sullivan 2013; the Stormont House Agreement 2014) but have failed to gain political and community consensus around issues of victims; national symbols, national security and historical justice. I return to this later.

Despite the lack of an overarching framework for dealing with the legacy of conflict, numerous initiatives have been launched on issues relating to past transgressions in Northern Ireland, both at the state and societal levels, to respond to the growing demands from victim and survivor groups: there have been official inquiries, human rights reports, public consultations, storytelling and oral history projects, memorial art and architecture and proposals for a 'legacy' or a 'truth and reconciliation' commission, all to recover from and redress the conflict (see McEvoy 2013; McEvoy and McGregor 2008).

Unsurprisingly, these various initiatives have different concerns and objectives and have emerged in the shifting circumstances of Northern Ireland's ambiguous transition. At the heart of many of these initiatives is an ambition to 'get to the truth about what happened' in order to have some form of recognition, justice and closure to move beyond conflict. However, not only are there different forms of truths to be recovered, there are also simply different versions of truth. This becomes especially evident and problematic in relation to establishing shared truths in divided societies. Similarly, the underlying motivations for 'getting to the truth' may rest on differing conceptions of justice. Navigating various forms of truth and justice in a context where the status of both is indeterminate insofar as an overarching framework may be introduced to capture them differently in the future is another particular characteristic of the Northern Ireland model. Part of this navigation is also to steer a course between 'micro-truths' (i.e. specifics of particular cases) and 'macro-truths' (contexts, causes and patterns) (Chapman and Ball 2001). These levels may be difficult to connect (but can also be difficult to separate) and might also require different forms of justice.

In Northern Ireland, different initiatives have pursued distinct lines and levels of 'truth inquiry'[1] and dispensations of justice. For instance, social truths have been pursued in public inquiries, and restorative truths have been searched for in public consultations aimed at locating the overarching mechanisms, provisions and discourses that may receive sufficient support from all sides. Establishing the forensic truths of individual cases has been pursued by state agents, such as the now defunct Historical Enquiries Team (under the Police Service Northern Ireland), as well as by human rights organizations and other NGOs. While forensic truths amount to evidence in individual cases and may lead to criminal justice, they are established at the micro level and, taken separately, might not necessarily alter the macro narrative of the conflict. In the same category of micro truths are narrative truths, which are defined as personal primary accounts of experiences. Allowing voices that have been suppressed or silenced to be restored to dignity has been the focus of much work done by victim and survivor organizations in Northern Ireland. Beyond the victim organizations, oral history and storytelling projects have become a prevalent form of capturing the voices of a plethora of actors as well as both the everyday and extraordinary aspects of the conflict (Hamber and Kelly 2016; McQuaid 2016). The EU programme for Peace and Reconciliation (Peace III) has awarded funding for a plethora of these projects, run by local community groups, recognizing that this approach to dealing with the past is one of the few to enjoy widespread popular support (McClelland 2002). While such stories offer anecdotal evidence, the myriad memories have the capacity to continuously challenge singular and hegemonic histories emerging over time in what remains an ambiguous transition in which political parties struggle to control the narratives of conflict and peace. However, these kinds of oral history projects have been impacted by the explosive developments of the Belfast Project at Boston College. The Belfast Project had collected life stories from the rank and file of paramilitary organizations for the historical record, but they were subpoenaed by law enforcements agencies in Northern Ireland to be used in potential trials. This slippage from narrative to forensic truth also entailed a shift in the status of the historical witnesses relied on as sources; they went from being protected sources to being named and liable.

The repercussions of the Belfast Project extend beyond the legal realm, however. While universities and researchers are presently much warier of the ethical and legal implications of doing conflict-related oral history, storytelling projects in Northern Ireland still abound; indeed, they have been embraced in policy discourses, as described later. However, the fate of the Belfast Project has had consequences for the kinds of narrative truths people want to share in such projects and so for the kinds of justice to which they can aspire as a result. Already, the firm focus on 'reconciling communities' and 'build[ing] positive relations at the local level' in the European PEACE III funding stipulates a significant boundary in terms of what can be remembered and how micro narratives can be articulated and weave their way into official macro discourses (McQuaid 2016). The Boston College case illustrates how an initiative purportedly serving the function of gathering narrative truths of former combatants for future reflection can be employed to establish forensic truths and dispense criminal justice (in subpoenaing and using these autobiographical narratives as legal evidence), with very real consequences for the course of the peace process.

While storytelling projects are concerned with allowing pluri-vocal accounts to coexist, other instruments of dealing with the past are concerned with explicitly reconfiguring the myriad of myths and veiled truths into definitive and singular accounts. An example is the Saville Tribunal, which was tasked with bringing private, public and official accounts of what happened on Bloody Sunday into sync: to establish, once and for all, the authoritative social truth about the events of 30 January 1972, when an anti-internment march organized by the Northern Ireland Civil Rights Association in Derry ended with 14 civilians shot dead by British paratroopers. When the report was published in 2010 after a 12-year inquiry, the Bloody Sunday Inquiry arguably managed to connect the micro and macro levels of recovering and establishing the truth about what happened in Derry on 30 January 1972, that is, providing forensic details of the individual event whilst also passing historical judgement on the broader importance of it (Saville 2010).

However, while the conclusions in the final report manage to engage with the macro level in terms of context and consequences, it has been argued that there is no higher consideration of patterns and structures in terms of, for example, security policy (see Ó Dochartaigh 2010). However, it is only possible to establish such patterns of systemic abuse or excessive use of violence by state forces if more, similar events were treated to the same thorough examination, which has been ruled out. While the Saville Inquiry succeeded in bridging different forms of truth and its findings resulted in an official apology from British Prime Minister David Cameron (2010), it was immediately announced that there would be no more open-ended inquiries like it. Additionally, some of the families wanted the inquiry not to be a substitute, but rather a precursor for criminal charges. The evidence emerging from the inquiry now forms part of a fresh probe into the killings, which has led to further contestations around the prosecution of former British soldiers. Veterans' associations, which have not otherwise been a conspicuous part of legacy debates, have recently held rallies against what they term a 'legal witch hunt' (Farmer, Belfast Telegraph 2017) in England, Scotland and Northern Ireland. They have been backed by British Prime Minister Theresa May, who, in a letter to army veterans, called the approach to dealing with the past in Northern Ireland 'unbalanced' (Morrison, BBC 2017) and by the Secretary of State for Northern Ireland, who said that investigations 'disproportionately' focused on the police and the army. This case illustrates both the enormous costs in time and the money involved in attempting to create shared accounts of the past in a context of radical disagreement as well as how these accounts have wider political consequences.

These brief examples underscore how struggles between past and present, justice and truth, are not merely about the legitimacy of the political order but also fundamentally regulated by resources in changing political economies. Dealing with the past also means dealing with radical disagreement in the shifting contexts of ambiguous transitions compounded by the lack of an overall policy framework.

Policies on the past between radical disagreement, ambiguous transition and reconciliation

Every new initiative for dealing with the past evolves at once in dialogue with previous initiatives but also in correspondence with unfolding events and the underlying political economy of the peace processes. In policy discussions about how to address the legacy of the violent past, there have been understandable concerns about how diverse processes could be suitably balanced, that is, not just between prosecution and reconciliation, truth and justice, recognition and reparation, but also between state and society and between communities. Part of coming to terms with the past is understood as the duty to rewrite the historical account to unearth and include what has been buried in the past, or even to rewrite the history of the nation in light of a new order and construct a shared account (Teitel 2000). This is a particularly complex task in protracted ethno-national conflicts marked by radical disagreement, where there are precious few shared frames, discourses and concepts – not least in relation to who and what historically constitutes the nation. As McGrattan argues, '(in Northern Ireland) [...] the past is used in many ways to mobilize political support in the present and power bases are constructed and maintained through the careful guardianship of historical narratives' (2009:166). In this respect, it is questionable whether major protagonists in the conflict can be objective facilitators of the establishment of a shared historical record, whether by narrative or legal mechanisms. This caution obviously extends to British and Irish state actors.

Still, a number of policy initiatives have attempted to navigate the tensions between institutionalized radical disagreement, ambiguous transition and a desire for reconciliation on and through the past. While the Agreement (1998) did not consider how to deal with the legacy of the conflict in institutional terms, the Consultative Group on the Past (2009) proposed establishing a legacy commission akin to a truth and reconciliation commission. However, objections that such a process might on the one hand be shunned by the paramilitaries (having been released under the terms of the peace agreement and perhaps refusing to criminalize themselves and delegitimize their actions) or on the other be a 'one-sided attempt to re-write history in a way that puts the RUC, the PSNI and our Armed Forces on the same footing as terrorists' (Paterson 2010) meant that this suggestion was rejected.

Nevertheless, in subsequent initiatives, a flexible architecture of legacy mechanisms was further pursued. This is where operational elements of the Northern Ireland model start to become clearer. In both the Haass/O'Sullivan talks (2013) and the Stormont House Agreement (2014), holistic and fractionalized approaches operate at the same time. The Haass/O'Sullivan proposals were holistic in the sense that they envisaged how to institutionalize multiple processes of dealing with the past at once whilst also compartmentalizing different forms of truth recovery and redress. Three mechanisms were proposed: the first was a historical investigations unit to deal with forensic evidence and criminal justice – a cold case squad akin to the Historical Enquiries Team established in 2005, and wound up in 2014. The second was an Independent Commission for Information Retrieval, which would deal in forms of limited immunity to increase the availability of information (including information from perpetrators volunteering further information) and assess broader themes and patterns. In other words, connecting micro and macro truths to offer a societal context for more detailed individual accounts. Recognizing the prevailing agonistic dualism, the Haass/O'Sullivan proposals made clear that the establishment of broader themes 'should not be suggested to pursue or protect narrow or vested interests. Nor should they be assumed to reflect the statistical reality of patterns of violence during the conflict' (Haass and O'Sullivan 2013:2). This last sentence should be seen in relation to discrete definitions of violence. In flat numbers, security forces were responsible for 10% of deaths, loyalist paramilitaries 30% and republican paramilitaries 60% (McKittrick 2001). If a guiding definition of victims of violence was to address only victims of direct violence, any mechanism to deal with the violent past might reflect these proportions, putting the onus on the acts of the paramilitary organizations. If violence was conceived in broader terms, however (i.e. as not only direct, but also structural and cultural) (Galtung 1990), it would also reflect culpability diffused between paramilitaries and the state. Furthermore, a narrow definition of violence attributed according to the scale introduced earlier would not address allegations of collusion between security forces and paramilitaries uncovered by successive inquiries (Stevens 2003). It remains the case that political unionists broadly support a narrow definition of violence (Lawther 2012), whereas republicans and nationalists advocate a much broader definition of violence in addressing issues of truth and justice. In other words, radical disagreement extends to the very conceptual terms of inquiries into the past.

The third and final suggestion was for the creation of an online archive for conflict-related oral histories to record individual experiences. The proposal stipulates that contributions to the archive will not be fact-checked, validated or corroborated and should not be relied on for 'truth' without further research and analysis. In this vein, the archive is conceived as a repository for first-hand accounts and narrative truths, preserving the past for the future and leaving the correlation and corroboration of accounts to the historians. It also obviously responds to the rise in oral history and storytelling projects described earlier.

The Stormont House Agreement of 2014 sets out the same three institutions: a Historical Investigation Unit (HIU), Independent Commission for Information Retrieval (ICIR) and an Oral History Archive (OHA). As opposed to the Haass/O'Sullivan document, however, there is an explicit and repeated line stipulating that these institutions need to operate in a way that is 'balanced, proportionate, transparent, fair and equal' and that these key principles should ensure that the new institutions 'must not seek to re-write history [...]' (Northern Ireland Office UK SHA 2014:6).

Further along these lines, the mechanisms for bridging individual cases and macro history are watered down significantly, as the ICIR will not provide an interpretive framework for the evidence collected. There seems to be a widespread perception that a process of truth recovery will work to the advantage of anti-state narratives (Lawther 2012; *cf.* Edwards 2012); this is further reflected in recent parliamentary debates in the House of Commons (Debate Pack 2017), which obviously has consequences for the establishment of cross-community support for policies on the past.

The most often-used principle to describe the 1996–1998 talks leading to the peace agreement in Northern Ireland is that 'Nothing is agreed until everything is agreed'. In the negotiation and mediation literature, this is sometimes understood to be a philosophical approach highlighting how the parties should feel free to generate all sorts of ideas and not be bound by any one of them until there is an agreement on all of the issues in question (Weiss and Rosenberg 2003). That is, the creation of an imaginative space to make room for manoeuvring beyond intractability. The principle was applied in a much more limited way in Northern Ireland, however, where it became more a case of linking or conjoining issues to settle them together: a mutual construction, obstruction and destruction clause, where each set of issues would have a champion. In this respect, it resembles the agonistic dialogue that goes with radical disagreement. As described later, the maxim of 'Nothing is agreed until everything is agreed' has been extended to political talks and policies about dealing with the past. Mirroring the political economy of the earlier peace process, multiple issues of culture and commemoration, dealing with the past, victims and reparation and even welfare reform have been bound together for joint solution (or mutual obstruction) in both the Haass/O'Sullivan talks and the Stormont House Agreement.

In the Haass/O'Sullivan talks, the conjoined issues pointed to the cultural struggles beyond the constitutional settlement. It was exceptionally difficult to move forward on two areas in the talks: one was on defining victims and the other was about which flags to fly, when and where. A year after the 'Flags Protest' (see Nolan et al. 2014), the Haass/O'Sullivan report recognized flags as symbols of sovereignty and identity, stating that 'without a larger consensus on the place of Britishness and Irishness a common position could not be reached'. In this respect, the radical disagreement (on the future constitutional status of Northern Ireland) at the heart of the agreement was offered as an explanation in the areas where agreement could not be reached.

In the Stormont House Agreement, the deadlocked political issue of welfare reform (introduced by the UK government) was added to the bundle. Here, 'welfare reform' as such was not an 'outstanding issue' in the peace process but entangled in the political culture of radical disagreement and government by brink politics. In this respect, the constitutional compromise allows political actors to hold the past hostage to the present with serious ramifications for recipients of policies on the past and reconciliation in the future.

Looking at this chain of texts in relation to the cases in the previous section, it becomes clear that the ongoing policy proposals presented here respond to emerging problems in the existing processes of dealing with the past by explicitly trying to establish a fixed relationship between categories of materials and levels of analysis: between forensic truths that can lead to criminal justice, social truths that can lead to restorative justice and narrative truths that may lead to historical justice.

Obviously, it would be naïve to think that historical dialogues can be neatly contained like this by writing out politics. As amply illustrated, mechanisms for dealing with the past can be politicized by vested interests, particularly when the future remains legitimately contested – in this context, there can be no retraining of the focus on the future, no fusion of horizons. Furthermore, attempts at separating different strands of truth recovery do not yield neat results, just as cordoning off various kinds of truth and justice may also fail, as distinguishable intentions and results bleed into rather than support each other. While this is hardly surprising, it is even more pertinent in a peace process where the political structures run on a continuum that fudges both the past and the future. The past remains volatile and is variously incorporated and consolidated by unionist and nationalist politicians into discordant constitutional political ambitions for the future. This contradiction continuity rather than discontinuity is haunting the process of dealing with the past in Northern Ireland.

In the Consultative Group on the Past, the Haass/O'Sullivan talks and the Stormont House Agreement, attempts at restorative justice clash with diverging social truths as well as with resistance to the transitional justice paradigm itself, which is feared to relativize, distort and possibly untether the past with consequences for the system of institutionalized radical disagreement. Partisan interests (material, cultural, social and spatial as well as political and constitutional) remain alongside international norms, and power-sharing works to compound them. Indeed, as we have seen, what I have called the Northern Ireland model very much emerges in this patchwork of processes of transnational justice, the peace agreement that frames it, and the local, partisan resistances to and negotiations with them.

Conclusion: the 'Northern Ireland model' of dealing with the past

As I have shown, dealing with the past in Northern Ireland has thus far been a fragmented process – not least because a comprehensive approach has proven a precarious political exercise in what remains a divided society. The spectrum of available stable rigging points is of course circumscribed by the immediate context, including the particular transition in question and the implicit hierarchies of truth and justice, with constitutional justice placed at the very top in Northern Ireland.

In many ways, an alternative incremental and proliferated approach can then be positive in a context of institutionalized radical disagreement, as it allows a degree of pluri-vocality and may be driven by both state agencies and civil society, by a mixture of universal and communitarian principles.

This is what we might call the 'Northern Ireland Model': an increasingly conscious process of addendum where important lines of enquiry into the past can be established and dealt with in multiple ways, even in default of comprehensive frameworks. In the absence of an all-encompassing architecture of dealing with the past, this 'Northern Ireland model' has nevertheless emerged, consisting of disparate policies and institutions, each invested in bringing particular forms of truth and justice to the fore. It is tempting to think of this in relation to Oakeshott's idea of a 'dry stone wall' (1999:102–103), a structure built by cobbling together antecedent and subsequent initiatives so as to layer and fit the right shapes into each other, thereby composing an organic structure. In Oakeshott's metaphor, the design of the wall is not premeditated but comes into view as a result of what the components constitute in touching. The components of the Northern Ireland model are not inert stones, however, but rather dynamic figures constituted by and constitutive of the particular and changing political realities in Northern Ireland – including shifting norms in international peacebuilding that test the core premises of the original peace agreement. The wall is built on unstable ground in which the latest tectonic shift is Brexit, which has brought the bracketed national, territorial question into full political consciousness again. The Northern Ireland model is, thus, a rather more precarious structure than the drystone wall imagined in Oakeshott's metaphor; nevertheless, it models a de facto approach to dealing with the past.

The requirements for reconciliation as formulated by Ramsbotham, Miall and Woodhouse (2011:251) entail sufficient consensus around the legitimacy of the rule of law, correlation of accounts of conflict and bridging of differences. These preconditions are not fully present in Northern Ireland, and attempts at dealing with the past have precisely foundered on some of them. Nevertheless, the Northern Ireland model has promoted the end of direct sectarian violence and allowed for imaginative community responses to come to terms with the past at many levels if not comprehensively in politics and policy. Furthermore, this model has arguably enabled a form of agonistic pluralism in the Mouffian sense as societal actors have ventured beyond the dualism in the agreement and even conducted agonistic dialogues in Ramsbotham's sense inasmuch as initiatives have not entirely distinguished between those inside and outside of the democratic agon.

What the future holds for the Northern Ireland model and indeed for the possibilities for reconciliation remains unclear. The preconditions Ramsbotham and colleagues raise are all increasingly in question. Challenges to the legitimacy of agents upholding the rule of law (state-led initiatives and indeed the British state itself) continue to exist, as does anger about former paramilitaries in political offices. Furthermore, the compromise that was supposed to deliver constitutional justice has thus far failed to deliver policies on the past and has been thoroughly shaken by the referendum on EU membership in 2016 and the collapse of the power-sharing executive in Northern Ireland in early 2017. As such, sufficient consensus on democratic legitimacy is no longer self-evident. Moreover, insufficient consensus prevails on the correlation of conflict accounts to create agreeable narratives even to define a category eligible for victims' services (with severe consequences for social justice) or what kind of language should be employed to describe violence (i.e. the omission of the word 'terrorism' in the Haass proposal was a sore point). In relation to bridging differences to deliver justice in the future, the discording constitutional aspirations obscure the horizon. While the Agreement (1998) supposedly provided a new framework for legitimate government, it was more a constitutional recognition of different aspirations than a full acknowledgement of anchored legitimacy. The Agreement not only recognized the main groups in Northern Ireland as culture bearers of different pasts and presents but also futures. While this was good for making peace, it is bad for making shared policies.

The primacy of constitutional justice in terms of institutionalizing radical disagreement by enshrining power sharing and recognizing future national aspirations has thus created a 'holding pattern' rather than a robust structure. This holding pattern is in continuous tension with the ambiguous status of Northern Irish transition and the ongoing shifts in political landscapes and peacebuilding norms shaping the possibilities for dealing with the past as well as for reconciliation more broadly. Placing mutually exclusive aspirations at the heart of the peace agreement has made it difficult to integrate micro and macro truths of the past, provide an immediate sense of justice in the present and project a shared future. In these terms, Northern Ireland is also a model of continuation of conflict by other means. That which also emerges from this, however, is a peculiar Northern Ireland model for dealing with the past, circumscribed and politically volatile, but also potentially fostering the sorts of agonistic pluralism beyond the dualism that have largely been locked in place by what was considered the necessary institutionalization of radical disagreement.

Note

1 The following categories of truth are taken from the Truth and Reconciliation Commission in South Africa. The categories were derived from the evidence and testimonies from thousands of victims of Apartheid. In a post hoc analysis, these statements were divided into four categories of 'truths' (forensic, narrative, social and restorative), which served different purposes and could be pursued in different ways (Truth and Reconciliation Commission of South Africa 1998).

References

Barsalou, Judy (2014) 'Reflecting the Fractured Past: Memorialization, Transitional Justice and the Role of Outsiders', in Susanne Buckley-Zistel and Stefanie Schafer (Eds.), *Memorials in Times of Transition* (47–65), Cambridge: Intersentia.

Barsalou, Judy and Victoria Baxter (2007) 'The Urge to Remember: The Role of Memorials in Social Reconstruction and Transitional Justice', *Stabilization and Reconstruction Series* 5: 1–22.

Cameron, David (2010) *House of Commons Hansard Debates for 15 June 2010.* www.publications.parliament.uk/pa/cm201011/cmhansrd/cm100615/debtext/100615-0004.htm (accessed 21 June 2017).

Campbell, Colm and Fionnuala Ni Aolain (2005) 'The Paradox of Transition in Conflicted Democracies', *Human Rights Quarterly* 27 (1): 172–213.

Chapman, Audrey R. and Patrick Ball (2001) 'Truth of Truth Commissions: Comparative Lessons from Haiti, South Africa, and Guatemala', *Human Rights Quarterly* 23 (1): 1–43.

Debate Pack (2017) 'Implementation of the Stormont House Agreement' Number CDP-2017-0008, House of Commons Library. http://researchbriefings.parliament.uk/ResearchBriefing/Summary/CDP-2017-0008 (accessed 15 May 2017).

Edwards, Aaron (2012) 'Fearful of the Past or "Remembering the Future and Our Cause"? A Response to Cheryl Lawther', *Irish Political Studies* 27 (3): 457–470.

Farmer, Ben (2017) *Veterans Stage Protest over Troubles 'Witch-hunt'.* www.telegraph.co.uk/news/2017/04/14/veterans-stage-protest-troubles-witch-hunt/ (accessed 22 June 2017).

Galtung, Johan (1990) *60 Speeches on War and Peace.* Oslo: PRIO.

Haass, Richard and Meghan O'Sullivan (2013) *The Haass Report: Office of the First Minister and Deputy First Minister.* www.northernireland.gov.uk/sites/default/files/publications/newnigov/haass-report-2013.pdf (accessed 21 June 2017).

Hamber, Brandon and Grainne Kelly (2016) 'Practice, Power and Inertia: Personal Narrative, Archives and Dealing with the Past in Northern Ireland', *Journal of Human Rights Practice* 8 (1): 25–44.

Lawther, Cheryl (2012) 'Denial, Silence and the Politics of the Past: Unpicking the Opposition to Truth Recovery in Northern Ireland', *International Journal of Transitional Justice* 7 (1): 157–177.

Lord Saville of Newdigate (2010) *Report of the Bloody Sunday Inquiry*, Volume I [Saville Report]. TSO. www.gov.uk/government/uploads/system/uploads/attachment_data/file/279133/0029_i.pdf (accessed 21 June 2017).

Mac Ginty, Roger and Oliver P. Richmond (2013) 'The Local Turn in Peace Building: A Critical Agenda for Peace', *Third World Quarterly* 34 (5): 763–783.

Mapendere, Jeffrey (2005) 'Track One and a Half Diplomacy and the Complementarity of Tracks', *Culture of Peace Online Journal* 2 (1): 66–81.

McClelland, Roy (2002) *Healing through Remembering: The Report of the Healing through Remembering Project*. http://healingthroughremembering.org/wp-content/uploads/2015/11/HTR-Report-2002.pdf (accessed 21 June 2017).

McEvoy, Kieran (2013) *Dealing with the Past? An Overview of Legal and Political Approaches Relating to the Conflict in and about Northern Ireland*. http://healingthroughremembering.org/wp-content/uploads/2015/11/Dealing-with-the-Past_2013.pdf (accessed 21 June 2017).

McEvoy, Kieran and Lorna McGregor (2008) 'Transitional Justice from Below: An Agenda for Research, Policy and Praxis', in Kieran McEvoy and Lorna McGregor (Eds.), *Transitional Justice from Below* (15–45), Oxford: Hart Publishing.

McGrattan, Cillian (2009) '"Order Out of Chaos": The Politics of Transitional Justice', *Politics* 29 (3): 164–172.

McKittrick, David (2001) *Lost Lives: The Stories of the Men, Women and Children Who Died as a Result of the Northern Ireland Troubles*. New York: Random House.

McQuaid, Sara Dybris (2009) *Ideas as Practicalities: A Discursive Exploration of the Relationship between Academic Output and Conflict Resolution in Northern*. Belfast: Queen's University Belfast.

McQuaid, Sara Dybris (2016) 'Passive Archives or Storages for Action? Storytelling Projects in Northern Ireland', *Irish Political Studies* 31 (3): 63–85.

Morrison, Catherine (2017) 'System for Dealing with NI's Past "Unbalanced", Says Theresa May'. *BBC*. www.bbc.com/news/uk-northern-ireland-39269468 (Accessed 15 May 2017).

Mouffe, Chantal (1999) 'Deliberative Democracy or Agonistic Pluralism?', *Social Research* 66 (3): 745–758.

Nolan, Paul, Dominic Bryan, Clare Dwyer, Katy Hayward, Katy Radford and Peter Shirlow (2014) *The Flag Dispute: Anatomy of a Protest*. http://pure.qub.ac.uk/portal/files/13748797/The_Flag_Dispute_report_PRINTED.pdf (accessed 21 June 2017).

Northern Ireland Office UK (1998) *The Belfast Agreement*. www.gov.uk/government/publications/the-belfast-agreement (accessed 21 June 2017).

Northern Ireland Office UK (2014) *The Stormont House Agreement*. www.gov.uk/government/publications/the-stormont-house-agreement (Accessed 15 May 2017).Oakeshott, Michael (1999) *On History*. Indianapolis, IN: Liberty Fund.

Ó Dochartaigh, Niall (2010) 'Bloody Sunday: Error or Design?', *Contemporary British History* 24 (1): 89–108.

Paterson, Owen (2010) *Building the Future: Dealing with the Past*. http://cain.ulst.ac.uk/issues/politics/docs/nio/op161110.htm (accessed 21 June 2017).

Ramsbotham, Oliver (2010) *Transforming Violent Conflict*. Oxon: Routledge.

Ramsbotham, Oliver, Hugh Miall and Tom Woodhouse (2011) *Contemporary Conflict Resolution*, third edition. Cambridge: Polity Press.

Stevens, Sir John (2003) *Stevens Enquiry. Overview and Recommendations*. http://cain.ulst.ac.uk/issues/violence/docs/stevens3/stevens3summary.pdf (accessed 8 November 2018).

Teitel, Ruti (2000) *Transitional Justice*. Oxford: Oxford University Press.

Teitel, Ruti (2008) 'Editorial Note-Transitional Justice Globalized', *International Journal of Transitional Justice* 2 (1): 1–4.

Truth and Reconciliation Commission of South Africa (1998) *Truth and Reconciliation Report*. www.justice.gov.za/trc/report/ (accessed 31 October 2014).

UN Security Council (2000) *Security Council Resolution 1325 (2000) [On Women and Peace and Security]*, 31 October 2000, S/RES/1325.

UN Human Rights Council (2014) *Summary of Panel Discussion on History Teaching and Memorialization Processes*, 22 December 2014, A/HRC/28/36.

Vandeginste, Stef and Chandra Lekha Sriram (2011) 'Power Sharing and Transitional Justice: A Clash of Paradigms?', *Global Governance: A Review of Multilateralism and International Organizations* 17 (4): 489–505.

Weiss, Joshua N. and Sarah Rosenberg (2003) 'Sequencing Strategies and Tactics', in Guy Burgess and Heidi Burgess (Eds.), *Beyond Intractability*. Boulder, Conflict Information Consortium, University of Colorado. www.beyondintractability.org/essay/issue-segmentation (accessed 21 June 2017).

10

THIRD PARTIES, CONFLICT AND CONFLICT RESOLUTION

The case of Sudan

Bjørn Møller

Introduction: third parties in conflict

This chapter offers a typology of an array of external actors, often referred to as 'third parties', describing the various roles they play in intra-state armed conflicts. Throughout the chapter, Sudan is used as a case study, occasionally supplemented with other cases from the (Greater) Horn of Africa, such as Somalia. In the context of this volume, a major contribution of this chapter is to show how the power of conflict is strong enough to regularly draw in such third parties, which thereby become de facto parties to the conflict. These dynamics unfold differently for different kinds of third parties, and a nuanced understanding of the many different species of the genus of third party is therefore important.

What and who are third parties?

While much has been written about the role of third parties in conflicts and wars, the term is rather unfortunate. Firstly, it seems to presuppose binary conflicts between two actors or parties – in intra-state conflicts typically a government and an opposition – but the reality is usually much more complex, involving multiple factions, often within government and opposition alike.

In Sudan, for instance, the government in Khartoum on more than one occasion succeeded in splitting its main opponent, the Sudan People's Liberation Movement/Army (SPLM/A), paradoxically by supporting the faction fighting for secession against the more moderate one, which was fighting for a 'New Sudan' (Johnson 2013). The government side also split with the fallout between President Omar Al-Bashir and his former religious mentor, the late Hassan al-Turabi (Natsios 2012:80–116). The latter then sided with the insurgent Justice and Equality Movement (JEM) in the Darfur region, which subsequently fractured.

Secondly, the term seems premised on a neat distinction between inside and outside, which is a legal fiction associated with the concept of sovereignty that only rarely corresponds to reality. Internal conflicts often become transnational by spreading, usually to immediate neighbours. This does not happen automatically, however, and Michael Brown is surely correct that analysts should avoid terms such as contagion, diffusion or spillover, as 'It does not help (...) to suggest that these mechanisms are bacteriological, mechanical, or hydraulic in character' (1996:594). Conversely, there is much to be said for a common language and terminology. Hence, in the following, we shall use the terms 'third parties' and 'external actors' (more or less synonymously) with the aforementioned considerations reduced to caveats.

Such third parties would have no role to play in a purely Westphalian order, as domestic affairs in other countries would simply be off limits to international organizations, other states and non-state actors unless explicitly invited by the sovereign state in question. Likewise, a purely cosmopolitan world would have no distinction between internal and external actors. The very category of third parties or external actors thus belongs to the hybrid order in which we presently live and for which the term 'globalisation' seems appropriate. While the entire world might well be more interconnected and interdependent than ever before, distance still makes a difference in most matters, not least armed conflicts, to which this chapter is devoted (Webb 2007).

Typology of third parties

Third parties come in many types and play many different roles in armed conflicts and their management, mitigation and resolution, as summed up in Table 10.1, which is less than exhaustive.

International organizations

International Governmental Organizations (IGOs) are found at every level of the international system and are the obvious candidates for the third-party role, if only because many of them were created for this very mission.

At the global level, we find the UN (Møller 2012:87–139) and its Security Council (UNSC), which is the supreme authority regarding the use of force, a mandate it frequently uses to dispatch peacekeeping forces (Bellamy and Williams 2010). On rare occasions, the UNSC has also mandated humanitarian interventions, as it did for Libya in UNSC Resolution 1973 in 2011. The UN has also been deeply involved in the various conflicts in Sudan and South Sudan since its independence in 2011 (Johnson 2011, 2016).

The regional level includes organizations such as the African Union (AU). While regional organizations are assigned important roles by the UN Charter, they explicitly do *not* have the right to use force without a UNSC mandate. Not only did the AU mediate the North-South conflict as well as that in Darfur, bringing into play its newly established 'Panel of the Wise' (Nathan 2004), it also followed up with a peacekeeping mission in Darfur (see below).

TABLE 10.1 Sudan: 'third parties' by category

IGOs				States			Non-state actors		
Global	Regional	Subregional	Misc.	Neighbours	Great Powers	Misc.	NGOs	Firms	Persons
UN	(OAU)	IGAD	EU	Egypt	USA	Israel	Humanitarian NGOs	Oil companies	Religious leaders
UN Agencies	AU	COMESA	NATO	Ethiopia Eritrea	(USSR)	(Libya)	HRW		
ICC			LAS	Kenya	China		ICG	PMCs	Celebrities
World Bank			OIC	Uganda Chad		Norway	Amnesty International		Academics
IMF									

Legend: AU: African Union; COMESA: Common Market for Eastern and Southern Africa; EU: European Union; HRW: Human Rights Watch; ICC: International Criminal Court; ICG: International Crisis Group; IMF: International Monetary Front; IGAD: Inter-Governmental Authority on Development; LAS: League of Arab States; NATO: North Atlantic Treaty Organization; OAU: Organisation for African Unity; OIC: Organisation of the Islamic Conference; PMC: Private Military Companies; UN: United Nations; USA: United States of America; USSR: Union of Socialist Soviet Republics; (): No longer exists or has ceased to be involved.

At the subregional level, we find the Inter-Governmental Authority for Development (IGAD), covering northeast Africa. Even though subregional organizations were supposed to play a central role in the so-called 'African Security Architecture', IGAD is much weaker than, say, its counterparts in western and southern Africa (Møller 2005), and has not managed to play any role in the AU peacekeeping missions, AMIS and AMISOM, in Sudan and Somalia, respectively (Jeng 2012:234–276). Nevertheless, IGAD was instrumental in bringing about the Comprehensive Peace Agreement (CPA) for Sudan in 2005 and has made an effort to mediate the post-independence conflict in South Sudan (Apuuli 2015).

Besides these IGOs, there are also various agencies (sometimes IGO affiliates) providing official development assistance (ODA), which can presumably help defuse conflicts. Traditional ODA may help reduce poverty, thereby reducing the statistical likelihood of the outbreak of armed conflict (Collier 2008:17–37). The World Bank (WB) and International Monetary Fund (IMF) possibly also play a role in addition to the various UN agencies (e.g. the United Nations Development Programme, UNDP). While the IMF only indirectly impacts security and armed conflicts (Hartzell, Hoddie and Bauer 2010), the WB (e.g. personified in Paul Collier as a research director) has displayed at least an academic interest in armed conflicts for many years and has proven eager to provide economic support to countries emerging from war, as in South Sudan, as soon as the civil war abates sufficiently to allow WB staff to return (De Waal 2014).

The IGO level also includes institutions such as international tribunals and courts (e.g. the International Criminal Court, ICC). While most African states initially welcomed and joined the ICC (Werle, Fernandez and Vormbaum 2014), several had second thoughts about it and came to view it as a neo-imperialist institution due to mounting evidence that the ICC was predominantly prosecuting Africans, whereas Westerners were apparently immune from prosecution. This perception is rather understandable given how, as of 2015, all of the cases in the ICC had been about Africa.

States

Even though the rules of the game in the aforementioned Westphalian Order prohibit it, individual states frequently meddle in other states' intra-state conflicts.

The most obvious category of such states includes neighbours, as they are usually affected most by the devastation and displacement caused by a given conflict, often having to host large numbers of refugees, Ethiopia, for example, being the obvious place of refuge for most Sudanese (Hammond 2004), even though large numbers have also been hosted by Kenya, Uganda and Chad (Kaiser 2008).

Resource scarcities sometimes also bring neighbouring states into the picture, as is the case with the Nile, upon which downstream countries such as Egypt are critically dependent – so much so, in fact, that the rulers in Cairo have made it abundantly clear that they would see any attempt at depriving their country of its 'fair' share of the Nile waters as a *casus belli*. The fact that water entitlements are only regulated in a bilateral treaty between Sudan and Egypt presents a serious obstacle to peaceful conflict resolution, even though the Nile Basin Initiative may facilitate negotiations in future disputes (Tvedt 2009).

Neighbouring states sometimes align themselves with insurgents, using them as proxies, as when Sudan supported the Lord Resistance Army in its fight against the government of Uganda, which was seen as retaliation for the latter having supported the SPLM/A (Prunier 2004). But by no means is this game limited to neighbour states, as the two rivalling superpowers excelled at it throughout the Cold War, also in the Horn of Africa.

While the Soviet Union lost interest in the Third World, including the African Horn, already in the late 1980s, convinced that 'the game wasn't worth the candle' (Patman 1990:289–306), the United States first did so after the debacle in Somalia in the early 1990s, due in part to the 'Black Hawk down' incident in October 1993 (Hirsch and Oakley 1995). While this led the USA to disengage almost completely from Africa, there was the exception of US national security interests possibly warranting engagement and even intervention. Under the auspices of its 'rogue states doctrine' (Klare 1995:130–168), Washington thus kept an eye on Sudan due to its Islamist regime and links to international terrorism. In the wake of 9/11, Sudan pledged its support to the USA. It has not yet managed to be stricken from the US list of 'state sponsors of terrorism', however, despite being lauded in the US State Department *Country Reports on Terrorism 2016* for its collaboration with the USA (United States State Department 2017).

More recently, China has also become a major player, both as a provider of development assistance and as a contributor to UN peacekeeping operations in Sudan, both UNAMID (UN-Africa Mission in Darfur) and UNMIS (UN Mission in Sudan), as well as in the rest of Sub-Saharan Africa (Zhengyu and Taylor 2011), apparently at least partly motivated by economic interests, not least a seemingly unquenchable thirst for oil (De Oliviera 2008). As far as Sudan and the insurgency in Darfur are concerned, China chose (either for principled or opportunistic reasons) to block any UNSC action (Contessi 2010), which may in fact have served as a convenient excuse for the USA and other Western powers to do next to nothing to stop what they labelled an ongoing genocide (Hagan and Rymond-Richmond 2009:32, 59, 78, 220).

Small states like Norway occasionally also play a role, as in the conflicts in Sri Lanka and Colombia, but also in Sudan, mainly by capitalizing on their reputation and lack of the vested interests that typically drive great powers, which enhances their credibility as 'honest brokers' (Johnson 2011, 2016). What they lack in military or other material leverage they may make up for in terms of impartiality and greater legitimacy. Libya has also been a key external player in several African countries, usually motivated by the bizarre ideology enshrined in Gadhafi's *Green Book*, but occasionally also for geopolitical reasons, in Sudan, for instance, in order to weaken its arch-enemy Chad (Ronen 2011).

Non-state actors

Various NGOs and other non-state actors sometimes also play important roles in conflicts. Firstly, NGOs are occasionally able to cast light on otherwise ignored conflicts and/or highlight particular aspects of them, as in the campaign against the oil companies in Sudan, eventually succeeding in forcing out the Western ones, although they were simply replaced by Asian oil companies (Patey 2007).

Most private companies are concerned about their public image and therefore prefer being associated with good causes rather than bad ones, hence an interest in 'corporate social responsibility' (Vertigans, Idowu and Schmidpeter 2016). This could, *mirabile dictu*, also be said about at least some private military companies (PMCs), some of which have founded an association of PMCs and Private Security Companies (PSCs) – the 'International Stability Operations Association' (ISOA), devoting itself to 'promoting appropriate regulation alongside industry standards to ensure the delivery of the highest quality services in fragile environments worldwide' (ISOA 2018. See also Brooks 2000).

Religious authorities, groups and/or institutions often also play a role, including religious fanatics such as those in *Al-Qaeda*, which Sudan hosted from 1991 to 1996 (Burke 2004:143–157). Religious authorities and institutions also occasionally play more constructive roles, preventing or ending armed conflicts, usually assuming a mediating role (Appleby 2001), typically in the later stages of a conflict, to help promote peaceful relations (Irving-Erickson and Phan 2016).

The same is the case with diasporas, which are usually seen by others as 'external actors' or a 'domestic abroad' as they are, by definition, outside of their countries of personal or ancestral origin (Varadarajan 2010). Diaspora members typically see matters differently, however, due to their (likewise definitional) emotional attachment to their homeland, which often also has more tangible manifestations, as in the form of occasional visits to relatives and kin and the sending of remittances to either the latter or to the homeland as such (Carment and Sadjed 2017). Some have argued that diasporas in OECD (rich) countries from Third World (poor) countries often intensify and prolong conflict in the homeland, as they provide the resources required for protracted war and tend to be more radical than their fellow countrymen in the homeland, who have to 'cut corners' and compromise on a daily basis as a coping strategy (Smith and Stares 2007). For better or for worse, throughout the GHoA, diasporas play important roles and are – among other, less savoury activities – engaged in peacebuilding (Laakso and Hautaniemi 2014). This may well also apply to the (rather scattered) Sudanese and (even more so) South Sudanese diaspora. The latter is even more complex than other diasporas, as many of those who are now South Sudanese were internally displaced persons (IDPs) within the united Sudan prior to 2011 (i.e. an 'internal diaspora'), who are now facing the choice between 'returning' to the new state of South Sudan or remaining a genuine (i.e. external) diaspora.

Numerous private actors are also involved in the side effects of armed conflicts, including the often-massive human displacement caused by such struggles, producing either IDPs or refugees, at least according to the more permissive criteria of the OAU refugee convention, which grants refugee status to people fleeing from dangerous locations, regardless of whether they are personally persecuted (Milner 2009:6–14). For several decades, this has been the case with humanitarian agencies in Sudan and Sudanese refugees in, for instance, Ethiopia. According to practitioners-turned-analysts such as Alex De Waal (1997:86–105), Mark Duffield (2001:202–256) and David Keen (2008), humanitarian aid has sometimes created more problems than it has solved by unwittingly favouring one side against the other and/or by allowing the conflict to become protracted and intractable.

A final category of non-state actors consists of celebrities, a good example being the American actor and filmmaker Don Cheadle, who has campaigned in favour of intervention in the Darfur conflict along with a renowned expert on the Horn (Cheadle and Prendergast 2007). They are merely one subcategory of what has aptly been labelled 'private peace entrepreneurs' (Lehrs 2016). Jimmy Carter is another such private peace entrepreneur, instrumental as he was in bringing about the 1999 Nairobi Agreement between Uganda and Sudan (Barltrop 2015:56–58).

Roles of third parties

It should be obvious from this mapping of third parties that their roles differ considerably. While this allows for a fruitful division of labour, it may also be a recipe for confusion and provide a welcome excuse for doing nothing. Conflict prevention, management and resolution thus face obvious 'collective action problems', as there is no link between the 'production' of peace and the enjoyment of this 'public good' (Møller 2019).

One way of mapping the various roles of external actors is to break down the evolution of a conflict into distinct phases: (1) early stages, (2) violent stages and (3) post-violent stages moving towards peace that will structure the following sections.

The early stages

Considering the human suffering created by armed conflicts, there is much to be said in favour of early – preferably even preventive – action.

At the very beginning of a conflict cycle, we find the latent stage where conflict behaviour is absent and the conflict thus unobservable. In fact, it is only by retrospective logical deduction that we arrive at the view that the conflict must have been latent before becoming manifest. Even though external observers may identify instances of oppression (e.g. of ethnic minorities) and, in the absence of actual evidence, predict this to provoke conflict, they may simply be mistaken. Interfering at this early stage may even provoke rather than prevent an open conflict.

Moreover, it is far from being self-evident that all latent conflicts should be kept 'under lid'. On the contrary, their becoming manifest may be a *sine qua non* of their resolution. For instance, protracted political struggles were necessary to enfranchise women and abolish slavery. With these caveats, it stands to reason that the prevention of *violent* conflict is almost always worthwhile. This endeavour is often subdivided into two elements, early warning and preventative action, or, in UN-speak, 'preventive diplomacy' (Lund 1996).

The former is intended to identify where (and perhaps also when and how) a conflict may erupt, which is a precondition of targeted action that actually makes a difference. There is no shortage of early warning 'mechanisms' in Africa, as the AU, IGAD and COMESA have all established such entities (Hassan 2013; Kasaija 2013). Early warning is essentially the product of an application of conflict theories to data, and the main complications relate to the lack or low quality of the latter. Indeed, while the conflict propensity is very high in places such as South Sudan, the administrative capacity is so deficient that statistical data are almost completely lacking. Hence, even the most sophisticated econometric models, such as those produced by Paul Collier and associates (2005), are unlikely to produce reliable warning (Nathan 2005).

Problems become even more severe when it comes to preventative action, mainly because the sovereignty issue looms large. Should an external intervention of sorts be contemplated in the initial stages of a conflict, it is almost certain to be perceived (certainly by the regime, perhaps also by others in the target country) as illegitimate 'interference in domestic affairs', regardless of the underlying intentions, as further exemplified by the early intervention in Burundi, as Engell and Jacobsens write in Chapter 8.

Third parties may play a role in containing the conflict at early stages of escalation either in the form of mediation (Zartman and Touwal 2007) or perhaps by 'naming and shaming' (Seidman 2016). Both activities are open to all of the above categories of external actors. NGOs may certainly play a role, both in bringing the parties together and by serving as honest brokers, and NGOs such as Human Rights Watch, Amnesty International and the International Crisis Group also engage in naming and shaming.

Both neighbouring and other states may, likewise, engage in mediation, as may IGOs such as the UN, AU or IGAD. In this connection, there may be trade-offs between leverage and legitimacy. Neighbours usually have some leverage simply due to their proximity, but they are rarely impartial, which detracts from their legitimacy (Kleiboer 1996), while small and/or distant states and IGOs may make up with legitimacy what they lack in terms of leverage. Actors such as the EU (certainly to a much greater extent than the United States) are in an intermediate position, perceived as being impartial in most conflicts in the Third World, including Sudan and the rest of the Horn of Africa, while possessing considerable leverage in terms of development aid and trade concessions (Ginsberg 1999).

The violent stages

It is often forgotten how many armed conflicts end in victory for one side and surrender by its antagonist (Afflerbach and Strachan 2012), either when the government crushes an armed insurgency or when the insurgents overthrow the government. Even though this form of conflict termination by surrender is often brutal, it may still be preferable to a protracted war. If so, the provision by third parties of plentiful arms to one side or the other (but obviously not to both) may be a lesser evil simply because it brings the fighting to an end. The worst eventuality is probably the Cold War pattern with one set of third parties supplying one side and another its adversary, which increases the intensity and destructiveness of the war without ensuring its swift termination. It may occasionally even make sense to 'give war a chance' by abstaining completely from any interference, as suggested by the always provocative Edward Luttwak (1999). With these caveats in mind, it is surely preferable in most cases to help bring about an end to the fighting through mediation. Whether efforts towards this end succeed or fail may be explained retrospectively by reference to whether the moment was 'ripe' or not – a term usually attributed to I. William Zartman.

Skilled and legitimate mediators also matter (Aquilar and Gallucio 2008:124–135). In some cases, useful first steps may be taken by the so-called 'track two' or even 'track three' talks, involving interlocutors capitalizing on their inability to decide and make commitment, which may help clarify the 'red lines' of the 'real' antagonists (Benziman 2016). There were actually numerous such third-party mediation initiatives leading up to the 2005 CPA for Sudan (Rolandsen 2013).

One obstacle to reaching a negotiated truce leading up to a peace agreement is often the security concerns of the warring parties, as it is dangerous to lay down one's arms when there is no trust between the parties. A safeguard against this eventuality is the deployment of peacekeepers, seen by all parties as impartial, of which there had, at the time of writing (October 2017), been three in Sudan (UNMIS, UNAMID and UNISFA) plus one (UNMISS) in now independent South Sudan (see Table 10.2). While UNMIS resembled a 'traditional' inter-positioning peacekeeping mission, deployed along a border or line of demarcation

TABLE 10.2 UN and hybrid peacekeeping missions in Sudan and South Sudan (based on www.un.org/en/peacekeeping/)

Acronym	UNMIS	UNAMID	UNISFA	UNMISS
Full title	United Nations Mission in the Sudan	African Union/ United Nations Hybrid Operation in Darfur	United Nations Interim Security Force for Abyei	United Nations Mission in the Republic of South Sudan
Mandate	UNSCR 1590 (2005)	UNSCR 1769 (2007)	UNSCR 1990 (2011)	UNSCR 1996 (2011)
Authorized size	c. 10,000 Mil. c. 700 Pol.	15,845 Mil. 3,403 Pol.	6,326 Mil. 50 Pol.	17,000 Mil. 900 Pol.
Duration	Until June 2011	Ongoing	Ongoing	Ongoing

(Van der Lijn 2010), the other three are more complex since there is no recognized line of demarcation.

Unfortunately, however, the aforementioned collective action problem also applies to peacekeeping, which explains the persistent undersupply of troops for such missions (Shimizu and Sandler 2002).

Towards peace

Presupposing that the violent struggle comes to an end, we enter the stage often referred to as 'peace-building', which includes the rebuilding of the war-ravaged society. As far as infrastructure is concerned, this is rather straightforward, albeit often horrendously expensive and usually far beyond the means of the country itself (Harris 1999), making both technical and external economic assistances indispensable. Considering that there must have been something wrong with the society and its political superstructure in the first place to give rise to the armed conflict, it would be manifestly unwise to simply recreate these societal structures in the reconstruction phase – but equally imprudent for 'Western' external actors to seek to transform them in their own image. Neither Sudan nor South Sudan will come to resemble the West, for example, nor would their respective peoples probably want them to do so.

An extremely important element in societal reconstruction is the building of trust among the members of society. A precondition for trust is often disarmament, both pertaining to the antagonistic armed forces and the general population. As far as the former are concerned, there is a need for DDR: *Disarmament, Demobilization* and *Reintegration*, with which Sudan actually has lengthy historical experience. This began with the scaling down-*cum*-integration of the opposing armed forces (i.e. the Sudan Armed Forces (SAF) and the *Anya-Nya*) following the 1972 Addis Ababa Agreement (Kasfir 1977). This was partly repeated following the 2005 CPA (Møller and Cawthra 2007). Compulsory disarmament may be especially difficult to swallow for the rural population, however, which feels (and probably has) an existential need for self-protection from cattle-rustlers, ordinary robbers and wild animals.

As far as the armed forces are concerned, there is also a need for what is usually called SSR – *Security Sector Reform* (Schnabel and Ehrhart 2005) – for transforming the country's armed forces, hitherto deployed for counter-insurgency warfare (COIN), into a defence force that is suitable for national defence and which is duly accountable to the civilian authorities and without 'praetorian' inclinations (Huntington 1991:231–251). There were plans for this during the 'interim period', where the Sudan People's Liberation Army (SPLA) was supposed to serve as a 'home guard' for the present South Sudan and form integrated units with the SAF (Møller and Cawthra 2007), but these worthwhile pursuits were fatally 'poisoned' by the subsidiary task of transforming the SPLA into a national defence force for the potentially independent South Sudan, the main enemy of which would obviously be Sudan.

Another important aspect of peacebuilding is state-building. All too often, however, there is no functioning state to resurrect or reform, and occasionally there is no nation – or there may be contending and irreconcilable 'imaginations' of the nation in the sense of Benedict Anderson (1991). Moreover, whatever 'sentimental ties' there may have been between and within nested communities prior to the armed conflict may well have been destroyed by it.

Hence, there is an urgent need for nation-building at the societal level as a precondition for successful state-building at the political level. The answers to the nation/state issue have never been self-evident in Sudan. This question was even debated in the run-up to the planned independence in 1956, where one of the options was a merger with Egypt and another one a loose federation (Deng 1995:101–134). It was also far from self-evident that South Sudan constituted a nation when it became politically independent in 2011, which goes a long way towards explaining the new country's rapid descent into internecine ethnic war in 2012–2013, pitting Nuer against Dinka (Johnson 2016:102–117, 179–223).

Even though South Sudan may thus be characterized as 'a state in search of a nation', this 'legitimacy deficit' might have been mitigated by good state performance, investing its institutions with at least a modicum of 'performance legitimacy' (Gilley 2009:3–11). This term is sometimes used about China, the 'economic miracle' of which may in fact have given the unelected regime some legitimacy. Unfortunately, however, what the citizens of South Sudan have experienced since 2011 has been almost the exact opposite of an economic miracle (Copnall 2014:227–229), i.e. a veritable kleptocracy (De Waal 2014).

State-building was heavily subsidized and *ipso facto* influenced by foreign actors, especially in their role as donors. This has become a major preoccupation for the proverbial international community as well as a veritable cottage industry in academia. Some analysts, such as David Chandler (2006), come close to dismissing the task as almost inevitably exacerbating rather than solving problems and as an 'empire in denial', where the external actors take almost complete control of the process, but without accepting the responsibility for the results. State-building is inevitably shaped by several dilemmas, including the following (Paris and Sisk 2009):

- Is it possible to reconcile the creation of a sovereign state with the de facto imposition of an international trusteeship over a territory, depriving its former institutions and citizens of all the vestiges of sovereignty, albeit only for a transitional period?
- Should one first ensure legitimacy and then proceed to building functioning institutions – or the other way around?
- Is it possible to build state strength without jeopardizing political legitimacy – considering that state-building in Europe was very bloody, proceeded step by step and took centuries to complete?

- Can the (understandable) insistence on the part of the external actors on an 'exit strategy' be reconciled with the need for building popular support for the state-building process?

Unfortunately, there is an almost irresistibly seductive way of seemingly reconciling most of these dilemmas: first, establish an international trusteeship, then prepare for a handover to indigenous authorities by training (however superficially) an ephemeral civil service, support the emergence of political parties, set an election day as early as possible, announce that the victor in this elections will be handed the reins of government of a sovereign state and let it be known that the wishes of the new government will be accommodated (e.g. if it wants the international actors to leave). For all the attractions of this strategy, it suffers from one problem: it has so far never worked, which makes it rather unlikely that it ever will. Either the internationals bid their farewell and once again the sovereign state falls apart (e.g. Afghanistan) or becomes dictatorial (Iraq); or the internationals must recognize that their exit plan has failed and they will be bogged down.

All of the above costs money that the post-conflict state usually does not have and which therefore must be provided by external actors – which exacerbates other problems. As mentioned above, South Sudan has thus developed into a veritable 'kleptocracy' (De Waal 2014, 2015:91–108) marred by what Jean-Francois Bayart (1989) aptly labelled *la politique du ventre* (i.e. the 'politics of the belly').

Conclusion

It is very difficult to conclude anything from the aforementioned analysis of the roles of a multitude of different third parties. The track record of their involvement is far from impressive and they have in quite a few cases made matters worse, even when their main motives have been unselfish.

Some of this record of failure can probably be attributed to a lack of understanding of the situation on the ground, as when Western powers are meddling in 'a quarrel in a far-away country between people of whom we know nothing', to quote Neville Chamberlain (1939:275). Hence, a recommendation may be to either seek to acquire sufficient understanding of the country, the protagonists and the culture – or refrain from intervening. In relation to this, third parties should be aware of their involvement in the conflict dynamics rather than perceiving themselves as somehow 'outside' the logic of conflict. A thorough analysis of the dynamics of third-party involvement in a particular case may very well improve the effort.

References

Afflerbach, Holger and Hew Strachan (Eds.) (2012) *How Fighting Ends: A History of Surrender*. Oxford: Oxford University Press.
Anderson, Benedict (1991) *Imagined Communities: Reflections on the Origin and Spread of Nationalism*, 2nd ed. London: Verso.

Appleby, Scott (2001) 'Religion as an Agent of Conflict Transformation and Peacebuilding', in Chester A. Crocker, Fen Osler Hampson and Pamela Aall (Eds.), *Turbulent Peace. The Challenges of Managing International Conflict* (821–840), Washington, DC: United States Institute of Peace Press.

Apuuli, Kasaija Phillip (2015) 'IGAD's Mediation in the Current South Sudan Conflict: Prospects and Challenges', *African Security* 8 (2): 120–145.

Aquilar, Francesco and Mauro Gallucio (2008) *Psychological Processes in International Negotiations: Theoretical and Practical Perspectives.* Heidelberg: Springer.

Barltrop, Richard (2015) *Darfur and the International Community: The Challenges of Conflict Resolution in Sudan.* London: I.B. Tauris.

Bayart, Jean-François (1989) *L'État en Afrique: La politique du ventre.* Paris: Fayard.

Bellamy, Alex and Paul D. Williams (2010) *Understanding Peacekeeping*, 2nd ed. Cambridge: Polity.

Benziman, Yuval (2016) 'Ingredients of a Successful Track Two Negotiation', *Negotiation Journal* 32 (1): 49–62.

Brooks, Doug (2000) 'Messiahs or Mercenaries? The Future of International Private Military Services', *International Peacekeeping* 7 (1): 129–144.

Brown, Michael (1996) 'The Causes and Regional Dimensions of Internal Conflict', in Michael Brown (Ed.), *The International Dimensions of Internal Conflict* (571–601), Cambridge: MIT Press.

Burke, Jason (2004) *Al Qaeda: The True Story of Radical Islam.* Harmondsworth: Penguin Books.

Carment, David and Ariane Sadjed (Eds.) (2017) *Diasporas as Cultures of Cooperation: Global and Local Perspectives.* Cham: Palgrave Macmillan.

Chamberlain, Neville (1939) *The Struggle for Peace.* London: Hutchinson & Co.

Chandler, David (2006) *Empire in Denial: The Politics of State-Building.* London: Pluto Press.

Cheadle, Don and John Prendergast (2007) *Not on Our Watch: The Mission to End Genocide in Darfur and Beyond*, 2nd ed. New York: Maverick House.

Collier, Paul (2008) *The Bottom Billion: Why the Poorest Countries Are Failing and What Can Be Done about It.* Oxford: Oxford University Press.

Collier, Paul, Anke Hoeffler and Nicholas Sambanis (2005) 'The Collier-Hoeffler Model of Civil War Onset and the Case Study Project Research Design', in Paul Collier and Nicholas Sambanis (Eds.), *Understanding War: Evidence and Analysis, Vol. 1: Africa* (1–33), Washington, DC: World Bank.

Contessi, Nicola P. (2010) 'Multilateralism, Intervention and Norm Contestation: China's Stance on Darfur in the UN Security Council', *Security Dialogue* 41 (3): 323–344.

Copnall, James (2014) *A Poisonous Thorn in Our Hearts: Sudan and South Sudan's Bitter and Incomplete Divorce.* London: Hurst.

De Oliviera, Ricardo Soares (2008) 'Making Sense of Chinese Oil Investment in Africa', in Chris Alden, Daniel Large and Ricardo Soares de Oliveira (Eds.), *China Returns to Africa: A Rising Power and a Continental Embrace* (83–110), New York: Columbia University Press.

De Waal, Alex (1997) *Famine Crimes: Politics and the Disaster Relief Industry in Africa.* Oxford: James Currey.

De Waal, Alex (2014) 'When Kleptocracy Becomes Insolvent: Brute Causes of the Civil War in South Sudan', *African Affairs* 113 (452): 347–369.

De Waal, Alex (2015) *The Real Politics of the Horn of Africa: Money, War and the Business of Power.* Cambridge: Polity.

Deng, Francis M. (1995) *War of Visions: Conflict of Identities in Sudan.* Washington, DC: Brookings Institution.

Duffield, Mark (2001) *Global Governance and the New Wars: The Merger of Development and Security.* London: Zed Books.

Gilley, Bruce (2009) *The Right to Rule: How States Win and Lose Legitimacy.* New York: Columbia University Press.

Ginsberg, Roy H. (1999) 'Conceptualizing the European Union as an International Actors: Narrowing the Theoretical Capability-Expectations Gap', *Journal of Common Market Studies* 37 (3): 429–454.

Hagan, John and Wenona Rymond-Richmond (2009) *Darfur and the Crime of Genocide.* Cambridge: Cambridge University Press.

Hammond, Laura C. (2004) *This Place Will Become Home: Refugee Repatriation to Ethiopia.* Ithaca, NY: Cornell University Press.

Harris, Geoff (Ed.) (1999) *Recovery from Armed Conflict in Developing Countries: An Economic and Political Analysis.* London: Routledge.

Hartzell, Caroline A., Matthew Hoddie and Molly Bauer (2010) 'Economic Liberalization via IMF Structural Adjustment: Sowing the Seeds of Civil War?', *International Organization* 64 (2): 339–356.

Hassan, Rania (2013) 'CEWARN's New Strategic Framework', *African Security Review* 22 (2): 26–38.

Hirsch, John L. and Robert B. Oakley (1995) *Somalia and Operation Restore Hope: Reflections on Peacemaking and Peacekeeping.* Washington, DC: United States Institute of Peace Press.

Huntington, Samuel P. (1991) *The Third Wave: Democratization in the Late Twentieth Century.* Norman: University of Oklahoma Press.

Irving-Erickson, Douglas and Peter C. Phan (2016) *Violence, Religion, Peacemaking: Contributions of Interreligious Dialogue.* Houndmillls, Basingstoke: Palgrave Macmillan.

ISOA (2018). *Our Work.* https://stability-operations.site-ym.com/page/work/ (accessed 8 November 2018).

Jeng, Abou (2012) *Peacebuilding in the African Union: Law, Philosophy and Practice.* Cambridge: Cambridge University Press.

Johnson, Douglas H. (2013) 'New Sudan or South Sudan? The Multiple Meanings of Self-Determination in Sudan's Comprehensive Peace Agreement', *Civil Wars* 15 (2): 141–156.

Johnson, Hilde F. (2011) *Waging Peace in Sudan: The Inside Story of the Negotiations that Ended Africa's Longest Civil War.* Eastbourne: Sussex Academic Press.

Johnson, Hilde F. (2016) *South Sudan: The Untold Story. From Independence to Civil War.* London: I.B. Tauris.

Kaiser, Tania (2008) 'Sudanese Refugees in Uganda and Kenya', in Gil Loescher, James Milner, Edward Newman and Gary Troeller (Eds.), *Protracted Refugee Situations: Political, Human Rights and Security Implications* (248–276), Tokyo: United Nations University Press.

Kasaija, Phillip Apuuli (2013) 'The Intergovernmental Authority on Development's Conflict Early Warning and Responsed Mechanism: Can It Go Beyond Pastoral Conflicts', *African Security Review* 22 (2): 11–25.

Kasfir, Nelson (1977) 'Southern Sudanese Politics Since the Addis Ababa Agreement', *African Affairs* 76 (303): 143–166.

Keen, David (2008) *The Benefits of Famine: A Political Economy of Famine and Relief in Southwestern Sudan, 1983–89,* 2nd ed. Oxford: James Currey.

Klare, Michael (1995) *Rogue States and Nuclear Outlaws: America's Search for a New Foreign Policy*. New York: Hill and Wang.

Kleiboer, Marieke (1996) 'Understanding Success and Failure of International Mediation', *Journal of Conflict Resolution* 40 (2): 360–389.

Laakso, Liisa and Petri Hautaniemi (Eds.) (2014) *Diasporas, Development and Peacemaking in the Horn of Africa*. London: Zed Books.

Lehrs, Lior (2016) 'Private Peace Entrepreneurs in Conflict Resolution Processes', *International Negotiation* 21 (3): 381–408.

Lund, Michael S. (1996) *Preventing Violent Conflicts: A Strategy for Preventive Diplomacy*. Washington, DC: United States Institute of Peace Press.

Luttwak, Edward N. (1999) 'Give War a Chance', *Foreign Affairs* 78 (4): 36–44.

Milner, James H.S. (2009) *Refugees, the State and the Politics of Asylum in Africa*. Houndmills, Basingstoke: Palgrave Macmillan.Møller, Bjørn (2005) 'The Pros and Cons of Subsidiarity: The Role of African Regional and Sub-Regional Organisations in Ensuring Peace and Security in Africa', in Anne Hammerstad (Ed.), *People, States and Regions: Building a Collaborative Security Regime in Southern Africa* (23–82), Johannesburg: South African Institute of International Affairs.

Møller, Bjørn (2019) 'Peace, R2P and Public Goods Theory', in Aigul Kulnazarova and Vesselin Popovski (Eds.), *The Palgrave Handbook of Global Aproaches to Peace* (47–68), Cham, Switzerland: Palgrave Macmillan.

Møller, Bjørn (2012) *European Security: The Roles of Regional Organisations*. Farnham, Surrey: Ashgate.

Møller, Bjørn and Gavin Cawthra (2007) 'Integration of Former Enemies into National Armies in Fragile States', in Louise Andersen, Bjørn Møller and Finn Stepputat (Eds.), *Fragile States and Insecure People? Violence, Security, and Statehood in the Twenty-First Century* (177–200), Houndmills, Basingstoke: Palgrave.

Nathan, Laurie (2004) 'Mediation and the African Union's Panel of the Wise', in Shannon Field (Ed.), *Peace in Africa: Towards a Collaborative Security Regime* (63–80), Johannesburg: Institute for Global Dialogue.

Nathan, Laurie (2005) 'The Frightful Inadequacy of Most of the Statistics: A Critique of Collier and Hoeffler on the Causes of Civil War', *Track Two* 12 (5): 5–36.

Natsios, Andrew S. (2012) *Sudan, South Sudan, and Darfur: What Everyone Needs to Know*. Oxford: Oxford University Press.

Paris, Roland and Timothy D. Sisk (Eds.) (2009) *The Dilemmas of Statebuilding: Confronting the Contradictions of Postwar Peace Operations*. Abingdon, Oxon: Routledge.

Patey, Luke A. (2007) 'State Rules: Oil Companies and Armed Conflict in Sudan', *Third World Quarterly* 28 (5): 997–1016.

Patman, Robert G. (1990) *The Soviet Union in the Horn of Africa: The Diplomacy of Intervention and Disengagement*. Cambridge: Cambridge University Press.

Prunier, Gérard (2004) 'Rebel Movements and Proxy Warfare: Uganda, Sudan and the Congo, 1986–99', *African Affairs* 103 (412): 359–383.

Rolandsen, Øysten H. (2013) 'Sudan: The Role of Foreign Involvement in the Shaping and Implementation of the Sudan Comprehensive Peace Agreement', in Mikael Erikson and Roland Kosić (Eds.), *Mediation and Liberal Peacebuilding: Peace from the Ashes of War?* (76–91), Abingdon, Oxon: Routledge.

Ronen, Yehudit (2011) 'Between Africanism and Arabism: Libya's Involvement in Sudan', *Journal of the Middle East and Africa* 2 (1): 1–14.

Schnabel, Albrecht and Hans-Georg Ehrhart (Eds.) (2005) *Security Sector Reform and Post-Conflict Peacebuilding*. Tokyo: United Nations University Press.

Seidman, Gay (2016) 'Naming, Shaming, Changing the World', in David Courpasson and Steven Vallas (Eds.), *The Sage Handbook of Resistance* (351–366), London: Sage.

Shimizu, Hirofumi and Todd Sandler (2002) 'Peacekeeping and Burden-Sharing, 1994–2000', *Journal of Peace Research* 39 (6): 651–668.

Smith, Hazel and Paul Stares (Eds.) (2007) *Diasporas in Conflict: Peace-Makers or Peace-Wreckers?* Tokyo: United Nations University Press.

Tvedt, Terje (Ed.) (2009) *The River Nile in the Post-Colonial Age: Conflict and Cooperation among the Nile Basin Countries.* London: I.B. Tauris.

United States State Department (2017) *Country Reports on Terrorism 2016.* Washington, DC: United States State Department.

Van der Lijn (2010) 'Success and Failure of UN Peacekeeping Operations: UNMIS in Sudan', *Journal of International Peacekeeping* 14 (1–2): 27–59.

Varadarajan, Latha (2010) *The Domestic Abroad: Diasporas in International Relations.* Oxford: Oxford University Press.

Vertigans, Stephen, Samuel O. Idowu and René Schmidpeter (Eds.) (2016) *Corporate Social Responsibility in Sub-Saharan Africa.* Heidelberg: Springer.

Webb, Kieran (2007) 'The Continued Importance of Geographic Distance and Boulding's Loss of Strength Gradient', *Comparative Strategy* 26 (4): 295–310.

Werle, Gerhard, Lovell Fernandez and Moritz Vormbaum (Eds.) (2014) *Africa and the International Criminal Court.* The Hague: Asser Press.

Zartman, I. William and Saadia Touwal (2007) 'International Mediation', in Chester A. Crocker, Fen Osler Hampson and Pamela Aall (Eds.), *Leashing the Dogs of War: Conflict Management in a Divided World* (437–454), Washington, DC: United States Institute of Peace Press.

Zhengyu, Wu and Ian Taylor (2011) 'From Refusal to Engagement: Chinese Contributions to Peacekeeping in Africa', *Journal of Contemporary African Studies* 29 (2): 137–154.

11

EXTERNAL INCENTIVES AND CONFLICT DE-ESCALATION

Negotiating a settlement to Sudan's North–South Civil War

Nikolas Emmanuel

Introduction: third-party conflict management tools

There is much to learn about the role of external actors in preventing violent conflict and helping to manage it when it occurs. Consequently, this chapter focuses on the range of third-party conflict management tools, examined in theory and more specifically in the context of U.S. efforts to facilitate a negotiated settlement in Sudan's North–South Civil War (1983–2005). This will primarily be done through the lens of an incentives approach. These externally applied policy options seek to manage conflict by facilitating bargaining between the conflicting parties. Such methods go beyond the purview of realist international relations scholars, who view intervention by external third parties as limited to military action or its threat (Finnemore 2003:9–10). I take a broader perspective and consider a range of foreign policy tools for external actors (Elbadawi and Sambanis 2001; Jentleson 2000). This chapter examines several types of commonly used intervention options that are available to external players that can have a significant influence in altering the behaviour of conflicting parties and encouraging peace (Rothchild and Emmanuel 2010). These options are referred to here as incentive strategies.

Outside parties (states and international organizations, but also individuals and nongovernmental entities) frequently make use of different types of incentives to manage conflict. I examine how external actors use incentives to facilitate negotiations and de-escalate intense internal conflict, specifically in the American role in helping to achieve a negotiated settlement in the North–South war in Sudan (1983–2005). Here, I argue that incentives are critical in conflict management. Without ignoring the key role of the East African Intergovernmental Authority on Development (IGAD) in pushing negotiations forward, along with the important parts played by five mediators and observers (United Kingdom, Norway, Italy, the African Union and the United Nations), the United States deployed a range of incentives at critical junctures to support the peace process, providing leverage to the negotiators. This entire process was not easy, especially in light of the growing conflict in Darfur, whose genocidal violence had begun to overshadow the fragile peace between Khartoum and the Sudan People's Liberation Army (SPLA), for not mentioning the growing rebellions in the contested areas of Abyei, the Nuba Mountains and the Southern Blue Nile. This was a turning into a constellation of wars throughout Sudan, not just limited to the North–South conflict (ICG 2003b). Nonetheless, this chapter limits itself to the primary conflict and the negotiations between the government in Khartoum and the SPLA, where the U.S. was able to build and use its leverage. Washington was never the central player in these discussions, however, as regional actors were out in front during much of the negotiations. Nevertheless, the Bush II administration was able to help push the process by using incentives at various junctures. The U.S. acted as a supporting actor, what American diplomat Robert Oakley called 'a catalyst' (Africa Confidential 2002:2).

I ask the following questions: What is an incentives approach to conflict management? What types of incentives are available? How are these strategies used in such interactions as between the U.S. and the various players in the negotiations to end the Sudanese North–South war? By addressing these questions, the study seeks three practical goals: (1) to fill a gap in the relevant literature by exploring the theoretical basis for the use of incentives in conflict management, (2) to develop a typology of incentives frequently used by external actors and (3) to examine how an incentives approach plays out in the Sudan case.

Incentives

It may be obvious that to reach a peaceful outcome, the conflicting parties themselves must learn to resolve their differences. Nonetheless, outside parties can help push (or pull) them in the direction of peace by using the incentives and pressures available to them.

An incentives approach consists of a variety of strategies that an outside actor may use to encourage conflicting parties to adopt a peaceful solution by easing the bargaining and compromise process (Emmanuel 2016; Rothchild and Emmanuel 2010). It is worth noting that encouraging such a shift in behaviour away from violent conflict towards bargaining cannot occur with military force alone, frequently also including the deployment of non-military options (Nye 2004), that is, this approach includes both rewards (noncoercive actions) and punishments (coercive actions). Rewards relate to soft intervention or noncoercive incentive strategies and are generally viewed more favourably by the targeted actor(s) than punishments. In other words, '[c]onciliatory gestures frequently lead to cooperative responses, while threats often initiate spirals of hostility and defiance' (Lapidus and Tsalik 1998:57). Incentives consist of a variety of 'structural arrangements, distributive or symbolic rewards or punishments (e.g. disincentives) aimed to encourage a target state or movement in a given conflict to shift their priorities and agree to compromise on the major issues in contention' (Rothchild 1997:19). Whether noncoercive or coercive, related to soft or hard power, non-military or military in nature, such incentives attempt 'to raise the opportunity cost of continuing on the previous course of action by changing the calculation of costs and benefits' (Cortright 1997:273). Here, an incentive is the act of granting a benefit with a clear expectation of receiving something in return (Emmanuel 2010, 2013). The overall objective of the incentives examined in this article has to do with managing conflict by facilitating bargaining relationships. These strategies can be used throughout the conflict cycle.

Incentives involve a trade-off between interference and the advancement of peace and protection (Nye 2002:8). These types of policy instruments are used to influence other people's behaviour. They do so by reducing uncertainty over the process leading to a peaceful resolution of conflict, helping to give credibility to the negotiations and easing uncertainty about their future intergroup relations (North 1990; Zartman 2001:300). As Rothchild (1997:148) indicates, 'determined mediators need not passively wait for a ripe moment to emerge'. Incentives can advance 'ripeness' for conflict resolution (Zartman 1985), but this is a delicate endeavour. Through the application of incentives, mediators can help advance the ripening process in some instances.

Incentives typology

External actors help manage conflict in a variety of ways. They use a wide spectrum of diplomatic, economic and security options to de-escalate conflict. This section highlights the main incentive categories, addressing their contributions to conflict management and resolution. As Power (2002:xviii) writes, there is a 'continuum of intervention'. As depicted later, at one end of the spectrum are the least coercive measures that can be implemented to facilitate peaceful bargaining (Rothchild 1997; Rothchild and Emmanuel 2010). One end includes purchase, insurance, legitimation and economic support. At the other end of the intervention continuum, the more coercive incentives include diplomatic pressure, a wide variety of sanctions and different types of military intervention. Although these coercive features are present in these options, they should be considered incentives that attempt to bring about cooperation. External actors use these policies to encourage the combatting factions to alter their calculations and de-escalate already tense relations. The objective involves making the adoption of more peaceful behaviour favourable to participants in a given conflict. Incentives are frequently applied together in packages, as with Sudan. However, the choice of which incentive(s) to apply in any given case depends on a third party's capacity, willingness to engage and assessment of what will prove effective in de-escalating the conflict and advancing peace.

Noncoercive incentives

Noncoercive incentives are more likely to result in a durable peace (Rothchild and Emmanuel 2010). Overall, the choice of incentive(s) is based on the diplomat's perception of their country's interests and the ability of their strategic approach to realize its desired purposes of conflict termination at a reasonable cost (Zartman 1995:7).

Importantly, making overarching generalizations about the use of different foreign policy approaches is rather difficult; each conflict has its own dynamics and specificities. That said, it is possible to glean vital information from previous uses of incentives in conflict management. It is valuable to consider past experiences to better inform possible incentive choices that may be relevant in each future context. To explore these experiences and any potential generalizations, the next few pages will examine four noncoercive incentives before proceeding to three more coercive ones.

Purchase

A number of relatively low-cost but effective means of facilitating cooperation are available. The noncoercive incentive strategy of purchase represents one of these options. Purchase refers to short-term, tangible fiscal rewards or side payments that can alter behaviour to help end conflict. Purchase differs from economic aid, which is much larger in terms of amount and scope. Even with such a limited option, the outside actor enlarges the pie in order to facilitate the possibility of reconciliation. It alters the payoff structure to transform a dispute from a constant-sum to a positive-sum game, thus enhancing the opportunity to achieve compromise (Rubin 1981:27; Touval 1982:327). More concretely, purchase can be used to make special arrangements with individuals or groups of individuals to encourage exit (i.e. leave the conflict). The hope is to eliminate the potential for spoilers that may undermine the move away from violent conflict.

Such special deals to encourage an exit can be seen in the successful effort to persuade former Ethiopian leader Mengistu Haile Mariam to leave Addis Ababa and depart for Zimbabsuwe in 1991. Furthermore, this technique can provide short-term financing to rebel movements to ease their transformation into legitimate political parties in the hope that they will become stakeholders in the political system. Purchase is widely used and, despite its relatively low cost, can contribute significantly to furthering conflict-prevention goals (Rothchild 1997:257). By themselves, such incentives are not likely to overcome the commitment problem in intense conflict situations; even here, however, their contribution to conflict management should not be dismissed lightly.

Insurance

Outside actors can play important roles by encouraging conflicting parties to adopt and respect inclusive political institutions and minority protection as well as to uphold negotiated settlements. Insurance incentives can help manage conflict by trying to alleviate the fears of disenfranchised groups. These measures are frequently offered during the peace-implementation phase in an effort to make possible more pacific interactions in the future. External parties can transform a dispute by promising protection for minorities and safeguarding their participation in the political institutions. The international community may have considerable capacity to reassure minority groups through promises of support for elections; political autonomy; inclusion of weaker interests on a proportional basis in the civil service and central government; the rule of law; judicial impartiality; rules on the proportional distribution of revenues and the protection of linguistic, religious and ethnic rights (Rothchild and Emmanuel 2010:129–130).

Encouraging as such promised guarantees are for minority security and well-being, there are limits to their efficacy, and the majority party cannot credibly commit future leaders to refrain from exploiting smaller parties at a later date (Fearon 1998:108). Additionally, considerable constraints on external actors may exist and undermine such incentives. Under pressure from their own domestic constituents to reduce overseas involvements (especially ones that they believe might not fit in their perceived 'national interests'), third parties find it difficult in practice to honour fully the 'guarantees' they give to uphold an agreement.

Legitimation

Perhaps one of the most powerful inducements for peaceful relations is the inclusion of a given actor as a part of the international community. Acceptance (or non-acceptance in some cases) by other states is a form of soft intervention that affects the credibility of the underlying negotiating process (Zartman 2001:300). Third parties can use such legitimacy incentives to induce the cooperation of a target state or movement in preventing violent conflict or helping to de-escalate it once it has emerged. In passing judgement on other actors' legitimacy, states and international organizations can affect the reputation of elites and their ability to enter into beneficial relations with other members of the international community and all of the benefits it entails. This option is a form of what Joseph Nye (1990:168) calls 'soft power'.

Given such opportunities for international action, on the one hand, it seems clear that legitimacy incentives represent a noncoercive means of considerable potential importance in various contexts, such as in the area of conflict prevention and de-escalation. On the other hand, the exclusion of a state from full participation or membership in an international organization involves elements of delegitimation that can be costly in terms of access and support from donors and potential investors. Consequently, states are willing to take serious measures to avoid a loss of international standing. The readiness of international organizations to hold out the prospect of inclusion or exclusion is clearly a powerful tool at their disposal.

Economic support

The prospect of donor economic support holds out the likelihood that increased economic opportunity for all will enhance mutual cooperation and lower the probability of future warfare. It seems clear that when a society and its elites anticipate gains from cooperation and bargaining, they should be more readily prepared to work through potential crises and try to build a more prosperous future. Using aid as an incentive can hold promise for peace (Emmanuel 2015).

Development aid can be especially useful in the early stages of conflict before widespread violence. Donor funds can help overcome group grievances that may lead to war by building the economy and redistributing the benefits of economic growth. Additionally, aid can be critical in the post-conflict phase, helping ease tensions and avoid a recurrence of violence (Doyle and Sambanis 2000:795). Further recent research does in fact indicate that in the sample of African cases in which international donors gave sustained developmental assistance after the signing of a peace agreement, the majority did not return to war within five years (Rothchild and Emmanuel 2005:24). When assistance was not sustained or decreased, however, the chances of a return to civil war increased noticeably. Note that such economic support packages are not personalistic, like the purchase option; instead, economic aid is offered to assist the wider national community with the hope of reconciliation and development.

The promise of aid represents a future peace dividend offered to parties to induce them to overcome their differences and agree on joint problem-solving approaches. The adversaries have an incentive to agree to peace and thus gain the benefits that follow from ending the uncertainty of protracted war and creating new possibilities for economic development (Emmanuel 2015). Here, incentives in the form of developmental assistance can prove critical in the negotiations process, while cultivating the ripening process and an eventual negotiated settlement.

Coercive incentives

In addition to noncoercive incentives, three coercive incentives are available to external parties for conflict management. Despite their coercive features, one should treat them as incentives for cooperation since external actors use coercive measures to change the calculations of costs and benefits of local parties and encourage them to alter policies accordingly (Rothchild and Emmanuel 2010). Treating such coercion *as* incentives strategies means to retain a focus on how the dynamics change among the parties to the conflict themselves (cf. the Introduction Chapter). This stands in contrast to the mode it is usually talked about in public debates, that is, whether 'we, the interveners' are able to 'enforce' our will, which implies that we ultimately take control as if the local parties could or should be cut out of the configuration of political forces. This inclusion of coercive actions among the corpus of incentive strategies is different from the narrower approach adopted by some scholars but seems justified in terms of the purposes of the sending actor(s) and how they go about achieving them. These approaches include diplomatic pressure, sanctions and military intervention.

Diplomatic pressure

Diplomats frequently act in a preventive manner by raising awareness of the potential future costs of escalating conflict. They attempt to alter the perceptions of the warring parties, shifting them towards more accommodating positions. The effective communication of the possibly negative impact of continuing conflict-prone behaviour is crucial to the success of this strategy. However, diplomats need leverage on the parties and the interests involved to be able to press for a more peaceful situation. Stern warnings alone are frequently not enough to facilitate bargaining. To build leverage, diplomatic efforts are often combined with other incentives. Some of the most effective courses of action include offering economic assistance or warning about an imminent cut-off of aid, as well as threatening to invoke or offering to remove other types of sanctions and deciding on the inclusion or exclusion of a target state from an international organization. This is clearly seen in the Sudan case described later in this paper.

Sanctions

Sanctions (e.g. conditionalities, targeted sanctions and economic sanctions) are an important resource for conflict management but call for careful application. The threat or actual imposition of sanctions on a state or movement represents an important coercive incentive strategy. Sanctions are designed to alter the behaviour of combatants in a desired direction, in this case towards a peaceful settlement of the conflict. These actions seek to punish those who violate widely held international norms and to provide incentives for cooperation if behaviour changes. Sanctions also have an important symbolic dimension, as they indicate the international community's displeasure with the target's behaviour. This second aspect of sanctions is frequently underestimated. If one views the impact of sanctions broadly and includes the psychological and symbolic effects they have on the bargaining environment, then it is critical to stress their potential contribution on peace negotiations as well.

Nonetheless, it is important to note that sanctions are widely viewed as ineffective tools. Broad-based economic sanctions have a problem targeting the precise groups deemed responsible for the offensive behaviour (Cortright and Lopez 2000:4). Moreover, sanctions have not historically proven to be relevant coercive instruments vis-à-vis authoritarian regimes, weak states or those with a certain level of autonomy from the influence of the sender (or more generally the influence of the international community). Sanctions, then, require careful application if they are to provide an incentive for change. Nonetheless, sanctions can be considerably strengthened when applied in a multilateral manner with demands for change that are limited in scope and with targeted states that have clear links to the global economy.

Military intervention

When other options fail to prevent conflict from escalating, external actors may have little choice other than threatening or using military force. Such actions should be viewed as a last resort. Yet, the threat or actual deployment of military power may at times prove indispensable to de-escalate dangerous situations and to further legitimate objectives. Under the proper conditions, military intervention can play a constructive role and alter the conflict trajectory, facilitate bargaining and protect vulnerable peoples (Jentleson and Whytock 2005–2006:52). Provided their troops are sufficient in number to achieve their purposes and are well trained and armed, third-party military actions or the threat of such actions may be indispensable in strengthening a political initiative (Craig and George 1995:258; Jentleson 2002:274).

Beyond protecting vulnerable populations, military enforcement can be an important element in overcoming the credible-commitment problem and information issues that frequently undermine peace processes (Lake and Rothchild 1998). In addition to monitoring the actions of adversaries and providing information, the third party's use of military enforcement can actually further buttress a peace process by raising the costs of attempting to break the new bargain. Supporting this conclusion, Barbara Walter (2002:83) finds that parties in a peace process are 20% more likely to follow through on an agreement if a third-party intervenes as a protector of the agreement. Thus, third parties are likely to play a critically important role in overcoming the uncertainties surrounding the consolidation process, providing much-needed support to the state and raising the costs for potential challengers (Hartzell, Hoddie and Rothchild 2001:203).

Obviously, military force can at times be helpful in third-party attempts to manage conflict. It may be able to protect at-risk populations from massive human rights abuses or genocide, as in the case of Rwanda or Darfur. War appears to be changing in the twenty-first century, however, in Africa and elsewhere, as militia groups replace regular armies on the battlefield. Readily available modern technology and guerrilla tactics combine, making military intervention and peace enforcement and peacekeeping difficult for conventional armed forces. The conflicts in Somalia and Mali underscore this concept. In such situations, the very notion of victory may have lost some of its meaning, as irregular forces simply avoid surrender and melt into their communities until another opportunity presents itself. Moreover, external military force may even prove counterproductive and bring about a nationalist rally-around-the-flag effect, undermining the third parties' efforts. Clearly, military intervention in many contemporary conflicts is a delicate task, especially while trying to protect at-risk peoples, remaining unbiased and either helping the parties involved reach an agreement or assisting them in the implementation of one. However, this task may be so delicate that it is virtually impossible.

As demonstrated with the peace process that ended Sudan's North–South war (1983–2005), the United States used a variety of non-military incentives to build leverage over the warring parties. Packages of noncoercive and coercive incentives were deployed during the negotiations in order to push the process forward. U.S. diplomats regarded their efforts as catalysts, assisting other mediators to prod the negotiating parties forward. As we will see, incentives can be powerful tools.

Sudan: the role of U.S. incentives

The second Sudanese North–South Civil War (1983–2005), which killed an estimated two million people, was ended by a negotiated settlement after years of mediation to get the warring parties (i.e. the Government of Sudan and the Sudan People's Liberation Army/Movement – SPLA/M) to agree on how to resolve their bitter conflict peacefully. But merely getting the parties to enter into dialogue was far from easy. After years of abortive efforts, IGAD negotiators from the East African subregion finally facilitated an agreement between Khartoum and the SPLA in early 2002. The U.S. would come to play a crucial role supporting the peace process.

Washington, like no other member of the international community, had built up leverage with Khartoum starting in the 1990s, when the Clinton administration

> slowly ramped up uniliateral pressures in response to Sudan's abysmal human rights recond, its prosecution of the war [in the South] and its support for terrorism. This culminated in the imposition of comprehensive unilateral sanctions in late 1997. [The Clinton administration was effective] in using its policy of isolation and containment to develop leverage with Khartoum.
>
> *(ICG 2002:62)*

Subsequently, the Bush II administration was able to use this leverage in its efforts to promote a negotiated settlement to the conflict. Additionally, after the 9/11 attacks and American military intervenion in Afghanistan and Iraq, the U.S. was able to play the terrorism card with Khartoum, further increasing its leverage to bring the warring parties to the negotiating table. Such an environment allowed American incentives to have an important impact on the Sudanese government, which was more than willing to comply in order to improve its flagging international reputation. The U.S. policy of isolating Khartoum provided mediators with sigificant leverage. The end of this isolation was used as an incentive, part of a package of incentives that would bring Karthoum and the SPLA to the bargaining table.

It is important to add that the U.S. was not the only outside actor in the peace process. It was the outcome of concerted efforts from regional and international mediation teams, which were led by the IGAD and the IGAD Partners' Forum, including the U.S., the EU, Norway, the Netherlands, Canada, Italy and the UN. During the mediation process, U.S. diplomats largely wielded influence indirectly and maintained a low profile, working together with other negotiating teams.

Nonetheless, during the peace process, the International Crisis Group (2003a:1) argued that 'sustained U.S. pressure on the parties' was 'the single most important factor' in moving the Sudanese negotiations forward after the initial ceasefire in early 2002. This preliminary ceasefire in the Nuba Mountains was signed by the Government of Sudan and the SPLA on 18 February 2002 in Bürgenstock, Switzerland. This event laid the foundation for the entire process of the negotiated settlement culminating in the Comprehensive Peace Agreement that was signed on 9 January 2005.

One of the key early objectives of the United States and the other external mediators was to push the combatants towards the realization that they were in a hurting stalemate (Africa Confidential 2002:1). U.S. Secretary of State Colin Powell and the group of American envoys led by former U.S. Senator John Danforth had to push hard to get Khartoum and the SPLA to accept this reality. This 'ripening' process was facilitated by the deployment of U.S. incentive strategies, including insurance and guarantees, legitimation, promises of economic aid, diplomacy and the manipulation of a tough sanctions regime. These actions provided leverage for the negotiators, bringing the parties together in order to reach a definitive negotiated settlement on the North–South conflict. For example, talks stalled shortly after the signing of the Machakos Protocol. However, the U.S. combined diplomatic pressure with threats to deepen the sanctions regime on Khartoum to increase the costs of the target if it did not alter its preferences (i.e. continue fighting and not to negotiate). The next several pages provide further detail on how the U.S. used incentives, as in the aforementioned example, to build leverage in relation to the negotiating parties in the Sudan conflict.

Incentives

During the peace process, the U.S. adopted a rather balanced approach, somewhat favouring noncoercives (see Figure 11.1). The International Crisis Group (2003a) indicated that American leverage in the Sudanese North–South peace process was derived mostly from diplomatic pressures and economic sanctions. From the empirical data presented in Figure 11.1 and Appendix, the U.S. approach was actually using a more balanced variety of incentive strategies, combining both noncoercive and coercive ones.

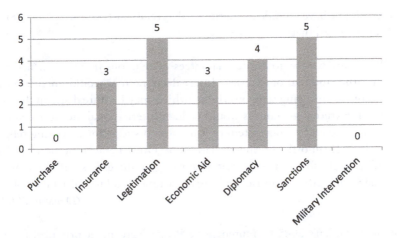

FIGURE 11.1 U.S. Use of Incentives during Sudanese Peace Process (2002–2005) (see Appendix).

It is important to note that the U.S. used an incentives approach to 'ripen' the situation and encourage the dialogue between the two primary combatants. During the negotiations, Washington used its leverage with Khartoum and the SPLA to play a constructive role in attempting to alter the priorities of these rivals. With the Sudanese government, the U.S. was able to offer aid, investment, international legitimation initiatives and looser sanctions. Washington was able to encourage the SPLA to negotiate by explaining that they would lose support with its American constituencies (especially its friends in the U.S. Congress) if it did not negotiate in good faith. As demonstrated earlier in Figure 11.1, U.S. diplomats used five different incentives strategies in the peace process: insurance, legitimation, the offer of economic assistance and sanctions.

Insurance

The problem of insuring the representation of minority interests in new post-conflict state institutions received considerable attention in the discussions during Sudan's North–South and Darfur peace processes. The final 2005 Comprehensive Peace Agreement between Khartoum and the SPLA represents such an effort. Outside actors helped with numerous protective measures in this negotiated settlement, including temporary power-sharing mechanisms in the central government in Khartoum, English and local language usage in the South, and the referendum for the independence of the South in 2011, leading to eventual autonomy for the planet's most recent independent state, South Sudan. Additionally, early in the Machakos negotiations, President George W. Bush's Special Envoy for Peace in Sudan, former U.S. Senator Danforth, pointed out that any peace process must explore ways of 'guaranteeing religious freedom' if Southern

Sudanese are to have confidence in the final agreement (Danforth 2002:28). His 2002 report stated that:

> "The key will be to create guarantees of religious freedom, which could be either internal or external. Internal guarantees would entail a judicial means of enforcing religious rights, which may be unrealistic in the short-term. External guarantees would include international monitoring of religious freedom with a system of 'carrots and sticks' for enforcing religious rights". [Danforth concluded that] "[t]he United States should consider in advance the form and extent of whatever guarantees it is willing to provide and which other countries and organizations could usefully be involved".
>
> *(Danforth 2002:30)*

Ultimately, Sudan's 2005 Comprehensive Peace Agreement provided for a variety of institutional protections for non-Muslim interests, assuring that Sharia Law would not be implemented in the South during the transition, coexistence of the Sudanese Armed Forces and the SPLA during the transition period, international monitoring of the ceasefire, formulas for wealth and power sharing, and specified Southern representation. These are important protections for threatened minorities and reassuring them in the future, helping them commit to a peace process.

Legitimation

U.S. negotiators recognize the powerful attractiveness of legitimacy incentives in their calls to governments and their opponents to negotiate and sign peace agreements. In the case at hand, Washington knew that it could play an important role and let Khartoum achieve some international acceptability, chiefly by removing Sudan from its list of countries not cooperating in 'the war on terror' (Africa Confidential 2004:2). Accordingly, after hinting at this incentive several times during the early Naivasha round of negotiations, the U.S. removed Sudan from this list in March 2004, playing a significant role in normalizing relations with Washington and the international community as a whole. Furthermore, the U.S. also held some leverage over Khartoum and its desire to normalize relations with the international community, as the U.S. was able to keep it from attaining membership to World Trade Organization. Furthermore, Washington held out the carrot of repealing International Monetary Fund restrictions, potentially granting it access to the Paris Club.

The fact that high-level U.S. officials such as former Secretary of State Colin Powell played such an important role in the negotiations that ended the Sudanese North–South war further demonstrated American commitment. Many even thought that Powell's presence provided the much-needed boost to the process (Africa Research Bulletin 2003b:15501). Nonetheless, Khartoum apparently wanted to improve its standing vis-à-vis the international community, and the U.S. was able to dispose certain incentives that would allow this change in status – in exchange for buying into the peace process.

Economic aid promises

A significant foreign assistance package can be a strong incentive to get negotiating parties to take a peace process seriously (Emmanuel 2015). Such economic assistance can be critical in rebuilding infrastructure in the aftermath of war. Pledges of aid played a central role in pushing the Sudanese negotiations from 2002 onwards. Not only did the U.S. offer economic assistance, it also coordinated with other key donors, the UN, and the World Bank on capacity building for the pre-interim period and setting programme priorities immediately after the CPA peace agreement was reached. The promise of a coordinated international response by aid providers can clearly be a strong incentive for peace.

Diplomatic pressure

Diplomatic pressure from various actors in the international community played a key role in pushing the peace process forward in Sudan, and U.S. mediators used skilful argumentation along with various types of incentives and rewards to ripen the situation. The main result of this was to convince the warring parties that they had indeed reached a mutually detrimental stalemate and needed to find a negotiated settlement. Later, in the 2003 Naivasha negotiations, former U.S. Secretary of State Colin Powell pointed out the reality of mutual exhaustion on the part of Khartoum and the SPLA together with the necessity of finding a mutually beneficial solution (Roeder and Rothchild 2005:106). The North was viewed as being weary of war. It could control the crucial oil fields in the South in good weather, but when the weather turned bad and the rainy season came, it struggled to do so. While Southern forces appeared less fatigued by the conflict, they too were unable to escape the back-and-forth fighting that was so closely influenced by the weather and seasons. The Southern leaders also perceived no 'victory' in sight. U.S. mediators used the idea of a hurting stalemate to influence the negotiations and push them forward. Secretary of State Powell gave his insight into official thinking on the timing of an American intervention: 'After a while', he stated, 'people start to wonder why they continue to fight when it is clear neither side will ultimately prevail, and a period of exhaustion sets in' (Susan 2003:2). Perceiving the time for a settlement to be propitious in the Sudan, U.S. diplomats facilitated the mediation process. To push the negotiations forward, the Bush II administration dropped Sudan from the list of countries considered non-cooperative in the War on Terror and held out the possibility of lifting U.S. sanctions. In this way, Washington sought to influence Sudanese leaders in the North to work towards a negotiated settlement with the South (Africa Research Bulletin 2004:15771; BBC News 2004). The Americans persuaded the parties to negotiate, offered alternatives and influenced the negotiating process with diplomatic incentives.

Clearly, mediators use their leverage over the parties involved in the conflict so that diplomatic pressures can work. In the case of Sudan, the mediators helped bring the parties into an agreement based on which I. William Zartman (1997:197) calls a 'mutually enticing opportunity'. When such a violent conflict is intense and third-party influence is needed, a mediator requires the capacity to raise the costs of proceeding with a given course of action (Cortright 1997:273).

Sanctions

Considering coercive incentives and the external efforts to influence the North-South Civil War in Sudan, the strongest international pressure by far was the U.S. sanctions regime (outlined in the Appendix), which was strengthened by the supposition that Sudan was supporting a number of terrorist organizations and destabilizing the region. The leverage created by the sanctions regime played a significant role in the success of the North-South peace process. The reward of removing the U.S. sanctions was used as a carrot, just as often as was the threat of the further strengthening of the sanctions regime. At specific times in the negotiations, however, when the Government of Sudan appeared obstinate, the U.S. mediators were able to push back and threaten to strengthen their sanctions on Khartoum (Africa Research Bulletin 2003a:15463). In April 2004, for example, the U.S. State Department expressed frustration over the slow progress in the peace talks and warned of further possible sanctions under the American 2002 Sudan Peace Act if the parties failed to reach an agreement soon (Gollust 2004). American negotiators understood the weight of the sanctions on Khartoum and were able to use it positively to reach a negotiated settlement.

Conclusion

A wide variety of incentive strategies are available for external actors in an attempt at managing conflict and facilitating negotiation settlements in even some of the most intractable civil wars. Nonetheless, external actors do not always consider the full range of options. The above-mentioned incentive strategies can give interveners leverage and aid them in their efforts to mediate and hopefully bring deadly conflict to an end. This leverage is frequently diplomatic in nature, not simply military, providing an advantageous basis for soft intervention in conflicts, especially when the extremes of withdrawal and military intervention are inappropriate and possibly even counterproductive. The problem is that these non-coercive/non-military incentives may not raise the costs of defiance sufficiently. Hence, as the previous discussions of economic sanctions and military enforcement suggest, it is necessary at times to link diplomacy with the threat of force to produce breakthroughs in the negotiation process. Regardless, evidence points to the fact that African elites, as well as scholars, policymakers and the public in the sender and target countries, generally prefer noncoercive incentives to their coercive counterparts because the sting of external imposition is less apparent and the resulting bargain has a voluntary quality about it (Rothchild and Emmanuel 2006). The chapter has therefore illustrated the general argument of the book: that the dynamics of the conflict itself are also often central throughout a transformation. The crucial impact of the incentives was to get the conflicting parties from a belief in the meaningfulness of continuing previous conflict behaviour to first see the conflict as a mutually hurting stalemate and ultimately as a 'mutually enticing opportunity'. Following on these realities, future research on this topic should examine the critical issues of: (1) the proper timing of the deployment of various incentives and (2) how packages of multiple incentive types have been combined and used successfully to encourage bargaining and resolve conflict.

APPENDIX: U.S. incentives & peace process to end the sudanese North–South war[1]

INCENTIVE TYPE	DATE	ACTION
Sanctions	1993	U.S. adds Sudan to list of countries which support terrorism and calls for mandatory US opposition to loans and aid from internal financial institution to Sudan.
Sanctions	3.Nov.1997	U.S. President Clinton imposes sanctions on Sudan for supporting terrorist groups, regional insurgencies, devastating civil war, and "abysmal human rights record".
Military Intervention	20.Aug.1998	U.S. bombs a-Shrifa pharmaceutical factory following terrorist attacks on U.S. Embassies in Kenya and Tanzania.
Sanctions	Nov.1999	U.S. extends unilateral sanctions against Sudan.
Sanctions	28.Sept.2001	Due to new found cooperation on terrorism U.S. agrees to lift UN sanctions by abstaining.
PEACE PROCESS	*18.Feb2002*	*NUBA MOUNTAINS CEASE-FIRE*
Economic Aid	2002	U.S. promises aid if the North enters into negotiations.
Insurance	26.April.2002	U.S. Special Envoy to Sudan John Danforth publishes report which emphasizes that peace process needs to include guarantees for religious freedom.
Diplomacy	Spring 2002	Secretary Powell authorizes US Embassy in Khartoum to resume normal operations after a four-year hiatus.
Diplomacy	July.2002	U.S. begins pushing idea of a "Mutually Hurting Stalemate".

(Continued)

INCENTIVE TYPE	DATE	ACTION
PEACE PROCESS	*20.July.2002*	*MACHAKOS PROTOCOL*
Diplomacy	30.Aug.2002	U.S. agrees to formal observer status in peace talks and drafting.
Sanctions	21.Oct.2002	Bush signs Sudan Peace Act into law threatening sanctions if Khartoum impedes relief efforts or is not negotiating in good faith.
Sanctions	2002	U.S. Secretary of State Powell notes during Machakos negotiations that sanctions will remain until comprehensive agreement is signed and implemented.
Insurance	2002	U.S. sends experts to assist in the development of the Machakos Protocol.
Economic Aid	10.May.2003	Sudanese parties, USAID, donors, UN, and World Bank met under US facilitation to talk about the capacity building for the pre-interim period and setting program priorities in the first 6 months after a peace agreement is reached.
Legitimation	14.May.2003	U.S. Assistant Secretary of State for Africa Kansteiner tells Sudanese Vice President Taha that normalization of relations is contingent on cooperation on peace, counter-terrorism, and relief access issues.
PEACE PROCESS	*25.Sept.2003*	*NAIVASHA AGREEMENT ON SECURITY ARRANGEMENTS*
Sanctions	21.Oct.2003	Powell suggests the U.S. might lift sanctions if Sudan reaches a peace accord.
Economic Aid	Dec.2003	U.S. senior official indicates that peace deal could bring in large quantities of aid (as much as $220m from US).
Legitimation	Dec.2003	U.S. indicates that if s successful peace deal is reached, they may remove Sudan from the US list of state sponsors of terrorism.
Diplomacy	15.Dec.2003	U.S. Sec. Of State Powell mentions the "mutual exhaustion" of both sides.
PEACE PROCESS	*7.Jan.2004*	*NAIVASHA AGREEMENT ON WEALTH SHARING*
Legitimation	Mar.2004	U.S. removes Sudan from list of countries in the not cooperating on the war on terror.
Sanctions	Mar.2004	U.S. removes Sudan from list of non-cooperating countries in the war on terror. Senior U.S. officials mentions the possibility of lifting sanctions.

INCENTIVE TYPE	DATE	ACTION
Sanctions	Apr.2004	U.S. warns of possibility of new sanctions under the 2002 Sudan Peace Act if parties do not reach an agreement soon.
Legitimation	14.May.2004	US State Department Representative Charles Snyder promises both sides that a prominent personality will attend the signing of a final agreement.
PEACE PROCESS	*26.May.2004*	*NAIVASHA PROTOCOL ON POWER SHARING*
PEACE PROCESS	*30.Oct.2004*	*NAIVASHA AGREEMENT ON PERMANET CEASEFIRE AND SECURITY ARRANGEMENTS*
Insurance	Nov.2004	U.S. discusses security arrangements with SPLA for final rounds of peace talks with Khartoum.
PEACE PROCESS	*31.Dec.2004*	*NAIVASHA AGREEMENT ON THE IMPLEMENTATION MODALITIES AND GLOBAL IMPLEMNTATION MATRIX AND APPENDICIES*
Legitimation	Jan.2005	U.S. Secretary of State Colin Powell attends the Comprehensive Peace Agreement signing ceremony.
PEACE PROCESS	*9.Jan.2005*	*COMPREHENSIVE PEACE AGREEMENT*

[1] *Foreign Policy in Focus* 2005, "Sudan: Recasting American Foreign Policy," 11 October, http://fpif. org/sudan_recasting_us_policy/; *Human Rights Watch* 2003, "Sudan, Oil, and Human Rights: The United States: Diplomacy Revisited," https://www.hrw.org/reports/2003/sudan1103/28. htm; *Human Rights Watch World Report 2002*, "Sudan", http://hrw.org/wr2k2/africa12.html; United States Department of State 2005, "Chronology of US Engagement in Sudan Peace Process Recapped," 8 January, http://iipdigital.usembassy.gov/st/english/texttrans/2005/01/ 20050108200607attocnich0.2324335.html#axzz477FCI9rG; *BBC* 2003, "Shadow over Sudan Peace Deal," 24 July, http://news.bbc.co.uk/1/hi/world/africa/3092869.st; *New York Times* 2003,"Powell Tries to Nudge Sudan Toward Peace.", 22 October, p. A14; Ellis, S 2003, "Let's not miss this opportunity," Powell Says of Imminent Sudan Peace," US Department of State, Washington DC, 21 October, http://usinfo.state.gov/topical/pol/terror/texts/031023007.htm; *BBC* 2003, "Sudan anger at sanctions renewal," 31 October; *BBC* 2004, "Bush Pushes for Sudan Peace Talks," 22 March, http://news.bbc.co.uk/1/hi/world/africa/3555435.stm; *Middle East Online* 2004, "Sudan Peace Talks Extended amid US Pressure," 22 March 22, http:// middle-east-online.com/english/?id=9348; Gollust, D 2004, "U.S. Expresses Frustration over Impasse on Sudan Peace Talks," *VOANews*, 12 April; *Christian Science Monitor* 2005, "Timeline: Sudan's long path from war to peace," 12 September, http://www.csmonitor.com/2005/0912/ p10s01-woaf.html; *BBC* 2005, "Country Profile: Sudan," 1 August, http://news.bbc.co.uk/ 1/low/world/middle_east/country_profiles/827425.stm

References

Africa Confidential (2002) 'Sudan: Calling the Shots at Machakos', *Africa Confidential* 43 (15): 1–3.

Africa Confidential (2004) 'Sudan: Peace without Honour', *Africa Confidential* 45 (12): 1–4.

Africa Research Bulletin (2003a) 'Sudan', 1–30 September: 15461–15463.

Africa Research Bulletin (2003b) 'Sudan', 1–31 October: 15500–15502.

Africa Research Bulletin (2004) 'Sudan: Last Minute Hitches', 1–31 May: 15770–15771.

BBC News (2004) *Bush Pushes for Sudan Peace Talks.* http://news.bbc.co.uk/2/hi/africa/3555435.stm (accessed 23 June 2017).

Cortright, David (1997) 'Incentives Strategies for Preventing Conflict,' in David Cortright (Ed.), *The Price of Peace: Incentives and International Conflict Prevention*, Lanham, MD: Rowman and Littlefield.

Cortright, David and George Lopez (2000) *The Sanctions Decade: Assessing UN Strategies in the 1990s.* Boulder, CO: Lynne Rienner.

Craig, Gordon and Alexander George (1995) *Force and Statecraft: Diplomatic Problems of Our Time.* New York: Oxford University Press.

Danforth, John (2002) *Report to the President of the United States on the Outlook for Peace in Sudan.* http://pdf.usaid.gov/pdf_docs/Pcaab158.pdf (accessed 23 June 2017).

Doyle, Michael and Nicholas Sambanis (2000) 'International Peacebuilding: A Theoretical and Quantitative Analysis', *American Political Science Review* 94 (4): 779–801.

Elbadawi, Ibrahim and Nicholas Sambanis (2001) 'How Much War Will We See? Estimating the Incidence of Civil War in 161 Countries, 1960–1999', *World Bank Policy Research Working Paper No. 2117*, Washington, DC: World Bank.

Emmanuel, Nikolas (2010) 'Undermining Cooperation: Donor-Patrons and the Failure of Political Conditionality', *Democratization* 17 (5): 856–877.

Emmanuel, Nikolas (2013) 'Evaluating a Political Conditionality Approach: The Role of Aid in Malawi's Democratic Transition', *African and Asian Studies* 12 (4): 415–434.

Emmanuel, Nikolas (2015) 'Peace Incentives: Economic Aid and Peace Processes in Africa,' *African Conflict and Peacebuilding Review* 5 (2): 1–32.

Emmanuel, Nikolas (2016) 'Third Party Incentive Strategies and Conflict Management in Africa', *Air and Space Power Journal – Africa and Francophonie* 7 (1): 14–29.

Fearon, James (1998), 'Commitment Problems and the Spread of Ethnic Conflict', in David Lake and Donald Rothchild (Eds.), *The International Spread of Ethnic Conflict* (107–126), Princeton, NJ: Princeton University Press.

Finnemore, Martha (2003) *The Purpose of Intervention: Changing Beliefs about the Use of Force.* Ithaca, NY: Cornell University Press.

Gollust, David (2004) *US Expresses Frustration over Impasse on Sudan Peace Talks.* www.voanews.com/a/a-13-a-2004-04-12-25-1-66345657/545252.html (accessed 23 June 2017).

Hartzell, Caroline, Mathew Hoddie and Donald Rothchild (2001) 'Stabilizing the Peace after Civil War: An Investigation of Some Key Variables', *International Organization* 55 (1): 183–208.

ICG, International Crisis Group (2002) 'God, Oil & Country: Changing the Logic of War in Sudan', *ICG Africa Report No. 39.* www.crisisgroup.org/africa/horn-africa/sudan/god-oil-and-country-changing-logic-war-sudan (accessed 23 June 2017).

ICG, International Crisis Group (2003a) 'Five Minutes to Midnight in Sudan's Peace Process', 8 August. reliefweb.int/report/sudan/five-minutes-midnight-sudans-peace-process (accessed 23 June 2017).

ICG, International Crisis Group (2003b) *Sudan: Towards an Incomplete Peace.* www.crisisgroup.org/africa/horn-africa/sudan/sudan-towards-incomplete-peace (accessed 23 June 2017).

Jentleson, Bruce (Ed.) (2000) *Opportunities Missed, Opportunities Seized: Preventive Diplomacy in the Post-Cold War World.* Lanham, MD: Rowman and Littlefield.

Jentleson, Bruce (2002) 'Use of Force Dilemmas: Policy and Politics', in Robert Lieber (Ed.), *Eagle Rules: Foreign Policy and American Primacy in the Twenty-First Century* (47–69), Upper Saddle River, NJ: Prentice Hall.

Jentleson, Bruce and Christopher Whytock (2005–2006) 'Who 'Won' Libya? The Force–Diplomacy Debate and Its Implications for Theory and Policy', *International Security* 30 (3): 47–86.

Lake, David and Donald Rothchild (Eds.) (1998) *The International Spread of Ethnic Conflict: Fear, Diffusion, and Escalation*. Princeton, NJ: Princeton University Press.

Lapidus, Gail and Svetlana Tsalik (Eds.) (1998) *Preventing Deadly Conflict: Strategies and Institutions*. Washington, DC: Carnegie Commission on Preventing Deadly Conflict.

North, Douglas (1990) *Institutions, Institutional Change and Economic Performance*. New York: Cambridge University Press.

Nye, Joseph (1990) 'Soft Power', *Foreign Policy* 80: 153–171.

Nye, Joseph (2002) *The Paradox of American Power*. New York: Oxford University Press.

Nye, Joseph (2004) *Soft Power: The Means to Success in World Politics*. New York: Public Affairs.

Power, Samantha (2002) *A Problem from Hell: America and the Age of Genocide*. New York: Basic Books.

Roeder, Phillip and Donald Rothchild (2005) *Sustainable Peace: Power and Democracy after Civil Wars*. Ithaca, NY: Cornell University Press.

Rothchild, Donald (1997) *Managing Ethnic Conflict in Africa: Pressures and Incentives*. Washington, DC: Brookings Institution Press.

Rothchild, Donald and Nikolas Emmanuel (2005) 'United States: The Process of Decision-Making on Africa', in Ulf Engel and Gorm Olsen (Eds.), *Africa and the North: Between Globalization and Marginalization* (55–69), London: Routledge.

Rothchild, Donald and Nikolas Emmanuel (2006) 'U.S. Intervention in Africa's Ethnic Conflicts: The Scope for Action', in Donald Rothchild and Edmond Keller (Eds.), *Africa–US Relations: Strategic Encounters* (65–97), Boulder, CO: Lynne Rienner.

Rothchild, Donald and Nikolas Emmanuel (2010) 'Soft Intervention in Africa: US Efforts to Generate Support for Peace', in Mathew Hoddie and Caroline Hartzell (Eds.), *Strengthening Peace in Post-Civil War States: Transforming Spoilers into Stakeholders* (123–143), Chicago, IL: University of Chicago Press.

Rubin, Jeffery (Ed.) (1981) *Dynamics of Third Party Intervention: Kissinger in the Middle East*. New York: Praeger.

Susan, Ellis (2003) '"Let's Not Miss This Opportunity", Powell Says of Imminent Sudan Peace', *U.S. Department of State*. https://allafrica.com/stories/200310240026.html (accessed 23 June 2017).

Touval, Saadia (1982) *The Peace Brokers: Mediators in the Arab–Israeli Conflict, 1948–1979*. Princeton, NJ: Princeton University Press.

Walter, Barbara (2002) *Committing to Peace: The Successful Settlement of Civil Wars*. Princeton, NJ: Princeton University Press.

Zartman, I. William (1985) *Ripe for Resolution: Conflict and Intervention in Africa*. New York: Oxford University Press.

Zartman, I. William (1995) 'Systems of World Order and Regional Conflict Reduction', in I. William Zartman and Victor Kremenyuk (Eds.), *Cooperative Security: Reducing Third World Wars* (3–24), Syracuse, NY: University Press.

Zartman, I. William (1997) 'Explaining Oslo', *International Negotiation* 2 (2): 195–215.

Zartman, I. William (2001) 'Negotiating Internal Conflict: Incentives and Intractability', *International Negotiation* 6 (3): 297–302.

12

ON THE CONTINUATION OF THE ISRAELI–PALESTINIAN CONFLICT

Martin Beck

Introduction: the puzzle of the continued Israeli–Palestinian conflict

The Israeli–Palestinian conflict appears as a protracted or intractable conflict *par excellence*. As we are accustomed to this perspective, the decades-long continuation of the Israeli–Palestinian conflict is often taken as a definite fact rather than understood as contingent. The aim of the present chapter is to seriously address the continuation of this conflict as something puzzling and thus an academic issue in need of being properly described and explained: How and why has the Israeli–Palestinian conflict continued for decades? When tackling this issue, rather than the causes, the dynamics of the conflict are to be emphasized.

The fruitfulness of this endeavour presupposes what is taken for granted too often: that it is productive and appropriate to apply the conflict paradigm to the issue(s) that Israelis and Palestinians have with one another. The critical discussion of applying the conflict paradigm to the Israeli–Palestinian conflict to be presented in the second main section serves the purpose of sharpening the idea of the Israeli–Palestinian issue(s) as a conflict in general and as a continuous conflict in particular, thereby emphasizing three facets: situation of contradiction, interaction and actors. This theoretical section will be followed by two empirical ones: in a diachronically oriented section, critical junctures of the Israeli–Palestinian conflict will be discussed. The subsequent synchronic section addresses the issue of continuation of the Israeli–Palestinian conflict in reference to the facets of situation of contradiction, interaction and actors.

The conflict paradigm and Israeli–Palestinian issues

Some scholars, most prominently Lisa Taraki (2006), have questioned the appropriateness of applying the conflict paradigm to the Israeli–Palestinian conflict. She argues that the conflict paradigm promotes a perspective of the Israeli–Palestinian issue as a 'dispute between two warring sides, each of which may have legitimate and valid claims' (2006:449). Such a perspective, however, leads to analyses based on 'even-handedness and balance' (Taraki 2006:453), thereby obscuring the highly asymmetric power relations between Israeli and Palestinian actors. Taraki addresses some severe flaws of many analyses of this conflict. By rejecting the conflict paradigm altogether, however, she throws out the baby with the bathwater. The argument of this chapter is that if the conflict paradigm is well conceptualized, it may serve as a productive tool to analyse issues between Israelis and Palestinians. Achieving this, however, requires seriously addressing potential flaws and assets in the conflict paradigm in its application to the Israeli–Palestinian conflict.

In the present chapter, conflict is strictly empirically defined as a social *situation* in which actors with non-harmonious goals on an issue struggle with each other, which implies a strict separation between conflict and the mode by which the actors deal with it (Mitchell 1981; Wallensteen 2007; Zürn 1992). This definition in no way presupposes that scholars who analyse a conflict commit themselves to the normative position that both conflict adversaries' claims and actions are equally (il)legitimate, as a naïve version of describing conflict narratives does (*cf.* Rotberg 2006). Therefore, in general, even-handedness is not a quality feature of conflict analysis: in some cases, such as conflicts between masters and slaves, the application of a balanced analysis may even be considered perverse. In particular in the present case, it should be taken into account that in the period of European colonialism, projects of colonizing areas of the Global South in general and the Middle East in particular – such as French settlement of Algeria and Zionist settlement of Palestine – were in the range of a mainstream value system which considered it legitimate when culturally 'enhanced' Europeans used their superior power to settle in 'underdeveloped' world areas. However, in the era of postcolonialism starting in the 1950s, the normative system shifted towards a value set which promulgated universal access to human rights (*cf.* Finnemore 1996). As social scientific research, including conflict analysis, may be normatively anchored in the validity of human rights, even-handedness is not a quality criterion of an analysis of the Israeli–Palestinian conflict because the occupational regime established by Israel in 1967 denies the Palestinians access to basic assets of human rights. Mainstream conflict research clearly favours the issue of violence as a relevant dimension of conflict modes, with peace as a normative point of reference. Yet, the dimension of how values are distributed also bears high relevance, and thus should not be neglected. The normative anchor of value distribution is justice. Thus, when discussing the normative implications of the Israeli–Palestinian conflict, not only peacefulness – in the sense of the absence of violence – but also justice – in the sense of a fair distribution of material and immaterial values between the conflict parties – is crucial.

This analysis highlights three basic characteristics of conflict formation: situation of contradiction, conflictual interaction and actors.[1] The social situation formed by the Israeli–Palestinian conflict varies among the different actors involved; yet, the constellation between Israel and the Fatah-led Palestinian Liberation Organization (PLO) can be represented as a graduated prisoner's dilemma (Beck 2004): the two parties strive to acquire effective and legitimate governance over Palestine.[2] Both parties have some incentives to cooperate (that is, to agree upon a rule over Palestine) but also some motives not to do so. The main barrier to cooperation in a simple prisoner's dilemma is the fear of being cheated: the lack of mutual trust has indeed been one of the issues that contributed to the failure of the 1993 Oslo negotiation process. However, in a graduated prisoner's dilemma, another fundamental problem of cooperation accrues, which is the distribution of means of authoritative rule over Palestine. In the present case, countless cooperative outcomes exist in terms of issues such as precisely what territory is to be governed by whom exactly with what kind of sovereignty restrictions.

Critical junctures in the history of the Israeli–Palestinian conflict: four wars and a 'peace process'

Louis Kriesberg (1989) shows in a methodologically sophisticated way that caution is demanded when attributing factors of conflict continuation as causal. In a comparative analysis of the refugee issues created in Central Europe and the Levant in the Second World War and in the first Arab–Israeli War, Kriesberg argues in a counterfactual manner: as parties in the conflict on Israel/Palestine were less influenced by fundamental ideological cleavages than East versus West European actors, in the case of a conflict settlement in the Levant, factors 'explaining' why the conflict on Israel/Palestine was settled would have been rather easily available. This also strengthens the argument of Wæver and Bramsen that when attempting to comprehend the continuation of a conflict, we should start with a look at the dynamics rather than at the roots of the conflict under examination.

For a better understanding of why the Israeli–Palestinian conflict is among the most long-lived ones, it helps to scrutinize critical junctures in its history. The five most significant critical junctures at which – had it not been for the intervention of dynamizing factors – a discontinuation of the conflict could have occurred are: First World War, the militant arguments following the issue of UN Resolution 181 in November 1947, the June War of 1967, the Lebanon War of 1982 and the Israeli–Palestinian negotiation process initiated in 1993 in Oslo. In the following, for every major juncture, two dynamizing factors (each of which is affiliated with one of the two basic parties of the Israeli–Palestinian conflict) are discussed.

The Zionist movement, which had started its nationalist colonization project in the last two decades of the nineteenth century, managed to link itself with British interests in the course of the First World War (Smith 2013: Chapter 2). When after the war the Ottoman Empire was dissolved and the European powers headed by the United Kingdom and France rearranged the political order of the Middle East through direct imperial power extension by establishing the mandate system, London empowered the Zionist movement when incorporating the Balfour Declaration into the Mandate of Palestine, thereby expressing its sponsorship of a Jewish 'national home'.[3] The promotion of Zionism by imperial Britain, in turn, strengthened anti-Zionist actors in the awakening Arab nationalism: in the elitist struggle between the notable families of the Husainis and Nashashibis on developing a political response to imperial penetration, the local Palestinian (rather than regional Arab) aspect of anti-Zionism gained ground in the 1920s. By the 1930s, a fully fledged nationalist Zionist–Palestinian conflict embedded in the imperial mandate system had emerged. Accordingly, the Arab Revolt (1936–1939) was directed against not only the United Kingdom but also the Zionist movement (Smith 2013: Chapter 3).

The UN Partition Plan as issued in 1947 in Resolution 181 triggered a civil war between Palestinians and Zionist Jews, in the course of which the latter gained control over the territory granted by the UN. They then managed to expand their territory in the first Arab–Israeli War in 1948/49, thereby benefiting from Soviet-approved weapon deliveries from Czechoslovakia. Armed hostilities induced the flight and expulsion of the vast majority of the Palestinian population and left its national organizations and leadership devastated (Smith 2013: Chapter 4). The reason why it appears that the Israeli–Palestinian conflict could have ended after the Arab defeat and the effective establishment of the State of Israel, respectively, is less the expectation of an agreement between Israel and the Arab actors (cf. Kriesberg 1989:111). The emergence of a meaningful Arab–Israeli peace was highly unlikely, as Israel was not ready to waive any part of the territory that had come under its control during the armed struggles from 1947 to 1949 (cf. Rabinovich 1991). Rather, an end to the conflict was prevented by the political elites of the Arab republics, under the guidance of Gamal Nasser, who headed the 1952 revolution in Egypt and launched the ideology of pan-Arabism, thereby exploiting the Palestinians' cause on the levels of foreign policy and paternalistic representation.

In June 1967, Israel crushed the Egyptian and Syrian armies, conquering and from then on controlling all territories of the former Mandate of Palestine. Similar to the situation in 1948/49, Israel's main conflict adversary was disempowered and its ideology of liberating Israel/Palestine through pan-Arabism was discredited. However, due to its incoherent interests and policies towards the occupied territories – Israel de facto (in 1980 de jure according to Israeli law) annexed East Jerusalem (without extending citizenship rights to its indigenous inhabitants), kept other parts of Palestine under military administration and confined co-operative attempts to Palestinian notables and the Jordanian regime, both of which enjoyed only low legitimacy among Palestinians – Israel could not fill the domestic Palestinian power vacuum created by the June War. Instead, a hitherto marginal but independent Palestinian political organization – Fatah under the leadership of Yasser Arafat – could lead the PLO, which had been founded under Egyptian tutelage in 1964.

In 1982 under the military-political leadership of defence minister Ariel Sharon, Israel aimed at solving the conflict by eliminating its adversary: the PLO. The campaign appeared to achieve Sharon's aim, as all that the militarily highly inferior PLO could achieve was safe passage of its headquarters from Beirut to distant Tunis. However, deprived of his last power basis in an Arab country neighbouring Israel/Palestine, the PLO accelerated its promotion of institutions suitable for resisting occupation in Palestine which had hitherto been considered of secondary importance by the PLO leadership (Bar-Siman-Tov 1994; Sahliyeh 1986). Thus, when, in late 1987, a spontaneous uprising occurred in the occupied territories, the PLO in Tunis was capable of institutionalizing it within a few weeks as 'Intifada'. At the same time, Arafat responded pragmatically to the 1982 defeat by *de facto* abandoning the militia concept and giving up claims to Israeli territories on the boundaries of 1949 by declaring in 1988 (virtual) Palestinian statehood in the territories occupied by Israel in 1967 only (Baumgarten 2005).

The immediate motivations of the political leaderships of the PLO and Israel, respectively, to sign the Oslo Accords were *not* to reach a final settlement of the conflict. Rather, Arafat saw putting his signature to the document as the only way out of an existential crisis triggered by the alienation of its financiers after the PLO's failure to support the Gulf States against Iraq's annexation of Kuwait in 1990. Israel agreed to Oslo because it combined low costs – no significant restrictions in terms of occupation practices – with high benefits – particularly in terms of legitimacy due to the PLO's full recognition of Israel (Beck 2004). Yet, as the 'peace dividend' for the Palestinian people turned out to be low – even extremely negative in terms of economic development and mobility as a basic freedom right – the Palestinian opposition managed to terminate Oslo by launching the Al-Aqsa Intifada. Israel, on its side, has blocked any advancement at the latest since the failed negotiations at Camp David (2000) and Taba (2001).

A three-dimensional analysis of the continuation of the Israeli–Palestinian conflict

The conflict definition presented earlier allows the structural analysis of the continuation of the Israeli–Palestinian conflict to unfold by applying the conflict trinity composed of a situation of contradiction, interaction (or: mode) and actors (or: parties). *Situation of contradiction* refers to the character of the contested issue; *interaction* relates to the way the conflict is handled; and *actors* deal with those who are in charge of the conflict.

Situation of contradiction

A graduated prisoner's dilemma, as which the conflict between Israel and the PLO has been presented earlier, constitutes a much more complex social situation than an ordinary prisoner's dilemma (Mayer 2006: Chapter 2; Snidal 1985). Why is that so? Consider for a moment that the conflict was an ordinary prisoner's dilemma, as which it is – explicitly or implicitly – actually often presented (Wright 2002). An ordinary prisoner's dilemma has only one cooperative outcome: peace. Power and power asymmetries do not play a role. If the parties just act in a reasonable way, the conflict may be settled. This is not to say that renunciation of violence is an easy target to meet. Yet, it is indeed more easily achieved than cooperation in a graduated prisoner's dilemma, which requires the conclusion of peace *and* a mutually accepted distribution of contested values.

Note that presenting the Israeli–Palestinian conflict as a graduated prisoner's dilemma by no means reflects excessive pessimism in terms of chances to settle the conflict. On the contrary, it presupposes that some rather optimistic assumptions are valid. First and foremost, the modelling of the Israeli–Palestinian conflict as a graduated prisoner's dilemma only makes sense for the period since 1967. Before that, it appeared rather as a zero-sum game: Israel did not consider any part of the territory inside the ceasefire border lines of 1949 as negotiable and the Palestinians and Arabs were not ready to unconditionally acknowledge Israel as a legitimate state. Second, concerning the Israeli–Palestinian conflict as it has appeared since the June War of 1967, actors are involved in it whose positions constitute a zero-sum game. On both sides of the conflict, this applies to (some) actors with a strong religious identity: (some factions of) Hamas and other Islamist groups such as Islamic Jihad and right-wing Jewish political parties and settlers' organizations, respectively.

Conflictual interaction

Material power is very unevenly distributed among the parties of the Israeli–Palestinian conflict: according to World Bank (2017) figures of 2015, Israel's GDP amounted to USD 35,729 per capita (slightly more than Japan's), whereas the GDP of the West Bank and the Gaza Strip was only USD 2,867 (slightly less than that of the Philippines). The Israeli army is one of the most powerful worldwide, whereas Palestine has only police forces and ill-equipped militias (Global Fire Power 2017).

The constellation of extreme power asymmetry has contributed to a continuation of the conflict insofar as cooperative outcomes which would potentially settle the conflict are very difficult to achieve: Israel has a simple alternative to accepting 'painful concessions', namely maintaining the status quo of occupation. From an Israeli perspective, occupation of Palestine has proven to be a rather functional and flexible concept over the last 50 years: Israel managed to *de facto* expand its borders to areas of cultural, strategic and/or economic interests. Resistance to the occupational regime could be rendered mostly ineffective. Until the early 1990s, area-wide direct military presence served as the major tool of occupation, which was effective but not efficient, as the direct control of the Palestinian population ate up large resources. The Oslo agreements then left the administration of the Palestinian population in most areas (except East Jerusalem and parts of Hebron) to the Palestinian Authority (PA) and focused occupation – beyond settling the West Bank and East Jerusalem – to controlling movements of Palestinian people and goods (Smith 2013: Chapters 10–11). This rearrangement also shifted major parts of the financial costs of occupation away from Israel towards Western states (*cf.* Brynen 2000: Chapter 1). In the twenty-first century,

Israel further diversified the occupational regime, thereby also preparing itself for Palestinian use of force: in the frame of the 'disengagement plan' of the Gaza Strip as implemented by dismantling its settlements in 2005, the Palestinian Mediterranean coastal area was sealed off and control of all movements of people and goods on land, air and sea was tightened. In the West Bank, a barrier that separated major Palestinian population centres from the big Israeli settlements in the West Bank, East Jerusalem and Israel was built and settlement activities were expanded (Smith 2013: Chapter 11).

Israel's major structural challenge related to occupation consists of a soft rather than a hard power problem: occupation of a people's territory is incompatible with postcolonial values of national self-determination and the idea that societies of the Global South should also enjoy full access to human rights. As former Western imperial powers adopted postcolonial values in their concepts of political communication, Israel has been challenged by the fact that its rule over Palestine has been exerted in an era of world history in which the (Western-dominated) international community promulgated occupation and settlement of conquered territories as being beyond the range of civilized policies. This aspect had a significant impact on actions, as it is part of the identity of mainstream Israel to be acknowledged as an integral part of the 'civilised' world.

Israel's violation of the spirit of the postcolonial age could, to a certain degree, be exploited by its main conflict adversary, who managed to present a timelier concept of ruling Palestine: under the leadership of Chairman Arafat, mainstream PLO in the 1980s and 1990s stripped all its socio-revolutionary and anti-imperialist elements, renounced violence and turned into a purely nationalist movement (Baumgarten 2005). This enabled the PLO to bring leverage to bear on the conflict with Israel, as the distribution issue of a graduated prisoner's dilemma cannot be dealt with by the infusion of only power, but also ideas such as a just settlement.

Due to the huge gap in power resources between Israel and the PLO, Israel, however, was not forced to compromise. Yet, in the late twentieth century, Western actors were, on the declaratory level, increasingly endorsing the demand for Palestinian self-determination in the territories conquered by Israel in 1967. Thus, Israel, in principle, came under pressure to provide its Western allies with legitimization for its occupational regime. Israel did so by securitizing occupation: by launching speech acts that constructed Israel as being exposed to threats endangering the survival of the 'Jewish state', Israel attempted to provide the international community with legitimization for its extraordinary measures of occupation.[4] Due to changing international, regional and local conditions, Israel's securitization strategy took different forms, all of which, however, had in common the idea that – given the claimed 'existential threats' to Israel – no reasonable alternative to the continuation of occupation was available. When the Palestinians terminated the Oslo process by launching the Second Intifada, Prime Minister Sharon attempted to legitimize drastic measures against the PLO, the PA and Hamas, by presenting them as actions of combating (global) terrorism. In the immediate aftermath of the attacks of 11 September 2001, Sharon presented Arafat as 'our Bin Laden' (Whitaker 2001:1) and managed to convince American President George W. Bush that Israel's policy of containing Palestinian organizations and their leaders served American interests of combating terrorism. When in 2004 the Israeli army assassinated the co-founding member of Hamas, Ahmad Yassin, Sharon uttered that 'the war against terror has not ended and will continue day after day, everywhere' (Guardian 2004:1). In the light of declining militant attacks committed by Palestinian actors, Prime Minister Benjamin Netanyahu put more emphasis on the issue of the Iranian nuclear programme and argued that the Israeli military presence in the occupied territories was necessary in order to prevent a takeover of Palestine by proxies of the Iranian regime (Sandler 2013:132). In his address to the audience of the 'Conference of Presidents of Major American Jewish Organizations' in February 2014, Netanyahu presented the option of mitigating occupation as a potential threat to the security of Israel: 'The whole land is convulsing, there are earthquakes everywhere you go. And how are we to be sure that areas that we cede to the Palestinians will not be taken over by Hamas and Hezbollah and Al-Queda and Salafis' (Prime Minister's Office 2014:1). Laurence Rothenberg and Abraham Bell present a scholarly version of this sort of securitization by claiming that 'the security fence … plays a crucial role in Israel's fight against the genocidal terror campaign against its citizens' (2004:1).

Even by those who claim that the 'peace process' is dead, the Oslo process and the subsequent negotiations are often presented as (failed) attempts to 'solve' the Israeli–Palestinian conflict by realizing the Palestinian right to self-determination through the establishment of a Palestinian state living in peaceful coexistence with Israel (Rubin 2012). However, the perspective of ending the Israeli–Palestinian conflict by solving it through bilateral negotiations is rather misleading, as the Oslo process and the subsequent bilateral negotiations have hardly restricted Israel in unfolding its highly superior power capabilities vis-à-vis the PLO. The Oslo Accords did not constrain the Israeli occupation policy in terms of settlement activities and measures claimed as relevant to Israel's security; the PA was created as a supplement rather than an opponent to occupation (Krieger 2015: Chapter 3). At the same time, reference to a Palestinian state feigns sovereignty of Palestine vis-à-vis Israel although there is hardly any doubt that Israel is reluctant to grant sovereignty to Palestine, particularly in the realm of security. Thus, Netanyahu clarified several times that Israel under all circumstances will maintain its military control of the Jordan Valley (Rettig Gur 2013), thereby reiterating basics of the plan designed by the Minister of Labour Yigal Allon in 1967.[5]

As on both sides 'spoilers' on the societal level were active – the settlers' movement and the nationalist right on the Israeli side and different militant groups on the Palestinian side – the negotiations process initiated in the Norwegian capital was not a smooth process at all (Beck 2016a). For the Palestinian people, the reality of occupation on the ground remained harsh, with living conditions even deteriorating in many respects, as mobility restrictions on persons and goods became sophisticated. On the Israeli side, the civilian population periodically suffered from militant attacks such as suicide bombings and shelling from the Gaza Strip. Thus, the question arises why both Israel and the PLO in their political communication strategies stick to the concept of the 'peace process'. Israel benefits from holding it up on a diplomatic level, as occupation thus appears potentially as a temporary regime. Yet, why did the PLO and the PA under the leadership of Mahmud Abbas show keen eagerness to regain Israel's recognition as a negotiation partner after the death of Arafat (2004) who – after falling in disgrace – had been put under house arrest for nearly three years? Abbas in fact resumed cooperation with Israel, particularly on the working level in the realm of security (Purkiss and Nafi 2015), thereby accepting the role as a junior partner of occupation. The cancellation of the negotiation process as the only alternative would have required publicly confessing that the mission of the PA to which Fatah had bound itself had failed. Due to the dependence of Palestinian society on Western foreign aid, such a move would have also had severe socio-economic consequences. It is a *topos* in conflict studies that the continuation of a conflict depends to a high degree on the existence of groups that make a living of it (Kriesberg 2005; Le Billon 2001). In the Israeli–Palestinian conflict, however, both main conflict actors have developed a vested interest in reproducing occupation by upholding the chimaera of negotiated peace.

At the same time, upholding the formula of a 'peace process' has given both sides some room to manoeuvre to embark on improvements created by unilateral measures. Israel sealed off the Gaza Strip after dismantling its settlements and erected a separation barrier in the West Bank. Palestinian unilateralism materialized in Initiative 194, which was supposed to establish Palestine as a full member state of the UN. Yet, the Obama Administration effectively blocked the endeavour, thereby lowering the sights of the PLO, which managed to get an upgrade from a 'non-member observer entity' to a 'non-member observer state' in the UN and full membership in the International Criminal Court. Palestinian policies related to Initiative 194 did not improve living conditions of the people enduring occupation. However, the PLO reaped significant gains on the diplomatic level, as its leadership and entourage were promoted from substandard to nearly adequate state bureaucrats (Beck 2016a).

Actors

As the Israeli–Palestinian conflict was unfolding in the heyday of European imperialism in the Levant, external actors have been an integral part of the conflict from the beginning. After the Second World War, Israel was massively supported in material and immaterial terms by European powers, particularly France and Germany in the critical post-independence years of Israeli state consolidation and the US ever since the late 1960s (Beck 2006). However, notwithstanding the fact that Western financial and moral support for Israel has facilitated its ability to unfold its capabilities, the material impact of Western support of Israel in maintaining the occupational regime is rather marginal: the power gap between Israel and Palestinian organizations such as the PLO and Hamas is enormous, regardless of Western support for Israel.

The impact of Western immaterial interference in the Israeli–Palestinian conflict is complex. On the one hand, the West – in particular the US and also leading European states such as Germany – has diplomatically backed Israel with unshakeable loyalty. Although Israel has never made a serious attempt to terminate occupation, the West has refrained from taking any significant measures against Israel and sheltered it from the diplomatic pressure of actors from the Global South and beyond that aimed at sanctioning Israel due to its occupation of Palestine. On the contrary, Israel could even afford to reject occasional American demands of de-escalating conflict behaviour without losing its support. A recent example is the policy of the Obama Administration towards Israel which – despite failing to convince Israel even to stick to a temporary settlement freeze – strongly supported Israel by *inter alia* blocking Initiative 194, averting the promotion of a nuclear-free zone in the Middle East (Bahgat 2015), and granting a record-high financial military aid package to Israel, which Netanyahu praised as a 'historic agreement' (as cited by Pileggi 2016:1; see also Beck 2016a). On the other hand, external diplomatic interferences contributed to the continuation of the Israeli–Palestinian conflict insofar as the West added to keeping the issue high on the international agenda in situations in which Palestinian organizations would have had trouble to achieve that out of their own strength. In the aftermath of the Israeli–Egyptian peace treaty that US President Jimmy Carter brokered in Camp David, the European Council declared in its 1980 summit in Venice that the Palestinians are people that are entitled to attempt national self-determination and furthermore demanded the incorporation of the PLO in negotiations. Thus, when Israel had succeeded in sidelining the PLO in the joint vision of 'A Framework for Peace in the Middle East Agreed at Camp David',[6] the Europeans paved the way for designing the idea of a two-state solution as diplomatically finally sanctioned by Resolution 1397 (2002) of the UN Security Council. In 1982, when Sharon attempted to liquidate the PLO in Beirut with massive force, the US pushed for a truce that guaranteed safe passage for the PLO to Tunis (Smith 2013: Chapter 8). Furthermore, when all that the PLO could achieve in bilateral negotiations with Israel in Oslo in 1993 was limited autonomy in Palestinian population centres completely surrounded by areas under full Israeli control, the West, particularly the EU, supported the PLO in its endeavour to promote the diplomatic idea of installing a sovereign Palestinian state in the frame of a final conflict settlement. Thus, if the distribution of material power between Israel and the PLO had been the only variable determining the outcome of the Israeli–Palestinian conflict, it could have been settled by Israel marginalizing or even liquidating Palestinian organizations that demanded the Palestinian right to self-determination.

When Israel conquered the Palestinian territories in 1967, the political leaderships and social elites in both Israel and Palestine were secular. Only thereafter did a settlers' movement emerge that combined religious and nationalist visions and attempted to consolidate Jewish-Israeli control over Palestine. Although the relationship between the secular Israeli establishment and representatives of diverse forms of politicized nationalist Judaism has never been smooth, a functional labour-sharing system emerged: the political leadership set the framework for colonizing Palestine, while the nationalist-religious movement ideologically supervised the endeavour and spearheaded the implementation in areas beyond the urban settlements in the West Bank close to Israel in the 1949 borders. The Oslo process intensified the cooperation and challenged it at the same time: in the Oslo Accords, the Israeli government avoided committing itself to any restrictions in terms of settling the occupied territories, thereby empowering the settlers' movement to accelerate its project. Still, the system did not find approval among all settlers and some turned to violence to obstruct the Oslo process: in February 1994, Baruch Goldstein massacred 29 Palestinians who were praying in the Ibrahimi Mosque in Hebron. While Prime Minister Yitzhak Rabin – who was politically at odds with the settlers' movement, despite holding contact with some of their leaders (Drori and Weizmann 2007) – would have then had the backing of the majority of Israelis to disarm the settlers, he refrained from doing so, as the potential costs of provoking a controversy with the militant settlers and their supporters in Israel would have been much higher than those Rabin had to pay as a result of an outraged but helpless PLO. After Rabin was assassinated by Yigal Amir in 1995, in the following elections for premiership, Netanyahu successfully mobilized different orthodox and secular right-wing groups, thereby at the same time facilitating accessibility to the Israeli establishment for the nationalist-religious right (Sprinzak 1998).

In Palestine, the politicization of Islam first culminated in the foundation of Hamas in 1987 in the wake of the first Intifada. The self-image of Hamas was originally to act as a sociopolitical movement whose task was *inter alia* to alter the direction of the PLO towards Islam rather than being its replacement in the struggle against Israel. However, with the establishment of the PA, Hamas *de facto* played the role of the major oppositional political party to Fatah. Hamas' rejection of the secular approach of the PLO played a significant role in the contest between the camps. Yet, the power struggle between Fatah and Hamas mainly became ignited by the issue of the appropriate nationalist strategy to combat occupation. Hamas (and other Islamist groups) were the driving political force behind the Al-Aqsa Intifada, which effectively terminated the Oslo process insofar as no substantial negotiations between Israel and the PLO have taken place in the twenty-first century (Beck 2016a). Hamas further gained legitimacy among Palestinians at the expense of Fatah, whom they beat in the parliamentary elections in 2006. Not the least encouraged by the Western refusal to accept Hamas' electoral victory and legitimacy to govern, the two major Palestinian organizations entered a fatal power struggle that ended in Hamas' and Fatah's takeover of domestic affairs in the Gaza Strip and the West Bank in 2007, respectively. Despite some cooperative elements between the two camps, all reconciliation efforts have so far failed (Tuastad 2013).

The growing influence of actors politicizing religion in the Israeli–Palestinian conflict induced new dynamics to the conflict in a twofold way. First, the religiously motivated actors in both conflict parties brought the legitimacy issue of the conflict opponent back on the agenda: Hamas and Israel refrained from recognizing each other as legitimate parties, the same holding true of the religious nationalist movement in Israel and Palestinian organizations. Although the major issue of the Israeli–Palestinian conflict has remained basically the same – governance over territory – the issue of contested legitimacy (of the other's territorial claims) further reduced the already small zones of potential agreement. Thus, second, the penetration of religion into a conflict challenged the basic principle of divisibility: by consecrating the land of Israel/Palestine, Hamas, the settlers' movement and other groups tend to transform the Israeli–Palestinian conflict into an issue over indivisible identities.

Conclusion

The present chapter has deliberately not applied a readily available theory on why and how a conflict continues to the Israeli–Palestinian case. The attempt was rather to conduct a thorough conflict analysis to retrieve and comprehend factors that may have contributed to the fact that the conflict has continued for 100 years or more. The diachronic and synchronic analysis based on the conflict trinity of contradiction, interaction and actors revealed that, in terms of parties, the interference of powerful external actors was most decisive: at several critical junctures, external actors have massively supported one conflict party that otherwise would have probably lacked the capabilities to continue the conflict. In combination with the dimension of contradiction, external actors could interfere in a particularly effective way, because the graduated prisoner's dilemma in which the conflict parties are involved provides leverage to both material and immaterial power.

Although it has been challenging for Israel to legitimize prolonged occupation, as this regime violates human rights, Israel was capable of maintaining it by extending its highly superior material power, supplemented by a policy of securitizing occupation. At the same time, the Israeli–Palestinian conflict has continued for so long because potential settlements that were considered acceptable from a normative point of view in the era of colonialism are not anymore. Thus, Israel could not solve the conflict by irrevocably enforcing its understanding of the system created in the Oslo negotiations as a reservation model, although there are quite some striking similarities to the American model of settling the conflict between the Americans of European origin and the native Americans: in both cases, a local population whose land was invaded by a colonizing power became entitled to regulate its domestic affairs in assigned areas whose outer borders were, however, kept under the sovereignty of the colonizer.

Scholars and politicians alike often present the Israeli–Palestinian conflict as if a peaceful solution would be likely to happen in the foreseeable future (provided that the two main actors, Israel and the PLO, were to act 'reasonably').

This not only ignores that in the face of 50 years of occupation, there is much more empirical evidence for the assumption that the current regime is quite robust than for the supposition that a profound transformation is right ahead – such a perspective also suffers from several analytical and normative shortcomings. In the first instance, to apply the peace paradigm is problematic, as there is no – and never has been – war between Israel and the PLO. Its previous identity as a militia movement notwithstanding the PLO was at no point in history capable of even moderately challenging Israel militarily. The fact that both Palestinian and Israeli actors tend to present it differently is due to their interest in appearing as a strong or potentially threatening actor, respectively. Furthermore, the peace paradigm overlooks that major issues of the Israeli–Palestinian conflict are divisible – in contrast to peace – which is why material and immaterial power come into the play. As Israel is rather well off with the status quo, its incentives to accept 'painful compromises' are limited up to a degree that any deal it would offer to the PLO is of so little benefit to the latter that the Palestinian side also prefers the status quo. At the same time, both the two main conflict adversaries and Western states as the major external actors have a vested interest in portraying negotiations on 'peace' as a promising strategy to settle the conflict: for Israel's ambition to be acknowledged as an integral member of the 'civilised' world, it is essential to portray itself as being ready to end occupation if circumstances allow. When signing the Oslo Accords, the PLO under the leadership of Fatah bound itself to a 'peace process' with Israel and thus would lose its current *raison d'être* if it revoked the idea. The Western community has a strong incentive to uphold the idea that the Palestinian right to self-determination is achievable through bilateral negotiations because recognizing an occupational regime as a legitimate steady form of governance contradicts postcolonial values. Last but not least, focusing on a final settlement may also be considered flawed from a normative point of view. Given the current circumstances, a likely 'solution' to the conflict would mean a non-desirable state of affairs for the Palestinians of Palestine: Graveyard peace.

Notes

1 Contrary to the SIT triangle as presented by Wæver and Bramsen in Chapter 1, in the present chapter, the component of *actors* rather than *tension* is scrutinized. This is done for two reasons. First, the focus on actors facilitates an examination of aspects of the Israeli–Palestinian conflict that are of particular relevance, such as the asymmetry between Israel and the PLO and the intervention of external actors. Second, insights of game theory are better applicable (*cf.* Wallensteen 2007; Zürn 1992).
2 If not otherwise indicated, from now on, "Palestine" refers to the Palestinian territories conquered by Israel in 1967, that is, the West Bank including East Jerusalem and the Gaza Strip.
3 Drafts and the final version of the Balfour Declaration from 1917 are reprinted in Smith (2013: 93–94).
4 For the concept of securitization, see Buzan, Wæver and de Wilde (1998); for Israel's policy of securitizing occupation, see Beck (2016b, 2017).
5 The Allon Plan is available at the Jewish Virtual Library (2017).
6 The document is reprinted in Smith (2013: 393–395).

References

Bahgat, Gawdat (2015) 'Prospects for a Nuclear-Weapon-Free Zone in the Middle East', *Center for Security Studies ETH Zürich*. www.ethz.ch/content/specialinterest/gess/cis/center-for-securities-studies/en/services/digital-library/articles/article.html/191392 (accessed 16 May 2017).

Bar-Siman-Tov, Yaacov (1994) 'The Arab-Israeli Conflict: Learning Conflict Resolution', *Journal of Peace Research* 31(1): 75–92.

Baumgarten, Helga (2005) 'The Three Faces/Phases of Palestinian Nationalism, 1948–2005', *Journal of Palestine Studies* 34(4): 25–48.

Beck, Martin (2004) *Prospects for and Obstacles to Achieving a Viable Palestinian State: What Can an Actor with Inferior Power Capabilities Do in a Graduated Prisoner's Dilemma?* Birzeit: Birzeit University.

Beck, Martin (2006) 'Germany and the Israeli-Palestinian Conflict', in Hanns W. Maull (Ed.), *Germany's Uncertain Power: Foreign Policy of the Berlin Republic* (260–272), Houndmills: Palgrave.

Beck, Martin (2016a) 'Failed Attempts or Failures to Attempt? Western Policies toward Palestinian Statehood', in Martin Beck, Dietrich Jung and Peter Seeberg (Eds.), *The Levant in Turmoil: Syria, Palestine, and the Transformation of Middle Eastern Politics* (167–189), New York: Palgrave.

Beck, Martin (2016b) '"Watching and Waiting" and "Much Ado about Nothing"? Making Sense of the Israeli Response to the Arab Uprisings', *Palgrave Communications* 2 (79): 1–10. www.palgrave-journals.com/articles/palcomms201679 (accessed 15 May 2017).

Beck, Martin (2017) 'Israeli Foreign Policy: Securitizing Occupation', in Robert Mason (Ed.), *Reassessing Order and Disorder in the Middle East: Regional Imbalance or Disintegration?* (173–193), Lanham, MD: Rowman and Littlefield.

Brynen, Rex (2000) *A Very Political Economy: Peacebuilding and Foreign Aid in the West Bank and Gaza*. Washington, DC: United States Institute of Peace Press.

Buzan, Barry, Ole Wæver and Jaap de Wilde (1998) *Security: A New Framework for Analysis*. Boulder, CO: Lynne Rienner.

Drori, Israel and Chaim Weizmann (2007) 'Prime Minister Yitzhak Rabin Against the Settlers: A Stakeholder Analysis', *Public Administration Review* 67(2): 302–314.

Finnemore, Martha (1996) 'Constructing Norms of Humanitarian Intervention', in Peter J. Katzenstein (Ed.), *The Culture of National Security: Norms and Identity in World Politics* (153–185), New York: Columbia University Press.

Global Fire Power (2017) *Israeli Military Strength*. www.globalfirepower.com/country-military-strength-detail.asp?country_id=Israel (accessed 16 May 2017).

Guardian (2004) *Sharon Vows to Continue 'War on Terror'*. www.theguardian.com/world/2004/mar/22/israel3 (accessed 16 May 2017).

Jewish Virtual Library (2017) *Maps of the Palestinian Territories: The Allon Plan*. www.jewishvirtuallibrary.org/map-of-the-allon-plan (accessed 17 May 2017).

Krieger, Helmut (2015) *Umkämpfte Staatlichkeit: Palästina zwischen Besatzung, Entwicklung und politischem Islam*. Wiesbaden: Springer.

Kriesberg, Louis (1989), 'Transforming Conflicts in the Middle East and Central Europe', in Louis Kriesberg, Terrell Northrup and Stuart J. Thorson (Eds.), *Intractable Conflicts and their Transformation* (109–131), Syracuse, NY: Syracuse University Press.

Kriesberg, Louis (2005) 'Nature, Dynamics, and Phases of Intractability', in Chester A. Crocker, Fen Osler Hampson and Pamela Aall (Eds.), *Grasping the Nettle: Analyzing Cases of Intractable Conflicts* (85–98), Washington, DC: United States Institute of Peace Press.

Le Billon, Philippe (2001) 'The Political Ecology of War: Natural Resources and Armed Conflict', *Political Geography* 20(5): 561–584.

Mayer, Peter (2006) *Macht, Gerechtigkeit und internationale Kooperation: Eine regimeanalytische Untersuchung zur internationalen Rohstoffpolitik.* Baden-Baden: Nomos.

Mitchell, Christopher R. (1981) *The Structure of International Conflict.* London: Macmillan.

Pileggi, Tamar (2016) *Netanyahu Thanks Obama for 'Historic' Military Aid Deal.* www.timesofisrael.com/netanyahu-thanks-obama-for-historic-military-aid-deal/ (accessed 16 May 2017).

Prime Minister's Office (2014) *Prime Minister Benjamin Netanyahu's Remarks at the Conference of Presidents of Major American Jewish Organizations.* www.pmo.gov.il/English/MediaCenter/Speeches/Pages/speechpre170214.aspx (accessed 15 May 2017).

Purkiss, Jessica and Ahmad Nafi (2015) *Palestinian Security Cooperation with Israel.* www.middleeastmonitor.com/wp-content/uploads/downloads/factsheets/20151028_Fact-Sheet-PalestinianSecurityCooperationWithIsrael-web.pdf (accessed 15 May 2017).

Rabinovich, Itamar (1991) *The Road Not Taken: Early Arab–Israeli Negotiations.* New York: Oxford University Press.

Rettig Gur, Haviv (2013) *PM: Israel Must Have 'Security Border' in Jordan Valley.* www.timesofisrael.com/pm-israel-must-have-security-border-in-jordan-valley/ (accessed 17 May 2017).

Rotberg, Robert I. (Ed.) (2006) *Israeli and Palestinian Narratives of Conflict: History's Double Helix.* Bloomington: Indiana University Press.

Rothenberg, Laurence E. and Abraham Bell (2004) *Israel's Anti-Terror Fence: The World Court Case.* www.jcpa.org/jl/vp513.htm (accessed 10 May 2017).

Rubin, Barry (2012) 'Is the Peace Process Dead?', *Middle East Review of International Affairs* 16 (2): 30–36.

Sahliyeh, Emile F. (1986) *The PLO after the Lebanon War.* Boulder, CO: Westview Press.

Sandler, Shmuel (2013) 'The Arab Spring and the Linkage between Israel's Domestic and Foreign Policies', in Efraim Inbar (Ed.), *The Arab Spring, Democracy and Security: Domestic and International Ramifications* (128–144), London: Routledge.

Smith, Charles D. (2013) Palestine and the Arab–Israeli Conflict: A History with Documents. Boston, MA: Bedford/St. Martin's.

Snidal, Duncan (1985) 'Coordination Versus Prisoner's Dilemma: Implications for International Cooperation and Regimes', *American Political Science Review* 79 (4): 923–942.

Sprinzak, Ehud (1998) 'The Politics of Paralysis I: Netanhyahu's Safety Belt', *Foreign Affairs* 77 (4): 18–28.

Taraki, Lisa (2006) 'Even-Handedness and the Palestinian–Israeli/Israeli–Palestinian "Conflict"', *Contemporary Sociology* 35 (5): 449–453.

Tuastad, Dag (2013) 'Hamas–PLO Relations Before and After the Arab Spring', *Middle East Policy* 20 (3): 86–98.

Wallensteen, Peter (2007) *Understanding Conflict Resolution.* London: Sage.

Whitaker, Brian (2001) *Sharon Likens Arafat to Bin Laden.* www.theguardian.com/world/2001/sep/14/israel.september11 (accessed 15 May 2017).

World Bank (2017) *GDP per capita (Current US$).* http://data.worldbank.org/indicator/NY.GDP.PCAP.CD (accessed 16 May 2017).

Wright, Robert (2002) *Both Sides Now.* www.slate.com/articles/news_and_politics/the_earthling/2002/05/both_sides_now.html (accessed 17 May 2017).

Zürn, Michael (1992) *Interessen und Institutionen in der internationalen Politik: Grundlegung und Anwendungen des situationsstrukturellen Ansatzes.* Opladen: Leske und Budrich.

13

ONTOLOGICAL SECURITY AND THE CONTINUATION OF THE ARAB–ISRAELI CONFLICT

Amir Lupovici

Introduction: dynamics of conflict continuation

I suggest that there are two main interrelated mechanisms that account for the continuation of conflicts. The first concerns securitizing moves, and in particular meta-securitizing moves that contribute to the perception that the threat remains, which justifies not only the specific measures necessary to address the (alleged) threat, but also the conflict itself. Second, once the conflict is (meta-) securitized, it becomes a constitutive element of the self, thereby validating the actors' ontological security. In this respect, de-securitizing moves that aim to end the conflict are challenging not only because of the uncertainties that accompany these steps as policy moves but also because they challenge the actors' selves. Once the conflict becomes part of the actors' identities, the peace process contests the ability of the respective parties to hold a coherent narrative of who they are as well as their ability to affirm their selves through their interactions with the enemy, their *significant other* (Mitzen 2006; Rumelili 2015).

But the point is that while the attachment to the conflict is rigid, changes in the reality on the ground bring the actors to reconstruct the conflict in order to credibly maintain it. This is done through securitizing moves that emphasize some threats while de-securitizing others. In this respect, new threats (and enemies) become part of the metanarrative of the conflict, while others disappear. This allows the continuation of the conflict and maintaining the narrative of the conflict despite the changes that have occurred throughout its duration.

I use the Arab-Israeli conflict to illustrate these dynamics. Although the Arab-Israeli conflict narrative is prominent, the threats that are part of it have in fact changed significantly over the years; while the major threats from some countries in the region have decreased significantly, other threats have been incorporated into the metanarrative of the conflict, including a number of non-state challenges (terrorism and immigration) and even a non–Arab country (Iran). While there are some (obvious) reasons for the incorporation of these challenges into the Arab-Israeli conflict, which has indeed contributed to the ability to securitize them as part of the meta-securitization of the Arab-Israeli conflict, they are clearly socially constructed and the threats could have been constructed differently.

I suggest that acknowledging these dynamics sheds light on how conflicts endure and, thus, they have further implications for conflict resolution. In a nutshell, one of the means to act towards ending conflicts is to block the attempts to fuel them by incorporating new threats into them. This requires clearly specifying what the conflict is about and, therefore, how other threats are not necessarily part of it. Second, it requires meta-de-securitizing moves that go beyond de-securitizing moves.

Securitization and the continuation of conflicts

The continuation of conflicts stems from the securitizing moves that perpetuate them. Securitization is a process whereby an issue is constructed as an existential threat. The process succeeds when a target audience accepts this framing and endorses the employment of extraordinary measures to address it, thereby removing the issue from normal politics to a mode of emergency. In this respect, the securitizing move involves an *enunciator* (a securitizing actor) who aims to convince a *target audience* that *an issue* poses an existential threat to a *referent object*.[1]

Basically, there are three interrelated kinds of securitizing moves that prolong conflicts. The first is a meta-securitization dynamic. According to Wilkinson (2011:94), meta-securitizations (or metanarratives of security) are the acts and narratives that contribute to a successful securitizing move. As such, meta-securitization is the context of this process; it constructs the conflict, defines its core elements and designates the 'enemy'.

Although meta-securitizing moves shape societies, these moves are also affected by the cultures, identities and histories of the involved societies. While the meta-securitization of the conflict is a somewhat self-fulfilling prophecy - and therefore part of the mechanisms that account for its continuation - it is also one of the main manifestations of continuous conflicts. Continuous conflicts, especially international ones, cannot be conducted clandestinely, as they require salient discourse to express them.

The second way through which securitizing moves affect the continuation of conflicts concerns more specific securitizing moves within which concrete threats are constructed. These securitizing moves allow the rejuvenation of the conflict and evoke a greater sense of urgency. In this respect, the meta-securitization of the conflict provides powerful means to securitize specific issues. By connecting concrete threats to the meta-securitization, it reaffirms the threats - whatever they are - and contributes to the success of securitization. At the same time, these concrete securitizing moves further justify and maintain the meta-securitization of the conflict and its narrative, thereby limiting the possibility that the conflict narrative wanes over time. Not only does it further confirm the meta-securitization and the severity of the situation, concrete securitizing moves also allow to adjust the meta-securitization dynamic, making it more accurate over time, and therefore also more acceptable given the changes to reality.

The specific securitizing moves allow adjustments to the meta-securitization over time by incorporating different or new kinds of threats and adding new enemies. The various securitizing moves are simultaneously securitizing and de-securitizing moves; on the one hand, they emphasize concrete threats and enemies that help to perpetuate the core elements, validity and justifiability of the meta-securitization, but many cases also involve a de-securitizing move in terms of a downplaying of the previous threats and enemies, so much so that it is hard to continue to see them as enemies anymore without de-securitizing the entire meta-securitization project.[2] As Buzan and Wæver (2003:489) argue, while de-securitization can be achieved via a discourse reconstructing a securitized threat as no longer existing, this is often an indirect process through which 'a shift in orientation towards other issues reduces the relative attention to the previously securitised issue'. In such situations, narrating other (more severe) threats replaces the previously securitized issues. For example, the Arab-Israeli conflict that was based on the conflict between the state of Israel and numerous Arab countries did not cease to exist following the peace agreements Israel signed with Egypt (1979) and Jordan (1994). Not only is Israel still seen by many in these societies as the enemy and is still constructed in this way, Israel itself has incorporated new actors and threats into the metanarrative of this conflict, such as Iran (which is not an Arab country).[3] Conversely, it became increasingly difficult to view Egypt as an existential threat given its growing security cooperation with Israel. This cooperation also challenges the previous narratives of the conflict, as the conflict with Egypt has long been constructed as a key element in the Arab-Israeli conflict.

By securitizing new threats, enunciators are able to uphold the meta-securitization as well as allowing the shifts that make the meta-securitization more credible given the changes to reality and, thus, more acceptable for the audience. Towards this goal, in addition to constructing threats, they also show how they are part of the metanarrative of the conflict.

The concrete securitizing moves incorporate additional actors into the metanarrative of the conflict, which interlocks the conflict, connecting its different elements and thereby making its resolution much harder. As Kriesberg notes, international conflicts are not limited to only having two rivals. First, they are linked to additional international actors. According to him, 'Each party to a conflict has allies or potential allies. Each adversary, therefore, has a somewhat different conflict with each member of the opposing coalition' (Kriesberg 1980:102). Second, they are linked to internal conflicts, reflecting domestic subgroups and struggles (Kriesberg 1980).[4] According to Kriesberg, the importance of acknowledging the interlocking characteristics of international conflicts stems from the fact that they have a number of effects that may burden the dynamics of conflict resolution: they encourage escalation because actors in such conflicts attempt to demonstrate resolve and because it is easier to solve an isolated conflict than one that it is part of a larger dispute (Kriesberg 1980:102–103). However, it should be emphasized that the interlocking characteristic of conflicts, which makes them all the more difficult to resolve, is a social process that is affected by the intersubjective meaning of insecurity and is a result of these securitizing moves, that is, the interplay between concrete securitization attempts and meta-securitization dynamics.

The third way through which securitizing moves affect the continuation of conflicts concerns the mutual influence of the securitizing moves that each rival performs on the other actor. In this respect, conflict continues not only because each actor securitizes the threats from their opponent but also because these securitizing moves reinforce each other. Mutual securitizing moves contribute to the continuation of conflicts in a number of ways: foremost, they become a powerful tool in legitimizing further securitization moves. When both sides securitize the other and see the other as an existential threat (see also Stritzel and Chang 2015), they provide ammunition for the opponent in their domestic struggle to legitimize the counter-threats, which presents an ultimate justification for the securitization move.

In addition, and following the previous point, the securitizing moves justify taking concrete security measures that further strengthen the perception of the threat to the other side, therefore requiring the justification of contra-measures to address them and additional securitizing moves.[5] The traditional security dilemma captures a similar dynamic within which the measures that actors employ to preserve their security threaten another country's security given the uncertainties in the anarchical system (see also Van Rythoven, forthcoming). As actors cannot be certain of their opponents' intentions, especially when they cannot distinguish between offensive and defensive means, military procurements will be perceived by their rivals as a threat – even if they are armaments that are for defensive purposes only (Booth and Wheeler 2007; Jervis 1978; Roe 2005:8–24). In fact, it can be argued that while an opponent's securitizing moves may even reduce the dilemma somewhat as they provide greater certainty about the opponent's aggressive intentions – as signalled through these very securitizing moves – it does not end the dilemma, as it is impossible to determine whether this is a genuine move. In fact, actors may use securitizing moves in order to enhance the credibility of the threat they pose even if they are unwilling to execute it (Lupovici 2016a).

These dynamics then influence both the concrete securitizing moves and the meta-securitization of the conflict. Concrete securitizing moves allow the justification of specific escalations and occasionally even the use of force, as noted earlier, which, in turn, contributes to the maintenance of the opponent as enemy, which further confirms the meta-securitizing move. Moreover, not only do specific securitizing moves contribute to the conflict metanarrative, creating an assemblage of securitizing moves that validate it, but enunciators can refer in general terms to the threats posed by the opponent while referring to the opponent's meta-securitizing moves that designate the other actor as an existential threat. For example, Israeli officials were able to securitize the Iranian nuclear project based on the rhetoric of the Iranian securitizing moves that justify the initiation of this project (Lupovici 2016a). Israeli officials justify presenting Iran as an existential threat based not only on this and other concrete securitizing moves, pointing out its support to Hizbullah and terrorism more generally (Schiff 2006), but also by pointing to the meta-securitization of Israel in Iran, as evident in how Iranian officials describe Israel as the little Satan (Kaye, Dassa and Roshan 2011:31). As Menashri (2006:115–117) claims, there is a consensus among mainstream Israeli politicians regarding the Iranian threat, an understanding that emerged in the late 1980s and early 1990s after the end of the Iran-Iraq War and the first Gulf War.

Ontological security and the continuation of conflicts

Once a conflict is meta-securitized, it becomes a constitutive element of the involved actors' selves. A future shift in the relationships to more cooperative lines may therefore actually lead to ontological insecurity. The emerging scholarship on ontological security and the different mechanisms through which actors attempt to validate their selves is thus useful in capturing the dynamics that cause conflicts to endure.

Ontological security concerns the need of actors to protect their identities and routines and thus to preserve their sense of *self*.[6] An inability to ensure ontological security may manifest itself in emotions such as frustration, shame, humiliation and anxiety (Lupovici 2016b:66), which actors attempt to avoid.

Basically, scholars distinguish between two main dynamics through which actors attempt to validate their selves. The first approach to ontological security emphasizes the relational dynamic. For these scholars, ontological security is achieved via routinized relationships with significant others (Mitzen 2006; Rumelili 2011; see also Hopf 2002:6–7; Ringmar 1996:13–14, 81). The second approach is internal and emphasizes how ontological insecurity is experienced through the actors' narratives. From this perspective, the ability to be ontologically secure depends on a coherent narrative of the self (Browning and Joenniemi 2013; Delehanty and Steele 2009; Kinnvall 2004; Steele 2008). However, these two approaches to ontological security overlap (Huysmans 1998:242–244; Kinnvall 2004; Krolikowski 2008; Zarakol 2010). While (from the internal approach perspective) specific interactions with other actors may challenge their ability to hold a coherent narrative, the relational approach is, for example, able to acknowledge that the other is not necessarily an external actor but possibly a former or *alternative* identity of an actor who challenges its current 'self' (Lupovici 2016b:61; see also Rumelili 2004:32).

These various dynamics have important implications for the continuation of conflict. First, and most prominently, scholars from the external approach to ontological security have pointed out the inherent difficulties in transforming conflict routines into cooperative ones. Mitzen argues that actors can become trapped in an ontological security dilemma in which they are forced to choose between physical security and securing their 'enemy identity'. She claims that states 'might actually come to prefer their ongoing, certain conflict to the unsettling condition of deep uncertainty as to the other's and one's own identity' (Mitzen 2006:342–343).[7] This directly explains enduring conflicts. Actors who are rigidly attached to their enemy identity must reaffirm it through the persistence of the conflict.

The internal approach also provides important insights as to how ontological security needs perpetuate conflicts. From this perspective, breaking away from conflictual practices challenges ontological security by creating a gap between reality and the actor's narrative. These dynamics can even be more complicated, as actors can have multiple (possibly even clashing) identities and narratives, which may lead them to adopting avoidance strategies that maintain the known conflict. This is because any other strategy, whether it be the escalation of an existing conflict or the ending of it, may further emphasize the contradictory elements of their self and lead them to experience ontological dissonance (Lupovici 2012).

The interplay between internal and external aspects of ontological security further contributes to the continuation of conflicts. When the conflict is a constitutive element of the self, cooperative interactions with 'the enemy' not only challenge the routines of enmity, but also create critical situations that challenge the ability to hold a coherent narrative of enemies. This becomes a mechanism that prevents in advance such cooperative practices aimed at avoiding the discomfort that accompanies ontological insecurity and the related emotions.

Studying these dynamics requires, first, establishing the meta-securitization of the conflict, as concrete securitizing moves refer directly to doing so. At the same time, the meta-securitization and metanarrative of the conflict are key aspects of the actors' ontological security. The meta-securitization creates a metanarrative, a collective narrative in Bar-Tal's terms, which provides the society with clear answers to key questions such as

> Why is the group in conflict? What are the goals in the conflict, and why they are existential? … How did the conflict erupt? What was the course of the conflict? Why is it so violent? Why does it still continue, and why can it not be resolved peacefully?
>
> *(Bar-Tal 2013:248)*

In answering these questions, it is methodologically useful to trace the collective narrative, which also allows the tracing of the meta-securitization, since, as Bar-Tal notes, part of it concerns questions regarding the existentiality of the conflict (Bar-Tal 2013:248), and it aims (among other things) to justify the negative measures towards 'the enemy' (Bar-Tal 2013:249).[8] In other words, it constructs the different aspects of the securitizing moves: the existential threats that need to be addressed and the extraordinary measures taken to deal with the alleged insecurity, as well as to justify them.

The continuation of the Arab–Israeli conflict

The Arab-Israeli conflict is a classic example of an enduring conflict in which multiple securitizing moves institutionalize it and make it part of the actors' identities and thus related to their ontological security. The point is, however, that while the core of the conflict has remained the Israeli-Palestinian conflict, it has attained additional dimensions and actors, and various kinds of threats over the years have been added into it, such as Iran.

Meta-securitization of the Arab–Israeli conflict

The Arab-Israeli conflict has received considerable attention from scholars who specifically point out its complexity and duration, describing it as a protracted (Azar, Jureidini and McLaurin 1978), interlocked (Kriesberg 1980) and intractable conflict (Bar-Tal 2013). All of these descriptions point in various ways to the meta-securitization of this conflict, as it becomes evident in the institutionalization of it in the respective political arenas of both sides. As Azar, Jureidini and McLaurin (1978:55) argue, '[t]he Arab Israeli conflict is a fundamental issue in the politics of each of the confrontation states'. The deep, successful securitization of the conflict is evident both in tangible aspects, such as the enormous amount of resources allocated to it by all parties (Maoz 2009:311, 331–332), and also in the parties' respective discourses, identities and culture. Bar-Tal, for example, argues that the conflict is institutionalized in various aspects of Israeli society, including the media, political arena, Israeli literature, the education system and popular culture (Bar-Tal 2013:262–269). In fact, not only has the conflict been successfully securitized since the 1930s, it has been internationally securitized through securitizing moves that interlocked it, that is, making the Arab countries part of the conflict. As Sela (1998) argues, the Palestinians attempted to mobilize Arab and Muslim support for their struggle against the threat to the country's Muslim-Arab character. According to him, while the involvement of Arab states in the conflict was related to the regional leadership and domestic pressure, the 'Defense of Palestine was thus presented as an Islamic and Pan-Arab national duty' (Sela 1998:36). In this respect, it was securitized as an interlocking conflict involving a number of actors.[9] In addition, according to Kriesberg (1980), the parties to the Arab-Israeli conflict seek to find allies. This not only enhanced the sheer amount of resources used in the conflict, but also led the parties to 'broaden their collective identity in order to gain support and in so doing generalize its grievance' (Kriesberg 1980:106–107).

Although the Arab-Israeli conflict is a key framework, its content has changed over the years. The Israeli-Palestinian conflict constitutes the core of the Arab-Israeli conflict. It began as a conflict between Jews and Palestinians and their respective national movements over territory in British-ruled Palestine, and violence occasionally erupted, beginning in the 1930s. It developed into an interstate conflict over the years, as became evident in the three main wars in 1956, 1967 and 1973 (Bar-Tal 2013:2). For a number of reasons, however, the

Arab-Israeli conflict has changed and the involvement of the Arab states waned over the years,[10] returning the conflict to 'its original dimension' of an ethnic conflict between two communities, and new actors such as Hamas, Hizbullah and Iran (Ben Yehuda and Sandler 2002:115; Menashri 2006), leading some to argue that the 'classic Arab-Israeli conflict' is over (Sela 1998:350).

While the characteristics of the conflict have thus changed significantly and while the level of violence has decreased (Ben Yehuda and Sandler 2002:169), the Arab-Israeli conflict has not ended; it has merely been transformed, allowing the inclusion of new threats and challenges, which, in turn, helped prolong it and maintain the Arab-Israeli conflict narrative rather than, for example, the Israeli-Palestinian conflict, which better captures its main characteristics.[11]

It should be noted, however, that the ongoing existence of this conflict provides both parties with ontological security in as much as it validates their routines as enemies (Mitzen 2006:362–363) while simultaneously affirming their self-narratives. In the Israeli case, the conflict (and its continuation) is a strong mechanism that allows Israel to maintain a coherent narrative of its self (Lupovici 2012), but at the same time, it also concerns additional and more specific identities Israel holds, such as that of a deterrer actor, a narrative that requires having enemies who confirm the self (Lupovici 2016b:70, 150–151).

The securitization of Israel in Iran (and of Iran in Israel) as part of the conflict

Elaborating on the securitization of Israel in Iran and of Iran in Israel as part of the conflict demonstrates how securitizing moves are one of the key sources of conflict perpetuation. While Menashri (2006) does not use these exact terms, he clearly points to how Israel has been successfully securitized in Iran and became 'the enemy' and existential threat – not just to Iran, but to all mankind. Since the Islamic revolution, a key theme prominent in Iranian politics is the call for 'Death to Israel' (Menashari 2006:108). In this respect, the Israeli threat has been institutionalized in Iran, that is, Israel has been meta-securitized. It should be noted, however, that these calls mark a shift in the interactions between the countries, as they had close ties prior to the revolution and even during the Shah Pahlavi era regarded each other as a natural ally, given that they are both non-Arab countries in the Middle East and share a history of hostility from their neighbours (Menashri 2006:108). From this perspective, it is quite remarkable that Iran is currently seen as a key actor in the Arab-Israeli conflict. Although the Iranian assertions against Israel resemble arguments made in the Arab political discourse, Iranian officials aimed to "'Islamize' the Arab-Israeli conflict, and to stress the religious obligations of all Muslims" (Menashri 2006:110). This securitizing move can be seen as a conflictualization process whereby actors construct what the conflict is about and frame it as part of the meta-securitization of the conflict and its institutionalization. Furthermore, constructing the conflict as a religious one further complicates the ability to resolve it.

At the same time in Israel, the Iranian threat has also been incorporated into the narrative of the Arab-Israeli conflict and more generally to the existential threats Israel is constantly facing (Bar-Tal 2007:249). The existentiality of the Iranian threat in Israel is empowered by the securitization of Israel in Iran and by connecting these issues to the Iranian nuclear programme, threats which have been securitized in Israel since the 1990s, culminating in a climax in 2012 (Lupovici 2016a:421–422). From this perspective, if Iran declares its willingness to destroy Israel and develop nuclear infrastructures (but see Kam 2004:417–422), then Israeli securitizing actors have effective tools to narrate this threat and justify taking extraordinary measures against Iran.

It is hardly surprising, then, that in this context, Iran is seen as an 'Arab' country simply because it is an enemy. A prominent example of this 'Arabnization' of Iran becomes evident in how Iran is covered in the Israeli media. Ram, for example, argues that those who speak and write about Iran in Israeli printed and electronic media "are the various 'correspondents of Arab affairs', whose knowledge about Iranian history, society, language, and culture is at best partial" (Ram 2007). In an article discussing the biased information on Iran in the Israeli media, Zvi Bar'el, Haaretz Middle Eastern affairs analyst, is interviewed. He explains this tendency claiming that 'there is no Iran desk in the Israeli media. Iran is perceived as another Arab country since it is the enemy' (in Persico 2007).

The Iranian threats have been securitized more specifically as part of the Arab-Israeli conflict by emphasizing Iran's close ties with Hizbullah and Hamas. In this respect, Iran's quest for nuclear capabilities enhance other perceived threats in Israel, such as Iran's support of terrorist groups and its increasing influence in the region (Kaye, Nader and Roshan 2011:25–31; see also Kam 2007:53–58). Israeli officials have constantly repeated the threat stemming from the Iranian involvement in the Middle East and its influence on the Arab-Israeli conflict, even when the words 'Arab-Israeli conflict' were not mentioned. Nonetheless, in some specific occasions, the rhetoric becomes more salient (e.g. during situations of violence). For example, Prime Minister Ehud Olmert, in an address to the Knesset early in the Second Lebanon War in the summer of 2006, stated that

> The campaign we are engaged in these days is against the terror organizations operating from Lebanon and Gaza. These organizations are nothing but 'sub-contractors' operating under the inspiration, permission, instigation and financing of the terror-sponsoring and peace-rejecting regimes, on the Axis of Evil which stretches from Tehran to Damascus.
>
> Radical, terrorist and violent elements are sabotaging the life of the entire region and placing its stability at risk. The region in which we live is threatened by these murderous terror groups.
>
> *(Olmert 2006)*

Likewise, while he admitted a few years later that 'there is no real reason for conflict between the State of Israel and Iran', he pointed to the serious, growing threat: the 'existence of an axis stretching from Tehran through Damascus to the Hizbullah in Lebanon and the Hamas in the Gaza Strip' (Olmert 2008). He declared that

> The Ayatollan regime, headed by an anti-Semitic and Holocaust-denying president, aspires to regional hegemony, and to a strong regional position. Its support of terror, its striving to achieve nuclear weapons, its develop-ment of long-range missiles, its resistance to all peace initiatives and its fanning of the *Arab–Israeli conflict* and of regional stability with the flame of religious fanaticism – all these are tools to achieve the megalomaniacal objective of this dark regime.
>
> *(Olmert 2008, my emphasis)*

These perceptions and the increasing involvement of Iran in the Arab-Israeli conflict was clearly acknowledged by then Haaretz military correspondent Ze'ev Schiff, who asserted that while the 2006 war in Lebanon 'may have looked to some like old news, just another battle in the long-running *Arab–Israeli war*', although Iran did not permit Hizbullah to launch a major operation, this war represented 'the start of a new war between Israel and Iran' (Schiff 2006:23, my emphasis).

These themes have also been reflected in recent years in speeches given by Israeli Prime Minister Netanyahu. Not only does Netanyahu often refer to the Iranian threat and their links to Hamas and Hizbullah (e.g. in Haaretz 2014; Keinon 2016), he also specifically points out how Iran is a key force prolonging the (Arab/Palestinian-Israeli) conflict. For example, in a February 2014 speech, he claimed that

> the strength of Iran weakens [the efforts to achieve a secure and enduring peace with the Palestinians], because Iran now controls one half of the Palestinian population. They control Hamas, they control Gaza through their proxies Hamas and Islamic Jihad, and of course they tell them what they say in Tehran, no peace with Israel, no reconciliation with Israel, con-tinuous war in Israel. That's what Hamas and the other terror proxies that Iran again, arms, funds and instructs are doing in Gaza. So one half of the Palestinian population is under the boot of Iran. And the other half, so far, has refused to confront the first half.
>
> *(Netanyahu 2014)*

Conclusion

In this chapter, I have considered mechanisms through which conflicts endure. I especially pointed to the securitization and meta-securitization dynamics and their effects on actors' ontological security. Acknowledging these dynamics has numerous implications. First, as the editors argue, the continuation of conflicts is not self-evident, depending on social processes that fuel them; otherwise, they may lose their momentum and wane overtime. Second, it also means that the 'content' of conflicts is socially constructed. As elaborated earlier, the Arab-Israeli conflict is a structure the meaning of which has changed over time to include different enemies and threats. Third, and following the previous points, while the distinction between conflict escalation and conflict continuation is important, it is also important to acknowledge how the recurring escalations evident in concrete securitizing moves and securitization climaxes contribute to conflict continuation. Fourth, de-securitization is not necessarily good – or more precisely, not good enough. As demonstrated earlier, the de-securitization of one threat within the context of the Arab-Israeli conflict did not contribute to end this conflict, but it actually contributed to its prolongation. The de-securitization of threats and enemies (e.g. Egypt and Jordan) with whom Israel signed peace treaties was part of the securitization of other threats, which helped maintain the conflict narrative.

This means that ending the conflict requires the de-securitization of the meta-securitization of the conflict; or in other words, it requires meta-de-securitizing moves that will allow the prevention of the usage of the conflict (meta-)narrative to incorporate into it new threats. Towards this aim, peace promoters must emphasize not only how the specific de-securitizing move contributes to security but also how it challenges the metanarrative of the conflict. In the Arab-Israeli case, for example, the peace with Egypt should be used as the basis for a counter-narrative emphasizing how not all the actors in the Middle East wish to destroy Israel.[12] Likewise, the ability to cooperate with such actors may also indicate that there is no logical validity to the connection often made between the historical enemies of the Jewish people and the current threats facing Israel. In other words, these challenges are not inevitable. Over time, success in these attempts will help challenge the narrative of the conflict itself and de-securitize it.

In addition, the supporters of conflict resolution should specify the exact characteristics of the conflict in order to challenge the ability of securitizing actors to integrate new threats into the conflict narrative. As noted earlier, this integration allows securitizing actors to preserve the conflict as well as empowering specific threats, which allows the conflict to colonize new issues or social relations. Clarifying the core elements of the Arab-Israeli conflict will allow the contesting of the attempts to conduct concrete securitizing moves by showing how the suggested securitizing move does not fit the conflict narrative. For example, it is possible to challenge the relevance of the Iranian threat to the Arab-Israeli conflict. While Iran has connections with some actors in the region and Iran does pose a threat to Israel, it does not necessarily need to be constructed as part of the Arab-Israeli conflict.

Notes

1 For some reviews of securitization scholarship, see Balzacq (2011), Gad and Petersen (2011), and Watson (2012). The original formulations are found in Wæver (1995) and Buzan, Wæver and De Wilde (1998).
2 According to Buzan and Wæver (2003:489), de-securitization is 'a process through which a political community downgrades or ceases to treat something as an existential threat to a valued referent object, and reduces or stops calling for urgent and

exceptional measures to deal with the threat'. See also Buzan, Wæver and De Wilde (1998:4), Huysmans (2006:143).

3 The distinction between meta-securitizing and securitizing moves overlaps with the distinction between master narrative of the conflict and specific narratives about particular events (Bar-Tal 2013:254).

4 It should be noted that Kriesberg (1980) discusses additional ways in which conflicts are interlocked, including in time and issues. However, for the purpose of this chapter, I focus on the above-mentioned ones.

5 For further discussion, through securitization theory, of the dynamics of the security dilemma, see Lupovici (2018).

6 For elaboration of the concept of ontological security, see Mitzen (2006), Steele (2005, 2008), Zarakol (2010), Croft (2012), Browning and Joenniemi (2013), and Solomon (2018).

7 For a similar argument, see Northrup (1989) and Huysmans (1998:239–240).

8 For further discussion of the narrative of the conflict, see Bar-Tal (2013:254–257).

9 It should be noted, however, that Great Britain also encouraged the involvement of the Arab rulers in the conflict, hoping that doing so would mitigate the tension (Sela 1998:37).

10 As Ben Yehuda and Sandler (2002:110) argue, the conflict has changed since 1973, as the destruction of Israel is no longer the ultimate objective.

11 The Israeli-Palestinian conflict concerns territorial aspects (including the Jewish settlements), security arrangements, the question of Jerusalem and the right of return of Palestinians who are living in that diaspora (Tessler 2009).

12 It should be noted, however, that while the political discourse towards Israel has significantly changed in countries like Egypt, there is a gap between the popular perception and attitude towards Israel in Egypt and that of the government. In other words, the peace with Israel has not been normalized (Zittrain and Caplan 2010:51).

References

Azar, E. Edward, Paul Jureidini and Ronald McLaurin (1978) 'Protracted Social Conflict: Theory and Practice in the Middle East', *Journal of Palestine Studies* 8 (1): 41–60.

Balzacq, Thierry (2011) 'A Theory of Securitization: Origins, Core Assumptions, and Variants', in Thierry Balzacq (Ed.), *Securitization Theory: How Security Problems Emerge and Dissolve* (1–30), Oxon: Routledge.

Bar-Tal, Daniel (2007) *Living with the Conflict: Socio-Psychological Analysis of the Jewish Society in Israel.* Jerusalem: Carmel [in Hebrew].

Bar-Tal, Daniel (2013) *Intractable Conflicts: Socio-Psychological Foundations and Dynamics.* Cambridge: Cambridge University Press.

Ben Yehuda, Hemda and Shmel Sandler (2002) *The Arab–Israeli Conflict Transformed: Fifty Years of Interstate and Ethnic Crises.* Albany: SUNY Press.

Booth, Ken and Nicholas Wheeler (2007) *The Security Dilemma: Fear, Cooperation and Trust in World Politics.* Hampshire: Palgrave Macmillan.

Browning, S. Christopher and Pertti Joenniemi (2013) 'From Fratricide to Security Community: Re-Theorising Difference in the Constitution of Nordic Peace', *Journal of International Relations and Development* 16 (3): 483–513.

Buzan, Barry and Ole Wæver (2003) *Regions and Powers: The Structure of International Security.* New York: Cambridge University Press.

Buzan, Barry, Ole Wæver and Jaap De Wilde (1998) *Security: A New Framework for Analysis.* Boulder, CO: Lynne Rienner.

Croft, Stuart (2012) *Securitizing Islam.* Cambridge: Cambridge University Press.

Delehanty, Will K. and Brent J. Steele (2009) 'Engaging the Narrative in Ontological (In) Security Theory: Insights from Feminist IR', *Cambridge Review of International Affairs* 22: 523–540.

Gad, Ulrik P. and Karen Lund Petersen (2011) 'Concepts of Politics in Securitization Studies', *Security Dialogue* 42 (4–5): 315–328.

Haaretz (2014) *Transcript of Benjamin Netanyahu's Address to the 2014 UN General Assembly.* www.haaretz.com/israel-news/1.618308 (accessed 23 June 2017).

Hopf, Ted (2002) *Social Construction of International Politics: Identities and Foreign Policies, Moscow, 1955 and 1999.* Ithaca, NY: Cornell University Press.

Huysmans, Jef (1998) 'Security! What Do You Mean? From Concept to Thick Signifier', *European Journal of International Relations* 4 (2): 226–255.

Huysmans, Jef (2006) *The Politics of Insecurity.* Oxon: Routledge.

Jervis, Robert (1978) 'Cooperation under the Security Dilemma', *World Politics* 30: 167–214.

Kam, Ephraim (2004) *From Terror to Nuclear Bombs: The Significance of the Iranian Threat and a Nuclear Iran.* Tel Aviv: Ministry of Defense [in Hebrew].

Kam, Ephraim (2007) *Nuclear Iran: What Does It Mean, and What Can Be Done.* Tel Aviv: The Institute for National Security Studies.

Kaye, Dalia Dassa, Alireza Nader and Parisa Roshan (2011) *Israel and Iran: A Dangerous Rivalry.* Santa Monica, CA: RAND.

Keinon, Herb (2016) *Netanyahu: Nuclear Deal Hasn't Stopped Iran's Support for Terror.* www.jpost.com/Israel-News/Politics-And-Diplomacy/Netanyahu-on-Iran-aid-to-Palestinian-martyrs-Nuclear-deal-hasnt-stopped-support-for-terror-446068 (accessed 23 June 2017).

Kinnvall, Catarina (2004) 'Globalization and Religious Nationalism: Self, Identity, and the Search for Ontological Security', *Political Psychology* 25: 741–767.

Kriesberg, Louis (1980) 'Interlocking Conflicts in the Middle East', in Louis Kriesberg (Ed.), *Research in Social Movements, Conflicts, and Change* (99–118), Greenwich, CT: JAI Press.

Krolikowski, Alanna (2008) 'State Personhood in Ontological Security Theories of International Relations and Chinese Nationalism: A Sceptical View', *Chinese Journal of International Politics* 2: 109–133.

Lupovici, Amir (2012) 'Ontological Dissonance, Clashing Identities, and Israel's Unilateral Steps Towards the Palestinians', *Review of International Studies* 38 (4): 809–833.

Lupovici, Amir (2016a) 'Securitization Climax: Putting the Iranian Nuclear Project at the Top of the Israeli Public Agenda (2009–2012)', *Foreign Policy Analysis* 12 (3): 413–432.

Lupovici, Amir (2016b) *The Power of Deterrence.* Cambridge: Cambridge University Press.

Maoz, Zeev (2009) *Defending the Holy Land: A Critical Analysis of Israel's National Security and Foreign Policy.* Ann Arbor: University of Michigan Press.

Menashri, David (2006) 'Iran, Israel and the Middle East Conflict', *Israel Affairs* 12 (1): 107–122.

Mitzen, Jennifer (2006) 'Ontological Security in World Politics: State Identity and the Security Dilemma', *European Journal of International Relations* 12: 341–370.

Netanyahu, Benjamin (2014) *Prime Minister Benjamin Netanyahu's Remarks at the Conference of Presidents of Major American Jewish Organizations. Prime Minister Office.* www.pmo.gov.il/English/MediaCenter/Speeches/Pages/speechpre170214.aspx (accessed 23 June 2017).

Northrup, Terrell A. (1989) 'The Dynamic of Identity in Personal and Social Conflict', in Louis Kriesberg, Terrell A. Northrup and Stuart J. Thorson (Eds.), *Intractable Conflicts and Their Transformation* (55–82). Syracuse, NY: Syracuse University Press.

Olmert, Ehud (2006) *Address by Prime Minister Ehud Olmert - The Knesset. Prime Minister's Office Communications Department.* www.pmo.gov.il/MediaCenter/Speeches/Pages/speechkneset170706.aspx (accessed 23 June 2017).

Olmert, Ehud (2008) *Address by PM Olmert to the TAU INSS Annual Conference.* http://mfa. gov.il/MFA/PressRoom/2008/Pages/Address_PM_Olmert_TAU_INSS_Annual_ Conference_18-Dec-2008.aspx (accessed 23 June 2017).

Persico, Tomer (2007) *Relax!* www.globes.co.il/news/article.aspx?did=1000263765 (accessed 23 June 2017).

Ram, Hagai (2007) *Iranophobia: The Logic of an Israeli Obsession.* Stanford, CA: Stanford University Press.

Ringmar, Erik (1996) *Identity, Interests and Action: A Cultural Explanation of Sweden's Intervention in the Thirty Years War.* New York: Cambridge University Press.

Roe, Paul (2005) *Ethnic Violence and the Societal Security Dilemma.* Oxon: Routledge.

Rumelili, Bahar (2004) 'Constructing Identity and Relating to Difference: Understanding the EU's Mode of Differentiation', *Review of International Studies* 30: 27–47.

Rumelili, Bahar (2011) *Identity and Desecuritization: Possibilities and Limits.* Paper Presented at Innupi's Research Seminar Series, Oslo, February 9.

Rumelili, Bahar (2015) 'Ontological (In)security and Peace Anxieties: A Framework for Conflict Resolution', in Bahar Rumelili (Ed.), *Conflict Resolution and Ontological Security: Peace Anxieties* (10–29), Oxon: Routledge.

Schiff, Ze'ev (2006) 'Israel's War with Iran', *Foreign Affairs* 85 (6): 23–31.

Sela, Avraham (1998) *The Decline of the Arab Israeli Conflict: Middle East Politics and the Quest for Regional Order.* Albany: SUNY Press.

Solomon, Ty (2018) 'Ontological Security, Circulations of Affect, and the Arab Spring', *Journal of International Relations and Development* 21 (4): 934–958.

Steele, Brent J. (2005) 'Ontological Security and the Power of Self-Identity: British Neutrality and the American Civil War', *Review of International Studies* 31: 519–540.

Steele, Brent J. (2008) *Ontological Security in International Relations: Self-Identity and the IR State.* London: Routledge.

Stritzel, Holger, and Chang Sean C. (2015) 'Securitization and Counter-Securitization in Afghanistan', *Security Dialogue* 46 (4): 548–567.

Tessler, Mark (2009) *A History of the Israeli–Palestinian Conflict*, 2nd ed. Bloomington: Indiana University Press.

Van Rythoven, Erik (Forthcoming) 'The Securitization Dilemma', *Journal of Global Security Studies.*

Watson, Scott D. (2012) ''Framing' the Copenhagen School: Integrating the Literature on Threat Construction', *Millennium* 40 (2): 279–301.

Wæver, Ole (1995) 'Securitization and Desecuritization', in Ronnie Lipschutz (Ed.), *On Security* (46–87), New York: Columbia University Press.

Wilkinson, Claire (2011) 'The Limits of Spoken Words: From Meta-Narratives to Experiences of Security', in Thierry Balzacq (Ed.), *Securitization Theory: How Security Problems Emerge and Dissolve* (94–115), Oxon: Routledge.

Zarakol, Ayşe (2010) 'Ontological (In)security and State Denial of Historical Crimes: Turkey and Japan', *International Relations* 24 (1): 3–23.

Zittrain, Laura E. and Neil Caplan (2010) *Negotiating Arab-Israeli Peace, Patterns, Problems, Possibilities*, 2nd ed. Bloomington: Indiana University Press.

14

HOLDING OUT FOR THE DAY AFTER TOMORROW

Futurity, memory and transitional justice evidence in Syria

Sune Haugbolle

Introduction: conflict continuation and futurity

One of the key dynamics of the war in Syria that scholarship has arguably over-looked is how expectations have shaped actors' willingness to engage in renewed conflict and their unwillingness to de-escalate. The expectations of combatants can range from defeat to victory, with many important variations. A defeat can either be the failure to defeat the enemy but still remain politically relevant in a post-conflict order; or it could be the complete denigration of influence. Conversely, a party to an armed conflict may see victory as complete replacement of the political system or set more modest goals, such as, in the case of the Syrian High Negotiations Committee, 'a politically negotiated departure for Assad' (Al Jazeera 2017, citing Bassma Kodmani, spokeswoman of the Syrian National Council (SNC)). Actors in military conflicts see shifting outlines of a possible outcome on the horizon. This explains why changing conflict dynamics do not just alter the original grievances that led to conflict and the social and political antagonisms between actors, but also refocus the ultimate imagined outcome. Without ignoring or belittling other reasons for conflict continuation, I want to highlight how reactions to possible futures can prolong conflict. A future horizon that promises an acceptable social order is necessary for actors to engage in meaningful negotiations. Such a horizon, it would seem, is yet to materialize in the six-year-long war in Syria. For the sake of understanding the conditions of continuing conflict, it is worth investigating expectations and their impact. In line with the general gist of this book, the present chapter therefore analyses the dynamics of conflict continuation and futurity in Syria since 2011 with a special emphasis on the collection of evidence for a transitional justice process. It then analyses how this information has influenced the political process. It also discusses the relation between what I call the 'archive' of evidence about a conflict and the narrative battles over its interpretation. Finally, I discuss the implications of my findings in relation to theories of conflict continuation and the possibility of transitional justice in Syria.

My point of departure is ethnographic. In 2013, while conducting fieldwork among Syrian revolutionaries in Lebanon, I had a heated exchange with an exiled Syrian friend. This was shortly after the regime and Hezbollah won the battle of Qusayr, cutting the supply lines between Lebanon and Homs and eventually forcing the 'capital of the revolution' to surrender in 2014. The Islamic State group had emerged on the scene as an important player, and an air of defeat hung over the Syrian revolutionary community in Beirut. From the perspective of my friend and many like-minded secular protestors, the tide had turned decisively on their revolution. Not only had their peaceful protests become militarized, while they were being brutalized by the regime. Worse yet, the turn to armed struggle had transformed their struggle into an intractable, endless muddle of regional and international powers slugging it out by proxy. It had become a protracted civil war, in which the other revolutionaries – Islamist in colouring – were stronger, better connected and therefore better equipped to drive the struggle against the Assad regime forward. In this disconsolate perspective – which has only become gloomier over the last four years – he hardly saw any point in talking about 'the revolution'. Protracted war had replaced it, and the war appeared to be a defeat for liberal revolutionaries. I suggested that what needed to be done was at least to document the atrocities committed against civilians in the hope that justice would be done after the war. I mentioned an organization called the Violence Documentation Centre (VDR), headed by the founder of the Coordination Committees, Razan Zeitouneh, which he was of course familiar with, as a model for revolutionary work in this protracted conflict.[1] That remark triggered the following rant:

> Transitional justice! This is for people who don't want to get their hands dirty. You can dream about transitional government like Kofi Annan [the UN Special Envoy to Syria 2011–12], but that's not what we need. This isn't what we needed. I mean Support the revolution now…not in some future. Like transitional government is already there and they're all sitting down together. It's not! And he [Bashar al-Assad] is laughing, you know? We don't need these sugar-coated words [hal-kalimat as-sukkariya]. He [Assad] will take them with his coffee, and say 'thank you very much [ya'tik al-afiye]'. No way. You know? We lost, maybe it was because of these lies.

My revolutionary friend was suggesting that the focus on social and political relations in a post-conflict setting actually impeded the necessary work to bring these relations about. At the time, I could not accept his despairing defeatism. In hindsight, however, the analysis raises a valid point for our understanding of protracted conflicts. How does the imagined aftermath influence how a conflict develops and is eventually settled? How does the future influence the present? How are futures created in a time with abundant digital documentation? What role should the collection of evidence play in conflict resolution? And what kind of unintended consequences can it have? These questions are addressed in this chapter. As regards Syria, one might argue that in the two first years of peace negotiations, whose failure was crucial for the continuation of the war, the international community, Western diplomats and Western governments never offered a vision that was realistic and acceptable to all parties. This was possibly due to a basic miscalculation of the strength and tenacity of the Syrian regime and its allies: Hezbollah, Iran and Russia. When the U.S. representatives and key allies of the armed groups fighting the regime have talked about Syria as they imagine it after the war, they consistently assumed the defeat of the Assad regime, summed up in John Kerry's slogans 'Assad must go' and 'Assad staying is a non-starter' (see Atlantic Council 2015). By weaving the thread of defeat into their diplomatic narrative, they hoped that it would become the accepted, expected outcome. Or perhaps they believed it so much as to not question it. Perhaps they were too taken with the narrative presented by the Syrian opposition, which, although strong and fairly united in 2012, has since fractured and weakened. The regime did not fall, Assad did not go and, as of 2017, transitional justice is still waiting in the docks. Since the summer of 2013, the apparent failure of the teleology has gradually meant that diplomatic scenarios jarred with reality and could not become a platform for the coveted 'political solution'.

Instead, all parties have opted for a military solution by entrenching positions and doubling up defences, even in the face of ongoing peace talks in Geneva, Vienna and Astana. Military and diplomatic dynamics have obviously determined the course of the conflict. National interests weighed in. Without Russian intervention and Hezbollah's assistance, the Syrian regime might indeed have crumbled on several occasions. Obama's decision to intervene against the Islamic State alongside the Syrian Air Force in September 2014 while not moving a finger to curtail the regime's daily attacks against civilians, including the infamous 'red lines' regarding chemical attacks, proved detrimental for those who sought regime change in Damascus. This indecision enraged the Saudi leadership and encouraged it to escalate brinkmanship and war by proxy with Iran. There are many other determining factors for the continuation of the conflict, such as the steady stream of weapons into the country, fragmentation of opposition forces and the Western obsession with the Islamic State. My argument is not simply that politicians and diplomats got it wrong when they imagined conditions for peace or that they perhaps unwillingly colluded to entrench positions and drag out the war. These are fairly obvious points.

Rather, I argue that a realist analysis of policymaking does not suffice when studying conflict continuation. We must also pay attention to the role of imagination and futurity. Contrary to my Syrian friend's advice, I think transitional justice warrants consideration, not because a process is about to leave the docks but because it is one of the ways actors attempt to shape a future scenario, which, in turn, helps determine events on the ground. As I show, transitional justice made what Zartmann (2008) calls a 'mutually hurting stalemate' with conditions that they could accept less likely – and certainly less appealing – for the regime. 'Futurity', as Jameson (2005), Tsing (2008), Koselleck (2004) and others have theorized it, describes the social constructions of the future. Different ways of imaging the future (or 'futurities') build on specific cultural heritages, but they 'go global' via the dissemination of various narratives and practices of communication technology. Modernist futurity is inscribed in narrative orders of progress and modernity, which simultaneously order memory and the use of remembering. In that sense, transitional justice can be seen as a modernist ideology seeking to transform memory – knowledge and documentation of the past – into a platform for particular futures as part of particular political projects. By analysing examples of transitional justice evidence (TJE) and memory culture in Syria, I reveal the complex nexus of political interests involved in imagining 'a day after tomorrow'. As a whole, I view this material as diverse evidence of violations in the Syrian War, which I call a hybrid archive. Rather than seeing this archive as an auxiliary effect of the war, I want to suggest that the act of imagining post-conflict scenarios can be significant for how a conflict develops. This act involves not just the regime and resistance groups but also a much wider struggle for a new political subjectivity, and new social and political relations – an act in which various international, transnational and national powers intervene.

War crime investigations and transitional justice evidence

The hybrid archive of the Syrian War is recorded in memory culture – films, videos, books, articles and other cultural production – and in TJE, which I define here as material collected for the distinct purpose of a post-conflict legal process. Here, I am primarily interested in TJE, although we should allow for some natural overlaps between memory culture and TJE. TJE is produced strictly with war crime investigations in mind. For all their virtues, war crime investigations have historically been bureaucratic efforts that often proceeded years after alleged violations took place. In the interim, witnesses and perpetrators can disappear. Tangible evidence can go up in flames. In short, the material necessity for a truth and reconciliation process – TJE – must be collated from various sources after the fact. From the outset of the popular uprising-turned-conflict in Syria, local lawyers and activists have been aware of this challenge. Imagining a 'day after tomorrow' when the Syrian War would end, preferably with a clear defeat of the Assad regime, they have been creating an archive for TJE since 2011. This is no organized archive, but rather a widely dispersed set of evidence that is preserved in multiple locations for later processing. The persistent imagining of a transitional process 'right around the corner' presumes the presence or near possibility of legality or the reality of a global truth and justice regime. This hope has also inspired a huge, if largely uncoordinated, campaign from the outside, which continues apace despite the seemingly intractable conflict in Syria.

Syria showcases an intense effort to collect TJE during conflict. While international and local advocacy organizations have researched atrocities during past wars, such as the Bosnian War in the 1990s, Syria is arguably the first time a wide range of local, transnational and international organizations are conducting full-fledged criminal investigations on the basis of digital evidence (see Wessels in Chapter 3). This raises a number of interesting comparative perspectives for our understanding of transitional justice in the Middle East more generally. The most important question might be whether a 'hybrid archive' of online material produced and analysed by a plethora of groups with different interests can find a focus and a geographical locus and eventually sustain a juridical process – or whether it is destined to remain a scattered effort. For the moment, the latter is certainly the case.

Syria has been called the most documented conflict in history, particularly due to social media. The Internet abounds with evidence of atrocities filmed with mobile phones. YouTube videos, blogs, webpages and the intense media coverage of the fighting in Syria provide raw material that organizations can mine for evidence. These violence documentation groups include the Kawakibi Center for Documenting Violations, the Center for Documentation of Violations in Syria, the Centre for Civil Society and Democracy, the Damascus Center for Human Rights Studies, Dawlaty, the Local Coordination Committees in Syria, the Syrian Center for Documentation, Syria Justice and Accountability Center, the Syrian Observatory for Human Rights (SOHR) and Syrian Shuhada. Some of them have been accused of skewed reporting and faulty methodology (Ray 2016). The question is not merely whether numbers are reliable (although inflated casualty numbers certainly can have political effects), but also whether third parties have verified information culled from informants on the ground in Syria. Activists, even if they reject these claims, acknowledge that their evidence would mostly be too flimsy for it to hold up in court (author's interview with the director of Dawlaty, Salma Kahale, Berlin, 12 December 2016). Organizations such as the Commission for International Justice and Accountability (CIJA) therefore collect more solid evidence of the chain of command from top officials in the regime to special police forces and soldiers who murdered and tortured protesters and opposition fighters. This documentation can supplement forensic evidence, news, satellite images and other sources. The documents obtained by CIJA's Syrian (and very brave) employees have been smuggled out of Syria and are now in multiple locations in Europe, Canada and the U.S. They can be supplemented by violence documentation, such as the so-called 'Caesar files', a collection of 53,000 photos smuggled out by a regime defector. Ultimately, a legal case can potentially be filed, either by the International Criminal Court or by Western countries against individual regime members residing in such countries. The photos show the abuse and murder of prisoners by the Syrian regime on a mechanical scale resembling the Third Reich. As an example of collaboration and cross-referencing by different organizations, Human Rights Watch has used satellite imagery and geolocation techniques to confirm that some of the Caesar photographs of the dead were taken in the courtyard of the 601 Military Hospital in Mezze, Damascus (Human Rights Watch 2015). A more recent case of documentation that may be used to cross-reference other material in a court case is the Amnesty International report of February

2017 detailing systematic extrajudicial killings of more than 13,000 inmates in the Syrian regime's Saydnaya prison (Amnesty International 2017). The report resulted from interviews with former inmates who managed to escape.

Other material, ranging from meticulous reports of every bombing and murder to forensic evidence gathering, is collated by a complex landscape of Syrian activists, foreign states, international and national non-governmental organizations (NGOs), as well as international institutions such as United Nations (UN) agencies. International organizations include the UN Office of the High Commissioner for Human Rights, international NGOs such as Alkarama, Amnesty International, Arabic Network for Human Rights Information, Médicins Sans Frontièrs, United States Institute of Peace, CIJA, Human Rights Watch, International Crisis Group, Justice for Syria, Reporters Without Borders, Syrian Emergency Task Force and Syrian Human Rights Committee. This list is far from complete. All in all, more than 40 prominent documentation groups exist. Together, they constitute a nexus of interests seeking to remember, restore and archive the war in Syria.

The motivation for seeking transitional justice varies. Syrians tend to have personal reasons for collecting TJE, and many of them have close connections to opposition groups. They want to maintain the momentum of the uprising and hope for justice to be done and for regime members to be tried as part of a transition of power (author's interview with Salma Kahale, director of Dawlaty, Berlin, 12 December 2016). Foreign members of international organizations with whom I have spoken tend to frame their intervention in terms of abstract notions of universal justice, preserving a workable international system, maintaining historical progression of humankind and similarly lofty ideals. Likewise, the director of CIJA, Bill Wiley, told *The New Yorker* in 2016 that his work to retrieve the documentation of crimes against humanity was not primarily about removing leaders such as Saddam Hussein and Bashar al-Assad, but rather 'about sending a signal to a conflict-affected society that, from here on out, this nation will be governed on the basis of the rule of law' (Taub 2016).

In many ways, of course, the interests of the Syrian opposition and foreign organizations do intersect, which explains the collusion between Syrian and international groups. But Syrian activists are generally more critical of the international system, the international donors and the UN and its inability to work with Syrians, including the organizations gathering TJE (Mansour 2017). At a general level, they are dismayed by what they see as the passivity of the West. In the words of the writer Yassin al-Haj Saleh, Syria is not just another conflict but a symptom of our time and the 'world's naked disgrace' (2016:2) in failing to address violations and injustice. Syria has become emblematic of the failure of the Arab uprisings as well as of the failure of international institutions to react adequately, to de-escalate conflict, to protect civilians and to pursue those guilty of war crimes. The human suffering that continues apace at a staggering level undermines faith in the ability of the international legal and diplomatic community to end the fighting and begin addressing the multiple emergencies in Syria and in the region more generally. Syria, in other words, is a moral problem as well as a policy problem, and the work of gathering TJE and archiving the memory of the war therefore touches on global moral concerns. The situation in Syria constitutes not a crisis for Syrians as well as also for international conflict resolution (Haugbolle 2016). It raises questions concerning the ability of the current international system to speak to the thousands of documented war crimes and crimes against humanity, the latter defined in the Rome Statute as acts such as murder, extermination, torture, etc., 'when committed as part of a widespread systematic attack against any civilian population' (Rome Statute of the International Criminal Court, article 7 (1)). The 'dilemmas of protection' (Stahn 2014) have not been resolved by existing measures such as the Responsibility to Protect doctrine and the UN Security Council. Many actors in the conflict, from the local level of peaceful activists alienated by the militarization of their struggle to international actors with no real belief in the diplomatic or military effort to stop the war, have instead turned to the collection of TJE as a way of addressing this crisis of morality. The archive they create has become an alternative location for ambitions of restoring global morality as well as for keeping the original revolutionary project in Syria alive. Most of all, it has become a tool for maintaining an alternative future from the one that seems to be materializing.

Archiving atrocities

What is this archive, then, and how can we begin to appreciate its political significance? By 'archive', I refer to intellectual, cultural and social work that seeks to contain, organize, represent, render intelligible and produce narratives about the past, telling us what is significant, valued and worth preserving – and what is not. Some of the archiving aims at precision: creating files, catalogues and building cases against named individuals. Other acts of archiving focus on human stories, emotions and evidence of lost social and material habitats. Artists, activists and professional transitional justice workers are all archivists in their own right. As archival scholars point out, all archives depend on interfaces (archivists or computer systems) to mediate between the past and the public (Laermans and Gielen 2007). While we might imagine the archive as a well-ordered system, it is only well ordered to the extent that intermediaries guide the user effectively through the often-colossal amount of source material that renders it possible to construct ideas about the past. And as Jacques Derrida (1998) writes in his essay *Archive Fever*, these processes of intermediary representation are never devoid of power relations. What may seem like neutral and objective processes are often revealed as places where archivists determine what constitutes legitimate evidence of the past and shape social memories. Memories and facts are excluded and included according to ideological, narrative ordering. Since much of the Syrian archive is produced by people sympathetic to the uprising, critics claim that they fail to cast light on crimes committed in regime-held territories or against regime supporters (Ray 2016). Before turning to this critique and reviewing some of the overlooked dynamics, a few words on the rationality behind transitional justice are in order.

The act of archiving, like all social facts, depends on rationalities that are produced and reproduced over time through deliberations in the public sphere. At the core of transitional justice lies a deliberation of moral order and humanity. Selected experiences from past conflicts are passed on (from the Holocaust in particular) to construct a progressive history of the world moving towards greater moral order, one conflict resolution at a time. These condensed experiences form the foundation of the international register of transitional justice on the basis of which international war crimes' tribunals work. One such lesson is that in order for conflict resolution to become the basis of lasting social peace, transgressors of moral norms must be punished, apologized or in other ways atoned for their sins. Archived memory must be put to work in a process that is seen as a transitional phase towards a more lasting, just social order. This process allows past violence to be recounted, either through the declassification of official documents or through public hearings. Truth about what happened must be established and embedded in a new master narrative for a reconstituting nation. This will not only heal injured social relations but also reintegrate the nation in question into (an idea of) a global community based on shared moral norms ('the international community'), from which contemporary Syria is seen as disconnected. By placing emphasis on multivocality and personal narratives, truth telling proclaims that the country in question will not accept such harms in the future (Phelps 2004). It performs reintegration into the global moral order. As Sriram (2007) has noted, transitional justice strategies are increasingly part of broader peacebuilding strategies and share a faith that other key goods (e.g. democracy and justice) can essentially stand in for, and necessarily create, peace. This rationality has been the basis of the vision for transitional justice that both Syrian and international actors pursue.

If Syrians were allowed to pause and reflect in their relentless conflict, they might be able to survey the local landscape of questionable transitional justice models in order to consider what to eventually do with the vast archive of war documentation. Looking at experiences in the region, transitional justice in Tunisia, Morocco, Lebanon and Iraq has tended towards what we can call performative politics of atonement (Haugbolle and Hastrup 2008). Performative politics of atonement seeks to integrate 'losers' into the moral community by laying their crimes bare in return for absolution and pardon. Some truth committees, as in South Africa, did not automatically provide amnesty; rather, perpetrators were invited to confess to crimes committed and apply for amnesty. In effect, however, truth committees have a limited punitive aspect. Very few people have been sentenced in any of the transitional committees and trials. As such, despite the apparent dichotomy between justice and amnesty, truth and reconciliation can be viewed as a variation of the approach to conflict resolution applied in Lebanon, Iraq and elsewhere in the Middle East that puts emphasis on blanket amnesty, initially in order to draw combatants to the negotiation table and later to pacify simmering conflict. From a peacebuilding perspective, many scholars now find this an inadequate and short-sighted approach, which rarely leads to long-term democratic transition or pacification (Lanegran 2005). Moreover, the state's application of absolute categories, such as truth and justice, is troubling because memory, upon closer examination, serves as a tool for particularly powerful agendas in most cases. In short, the local application of lofty notions of universal justice is always messy and often contradictory (Shaw and Waldorf 2010).

Legal frameworks

All of the mentioned and well-known problems inherent to the process of localizing universal notions of transitional justice play out in the Syrian case. They can be seen in the way Syrians debate and negotiate the terms of a coming settlement. The SNC, which formed in 2011 and entered into the Syrian National Coalition of Revolution and Opposition Forces in 2012 (only to exit it again in 2014), has produced not just a shadow government in exile but elaborate constitutional blueprints for a new Syria that also include the question of transitional justice. In its basic principles, the Coalition states that it is

> aiming at a political solution and a transition in Syria on the basis that Bashar al-Assad and his close associates cannot take part in it or be part of this solution for Syria. The exclusive authority mandated to discuss any political solutions or initiatives is the political committee of the Coalition.
> *(National Coalition of Syrian Revolution and Opposition Forces*
> *n.d.: principle 5)*

Furthermore,

> There will be no place in new Syria for individuals who belong to the regime with blood on their hands and are involved in corruption. They will be held accountable for crimes they have committed through fair trials overseen by an independent judiciary.
> *(National Coalition of Syrian Revolution and Opposition Forces*
> *n.d.: principle 9)*

This does not hint at soft-handed performative politics, but rather mass trials and comprehensive purges.

As mentioned, the regime and its supporters have not completely ignored legal reckoning with war crimes. The Syrian government has indeed engaged in a conversation about possible reforms. It obviously rejected the SNC's idea of complete transition from the beginning in 2011, instead proposing constitutional amendments in line with what it presents as a gradual policy of political liberalization under Bashar al-Assad (Leenders 2013). One might also argue that six amnesties granted by the Syrian government to non-violent demonstrators from May 2011 to October 2012 at least formally constitute transitional justice measures, even if they have not been implemented (see Al-Jazeera 2011). This internal negotiation between Syrian parties (rather than between the regime and international actors) was further mediated through the Geneva process, but essentially started at the beginning of the conflict. However, it has neither led to any tangible plan for transition nor has it bridged the fundamental disconnect between how opposition groups and regime representatives view the conflict. The regime's media and opposition-friendly media produce contradicting facts about casualty figures, the time of attacks and often also the identities of combatants.

In a conflict where international reporting has often been difficult and dangerous, social media networks have functioned as filtering devices. As a comprehensive study of tweets about Syria in English and Arabic in 2013 shows, this filtering created a clustering of like-minded users, where certain media activists became gatekeepers of images and facts about the war (Lynch, Freelon and Aday 2014). The study also suggests that the filtering skewed the Western understanding of the uprising towards liberal democratic registers. Videos of Islamist calls for martyrdom that circulated among Islamist online networks were rarely, if ever, picked up by English-speaking journalists (Lynch, Freelon and Aday 2014:8). Particular groups in the opposition thereby gained a hegemonic position in creating the facts and images that flowed to mainstream Western and Arab news networks. On the other side of the divide, the official media of Russia, Iran, Hezbollah, the Syrian government and pro-Syrian Arab outlets, such as the Arabic satellite channel al-Mayadeen, have persistently contested the narrative, and often the facts, of Western and pro-opposition media. Consequently, two different narrative frameworks based on two different archives came into being. While the Syrian opposition struggled to develop a narrative for the international media of a predominantly peaceful and pro-Western uprising, victimized by indiscriminate regime violence, the Syrian regime and its allies portrayed them as Islamist stooges controlled by rich Salafi puppet masters in the Gulf.

In order to appreciate fully the roots of this fundamental disconnect between two global publics that fail to agree on a factual basis for evaluating the war, we must remember that the contestation over truth and war crimes, and how to archive and remember them, has a longer trajectory in Syria. The human rights movement dates back to the 1978–1982 protests against the Ba'ath regime, which famously involved a regular armed rebellion from the Muslim Brotherhood, culminating in the destruction of Hama in 1982, but also a secular movement of activists, many of them belonging to Communist movements and various professional unions. Hundreds were imprisoned and first re-emerged in the 1990s, when some of them became leading figures in the so-called Damascus Spring in 2000–2001. This movement also included the foundation of human rights institutes and other legal practices aimed at recording human rights violations. Some were tolerated because they toed the government line. Others were periodically shut down and their staff imprisoned. At the core of this movement was the aspiration that a liberal democratic Syria would emerge in the future. When protests broke out in March 2011, some of these NGOs merged into revolutionary movements. A good example is the previously mentioned Violations Documentation Centre in Syria (VDC). Its founder Razan Zeitouneh, a human rights lawyer, had run a small Damascus-based centre since the mid-2000s providing legal advice to the relatives of prisoners. Zeitouneh also co-founded the Local Coordination Committees, which played a key role in connecting the local protests on the national level. By pursuing a rights-based form of activism, she insisted on the necessity of creating a viable legal environment in Syria in which individual rights are protected. She transferred this ambition to the Local Coordination Committees and even more so to the VDC. Its offices in Douma outside Damascus were destroyed by missiles in May 2016, but the VDC continues to publish statistics on killings and violence in the form of reports and testimonies. Zeitouneh was kidnapped from Douma in November 2013 and remains missing.

If the hybrid archive is a nexus of Syrian and transnational interests, VDC represents one part of the nexus, namely the civil society organizations borne out of long struggle, transformed by popular uprising and, since 2013, facing an increasingly difficult task in both the government-controlled and so-called liberated areas alike. While their work prior to the uprising focused on documenting violations in order to push for political reforms, their main task has become documenting war crimes as they occur in order to prepare the ground for transitional justice. Others, such as Rami Abdulrahman, who almost single-handedly runs the SOHR out of Great Britain, became politicized by the uprising and joined the documentation effort from a distance through the access facilitated by electronic media and communication. Based in Europe, the U.S., Turkey and the Arab countries, old and more recent Syrian exiles have played a major role in establishing monitoring units. Even so, they depend on colleagues on the ground in Syria. Because of their direct access, Syrian groups have spearheaded efforts to collect real-time information about the conflict, and they remain essential for foreign-based groups, Syrian, intergovernmental, governmental and international alike. In addition to the VDC, the SOHR, Syrian Centre for Media and Freedom (SCMF), the Sham News Network and Syrian Shuhada all played a crucial role in feeding Arab and international media with statistics and information that they hoped would sway international opinion. This political ambition has attracted criticism (e.g. of the SOHR's alleged connections to the Muslim Brotherhood). More worryingly for the advocates of transitional justice, far from all reports demonstrate knowledge of what is needed for information to serve as evidence in legal proceedings.

International NGOs, some of them strongly supported by Western governments, understand this problem and have focused their efforts on training Syrian human rights activists to enhance the usefulness of the TJE information they are collecting for future accountability mechanisms. In the words of the pro bono law firm PILPG (supported by the U.S. government), the aim is to achieve 'legal consistency' in the documentation of abuse and to help 'ensure that information is collected on all types of violations, rather than just a few' (PILPG and SJAC, Public International Law & Policy Group and Syria Justice and Accountability

Centre 2013:31–32). With more consistent collection, PILPG recommends that outside actors stand a better chance of undertaking 'efforts to re-compile TJE and simultaneously re-label according to a comprehensive legal framework' (PILPG and SJAC, Public International Law & Policy Group and Syria Justice and Accountability Centre 2013:36). In so many words, PILPG here envisions an international legal process, either in the form of a hybrid courts tribunal, as in the case of the Special Tribunal for Lebanon (STL), or a purely international process, such as a court case at the International Criminal Court. The idea of a Syria-based process based on a Syrian legal framework appears to be precluded from the beginning.

Precedents for transitional justice in Syria and the region

Even if its history is flawed by obvious transgressions, there is a legal framework in Syria that could, in the event of regime change and a comprehensive legal reform, become the basis of a truth and justice process. The most likely location for such a process would be the secular courts in Syria, in particular the Courts of Peace of Conciliation (*mahakim al-sulh*) (United Kingdom: Home Office 2012). Today, their mandate only extends to minor offenses but it could be extended and become a venue for the prosecution of war crimes at the national level. This would obviously require a formal overhaul of both the legal and political systems, the latter of which currently renders the legal system everything but independent of the government. Even if it is an unlikely scenario, the a priori assumption of a legal process outside of Syria is problematic, not least given the legacy of international involvement in Iraq and Lebanon, where tribunals have been hybrid in nature, incorporating both international and domestic structures and personnel. Several scholars are sceptical of the degree to which such international criminal trials realize justice or reconciliation. Eric Stover and Harvey Weinstein (2004), for example, assert that while criminal trials promote retributive justice, they can divide multi-ethnic communities such as Iraq, Lebanon and Syria. Meanwhile, many survivors of mass atrocity view justice not as a verdict from The Hague but rather as a host of remedies that are integral to reconciliation, such as apologies, reparations, the return of stolen property, location of missing bodies, meaningful employment and education, and recovery help for trauma victims. In short, restoration should include compensation and not just symbolic justice, such as the imprisonment of a few leaders after long, expensive trial proceedings at the International Criminal Court. The archive should not merely channel forensic and other high-precision forms of evidence; rather, it should be the basis for a reconciliation process and a process of understanding. This 'ecological model' of social reconstruction, as developed by Stover and Weinstein (2004), does not rule out trials altogether, instead viewing trials as just one part of the puzzle – and a possibly destabilizing one at that.

In the cases of Iraq and Lebanon, several scholars have argued that transitional justice mechanisms imposed by international actors, while aimed in theory at promoting reconciliation and delivering justice, exacerbated the risk of communal violence and only made minimal gains in terms of holding the perpetrators of past abuses accountable. These are important examples, as the multi-sectarian composition of Syrian society resembles its neighbours to the east and west. The Iraqi case might offer the best illustration of how dangerous assumptions about sectarianism can produce dangerous sectarian realities. Shortly after the American invasion of Iraq, the Iraqi Governing Council established the Iraqi Special Tribunal (IST). The IST was given jurisdiction to try suspects for genocide, crimes against humanity and war crimes committed between 1968 and 2003. It was responsible for the trial of Saddam Hussein and other senior officials in the overthrown Ba'athist regime. Functionally a hybrid court, the IST proved to be highly politicized and divisive among Iraqis, fanning the flames of Shiite and Kurdish retribution and creating a sense among Sunnis that they were being targeted as a community. The American occupational authorities were unfamiliar with the Iraqi legal system and had de-prioritized transitional justice planning. The result was a string of politically biased trials that effectively meted out victors' justice.

If Syrians instead look to their Western neighbour Lebanon for inspiration, the case of the STL highlights the political biases of international politics and how they translate into sectarian divisions on the ground. The result of the STL's imposition on Lebanon was disastrous from the standpoint of social reconciliation. Political conflict in Lebanon between the March 8 coalition (of which Hezbollah is a member) and the March 14 alliance intensified as the STL pushed political actors into even more rigid camps – either to resist U.S.–Israeli ambitions or against the Syrian grip on Lebanon (Knudsen 2012).

Even if the success of international actors to assist in transitional justice in the Levant has been questionable thus far, most observers realize that Syria will need some form of outside support. Some writers stress that because Syria has become a divided society, irreparably split between sectarian loyalties, international trials are the only option (Dalton 2016). International trials would depend on a full or partial opposition victory, the establishment of a new system and an interim government to oversee a transitional period. The scenario of a full or partial victory is the sine qua non of many of the plans drafted in 2012 and 2013. Already in May 2011, the UN High Commissioner for Human Rights established The Independent International Commission of Inquiry (IICI) on the Syrian Arab Republic. It was mandated to 'investigate all alleged violations of international human rights law since March 2011 in the Syrian Arab Republic' (United Nations, Human Rights Council 2011). The Commission was also tasked

> to establish the facts and circumstances that may amount to such violations and of the crimes perpetrated and, where possible, to identify those responsible with a view of ensuring that perpetrators of violations, including those that may constitute crimes against humanity, are held accountable.
>
> *(OHCHR n.d.)*

The IICI has produced four detailed reports, culling information from Syrian groups as well as independent research, such as forensic analysis, interviews in the region and over Skype. The most detailed report relates to the massacre of 108 civilians in Houla in May 2012. Although the IICI's work has been downscaled since 2013, many diplomats view it as the best platform for a potential ad hoc international tribunal for Syria similar to the tribunals established for Rwanda and the former Yugoslavia. At an informal meeting at the UN Headquarters in New York on 16 April 2016, the General Coordinator of the Syrian National Coalition's High Negotiations Committee, Riad Hijab, reiterated calls for bringing Assad before an international court for the war crimes he committed in Syria and for IICI to be its institutional locus (National Coalition of Syrian Revolution and Opposition Forces 2017). The arrival of a new Secretary General of the UN in January 2017 appears to have revived the efforts of the IICI, which in February produced a report on the Russian, Iranian and Syrian governments' siege and bombardment of East Aleppo. At a time when the Syrian regime appears to emerge victorious more than ever before in the conflict, international and Syrian advocates of transitional justice still pursue an alternative future.

Conclusion

In conclusion, this chapter has suggested that studies of conflict continuation should pay more attention to how future scenarios are discursively constructed. Through the case of transitional justice advocacy and archiving in Syria, the chapter has shown how such scenarios result from a nexus of national and international organizations. Since 2011, they have worked together to procure evidence of violations to be used in future legal proceedings. While this process has given hope to the victims of state violence, the analysis suggested that it has also played a role in creating two adverse global camps in relation to the Syrian War that disagree fundamentally on how the conflict could be de-escalated and eventually resolved, and how combatants and mediators alike can reach agreement on basic facts about the war. The intention has not been to exonerate Russia, Iran or the Syrian regime for their lies and deceit, and the negative role this has played in protracting the war. Clearly, the fact that the Syrian regime categorically denies committing well-documented war crimes has not helped diplomats carve out any common ground for negotiations that could end conflict continuation. Rather, the aim of my analysis has been to show the level of institutional and ideological investments in transitional justice from the beginning of the conflict. I have argued that this investment has made it nearly impossible for diplomats to bridge competing narratives about the war. When a rationality of revolutionary change is inscribed into global norms of transition in a reality where compromise may be the only way to end conflict continuation, the result is war without end.

Note

1 The initial CRIC research agenda from 2012 likewise expected that the Syrian War would soon end and that our research would focus on how to prepare for transitional justice.

References

Atlantic Council (2015) *Kerry Reaffirms: Assad Must Go.* www.atlanticcouncil.org/blogs/natosource/kerry-reaffirms-assad-must-go (accessed 9 June 2017).

Al-Jazeera (2011) *Syrian President Issues Amnesty.* www.aljazeera.com/news/middleeast/2011/05/2011531173212337652.html (accessed 8 June 2017).

Al-Jazeera (2017) *Has Syria's Opposition Lost to Assad?* www.aljazeera.com/programmes/upfront/2017/05/syria-opposition-lost-assad-170505082253753.html (accessed 15 May 2017).

Amnesty International (2017) *Syria: Secret Campaign of Mass Hangings and Extermination at Saydnaya Prison.* www.amnesty.org/en/latest/news/2017/02/syria-investigation-uncovers-governments-secret-campaign-of-mass-hangings-and-extermination-at-saydnaya-prison/ (accessed 7 June 2017).

Dalton, Melissa (2016) *What Options Do We Have in Syria?* www.csis.org/analysis/what-options-do-we-have-syria (accessed 9 June 2017).

Derrida, Jacques (1998) *Archive Fever.* Chicago, IL: University of Chicago Press.

Haugbolle, Sune (2016) *A Militant Humanism for the 21st Century.* http://aljumhuriya.net/en/critical-thought/a-militant-humanism-for-the-21st-century (accessed 3 June 2017).

Haugbolle, Sune and Anders Hastrup (2008) *The Politics of Violence, Truth, and Reconciliation in the Arab Middle East.* London: Routledge.

Human Rights Watch (2015) *If the Dead Could Speak: Mass Deaths and Torture in Syria's Detention Facilities.* www.hrw.org/report/2015/12/16/if-dead-could-speak/mass-deaths-and-torture-syrias-detention-facilities (accessed 7 June 2017).

Jameson, Fredric (2005) *Archaeologies of the Future.* London: Verso.

Knudsen, Are (2012) 'Special Tribunal for Lebanon: Homage to Hariri?', in Are Knudsen and Michael Kerr (Eds.), *Lebanon after the Cedar Revolution* (219–234), Oxford: Oxford University Press.

Koselleck, Reinhart (2004) *Futures Past: On the Semantics of Historical Time.* New York: Columbia.

Laermans, Rudi and Pascal Gielen (2007) 'The Archive of the Digital An-Archive', *Image & Narrative* 17 (1).

Lanegran, Kimberly (2005) 'Truth Commissions, Human Rights Trials and the Politics of Memory', *Comparative Studies of South Asia, Africa, and the Middle East* 25 (1): 111–121.

Leenders, Reinoud (2013) 'Social Movement Theory and the Onset of Popular Uprising in Syria', *Arab Studies Quarterly* 35 (3): 273–289.

Lynch, Marc, Deen Freelon and Sean Aday (2014) *Syria's Socially Mediated War.* www.usip.org/sites/default/files/PW91-Syrias%20Socially%20Mediated%20Civil%20War.pdf (accessed 9 June 2017).

Mansour, Kholoud (2017) *UN Humanitarian Coordination in Lebanon: The Consequences of Excluding Syrian Actors.* www.chathamhouse.org/publication/un-humanitarian-coordination-lebanon-consequences-excluding-syrian-actors (accessed 15 May 2017).

National Coalition of Syrian Revolution and Opposition Forces (n.d.) *Declaration by the National Coalition for Syrian Revolutionary and Opposition Forces.* http://en.etilaf.org/coalition-documents/declaration-by-the-national-coalition-for-syrian-revolutionary-and-opposition-forces.html (accessed 8 June 2017).

National Coalition of Syrian Revolution and Opposition Forces (2017) *Seif to Meet EU Foreign Policy Chief Mogherini Friday to Discuss EU Support for Opposition.* http://en.etilaf.org/search.html?searchword=transitional+justice&categories=&format=html&t=1472112980475&tpl=search) (accessed 8 June 2017).

OHCHR, The Office of the United Nations High Commissioner for Human Rights (n.d.) *Independent International Commission of Inquiry on the Syrian Arab Republic.* www.ohchr.org/EN/HRBodies/HRC/IICISyria/Pages/AboutCoI.aspx (accessed 8 June 2017).

Phelps, Teresa Godwin (2004) *Shattered Voices: Language, Violence, and the Work of Truth Commissions.* Philadelphia: University of Pennsylvania Press.

PILPG and SJAC, Public International Law & Policy Group and Syria Justice and Accountability Centre (2013) *Mapping Accountability Efforts in Syria.* www.documentcloud.org/documents/627591-mapping-accountability-efforts-in-syria.html (accessed 8 June 2017).

Ray, Alex (2016) *The Death Toll in Syria: What Do the Numbers Really Say?* www.counterpunch.org/2016/05/26/the-death-toll-in-syria-what-do-the-numbers-really-say/ (accessed 7 June 2017).

Saleh, Yassin al-Haj (2016) *The World's Naked Disgrace.* www.yassinhs.com/2016/08/22/the-worlds-naked-disgrace/ (accessed 25 May 2017).

Shaw, Rosalind and Lars Waldorf (2010) 'Introduction: Localizing Transitional Justice', in Rosalind Shaw and Lars Waldorf with Pierre Hazan (Eds.), *Localizing Transitional Justice: Interventions and Priorities after Mass Violence* (3–26), Stanford, CA: Stanford University Press.

Sriram, Chandra (2007) 'Justice as Peace? Liberal Peacebuilding and Strategies of Transitional Justice', *Global Society* 21 (4): 579–591.

Stahn, Carsten (2014) 'Between Law-Breaking and Law-Making: Syria, Humanitarian Intervention and "What the Law Ought to Be"', *Journal of Conflict and Security Law* 19 (1): 25–48.

Stover, Eric and Harvey Weinstein (Eds.) (2004) *My Neighbor, My Enemy: Justice and Community in the Aftermath of Mass Atrocity.* Cambridge: Cambridge University Press.

Taub, Ben (2016) *The Assad Files: Capturing the Top-Secret Documents that Tie the Syrian Regime to Mass Torture and Killings.* www.newyorker.com/magazine/2016/04/18/bashar-al-assads-war-crimes-exposed (accessed 8 June 2017).

Tsing, Anna Lowenhaupt (2008) 'The Global Situation', in Jonathan X. Inda and Renato Rosaldo (Eds.), *The Anthropology of Globalisation* (66–98), Oxford: Oxford University Press.

United Kingdom: Home Office (2012) *Country of Origin Information Report: Syria.* www.refworld.org/docid/50374cf72.html (accessed 8 June 2017).

United Nations, Human Rights Council (2011) *Resolution S-16/1, The Current Human Rights Situation in the Syrian Arab Republic in the Context of Recent Events*, adapted April 29, 2011. https://digitallibrary.un.org/record/704169

Zartmann, William (2008) 'The Timing of Peace Initiatives: Hurting Stalemates and Ripe Moments', in John Darby and Roger Mac Ginty (Eds.), *Contemporary Peace-Making: Conflict, Peace Processes and Post-War Reconstruction* (22–35), New York: Palgrave MacMillan.

15

CONCLUSION

Poul Poder and Isabel Bramsen

Throughout this book, we have turned self-evident assumptions about the escalation and continuation of conflicts into puzzles: Why and how do conflicts escalate? Why and how do they continue? The individual chapters have identified numerous and very diverse dynamics and processes that fuel escalation and support the continuation of conflicts, and we have shown how conflictualization generates and rebuilds emotions, subjectivities and social identities. In this concluding chapter, we briefly recapitulate the basic insights and crosscutting themes in an overall discussion of conflict escalation and new conflict dynamics as well as the implications for conflict resolution and transformation. We revisit the theoretical framework presented in the introduction – the SIT conflict triangle – and show how the different chapters draw on, modify and challenge this framework.

Conflict escalation, continuation and termination in Syria

First, we exemplify how conflict escalation and continuation are dynamic processes in the Syrian conflict, which has served as the primary case in several of the chapters. Prior to the popular uprising in 2011, the situation in Syria could be characterized as one of *domination*, where the regime encountered fairly limited resistance, and which the regime promptly repressed (George 2003). As argued in Chapter 2, mobilization is really about turning a situation of domination into one of *conflict* by responding to domination with resistance. When the revolution began, it was not a question of regime change that mobilized large groups of people but rather one of rage over unjust and brutal regime repression and domination, namely the torturing of youngsters and humiliation of their parents and tribal leaders. As the regime responded to the unrest by killing demonstrators, this turned the contradiction into one of regime brutalities in general, and more provinces joined the conflict in solidarity with Deraa. Corresponding to the SIT triangle, the contradiction therefore did not remain the same, as it became increasingly comprehensive throughout the initial escalation of the conflict, with demands evolving from being concerned with justice and police brutality to regime change. As argued in Chapter 5, the velocity and range of the distribution of grassroots videos enabled the rapid and simultaneous spread of opposition activity against the authoritarian forces, such as street protests, which were violently suppressed by the Assad regime. Moral outrage as a reaction to the subsequent videos of suffering and violence thus contributed to the escalation of conflict over great distances throughout Syria, leading to a spiral of violence. This effect was only felt among specific audiences who identified with the pain, suffering and moral outrage expressed in the grassroots videos. Motivation stemming from moral outrage can thus be diffused from various places at the same time, which questions both the linearity of conflict escalation and the established notions of centre and periphery.

The increased moral outrage and mobilization also contributed to new demands regarding reform, the lifting of the state of emergency and the release of political prisoners. The conflict thus escalated both in terms of the number of people engaging in the conflict, how strongly it affected people's lives in general, and in terms of the situation of contradiction. Some people who supported the regime prior to 2011 joined the dissent not because of previous grievances but rather due to indignation over the injustice. Violence is a form rather than degree of escalation. If perceived as unjust and spectacular, however, violence tends to increase tension and escalate conflict. An important reason why regime violence increased tension and conflictual action in Syria is that it brought people together at funerals to grieve the martyrs, which inevitably led to protest marches and increased group solidarity and energized participants as shown by Bramsen in Chapter 3.

Initially, the protesters did not necessarily link the brutality of the security forces to Al-Assad. They hoped that he would punish the responsible officers and the head of the security branch. In his speech on 30 March 2011, however, it became apparent that he was behind or at least supported the crackdown. One Syrian activist describes how this speech was the turning point for himself in terms of joining the revolution (interviews conducted by Isabel Bramsen 2015). Bashar al-Assad's speech further escalated the conflict as popular anger increased and the contradiction expanded to include change vs. 'non-regime-change' rather than just the reform and punishment of the responsible officers.

As argued in Chapter 3, the mundane drivers of sectarianism show how factors that are otherwise considered root causes (e.g. the sectarian composition of a society) should instead be studied in its everyday practice. Neither ancient hatred nor deep-rooted religious splits contributed to sectarianism; to the contrary, in fact, protesters in both Syria and Bahrain did an impressive job of countering sectarianism. Rather, sectarian divisions were generated through everyday practices that unwillingly promoted othering, such as having different rhetoric or religious utterings that generated confidence and solidarity in threatening situations. In Chapter 6, Jakob Skovgaard Petersen explains how religious actors who were not part of a strong hierarchical church played a central role in the development of the conflict. Their role varied depending on historical dynamics as well as situational dynamics; some of them stressed their obligation to be obedient to the ruler, whereas other ulama went along with the uprising to address the people's legitimate demands. The involvement of religious actors together with the everyday religious dynamics (e.g. activists assembling after Friday prayers or at funerals) expanded the contradiction to not only being a question of status quo vs. regime change but also a sectarian issue. The process of escalation is, thus, one of increasing contradictions, increasing tension and increasing conflictual action.

Since the initial phase, the Syria conflict has escalated much further, involving even more issues, actors and parties, many of them adding to the continuation rather than the resolution of the conflict. At the time of writing, the most likely route to an end of the war requires regenerating energy and building up momentum for conflict resolution. At various stages, the conflict was close to a real possibility of an end: sudden concessions by one party not being picked up by the opponents or negotiations in the shadow of various partial military victories, especially by the regime and its main allies, in a best-of-the-worst-case scenario supplemented by a military setback for the regime at an optimal moment of global politics. With the widespread tendency to treat non-events as impossible (i.e. to ignore near misses), it is probably underestimated today that a solution was close to materializing on numerous occasions, a solution that would have been considered bad by all parties but potentially involved the major parties sufficiently in the negotiated final element to include both mechanisms against returns to violence and provisions for future processes that had secured a transition beyond the current regime. In contrast, there is now an indication of an even more unjust and enforced conflict termination, where the military decision is only modestly mixed up with a minor element of negotiation. However, this 'end' is ultimately an expression of the mechanism posited as central in the present book: an inability to regenerate the energy for conflict. Only, the internationalization and transnationalization of the conflict mean that this change is happening not primarily by the local population and groups grudgingly accepting the outcome, but by the interlinked constellation of international and internal actors losing focus. When the war in Syria ends, it will be necessary for the many different parties to deal with the massive loss of life and widespread grievances and to establish an effective form of (most likely, largely informal) transitional justice to engender a situation where oppositional parties can live together in peace without lingering grievances. Post-war conflict transformation in Syria is going to be a very long-term process, any significant healing between the affected groups and parties likely taking decades. While the prevention of a return to fighting is mostly determined in the short term by the emerging political arrangement, especially regarding the inclusion and control of the power agencies, long-term stability also demands a favourable reconstruction of collective memories, which, in turn, depends on the low-level continuation of the conflicts. The fact that the likely end will have such a comparatively minor element of being negotiated and/or mediated and a higher element of victory/ defeat and exhaustion does not bode well.

Expanding the notion of conflict dynamics

Throughout this book, the different chapters have shown how conflict dynamics should not be considered a narrow category; rather, conflicts are shaped by varied dynamics relating to emotion, securitization, incentives, digital technology, violence and third parties. Even attempts at monitoring, resolving or remembering a conflict may end up contributing to its escalation or continuation, as described in several chapters.

Emotional dynamics receive particular attention in Chapter 2, where Bramsen and Poder explore what they refer to as three basic emotional formations of conflict: (1) domination rituals that de-energize the dominated part and energize the dominating part; (2) solidarity interaction that energizes the involved actors; and, finally, (3) conflict rituals that energize two parties to a conflict with negative emotional energy. While these rituals may occur simultaneously in conflicts, some are often more central than others. As described in Chapter 4, for example, domination and humiliation dynamics often serve as an enduring motivation for actions to engage in conflict. The chapter shows how various sources give rise to humiliating dynamics that can motivate people to stand up for their dignity, which can be considered a fundamental drive in humans, albeit what defines self-worth varies culturally.

Violence is a central dynamic in many conflicts. Chapter 3 explores how the visibility and perceived brutality of the violence perpetrated by the Syrian regime was a crucial force in the escalation of the conflict, as witnessing violence in the streets and on YouTube mobilized many people, and gathered people at funerals. Conversely, the regime in Bahrain adopted a new strategy, no longer killing people in the streets and instead injuring and torturing them in prisons, which over time has de-energized and demobilized the resistance movement. Chapter 7 likewise addresses the dynamics of violence, although from a different angle. In the chapter, Jung argues that violent persons fighting in foreign countries should be understood in terms of the alternative construction of meaningful modern selfhoods and not exclusively in terms of the radicalization of their minds and behaviour. In order to understand conflict dynamics involving violence, we must therefore acknowledge how various cultural notions of meaningful selfhoods also contribute to how conflicts arise and escalate. Jung's core argument is that we should consider violence not only as a *result* of social action, but also as an independent *cause*. In the broader theoretical picture, taking violence seriously as an independent variable should lead to the revision of the liberal imagination of modernity, which tends to neglect the 'dark sides' of modernity in which violence plays a central role.

Several chapters have shown how the relatively recent introduction of mobile phones and digital video cameras chronicling the events of violence, war and conflict on the grassroots level has added extra complexity and dynamics to conflicts and how they escalate over time and space. Chapters 3 and 5 show how digital technology was a crucial factor shaping how the Arab Uprisings of 2011 developed and spread throughout the Arab world. In addition to being testimonials of grief and moral outrage, the grassroots videos from Syria indicate where violence took place geographically and which particular groups of people had been severely affected by violence in Syria. These audiovisual records may form part of a body of complementary evidence to serve in future war-crime tribunals concerning the Syrian War. As shown in Chapter 14, however, Sune Haugbølle's gathering of data for potential, transitional justice was part of but also contributed to the impression among protesters and their Western supporters that the regime would soon be toppled, implying a full and total victory for the opposition. This provided fuel to continue the conflict and contributed to creating two irreconcilable visions for how a future solution should take form. The monitoring of human rights violations supported the parties in their perceptions of justice, right and wrong, which posed great challenges for the finding of any common ground and contributed to the continuation of the conflict. In this sense, future scenarios became part of the dynamics feeding into conflict escalation and continuation. This shows how even attempts at addressing and monitoring a conflict may actually end up adding to its escalation and continuation.

A similar point about how conflict resolution practices may contribute to the conflict is reflected in Chapter 9, where Sara McQuaid explains how attempts in Northern Ireland at dealing with the past are both constituted by the peace agreement of 1998 and themselves, in turn, constitutive of peacemaking. Here, she exposes some fault lines in the constitutional compromise in the tensions between enshrining radical disagreement and the constructivism of an ongoing transition. Changes in the basic power balances upon which the principles of the peace agreement were based (both in terms of internal NI dynamics and in/external relations to the UK, Republic of Ireland and the EU and between them) have made the peace agreement seem increasingly out of step – yet constantly setting the pace in Northern Ireland, where it continues to give shape to contradictions, interactions and tensions.

Third parties can also change the dynamics in conflicts, and not always for the better. In Chapter 10, Bjørn Møller shows how third parties can in fact be part of prolonging rather than ending a conflict, either by supplying the weaker part in a conflict to continue fighting despite asymmetry or, as in the Cold War, where one set of third parties supports one side, while another supports its adversary, thereby increasing the intensity and destructiveness of the conflict. Obviously, third parties can potentially play multiple constructive roles in conflicts through mediation, diplomacy and preventive measures. Either way, third parties change the construction and dynamics in the conflict, sometimes by changing the power balance or by intervening in rhythms of action-reaction.

Conflict transformation

Peace and conflict research often focuses on not only understanding but also *changing* the world by producing practical ideas for how to solve conflicts or improve existing peacebuilding practices. This book is no exception. While efforts at addressing conflicts surely may end up creating more problems than they solve, as described earlier, it is nevertheless crucial to explore ways of responding to conflicts constructively.

On the one hand, most contemporary, resolution–oriented conflict analysis places emphasis on either structural transformation or reaching agreements. The widespread assumption that 'causes' (in the sense of 'origins' or 'roots') is the main issue for conflict analysis leads our attention to the underlying factors that do indeed influence the likelihood of conflict and which is therefore relevant for conflict prevention and peacebuilding. Such lessons deserve to be applied more structurally, both at the systemic level in order to shape a world generating fewer destructive conflicts and in terms of helping to prevent relapse in the violent conflicts today. But they often miss the target in relation to active conflicts, where such structural policies are often overpowered by dynamics already unleashed.

Conversely, conflict resolution often has a relatively narrow focus on reaching agreement among the main parties. This, too, has an important role to play in conflict resolution, as have the more structural approaches. However, this approach is often too superficial and only able to interrupt the dynamics of the conflict itself when attuned specifically to them.

Our approach aims at the missing link between the two. As a continuation of the 'dynamic conflict theory' tradition (from Johan Galtung, especially in his 1970s incarnation), we ask what would break the vicious circles that have made a conflictualization take hold of the situation and relationship. Making dynamic conflict theory even more dynamic (Bramsen and Wæver, Chapter 1), we recast that question as the challenge of intervening in the conflict situation, reducing tension or changing forms of conflictual interaction. With the SIT framework, we argue that conflict is structured around contradiction and opposition and that conflict transformation should therefore aim at changing the structure of the situation, that is, the opposing positioning of the parties.

One way to change the situation is to change the incentive structures shaping the contradiction of the conflict. As Nik Emmanuel argues in Chapter 11, conflict dynamics can be transformed by increasing the incentives for not engaging (violently) in conflict as well as by ripening a situation to be more favourable for conflict resolution. Incentives are dynamic and not necessarily rooted in basic needs; they can change, depending on the situation. Nor are they necessarily economic or rational, at least not according to a very strict understanding of these notions, as incentives can also be emotional in terms of gaining (or not losing) acknowledgement and pride vis-à-vis other actors. In the SIT triangle, conflicts are considered a particular structure of contradiction generating tension and conflictual interaction. A change in incentive structures (e.g. with a third party offering economic support and legitimation, as in South Sudan) produces a new situation where the something else (foreign support or acknowledgement) may be more important than what the conflict is believed to be about. The challenge, however, is to change the incentives and situation, not only at the elite level but also amongst ordinary people or fighters who may otherwise continue the fighting (in some cases, only one act of violence may jeopardize the peace process).

The importance of incentive structures also becomes evident in Chapter 12, where Martin Beck shows how the Israel-Palestine conflict continues due to a lack of incentives, especially for the top dog in the conflict - Israel - to change the status quo. Here, international attempts at solving the conflict in the form of the Oslo Accords have ended up de facto continuing if not prolonging the conflict, as the Palestinian Authorities de facto end up managing great parts of the occupation of the West Bank at the same time as they have become economically dependent on Western funding, which has limited their incentives to change. Should it come at all, change should therefore come from the people most affected by the conflict, who are those with the greatest incentive to challenge the status quo, namely great parts of the Palestinian people. While challenging indeed, constructive options for oppressed peoples amount to nonviolent resistance, civil resistance and lobbying for outside pressure. In the Palestinian case, this would amount to pressure on Israel and perhaps the Palestinian Authorities through escalatory actions to increase the incentive to change the status quo. From a dynamic perspective, conflicts are not determined by their root causes and bound to continue but rather possible to change (e.g. by increasing tension or changing modes of interaction).

As regards nonviolent resistance, an important lesson to draw from the uprising in Bahrain (Chapter 3) is the importance of momentum. The protesters initially enjoyed great momentum that resulted from the reactions to the killing of demonstrators, which gathered people in energizing funeral rituals and the revolutionary winds from the successful overthrow of regimes in Tunisia and Egypt. However, the regime changed its strategy and waited until the momentum had decreased before their second attempt to crack down on the movement. Thus, it is important for protesters and third parties alike to be aware of, take advantage of and promote momentum.

That said, the Israeli-Palestinian conflict is probably *the conflict* that most observers would think of as continuing endlessly. Beck's chapter points out many reasons why this seems to be the most realistic prospect, not least due to Israel's very powerful position on many levels (material and immaterial power on the local, regional and global levels) and its lack of interest in changing the status quo. History has shown, however, that even a relatively disempowered group (e.g. the people of India or black community in South Africa) can find ways to effectively challenge an oppressor that no conflict is set to continue in eternity, and conflict dynamics and momentum can be exploited in unexpected ways.

Another way to challenge the continuation of the Israeli-Palestinian conflict is to consider what fuels the conflict and energizes the parties, in particular Israel (due to its powerful position in maintaining the status quo) and, thus, how this basis for continuation can be challenged. Here, ontological security and identity play a significant role, as discussed in Chapter 13. In the chapter, Lupovici shows how the continuation of the Arab-Israeli conflict is not self-evident but depends on the social processes that fuel conflictual interaction and sustains their momentum. Lupovici explains how giving up seeing the other party as an enemy engenders ontological insecurity – the destabilization of one's identity – and avoiding this unpleasant experience works as an incentive to remain in the known and secure adversarial relationship rather than engaging in a serious resolution move. A wider narrative of the conflict binds up the identities of parties, and this narrative provides a certain sense of value and direction that people live by. As described in the introduction chapter, the contradiction in a conflict often develops as a central dimension of conflict escalation. This is also the case in the Arab-Israeli conflict, where securitizing actors inject more and more threats and issues to the conflict narrative, such as the threat of Iran. A de-securitizing move is therefore to challenge and problematize this process. Likewise, counternarratives can challenge the common beliefs that contribute to the continuation of the conflict; for example, the peaceful relations that have developed between Egypt and Israel show that not all Arab nations aim to destroy Israel.

Chapters 8 and 9 make us rethink (in different ways) how the SIT model can be applied in conflict transformation. Both the preventive efforts in Burundi and the management of the conflict in Northern Ireland have focused on transforming violent interaction into nonviolent interaction, corresponding to our suggestion of conflict transformation in the introductory chapter. But this approach is not without challenges. In Chapter 9, it is argued that the goal of the Northern Ireland peace agreement of 1998 was not to resolve the key contradiction but to make it manageable within the democratic arena, that is, to change the interaction without transforming the contradiction. By privileging the key conflicting positions of unionism and nationalism (and as such two specific communities rather than others), however, the peace agreement has entrenched antagonistic political interactions: political elites are positioned as guardians of communities, which for the most part has perpetuated 'power-splitting' rather than 'power-sharing' amongst political elites. While the parties in Northern Ireland have agreed since 1998 to disagree on the future status of Northern Ireland, the conflict continues on other levels, because it remains structured around opposing nationalist and unionist political and cultural identities within Northern Ireland. Recently, Brexit has brought the main constitutional contradiction back as a matter of urgency with serious repercussions for the peace process.[1] While the peace process and agreement in Northern Ireland is a good case of moving from violence to non-violence, it leaves more to be desired in terms of being able to transform the interactions at the political level and address tensions beyond violence. This is not least evident from the attempts at dealing with the violent past and efforts at reconciliation and integration.

In the case of Burundi, the change in interaction is likewise paradoxical, although in a different manner. The violent riots characterizing the escalation of the conflict in 2015 have been transformed, not into powerful peaceful demonstrations but rather into more hidden yet lethal violence, such as assassinations. From the perspective of human rights and non-violence, this development is also not preferable. As the authors mention, one of the problems with the attempts at transforming the conflict in Burundi is that the power imbalance between the government and the opposition was not sufficiently challenged at the time of international intervention. In terms of lessons for third parties, it can be argued that changing forms of interaction does not necessarily or merely mean initiating elite negotiations but can also imply non-violence training among rioters that can equip and empower them to fight for their rights by other means.

Focusing more on the *dynamics* of conflict (and less on their deep roots) helps not only to make sense of such strategies; more fundamentally, it opens for attention to the potential value of interventions at any stage of a conflict and through many different strategies. If the main cause of conflict is conflict, there is always a chance that a de-escalation or reconfiguration that initially seems superficial can prove to be of more lasting value. In relation to the triggering of conflict, it is well known how seemingly minor incidents can become what 'lights a tinderbox'; and – as illustrated by the metaphor – it is not seen as generally plausible that this works in reverse. However, a focus on conflict dynamics points to the possibility that seemingly minor incidents likewise can evolve into greater changes that can shape conflicts in more peaceful directions. This is seen in the escalating conflict in Tunisia in 2013, where assassinations and tense demonstrations threatened to destabilize the young democracy and was worrying not only when taking into account the general tendency in the remaining countries, which had likewise been affected by the Arab Uprisings. To manage the increasing conflicts and democratic challenges through dialogue, a coalition of civil society organizations was formed: The Tunisian National Dialogue Quartet. Through negotiation and dialogue sessions, this quartet was able to reduce tension and ensure democratic progress, efforts for which they were awarded the Nobel Peace Prize in 2015.

Another illustration works on two levels: in 1905, when the issue of Norwegian independence had triggered the mobilization of the Norwegian and Swedish armies, at least one interpretation has it that a narrow decision among Swedish political and military leaders not to escalate further created a self-reinforcing process that ended in the peaceful divorce. In turn, this became the foundational Nordic 'non-war' that set a precedent for later territorial conflicts of a magnitude that usually turns to war in other regions, which ultimately led to the Nordic security community (Archer and Joenniemi 2003; Wiberg 1986).

The challenge for future research and policymaking is to further grasp how micro-interactional conflict patterns can be redirected along peaceful avenues, be that through disengagement, dialogue processes, negotiations or nonviolent resistance.

Note

1 While the constitutional question has simmered comfortably on the back burner – since 1998 it has been a question for the future, not the present – the British decision to leave the EU has brought it back with increased urgency and the capacity to further polarize and destabilize. Northern Ireland voted to remain in the EU but will now be forced to leave with the rest of the UK. In this context, the border again becomes a focal point; and with it, the constitutional status of Northern Ireland and questions of sovereignty in more undiluted terms.

References

Archer, Clive and Pertti Joenniemi (Eds.) (2003). *The Nordic Peace*. Farnham: Ashgate.

George, Alan (2003) *Syria: Neither Bread nor Freedom*. New York: Zed Books.

Wiberg, Håkan 1986. 'The Nordic Countries: A Special Kind of System?', *Current Research on Peace and Violence* 9 (1–2): 2–12.

INDEX